The American Political Process

The American Political Process examines both the formal institutions of government and organisations such as political parties and pressure groups. It analyses how these bodies interact in the making of public policy in the United States in order to provide an understanding of contemporary American politics.

The new seventh edition of the text, published for the first time by Routledge, has been thoroughly updated and substantially revised to take account of such important events as the 2000 presidential election, the terrorist attacks on the United States on 11 September 2001, the 2002 midterm elections and the war against Iraq. It looks at political development in the new century against the background of a long-established constitutional structure and a distinctively American political culture.

Each chapter includes a variety of useful tables and figures as well as suggestions for further reading and there is an extensive glossary of terms in American politics which provides an easily accessible reference for the reader. New features of the seventh edition include details of relevant web sites, summaries of each chapter and questions designed to encourage thought and reflection on the key issues. *The American Political Process* will appeal to all those students who want a well-established and comprehensive introductory text that explains how American politics really works.

Alan Grant is Principal Lecturer in Politics at Oxford Brookes University. He is the editor and co-author of *Contemporary American Politics* (1995) and *American Politics: 2000 and Beyond* (2000) and co-author of the *'Politics Today' Companion to American Government* (2002).

The American Political Process

Seventh edition

Alan Grant

Routledge
Taylor & Francis Group

LONDON AND NEW YORK

First published 1979
Second edition 1982
by Heinemann Educational Books

Reprinted 1985
Third edition 1986
by Gower Publishing Company Limited

Fourth edition 1991
Fifth edition 1994
Reprinted 1996
by Dartmouth Publishing Company Limited

Sixth edition 1997
by Ashgate Publishing Company

Seventh edition published 2004
by Routledge
11 New Fetter Lane, London EC4P 4EE

Simultaneously published in the USA and Canada
by Routledge
29 West 35th Street, New York, NY 10001

Routledge is an imprint of the Taylor & Francis Group

© 1979, 1982, 1986, 1991, 1994, 1997, 2004 Alan Grant

Typeset in Sabon by
Keystroke, Jacaranda Lodge, Wolverhampton
Printed and bound in Great Britain by
T.J. International Ltd, Padstow, Cornwall

British Library Cataloguing in Publication Data
A catalogue record for this book is available from the British Library

Library of Congress Cataloging in Publication Data
Grant, Alan R.
    The American political process / Alan Grant. — 7th ed.
        p. cm.
    Includes bibliographical references (p.) and index.
    1. United States—Politics and government. I. Title.
    JK271.G727 2003
    320. 473—dc21   2003005179

ISBN 0–415–28820–7 (hbk)
ISBN 0–415–28821–5 (pbk)

Contents

Illustrations

Figures

Tables

Boxes

1   The framework of American politics

There have been many attempts to find a suitable definition of politics, but most people seem to agree that it is an activity that is related to the governing of a society. David Easton believes that politics is the 'activity of trying to influence the direction of social life and public policy',[1] and he emphasises that politics is not merely a struggle for power, but that it is related to the goals and direction of a society. The United States is usually described as a 'liberal democracy' and in such societies, where freedom of expression and association are encouraged, there is a more open and active display of political activity than in the closed autocratic systems within which governments do not allow groups to canvass support for alternative policies. As a pluralist society, America has thousands of different factions who wish to promote their own interests and objectives, and the study of American politics can therefore be seen as an examination of the continuous process of groups competing to influence the formal institutions of government in order that official policies reflect their preferences and goals.

The people of the United States

Any consideration of American politics should start with the people of the United States who as individuals and groups affect and are affected by the policies of government. The 2000 census counted 281.4 million people, making the United States one of the world's largest nations in population terms. In 1800 there were only five million people but in the two centuries since then a vast expansion has taken place, with the population almost quadrupling in the twentieth century alone (see Table 1.1).

Table 1.1 Population growth in the United States 1790–2000

1790	3,929,214
1810	7,239,881
1830	12,860,020
1850	23,191,876
1870	39,818,449
1900	75,994,575
1920	105,710,620
1940	131,669,275
1960	179,323,175
1980	226,542,199
1990	248,718,301
2000	281,421,906

Source: *Statistical Abstract of the United States 2001*, No. 1, p. 8.

Immigration was the major factor in explaining the tremendous growth in the American population. The United States is, in the words of John F. Kennedy 'a nation of immigrants' since, with the exception of the American Indians, the people of America are the descendants of immigrants. The settlers who arrived on the *Mayflower* in 1620 were religious fugitives from Europe, and the early colonists had both a Protestant background and tradition of individualism and resistance to authority. The 'WASPs' (White Anglo-Saxon Protestants) are still the dominant group in American society today in terms of holding positions of power and responsibility, even though they are now a minority numerically. America's heterogeneity and diversity of ethnic groups arose initially from the 'open-door' policy of immigration in the nineteenth century. From 1815 to 1914 there were over 30 million newcomers to the country; in the first part of the century they sailed mainly from Britain, Ireland and Germany, but by 1900 over a third were arriving from Southern and Eastern Europe.

Fears and hostility among the established population were aroused as masses of people, many poverty-stricken and speaking strange tongues, arrived at ports on the Eastern seaboard, and after the First World War restrictions on entry were introduced. In the 1920s quotas were fixed for each nationality, but as the system favoured Northern Europeans, critics charged that it was based on racial prejudice. In 1965 a new system was adopted and, as amended in 1976 and 1980, an annual limit was established. Preference was given to family members of US residents. The main impact was to reduce the flow from Northern Europe and to markedly increase the numbers from Asia (see Table 1.2).

The main motivation to come to America for the majority of immigrants was, and still is, a desire to seek a better life and standard of living than they could find in their own countries. Stories began to spread about the opportunities in America and were particularly attractive to those living in rigidly stratified European societies, where there was little hope of personal improvement. Some people fled from the autocratic governments in Eastern Europe to find political or religious freedom in America, while the development of cheaper steam transport made the journey a practical, if still dangerous, proposition.

Immigrants tended to settle in almost self-contained communities within the Eastern cities and they retained their own languages, dress and customs. Gradually over a couple of generations these groups became thoroughly assimilated into American society, while at the same time developing their own political leaders and remaining aware and proud of their ethnic origins. Although at various times there was tension and even violence, in broader perspective it is remarkable that so many millions of people were able to come from so many diverse backgrounds without more social and political instability. America has often been called for this reason 'the melting-pot society' although in recent times it has become fashionable to see the country as a mosaic with minority groups retaining their own identities and cultures while being part of the nation as a whole.

Table 1.2 Immigrants to the United States 1820–2000

(In thousands)	1820–1978	1961–70	1971–80	1981–90	1991–2000
Total	48,664	3,321.7	4,493.3	7,338.1	9,095.4
Europe	36,203	1,123.4	801.3	705.6	1,311.4
Asia	2,855	427.8	1,633.8	2,817.4	2,892.2
Americas	9,051	1,716.4	1,929.4	3,580.9	4,457.3
Africa	131	29.0	91.5	192.3	383.0
All others	427	25.3	37.3	41.9	48.0

Source: *Statistical Abstract of the United States 2002*, No. 8, p. 11, and various earlier editions.

Following legislation in 1980 almost two million refugees were admitted as permanent residents from countries such as the former Soviet Union, Vietnam, Cambodia and Cuba. In 1990 Congress passed a major new immigration law which increased the total number of visas available, permitted more European entrants and gave priority to people with particular skills. As a result America experienced its second great wave of legal immigration: the 1990s saw more immigrants coming to the United States than any other decade in American history.[2] By the beginning of the twenty-first century the country was considerably more diverse than it was even in 1990.

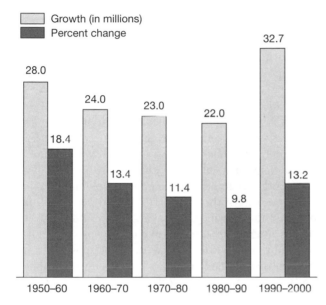

Figure 1.1 US Population Growth 1950–60 to 1990–2000

Source: 'Population Change and Distribution 1990 to 2000', *Census 2000 Brief*, US Census Bureau, April 2001.

Between 1860 and 1920 the proportion of the population that had been born outside the United States ranged from 13 to 15 per cent, reflecting the large-scale immigration from Europe. The 2000 census showed that the percentage of residents who were foreign-born had risen to 11.1 per cent (31.1 million) compared with 4.7 per cent in the 1970 count. More than half of the new arrivals, 51.7 per cent, came from Latin America, with 8.2 million from Asia and only 4.9 million or 15.8 per cent from Europe. As a result of this immigration there has been a marked increase in the number of people of five years and over who spoke a language other than English at home: 47 million in 2000 compared with 31.8 million in 1990. Of these, 21.3 million reported that they spoke English less than 'very well'. Almost 60 per cent of those not speaking English at home spoke Spanish.[3]

By 1996 there were approximately five million illegal aliens residing in the United States[4] with around 300,000 more arriving each year, mostly across the long land border with Mexico. Legislation passed in 1986 and 1996 has attempted to deal with this problem by increasing border patrols, speeding up detention and deportation procedures and improving methods of identifying illegal immigrants in the workplace, while also offering amnesty to around two million 'undocumented' immigrants who took up the opportunity to gain legal residency. Many observers believe that restrictionist measures are doomed to failure unless accompanied by a national database and the requirement that employers verify the legal status of every job applicant – moves that have been resisted by both business and civil liberties lobbies. While many Americans have shown their resentment at the mounting cost to the taxpayer of illegal immigration (for example, in California in 1994 voters passed a direct democracy measure, later declared unconstitutional by the courts, denying public services to illegal aliens), a growing coalition of politicians, business and trade union leaders have supported proposals which would allow some longstanding illegal immigrants to apply to become legal residents of the United States. Both Republican and Democratic leaders, conscious of the growing importance of Hispanic voters, were promoting such legislation in the 107th Congress (2001–2). Following the terrorist attacks in New York and Washington, DC on 11 September 2001 there were also demands for tighter security at US borders, an overhaul of the visa system to enable the authorities to keep track of individuals admitted legally to the country and a thorough reorganisation of the Immigration and Naturalization Service.

There has also been a vigorous debate as to whether there should also be a substantial tightening of restrictions on legal immigration or further liberalisation of the regulations. Some politicians and business leaders continue to argue that immigration helps fuel economic growth and fills jobs ranging from unskilled agricultural work to computer engineer positions which too few Americans are willing, or able, to do. Some also believe that America has an historic mission and duty to be open to people seeking opportunities denied to them at home. However, there has also been criticism about the impact of immigration on the availability of jobs and the wage levels available to American citizens, and concern has been expressed that many of the new wave of entrants are not being effectively assimilated into society and that this will have worrying implications for the future stability of the nation.[5] Some observers have gone as far as to suggest that there is a danger of 'Balkanisation' with the erosion of a common culture and language leading to the fragmentation and eventual disintegration of the United States.[6] This has led to attacks on the development of multiculturalism and bilingualism, with a growing movement demanding that English be named as the country's official language. In 1998 Californians voted to abolish bilingual education in the state's schools and required that all classes be taught in English with non-English speaking pupils being given intensive courses in the language.

One section of American society that has not been integrated so easily has been the African-American or black community which constitutes just under 13 per cent of the total population.[7] Sixty per cent of the 36.4 million black Americans live in ten states: New York, California, Texas, Florida, Georgia, Illinois, North Carolina, Maryland, Michigan and Louisiana. It is not surprising that the legacy of slavery, and the subsequent attempts to prevent blacks from participating in the political system, led to apathy and alienation. In the 1980s and 1990s black Americans increasingly played an important role politically and the number of black elected officials rose rapidly. In 1993 there were 7,984 compared with 6,056 after the 1984 elections, 4,963 in 1980 and only 1,479 in 1970.[8] The biggest rises have been in the South where until the 1960s segregation of the races was openly practised. This change was symbolised by the election in November 1989 of Douglas Wilder, a descendant of slaves, to be Virginia's Governor, the first elected black Governor in American history.

The 108th Congress, elected in 2002, included 37 black members in the House of Representatives or 8 per cent of the total, but Carol Moseley Braun, who in 1992 became the first black US Senator since 1978 as well as becoming the first black woman to serve in the upper chamber (see Table 1.3), lost her seat in 1998. The most dramatic increase has been among black mayors who now number over 300 compared with 86 in 1972. In recent times many major cities, including Washington, DC, Philadelphia, Los Angeles, Detroit, Atlanta and Baltimore, have had black mayors. The election of New York's first black mayor, David Dinkins, in 1989, after defeating three-term incumbent Ed Koch in the Democratic primary, was also seen as a landmark, while the election of black mayors in Seattle and New Haven was notable in that they are cities with relatively small black populations. Since the Voting Rights Act of 1965 which led to federal supervision of elections in areas which had used discriminatory methods to deter them from registering to vote, millions of blacks have been added to the electoral rolls and this was further stimulated by the presidential primary campaigns in both 1984 and 1988 of the Reverend Jesse Jackson who inspired many blacks to take part in politics for the first time. In the 1996 presidential election there was both a notable increase in the turnout of black voters and a decline in overall participation.

Table 1.3 Black and Hispanic members in Congress

Black		Senate	House
96th	(1979–80)	0	16
99th	(1985–86)	0	19
101st	(1989–90)	0	23
102nd	(1991–92)	0	25
103rd	(1993–94)	1	38
104th	(1995–96)	1	38
105th	(1997–98)	1	37
106th	(1999–2000)	0	39
107th	(2001–2)	0	36
108th	(2003–4)	0	37

Hispanic		Senate	House
96th	(1979–80)	0	6
99th	(1985–86)	0	11
101st	(1989–90)	0	11
102nd	(1991–92)	0	10
103rd	(1993–94)	0	17
104th	(1995–96)	0	18
105th	(1997–98)	0	18
106th	(1999–2000)	0	20
107th	(2001–2)	0	19
108th	(2003–4)	0	23

Source: *Congressional Quarterly Almanacs*, various dates.

Note: Does not include non-voting delegate from District of Columbia.

This increase in political power has been accompanied by the growth of a substantial black middle class which has been helped by anti-discrimination legislation and affirmative action programmes that have led to improved access to higher education and professional and managerial jobs. The contrast between the success of these black Americans, most of whom are among the 25 per cent of black families living in the suburbs, and the problems of an increasing 'underclass' based in decaying city centres and afflicted with drug addiction, violence, widespread illegitimacy and the threat of AIDS is indeed a stark one.

America's fastest growing minority group is the Hispanic or Latino population (mainly Mexican-Americans, Cubans, Puerto Ricans and Dominicans). The 2000 census showed 35 million Hispanics living in the United States, a 58 per cent increase over the previous decade and more than 12 per cent of the total population, very similar to the proportion of black Americans. The Bureau of the Census reported that by July 2001 the Hispanic population had risen to 37 million and was greater than the number of African-Americans which stood at 36.1 million. By 2050 it is estimated that the Hispanic population will have grown to almost a quarter of the total population of the country as a result of continuing immigration and the relative youth and high birth rates of its peoples. Some demographers have predicted that if the rate of growth continues Hispanics could even become the majority population by the end of the twenty-first century; at present whites constitute 70 per cent of the total US population.

The Voting Rights Act has also been important for Hispanics because it bans literacy tests and requires certain states and localities to provide assistance in voting in languages other than English. In 1994 5,459 Hispanics held public office,[9] while the 108th Congress had 23 Hispanic members or 5 per cent of the total. Leaders of the Hispanic communities saw increasing voter registration and participation among their people as their major political task in the next decade. Four out of ten Hispanics residing in the United States are not citizens and therefore not entitled to vote. Of those who are citizens only 57 per cent are registered to vote and therefore, although they make up 11 per cent of the voting age population, they comprise only 5.4 per cent of the electorate.[10] Politicians, however, have become very aware of the huge potential importance of Hispanic voters. While they were traditionally concentrated in California and Southern states such as Texas and Florida and a few Northern cities such as New York and Chicago they have now established a substantial presence in states such as Oregon, Utah, Georgia and North Carolina.[11] In recent years even Midwest states such as Wisconsin and Minnesota, whose long cold winters and Northern European heritage attracted few Latinos, have seen increasing numbers of Hispanic settlers, including many newly arrived immigrants.

The Asian population is also fast-growing and diverse and constitutes just over 4 per cent of the total population. In recent years China (including Taiwan), India, the Philippines, Vietnam and Korea have been among the top sources of immigration to the United States.

Blacks and Hispanics have registered substantial gains in membership of the House of Representatives, thanks in large measure to judicial interpretations of the Voting Rights Act that have led to 13 states redrawing their congressional district maps specifically to provide minority groups with the maximum opportunity of electing members of their own ethnic background to Congress. This had a marked effect in the 1992 elections but in a number of cases in Georgia, Texas and North Carolina the US Supreme Court found that the priority given to race in the drawing of electoral boundaries was unconstitutional and ordered that new districts be created (see Chapter 4). Despite the fact that some of the 'majority-minority' districts disappeared in subsequent elections most incumbent legislators from minority groups retained their seats and the total number of black and Hispanic members has remained stable since 1993.

There was also a growing backlash in the 1990s among white males against affirmative action programmes that are seen to discriminate in favour of racial and ethnic minorities as well as women.[12] Resentment against measures that provide for quotas with reserved places for these groups in higher education or in employment led to challenges in the courts and to voters in California passing a measure in 1996 that would end such practices in state government and public education. President Clinton was aware of this public mood and ordered a review of federal government affirmative action programmes. Although he made some modifications, the President announced that the overall goals of the policy remained sound and that the structure would remain.

Box 1.1 Women in American politics

In the last two decades the number of women playing a prominent role in American politics has increased considerably. In 1979, for example, there were only 16 female members of the House of Representatives and one Senator; by 2002 a record 59 women were serving in the House and there were 13 female Senators. The biggest jump happened in 1992, the so-called 'Year of the Woman', when an unusually large number of incumbents, mostly male, retired and women candidates were able to win many of the resulting open seats. Women are still considerably under-represented in Congress in relation to the population as a whole but the progress seen in recent years is also reflected in state government and in the executive and judicial branches of the federal government. George W. Bush appointed four women to his Cabinet in 2001 and two of the nine Supreme Court justices are female (Sandra Day O'Connor, appointed by Reagan in 1981, and Ruth Bader Ginsburg, appointed by Clinton in 1994).

Four prominent women in American politics

Madeleine Albright, Secretary of State 1997–2001

Mrs Albright was born in Czechoslovakia in 1937 but her family fled to London when the Nazis invaded her country and then sought asylum in the US when the Communists took over after the war. Her father became a lecturer in International Relations at the University of Denver. She later taught IR at Georgetown University. Having worked for Senator Ed Muskie and for the Carter White House she became the US Ambassador to the United Nations in the first Clinton administration. In 1997 she was promoted to Secretary of State, the highest position held by a woman in American government.

Hillary Clinton, First Lady 1993–2001 and US Senator for New York since 2001

Hillary Rodham was raised in Illinois and met Bill Clinton at Yale University. When they married she became a prominent lawyer in Little Rock while he served as Governor of Arkansas. During Bill Clinton's years as President, Hillary was criticised for becoming too involved in politics and downplaying the more traditional roles of the First Lady. She was the architect of the administration's ill-fated health care reform proposals in 1993–94, and also had to endure the embarrassment of a number of scandals to afflict the White House such as the Whitewater affair. Her relationship with the President was placed under great strain by the Monica Lewinsky scandal. Despite criticism that she had no connections to the state, Hillary Clinton won a comfortable victory to become a Senator for New York in 2000. As soon as she entered elective politics speculation was rife that her objective was to return to the White House as President in her own right and that she would become a candidate in 2008, or possibly even 2004 if pressure on her to run from the Democratic Party became too great to resist.

Nancy Pelosi, House Minority Leader since 2002

Nancy Pelosi has represented a House district covering most of San Francisco since 1987. Her liberal voting record is extremely popular in a constituency which she regularly wins with more than 80 per cent of the vote. She became the Democratic Minority Whip in 1999 and earned a reputation as an effective organiser and fund-raiser. She was elected Minority Leader in November 2002 following the resignation of Richard Gephardt who stood down after disappointing election results for the party. She became the first woman to lead a congressional party.

Condoleezza Rice, National Security Adviser since 2001

Brought up in Birmingham, Alabama when it was still racially segregated, Condoleezza Rice made a career as a highly successful academic specialising in International Relations. She became Provost of Stanford University at the age of 38 and wrote books on German reunification and the Czechoslovakian army as well as becoming an authority on the Soviet Union. She became an adviser to President Bush Senior and then to his son when he was running for the presidency. George W. Bush appointed her as his National Security Adviser in January 2001, making her not only the youngest but also the first black person and first woman to hold this senior post. Ms Rice has become one of the President's inner circle of advisers and played a key role in devising US policy in response to the 11 September terrorist attacks.

The median age of Americans in 2000 was 35.3 years and, as a result of a declining birth rate in the 1960s and increasing life expectancy, this will continue to go up. An ageing population has brought into focus the issues of the future of social security (retirement pensions) and the Medicare programme which provides for the health care costs of the elderly. With 35 million Americans over 65 years old the political influence of senior citizens and in particular the American Association of Retired Persons, the largest pressure group in the country, has grown substantially in recent times. As the 'baby-boomer' generation, those born between 1946 and 1964, approach retirement this trend will inevitably continue.

Table 1.4 Profile of the population 2000

281.4	million total
143.4	million females
138.0	million males
211.5	million whites
34.7	million blacks
35.3	million Hispanics
31.1	million born outside the USA
226.0	million residents of urban areas
72.4	million under 18s
35.0	million over 65s
15.0	million in college or university
116.7	million married
43.9	million single
17.6	million divorced
13.4	million widowed
104.9	million total households
27.7	million single person households

Source: *USA Statistics in Brief*, US Census Bureau,
http://www.census.gov/statab/www/poppart.html, accessed 20 August 2002.

A mobile society

The United States has always been a mobile society, geographically and socially. These two aspects of mobility have been closely connected as settlers have moved within America primarily in search of a better standard of living and future for themselves and their families. In 1992–93 16 per cent of Americans moved house, with 3 per cent settling in a new state. Mobility was greatest in the West (20 per cent) and the South (18 per cent) and least in the North-East (11 per cent) and Midwest (16 per cent).[13] However, the 2000 census showed that over two-thirds of Americans still lived in the state in which they were born.

In regional terms, the main trend historically has been the move to the West. The pioneers who with rugged determination developed the country westwards are part of American legend, but their hard-won paths to the Midwest and the Western coast have been followed, albeit more comfortably, by thousands and millions searching for the promised land of opportunity. The Western United States (the states of California, Oregon, Washington, Arizona particularly) grew at a rate of 500 per cent in population in the first half of the twentieth century, compared with a 67 per cent increase in New England.

Overall the population growth of 32.7 million people between 1990 and 2000 represented the largest census-to-census growth in American history and the only decade in the twentieth century in which all 50 states gained population.[14] However, the growth varied significantly by region with much higher rates in the West (19.7 per cent) and the South (17.3 per cent) than in the Midwest (7.9 per cent) and the North-East (5.5 per cent). In the last 50 years the South's share of the total population has increased from 31 to 36 per cent and the West from 13 to 22 per cent. Despite overall growth in each of the past five decades the Midwest's share fell from 29 to 23 per cent and the North-East's declined from 26 to 19 per cent.

Nevada, which has been the country's fastest-growing state for each of the past four decades, recorded a 66 per cent increase in the 1990s. It was followed by Arizona (40 per cent), Colorado (31 per cent), Utah (30 per cent) and Idaho (29 per cent) while California, Texas and Florida had the largest actual increases in numbers of residents. At the other end of the scale the slowest-growing states were North Dakota (0.5 per cent), West Virginia (0.8 per cent), Pennsylvania (3.4 per cent), Connecticut (3.6 per cent) and Maine (3.8 per cent).[15]

Political power has shifted with the population, to the more conservative areas of the South and West and away from the cities of the North-East, long the bastions of New Deal liberalism. The reapportionment of the House of Representatives seats to take

Table 1.5 US population by region 1960–2000

| | 1960 | | 1980 | | 2000 | |
	Millions	*%*	*Millions*	*%*	*Millions*	*%*
US	179.3	100	226.5	100	281.4	100
North-East	44.7	24.9	49.1	21.7	53.6	19.0
Midwest	51.6	28.8	58.9	26.0	64.4	22.9
South	55.0	30.7	75.4	33.3	100.2	35.6
West	28.1	15.6	43.2	19.1	63.2	22.5

Source: Compiled from the *Statistical Abstract of the United States 1996*, pp. 29 and 31 and *USA Statistics in Brief*, US Census Bureau, http://www.census.gov/statab/www/poppart.html, accessed 20 August 2002.

account of the demographic changes revealed in successive censuses has led to substantial changes in the representation of different states and regions. The total number of seats has remained at 435 since 1910 except for a temporary period of two years in the late 1950s following the admittance of Alaska and Hawaii to the Union. Reapportionment following the censuses from 1950 to 2000 resulted in California increasing its representation in the House by 23 to 53 seats, while Florida's went up by 17 to 25 and Texas by 10 to 32. On the other hand New York now has 29 seats, 14 less than in 1950, while Pennsylvania's representation has dropped from 30 to 19. As a result of the 2000 census 12 seats were redistributed, with Arizona, Florida, Georgia and Texas each gaining two seats and four other states each acquiring one. New York and Pennsylvania lost two seats each and eight other states now have one less representative. Although the lower house of Congress is affected by demographic changes the Senate continues to represent states equally regardless of population. Therefore although the ten most populous states contain 54 per cent of the people in 2000 they have only 20 Senators, the same number as the ten least populated states which only have 3 per cent of the American people.[16]

Another important trend in population mobility was the movement of blacks from the Southern states to the Northern cities in search of jobs and racial equality. In the 1970s, however, this trend slowed down and was even reversed as industrialisation and reform of racial laws took place in the South.

The most marked change in population structure has been the movement from rural to urban areas and, more recently, from city centres to suburban developments. In 1900 the population of America was approximately 60 per cent rural and 40 per cent urban (people living in towns of over 2,500). By 2000 there had been a complete transformation with 80.3 per cent of the population living in metropolitan areas, a total of 226 million Americans.

The movement of middle-class white people to the suburbs has left many cities increasingly unbalanced socially and often inhabited by the poor, the elderly and ethnic minority groups; the political and economic problems have multiplied as services have declined, property tax revenues have slumped and businesses, and with them employment, have moved out to the suburbs. By the 1980s only 25 per cent of white Americans lived in central city areas and 48 per cent resided in the suburbs; on the other hand 58 per cent of blacks had their homes in metropolitan centres and only 23 per cent lived in the suburbs. By 2000 non-Hispanic whites accounted for only 44 per cent of the 58.4 million people living in America's hundred biggest cities and were in a majority in only 52 of these.

Social mobility has been helped to a large extent in the past by the continually expanding economy and wealth of the country. With the development of service industries there are more white collar than manual jobs and many people have been able to move up the social ladder to a higher income bracket and the attributes of a middle-class lifestyle. With the recession in the early 1990s many Americans began to feel increasingly economically insecure and more people worried whether 'the American Dream' of improving living standards and upward mobility would be available to their children in the future. More families relied upon two wage packets to make ends meet, and changes in the economy reduced the number of secure and well-paid blue-collar jobs. Such factors contributed to the defeat of George Bush in the 1992 presidential election and the rise of populist politicians such as Ross Perot and Pat Buchanan who blamed US free trade policies and accused American business of exporting jobs to countries with lower labour costs. On the other hand, the American economy continued to create jobs, with 10 million more becoming available between 1992 and 1996. The unemployment rate, at 5.3 per cent for example in July 1996, was less than half the average for the European Union. There was also evidence that opportunities still existed for most people in the lowest income groups to move up the social and economic scale over time.[17] The booming economy of the mid to late 1990s led to renewed optimism about the future with consistently strong growth and low inflation. However, the aftershocks of the 11 September terrorist attacks, a falling stock market and corporate accounting scandals during 2002 gave rise to further concerns about an economic slowdown.

Class consciousness has not been as prevalent as in Europe and although there have been greater economic inequalities than in most European countries, many visitors to America, going back to the Frenchman Alexis De Tocqueville writing in the 1830s, have noted the markedly more egalitarian nature of social relationships. This was partly a result of the absence of feudalism with its established hierarchies and aristocracy, hereditary landed wealth and titles. The nation was fortunate to start with a clean slate and the history of fierce class divisions with the need to struggle for universal suffrage and basic political and economic rights for the working classes have not been so much a part of the American heritage. The possibility of social mobility and sustained economic growth was enhanced in America by two major factors. The size of the United States territory has grown considerably since the early days of the Republic. In 1800 the United States covered 888,811 square miles and 16 states and this had grown to 3,615,211 square miles and 50 states by 1970. At the same time America was fortunate in possessing enormous reserves of raw materials and its coal, iron ore and oil have been the bases of America's development as a 'Super-Power' militarily and industrially.

The American economic system is usually described as 'capitalist', and the United States Constitution was drawn up partly to protect private property rights and provide the right governmental framework for an expanding economy based on private ownership of capital and land. However, America certainly cannot be said to have a *laissez-faire* economy; even in the nineteenth century the federal government carried out policies designed to build up the economy and in the 1880s and 1890s considerable regulatory legislation was passed. American government has favoured regulation of business and commerce by specialist agencies and boards while leaving the means of production in private hands, rather than the direct nationalisation of industries experienced in Europe. Federal government intervention in the economy increased markedly in the 1930s. Large-scale unemployment and the slump in economic production led President Franklin D. Roosevelt to instigate a series of measures known collectively as the 'New Deal' in order to mitigate the worst effects of the Depression. In the period after the Roosevelt era (1933–45) Washington became closely concerned with managing the economy and a Republican President, Richard Nixon, even introduced a series of wage and price controls in the early 1970s. A reaction against widespread federal government intervention took place in the 1980s under the presidency of Ronald Reagan, but regulation by agencies concerned with, among other things, environmental protection, consumer safety and civil rights is widespread, and the federal government continues to spend large amounts of public money on subsidies to particular industries.

The federal government not only increased in size and scope but the balance of its spending also altered substantially in the thirty years between 1962 and 1992. Figure 1.2 shows that, despite the rapid build-up of America's armed forces in the 1980s, defence spending accounted for only one-fifth of the budget in 1992 compared with almost half in 1962. The major reason for this change is the huge increase in spending, both in absolute and proportional terms, on 'entitlement' programmes such as social security (pensions), health care and welfare payments to individuals.

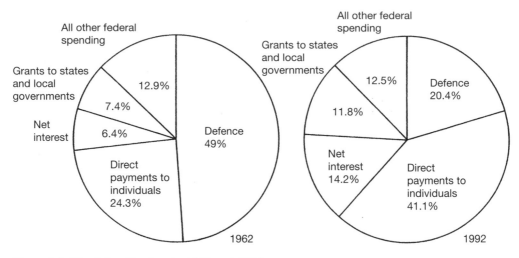

Figure 1.2 The federal budget in 1962 and 1992

Source: *Congressional Quarterly Guide to Congress*, 4th edition, 1991, p. 146.

Note: Grants to states and local governments include federal payments to states for social programmes such as Medicaid.

There can be no doubt that the market economy has allowed a rapid development of America's vast natural resources and produced the wealth that gives most of its citizens a high standard of living in comparison with the rest of the world. Capitalism is not without its critics, of course, but there is little real support for socialism or nationalisation, and the most that critics of the American system usually demand is that government more strictly regulate business activity so that profits are limited in the interests of the community as a whole. The oil crisis of 1973–74 and the increasing US dependence on imported oil damaged the self-confidence of Americans in the ability of their economy to expand continually. Public awareness of the dangers of environmental pollution and the need for conservation of natural resources also acted as a check on economic and industrial development in the 1970s.

By the 1980s it had become increasingly clear that the economic dominance enjoyed by the United States in the immediate post-war period was at an end. America has become far more interdependent with the rest of the world while the dollar fluctuated wildly and the US share of world trade declined. The productivity of American industry deteriorated in relation to most other industrial nations. The Reagan years saw increasing prosperity as a result of strong economic growth with low inflation and increasing numbers of jobs, but also a spiralling federal budget deficit and a trade deficit such that the United States for the first time became a net debtor country. The federal budget deficit cast a shadow over the American economy and arguments about how to deal with the problem and related issues of taxation and spending dominated American political debate in the early 1990s.[18] Figure 1.2 demonstrates that the net cost of servicing that debt accounted for 14.2 per cent of total federal expenditure in the 1992 fiscal year.

Improved economic growth in the mid-1990s allowed President Clinton to benefit in the 1996 presidential election from a reduction in the deficit from $290 billion when he took office to $107 billion, the lowest annual figure since 1981. However, the trend was projected to turn upwards again in the later years of the decade unless action was taken. The debate between Clinton and the Republican-controlled Congress on how to balance the budget created a major conflict between the two branches in the winter of 1995–96 and led to renewed demands for a constitutional amendment requiring the government to balance its expenditure with its revenues (see below, page 19). The President and Congress reached a compromise plan for deficit reduction in 1997. In practice the federal budget had moved from deficit to surplus by 1998, aided by particularly strong economic growth and the consequent increase in tax revenues and reductions in some areas of public expenditure. The nature of the political debate therefore was transformed with some (mostly Democrats) arguing that there was now scope for more spending on pro-grammes such as Medicare, federal health assistance for the elderly, while others (mostly Republicans) called for substantial tax cuts. By 2000 the annual surplus had reached $236 billion and the non-partisan Congressional Budget Office was forecasting cumulative surpluses totalling $5.6 trillion by 2011. However, partly as a result of the economic slowdown and the events of 11 September and partly because of the $1.3 trillion package of tax reductions promised by President George W. Bush in his election campaign and passed by Congress during 2001, the CBO's revised forecast in 2002 saw a fall of 71 per cent in the projected surpluses to $1.6 trillion, with actual deficits in the 2002 and 2003 fiscal years. Substantial proposed increases in defence and security spending as part of the 'War on Terrorism' and the projected costs of future costs of retirement pensions and medical care also raised fresh concerns about the federal government's ability to fund its expenditure without returning again to an era of deficit financing.

The historical framework: from Independence to Philadelphia

> We hold these Truths to be self-evident, that all Men are created equal, that they are endowed by their Creator with certain unalienable Rights, that among these are Life, Liberty and Pursuit of Happiness. That to secure these Rights, Governments are instituted among Men, deriving their just Powers from the Consent of the Governed that whenever any Form of Government becomes destructive of these Ends, it is the Right of the People to alter or to abolish it, and to constitute new Government . . .

In these famous words the Declaration of Independence, drafted by Thomas Jefferson, sets out the basic arguments that justified the act of rebellion by the 13 American colonies in breaking away from allegiance to the British Crown in July 1776. The settlers had a growing list of grievances including imprisonment of people without trial, cutting off their trade and quartering soldiers in their homes. However, it was the decision by the British that the colonies should pay part of the cost of protecting them militarily, but without representation in the Westminster Parliament, which acted as a catalyst in uniting them in opposition to George III. The Declaration of Independence explained to the world why the revolution had taken place.

It is important to remember that this statement was a revolutionary one because, at a time when most nations had hereditary monarchs who ruled on a 'divine right' basis, it was declaring that the only real and legitimate basis of government is the consent of the governed. The argument, and indeed the language, of the Declaration owed a great deal to the British political writer, John Locke. His theory of 'natural rights' and the idea of a social contract between government and the people had wide support among the liberal and educated classes in America.

By 1781 a plan for a confederation had been ratified by the 13 states which, although only a weak association with little central authority, did show that fighting and winning the war against Britain had succeeded in integrating the colonists into a viable political community. The Articles provided for a Congress in which each state would have one representative, but there would be no separate executive or judicial bodies. The Congress would have jurisdiction over foreign policy and defence, territorial disputes between the states, coinage, weights and measures, the Post Office and relations with the Indians, but the states would retain their independence and sovereignty over all other matters.

Within a few years it became clear that the Articles did not provide a sufficiently strong national authority or central leadership for the future development of America. The Congress had been unable to prevent commercial rivalries between the states and the imposition of tariffs, and there was very little development of a national identity. What is more, the Congress could not raise taxes itself but had to rely on contributions from the state legislatures to meet its expenditure.

By 1786 disillusionment with the Articles was rife and it was decided to hold a constitutional convention where proposals to reform the system could be considered. Most of the delegates who attended the Philadelphia Convention in May 1787 were young, fairly wealthy landowners, lawyers and businessmen and were committed to the notion of a stronger union. These men, who have been subsequently known as the 'Founding Fathers', went beyond their strict terms of reference and proceeded to write a completely new constitution.

Throughout the long summer of 1787 these men tackled three main problems. First, how to strengthen national identity through a more effective central government and, at the same time, recognise the diverse interests of the states. Second, they also had to remember that they should not, in creating this new central authority, allow individual rights to be threatened by too strong a government. Last, they had to establish a republican and representative system of government that would be acceptable to the peoples of the 13 states. The answer that the Philadelphia Convention arrived at has been called 'the Great Compromise'. A practical accommodation was achieved between those wanting a strong national government and those seeking to defend the powers of the state authorities, and the conflicting interests of the large and small states. A federal system was therefore created so that national and state governments would each have their own responsibilities (see Chapter 8). At the same time a bicameral national legislature would be established; one chamber would be elected directly by the people with the number of representatives apportioned on the basis of population, while in the upper chamber each state would have two indirectly elected members regardless of size and thus the interest of the smaller states would be protected. Other compromises in the package-deal included a more flexible amendment process, the promise of an early inclusion of a bill of rights to safeguard the freedom of individuals and the powers of the states and a system of electing a single-person executive which avoided both the selection by Congress and direct popular election by the public. Eventually all 13 states ratified the document in special conventions, with Rhode Island, which had boycotted the Philadelphia meeting, giving its support in May 1790. It is worth reading the full text of the Constitution, contained in Appendix I, to see how the Founding Fathers set out the powers, responsibilities and constraints on the institutions they created.[19]

Amendments to the Constitution

It was agreed at Philadelphia that proposals for amendments were to be made by either a two-thirds vote of both houses of Congress or by a national convention called by Congress at the requests of two-thirds of the state legislatures. An amendment could not

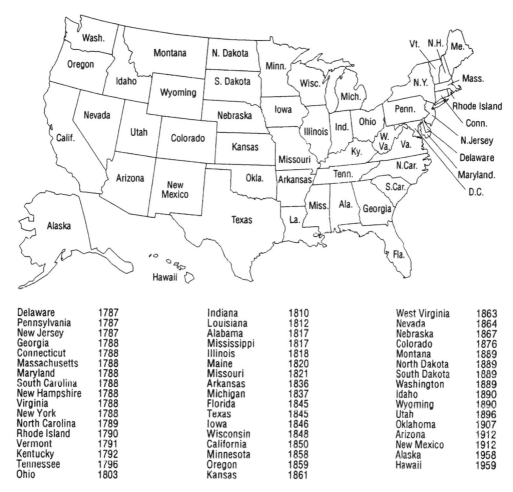

Delaware	1787	Indiana	1810	West Virginia	1863
Pennsylvania	1787	Louisiana	1812	Nevada	1864
New Jersey	1787	Alabama	1817	Nebraska	1867
Georgia	1788	Mississippi	1817	Colorado	1876
Connecticut	1788	Illinois	1818	Montana	1889
Massachusetts	1788	Maine	1820	North Dakota	1889
Maryland	1788	Missouri	1821	South Dakota	1889
South Carolina	1788	Arkansas	1836	Washington	1889
New Hampshire	1788	Michigan	1837	Idaho	1890
Virginia	1788	Florida	1845	Wyoming	1890
New York	1788	Texas	1845	Utah	1896
North Carolina	1789	Iowa	1846	Oklahoma	1907
Rhode Island	1790	Wisconsin	1848	Arizona	1912
Vermont	1791	California	1850	New Mexico	1912
Kentucky	1792	Minnesota	1858	Alaska	1958
Tennessee	1796	Oregon	1859	Hawaii	1959
Ohio	1803	Kansas	1861		

Figure 1.3 The states and dates of admittance to the Union

be effective until ratified, either by the legislatures or special conventions in three-quarters of the states. The President does not play a formal role in the process and he has no power to sign or veto a proposal passed by Congress. He can, of course, try to use his influence with the legislature and the public in advocating or opposing particular measures. There have been over 10,000 suggested amendments to the Constitution introduced in Congress since 1787, but less than 40 have been submitted to the states and only 27 have actually been ratified. This testifies to the fact that the framers introduced a system which could only be successful if an overwhelming number of people were behind the change. No amendments have ever been proposed by the convention method although by 1985 32 states (two short of the number necessary) had petitioned Congress for such a convention to write a new amendment backed by President Reagan requiring the federal government to maintain a balanced budget and restrict public spending to the levels of revenues raised. There are no rules for a Constitutional Convention and opponents of the move feared that such an assembly might propose much wider changes in the Constitution. Of the successful 27 amendments all but the Twenty-First, repealing prohibition, were ratified by state legislatures rather than by state conventions.

Some amendments have added to the Constitution and others have revised the provisions of the original constitutional document. It should be remembered that ten of the 27 amendments were ratified by December 1791, as the 'Bill of Rights' which was promised in order to ensure the ratification by some states of the new Constitution.

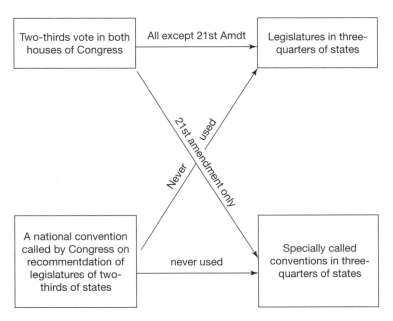

Figure 1.4 Amending the Constitution

The Bill of Rights – the first ten amendments

The first eight amendments set out restrictions on the federal government, specifically limiting its authority over the individual citizen. Many of the restrictions repeat similar limitations already in state constitutions, and they were designed to prevent the growth of a tyrannical dictatorship. The First Amendment sets out guarantees of freedom of speech, assembly and press, as well as the rights of petitioning the government and the free exercise of one's religion. The Second Amendment proclaims the right of the people to keep and bear arms, 'a well-regulated militia being necessary to the security of a free state'. This has been a controversial provision, as supporters of gun control and those groups opposed to legislation restricting the ownership of firearms have disagreed fiercely over how it should be interpreted. There is also protection against the government quartering soldiers in private homes and against unreasonable searches and seizures of people, their homes, or papers (Third and Fourth Amendments). The next four amendments are concerned with the rights of accused persons, and include the right not to testify against oneself, the right to trial by jury for major crimes and the provision that no one shall be deprived of 'life, liberty and property without due process of law'. There is the right to a speedy and public trial and the banning of excessive fines or bail, and 'cruel and unusual punishments'. These basic rights are, of course, fundamental to a free society and they retain their importance to this day, although the wording of the amendments has to be interpreted by the courts to fit in with present-day conditions.

The Tenth Amendment was important to the states accepting the new Constitution as it provides that, apart from the enumerated powers of federal government and those specifically denied to the states, all other government powers are retained by, or reserved to, the states or the people. It was supposed to guarantee the states that, although they had given up some powers in comparison with the Articles of Confederation, they were still major participants in the new federal system.

Amendments to extend voting rights

The states still retain today the right to determine exactly who is eligible to vote in elections within their boundaries, but they must not infringe any of the various constitutional amendments which have, since 1787, broadened the electorate. The Fifteenth Amendment, passed after the Civil War, laid down that no one should be denied the right to vote on the grounds of race or colour or previous condition of servitude. This was not effective for decades, and in 1964 the Twenty-Fourth Amendment prohibited the payment of poll taxes as a qualification, as this had been used in the Southern states to prevent blacks from voting.

In 1920, the Nineteenth Amendment ensured that women could not be denied voting rights on the grounds of their sex, and the Twenty-Sixth Amendment (1971) guaranteed all citizens over the age of 18 years the right to vote. This amendment holds the record for speed of adoption, being proposed in April 1971, and ratified by three-quarters of the states by July 1971.

Citizens living in Washington DC, the federal capital, were allowed to participate in the electoral process for President and Vice-President by the Twenty-Third Amendment (1961) and in 1978 Congress passed a proposal to give the District full representation in Congress, but it died in August 1985 with only 16 states having ratified it.[20]

Amendments to advance individual rights

As we have seen, the Constitution guarantees other rights of the individual as well as voting. In the original document there was no restriction on slavery, as the Southern states would certainly not have ratified the Constitution if this had been included. This great moral question, avoided at Philadelphia, was eventually put to the test in the bloody Civil War of 1861–65 and, as a result of the Northern victory, the Thirteenth Amendment abolished slavery in the United States. The Fourteenth Amendment was a very important and major alteration in the Constitution, because it extended the limitations on the federal government, mentioned in previous amendments, to the states as well. It says that states must not abridge 'the privileges or immunities of citizens of the United States', 'deprive any person of life, liberty or property without due process of law' nor deny to any person the 'equal protection of the laws'. The last restriction was later to allow federal intervention in states' affairs, like education, when it was felt that the states were not providing equal opportunities for all citizens.

Amendments to alter government

As the nation developed, so did the need to change some of the institutions and their powers, as set out in the original Constitution. Some amendments were passed to make the system more democratic as the country became more mature; others were necessary as a result of experience which showed the need for improvements and modifications, but none has changed the basic structure of government established at the Philadelphia Convention.

The Twelfth Amendment (1804) was necessary after the deadlocked presidential election of 1800 and provided that, in future, the Electoral College vote separately for the offices of President and Vice-President. The Sixteenth Amendment (1913) allowed the federal government to raise revenue by a graduated individual income tax, thus vastly expanding the amounts of money it could raise and spend. In the same year, the Seventeenth Amendment changed the nature of the Senate by making it a directly elected chamber.

In 1951, after President Franklin D. Roosevelt had been elected four times to the presidency, the Twenty-Second Amendment was passed, restricting any individual to two four-year terms in the White House. This was due to fears that a President elected too often to the office would become over-powerful but in August 1986 President Reagan argued for the repeal of the Amendment. Reagan said he did not want to serve a third term himself (he was 78 years old on leaving office in January 1989) but he felt that a restriction to two terms was 'a violation of the people's democratic rights'.

The Twenty-Fifth Amendment (1967) lays down the procedure for filling the post of Vice-President if it becomes vacant between elections. The President makes a nomination which must receive majority approval in both Houses of Congress. This procedure was used by President Nixon to replace Spiro Agnew with Gerald Ford as Vice-President in 1973; in the next year Ford himself as President was able to appoint Nelson Rockefeller.

The amendment also sets out the circumstances when a Vice-President may take over the leadership from the President in the event of the Chief Executive becoming mentally or physically ill or disabled. In July 1985 President Reagan became the first President to invoke this provision by transferring his powers temporarily for an eight-hour period to Vice-President Bush when undergoing surgery. In June 2002 Vice-President Dick Cheney assumed executive power for just over two hours while President Bush underwent a colonoscopy examination. The amendment was passed after the heart attack suffered in office by President Eisenhower and the assassination of President Kennedy.

Recent proposals

In 1992 a new amendment was added to the Constitution which delays the implementation of an increase in congressional salaries until after an election has been held. What made this development unique was that the proposal had originally been submitted by James Madison in 1789. Only six states had ratified it by 1792, a seventh ratified in 1873, an eighth in 1978 and 32 more by May 1992. Interest in the proposal had been revived by the public outcry against a recent large increase in congressional pay (see Chapter 2). Despite initial scepticism as to whether an amendment that had taken over two hundred years to complete the ratification process was valid and represented 'a contemporaneous consensus', as required by the Supreme Court, Congress somewhat reluctantly accepted it.[21]

In recent years a number of other proposals for amendments have been initiated but none of them has been able to obtain the necessary support for incorporation as part of the Constitution. A proposal known as the Equal Rights Amendment (ERA) which would require that equality of rights under the law should not be denied by the federal or state governments on the grounds of sex was first passed by Congress in 1972 but died in June 1982, three states short of the necessary 38 for ratification. An identical proposal fell six votes short in the House of Representatives in November 1983.

As we have seen, a call by state legislatures for a balanced budget amendment fell short of the 34 required for Congress to call a Constitutional Convention. In Congress itself, supporters of a balanced budget amendment fell short of the necessary majorities on several occasions during the 1990s. However, public concern about the federal budget deficit did keep the proposal alive and, once the Republicans gained control of both houses of Congress after the 1994 mid-term elections its prospects of success improved markedly. The party's 'Contract with America' for House elections contained a proposed amendment that would require a balanced annual budget from the year 2002, permitting a deficit only in times of war, if there was a threat to national security or if there were to be a three-fifths majority in both chambers. In January 1995 the House passed the proposal by 300–132, 12 more votes than required, and with all but two Republicans supporting it. However, in March 1995 the Senate failed to muster the necessary two-thirds majority by the slimmest of margins when one Republican Senator, Mark Hatfield of Oregon, refused to support his party colleagues, along with 33 Democrats. With the Republicans' majority in the Senate increased by two seats following the 1996 elections, supporters were optimistic that the proposal would pass in the 105th Congress, but in March 1997 it failed again by one vote in the Senate. Concerns that social security payments might be cut in future to bring the budget into balance influenced some wavering Democratic Senators to vote against the amendment.

Concern about congressional spending bills being loaded with 'pork-barrel' projects favouring particular districts and other unnecessary expenditure led to calls for the President to be given a line-item veto, allowing him to strike out specific parts of appropriation bills rather than accept all or nothing of the legislation. This proposal, which would have given the President similar powers to those enjoyed by many state governors, was also opposed in Congress by those who argued that it would shift power from the legislature to the executive branch, would have little impact on the deficit problem and would merely substitute presidential spending preferences for those of the Congress. The Republican 'Contract with America' included a commitment to introduce a line-item veto, but it was decided to avoid the problems associated with proposing and ratifying a constitutional amendment on the issue by passing legislation that would provide the President with 'enhanced rescission' authority. This means that he has the power to rescind any spending item contained in appropriations bills or in congressional reports unless both houses pass a 'disapproval bill' that would overturn his decision. The President could veto such a measure. After strong opposition in the Senate was overcome, President Clinton signed the bill into law in April 1996 and the powers came into effect in January 1997. The President used his new authority on several occasions to delete certain projects from the budget. Opponents immediately challenged the constitutionality of the statute in the courts. They argued that it gave the President, acting alone, the authority to cancel or repeal a federal law, that in so doing, he would be acting in a legislative capacity – a power not given him by Constitution – and that an amendment to the Constitution was necessary in order to make such a change. In June 1998 the Supreme Court voted by 6 to 3 to declare the law unconstitutional with the majority accepting the arguments made by those opposed to the new legislation.

Discontent with Congress in the wake of scandals, increased salaries for its members and a seeming inability to deal adequately with the nation's problems led to an upsurge in popular support for legislative term limits in the early 1990s. Proponents of term limits argued that such a radical measure was necessary to remove the power of incumbency which, they maintained, distorted the electoral process. In the 1990s voters in over 20 states passed referendum proposals to restrict the number of terms that legislators could serve in Washington; these were similar to the Twenty-Second Amendment which limits the President to two four-year terms.[22] Many areas had already introduced such restrictions for their state politicians and local government officials. However, in May 1995 the Supreme Court ruled that states did not have the power to set term limits for federal legislators, arguing that to do so would add to qualifications for office established in Article 1, Sections 2 and 3 – namely age, citizenship and residency. Supporters of term limits therefore saw their only way forward to be the passage of a constitutional amendment. Despite being included in the 'Contract with America' the House of Representatives failed by 61 votes to support passage by the necessary two-thirds majority in March 1995, the only Contract item not to succeed in the chamber. Opposition from many senior Republican members led to an unusual number of defections from the party line, as legislators claimed the measure would deprive Congress of experience and expertise and the voters of democratic choice of candidates. Supporters of the movement were also divided as to whether House members should be able to serve for six or 12 years, while agreeing that Senators should be limited to two six-year terms. The Senate failed to come to a vote on the issue after a debate in April 1996. At the beginning of the 105th Congress a new attempt to pass the proposal fell 69 votes short in the House and gained ten votes less than in 1995.

In two separate 5–4 decisions in June 1989 and June 1990 the Supreme Court declared state and federal legislation outlawing the burning or desecration of the US flag unconstitutional despite its symbolic importance to Americans. Justice William Brennan, writing for the majority, said:

> If there is a bedrock principle underlying the First Amendment, it is that the government may not prohibit the expression of an idea simply because society finds the idea itself offensive or disagreeable.

President Bush argued that a constitutional amendment was required to give special protection to the flag but such a proposal failed to achieve the necessary two-thirds majority in either house in June 1990. In 1995 the House passed an amendment prohibiting desecration of the flag by 312–120 but, despite confident predictions of success by its supporters, a similar proposal fell three votes short in the Senate. In 2000 the House again passed the proposal but the Senate vote was 63–37, four less than the number required to pass it to the states.

In 1998 an attempt to introduce an amendment guaranteeing the right to pray and practise religious beliefs in public property, including schools, as well as prohibiting the establishment of an official religion, failed in Congress. Supporters such as the Christian Coalition had hoped that such a proposal would overrule Supreme Court decisions in the 1960s which had interpreted the First Amendment as banning prayers being said in state-run schools (see Chapter 4).

In 2002 Republicans in the House of Representatives failed for the seventh year in a row since taking control of the chamber in 1995 to muster the necessary support for an amendment which would require both houses to pass by two-thirds majorities any proposals to increase taxes.

The separation of powers

The Founding Fathers were concerned not only with creating an American national government structure that would satisfy the states and the people, but also with avoiding the dangers of an over-powerful government. They felt that the experience of absolute monarchies in Europe showed that centralised control inevitably meant a concentration of power and the creation of a tyranny. The distribution of power between the federal and state governments would prevent excessive centralisation but how could an autocracy be avoided within the national government itself? They were determined to prevent any one individual or group securing control over all the powers of government – making the laws, executing or administering them, and settling disputes or adjudicating the law. The Framers turned to the principle enunciated by the French writer, Montesquieu, who felt that if the three processes were divided so that they were each the responsibility of a separate group of people, then a concentration of power could be avoided.

It would be unwise to build a system of government on the basis that office-holders would always be good and honest public servants, but if his plan was followed each institution would act as a check on the other. What is more, the President, Senate and House of Representatives would be elected by different constituencies for terms of different length and at different times.

The separation of powers system means therefore that no one can be a member of more than one branch of the federal government at any one time; in contrast the British Parliamentary system, for example, requires that the executive, the Prime Minister and Cabinet, *must* be members of the legislature. Negativity is the chief characteristic of the separation of powers doctrine as it is concerned with producing limitations and constraints on government rather than looking at the positive use to be made of such authority.

Checks and balances

Having separated the three main branches of government, the Framers proceeded to allow a certain amount of participation in, and checking of, each branch by the other two. This was because it was clear that a system of government would be unworkable and inflexible without some connecting links between those people making the laws, those enforcing them and the law adjudicators. In effect, the Founding Fathers created 'separated institutions sharing powers'. Since the Constitution was written, other institutions have developed which may bridge the gaps between the formal branches and help the system to operate. Two examples are political parties and congressional committees. The President and Congressmen are members of political parties and the ties between members of the same party in the two branches have often helped the passage of legislation by the development of common objectives. Congressional committees, which are not mentioned in the Constitution, are able to question executive branch officers, such as Cabinet Secretaries, about the administration's policies, even though the separation of powers doctrine prevents the President or any of his[23] subordinates being members of Congress.

There are many of these 'checks and balances', mostly written into the Constitution itself, although some important ones have grown up as matters of convention later. Some significant examples include:

Congressional checks on the President

(a) Many presidential appointments have to be confirmed by a majority of the Senate.
(b) The President's budget and appropriations for the executive departments have to be approved by Congress.
(c) All legislation the President wishes to see enacted has to pass the Congress.
(d) Congress has inserted in legislation the provision that executive action may be reviewed and approved by the legislature. The 'congressional veto' included in some

200 laws over the past 50 years was declared unconstitutional by the Supreme Court in June 1983. (See Chapter 2 for details.)

(e) The President's officials have to explain and defend their policies before congressional committees. (In an exceptional case President Ford himself appeared before a House Judiciary sub-committee to answer questions about his pardon of former President Nixon.)

(f) Congress can impeach and remove the President from office for 'high crimes and misdemeanors' (or force his resignation by the threat of impeachment, as occurred in the case of President Nixon in August 1974).

(g) The Senate has the power to ratify foreign treaties made by the President, with a two-thirds majority.

(h) Congress can override a presidential veto on legislation by a two-thirds majority in both houses.

Judicial checks on the President

(a) The Supreme Court can rule that the President has acted unconstitutionally or beyond his powers. (For example, the Supreme Court decided that President Nixon acted unconstitutionally in 'impounding' funds appropriated by Congress for particular legislation; President Nixon had refused to spend the money on these purposes.)

(b) The Supreme Court and federal judiciary can decide against the executive branch in court cases. (For example, the Supreme Court upheld the right of the *New York Times* to publish the Pentagon Papers taken by Daniel Ellsburg from the Defense Department, despite the opposition of the Attorney-General and the President.[24])

Presidential checks on Congress

(a) The President has the power to recommend to Congress measures he feels to be necessary; therefore, he can propose important legislation.

(b) As a recognised head of one of the major parties, he has influence throughout the legislative process.

(c) The President can veto bills which have passed the Congress but which he feels are unnecessary or undesirable.

(d) The President has the power of the 'pocket veto'; this means that he can refuse to give assent to legislation he receives after the adjournment of the legislative session and, there being no legislature to consider overriding the veto, the bill dies.

(e) The President has the right to convene extraordinary sessions of Congress so that it will consider matters he believes to be important. These are special meetings outside the normal congressional sessions.

Presidential checks on the judiciary

The President makes nominations for the appointment of all federal judges including the Supreme Court. If sufficient vacancies become available during his term, the President may be able to 'reshape' the Supreme Court politically.

Congressional checks on the judiciary

(a) The Senate has to approve all federal judicial appointments by a majority vote. The Senate Judiciary Committee particularly scrutinises appointees to the Supreme Court.

(b) Congress has the power to determine the size of the Supreme Court, and the number of inferior courts.

(c) Congress can impeach a judge and remove him from office for misbehaviour.

Judicial checks on Congress

(a) The Supreme Court can decide that an Act passed by Congress is 'unconstitutional' and thus null and void.

(b) The judiciary can interpret the meaning of Acts of Congress, and influence how they are carried out.

Whereas partisan connection may help to bridge the separation of powers when the President and Congress are controlled by representatives of the same party, divided party control of the two branches, which has been a feature of American politics in recent decades, may actually serve to reinforce the formal checks and balances in the constitutional system. For much of the post-war period Republican Presidents have been elected while the Democratic Party enjoyed majorities in one or, more often, both houses of Congress. In the period from 1995 to 2001 a Democratic President faced Republican control of both chambers on Capitol Hill and there is strong survey evidence to suggest that, in the 1996 elections, many voters consciously acted to try to secure such a result. By so doing they hoped to achieve a check on partisan extremism and, in effect, voted for a form of coalition government with moderate conservative policies. (See Chapter 3 for analysis of divided party government and Chapters 6 and 7 for discussion on split-ticket voting.)

Box 1.2 Political culture

To understand the working of any political system it is important to gain an appreciation of a nation's political culture – that is, the citizens' collection of beliefs and attitudes towards government and their feelings about their own place within the system. The political culture of the United States has a number of distinctive features which have evolved as a result of its particular historical development. The term 'American exceptionalism' has been coined to emphasise the peculiar and unique characteristics of the nation's culture and society that set it apart from other liberal democracies. The introductory survey in this chapter has pointed out the importance of the belief in the freedom of the individual and the suspicion and distrust of government control. Together these may be said to have given rise to an anti-authority political culture that has underpinned such movements as those opposing gun control and expressing hostility to taxation on the basis that it will be used wastefully by inefficient government bureaucracy. There has been a marked decline in trust in the federal government since the 1960s. Some of this may be accounted for by the upheavals and discontent following the Vietnam War and the Watergate scandal and the more adversarial role taken by the media since that time. However, the failure of government to deal effectively with major social problems and to meet public expectations have also played their part. Many surveys have demonstrated this trend. A *Washington Post*-ABC News poll in August 1997, for example, found that three-quarters of Americans distrusted the federal government despite the nation enjoying a prosperous economy at the time.[25] The crisis following the 11 September attacks led, at least temporarily, to more people expressing confidence in the national government and backing measures to give it more power to protect the nation from further terrorist assaults.

Americans have usually had a sense of optimism and confidence in the nation's future which has been accompanied by a belief that individuals can succeed in America by their own efforts. A lack of deference and a relatively high degree of social equality have been associated with social and geographical mobility. A strong belief in equality of opportunity has coexisted with a substantial degree of economic inequality and lack of support for a socialist movement. A firm commitment to democracy and representative government has been counterbalanced by restraints on majoritarianism and a powerful appointed judiciary that can override the decisions of the elected branches. Finally, the esteem in which the Constitution and the rule of law are held has led to a society in which recourse to the courts to settle disputes and protect rights is commonplace.

Chapter summary

- The United States has experienced large-scale immigration to the country which continues today. As a result the US is a hugely diverse society that is changing demographically all the time. The Hispanic population, for example, is likely to grow to approximately a quarter of the national total in the next 50 years.
- The US has always been a mobile society, geographically and socially. The fastest-growing regions in recent times have been the West and the South which have gained seats in the House of Representatives and in the Electoral College for the presidency at the expense of the Midwest and North-East.
- American wealth has been based upon a successful market economy and the country's vast natural resources. Government intervention in the economy has grown since the Great Depression of the 1930s but in overall terms regulation and taxation has been less than in European economies.
- The United States of America was created by the 13 American colonies which broke away from the British Crown with the Declaration of Independence in 1776. The Articles of Confederation which were ratified by the new states as the original basis for union proved to be too weak an association to survive. It had a central authority that had few powers and no ability to raise its own revenues.
- Delegates to the Philadelphia Convention in 1787 decided to propose a totally new constitution and replace the Articles with a stronger form of national union. The Founding Fathers thus created a federal system of government which divided law-making power between a new federal or national government and the states.
- The Founding Fathers also established a system for amending the new constitution which made it difficult but not impossible to alter the original document if circumstances required it. By doing so they ensured stability but also the survival of the US Constitution as the basis for American government for centuries to come. Amendments could only be made if there was overwhelming support for change in both Congress and the states. Following the Bill of Rights (made up of the first ten amendments) which was ratified by December 1791 there have only been a further 17 amendments since.
- Amendments have been passed to extend voting rights, to advance other individual rights of citizens and to reform government institutions established in 1787 in the light of subsequent experience or to make them more representative in a democratic age.
- The governmental system established at Philadelphia is one based on a separation

of powers principle whereby no one can serve as a member of more than one of the branches of the federal government – the legislature, the executive and the judiciary – at any one time. Power was therefore divided between different groups of people rather than concentrated in the belief that this was the best way of avoiding a tyranny becoming established.

- Although the Founding Fathers created a separation of powers they allowed for a certain amount of participation in the activities of each branch by the others. The sharing of powers in this way leads to the 'checks and balances' in the US Constitution.

Think points

- How has demographic growth and change affected the nature of American politics?
- Why have Americans traditionally had a mistrust of government?
- What are main principles underlying the design of the US Constitution?
- Which of the constitutional amendments passed since the Bill of Rights do you think has had most impact on the working of American government?

Some further reading

Edward Ashbee, 'America Divided: the Politics of Balkanization', in Alan Grant (ed.) *American Politics: 2000 and Beyond* (Ashgate 2000)

Edward Ashbee, *American Society Today* (Manchester University Press 2002)

Philip John Davis and Frederic A. Waldstein (eds), *Political Issues in America Today: the 1990s Revisited* (Manchester University Press 1996)

A. De Tocqueville, *Democracy in America* (Vintage 1965)

Michael Foley, *American Political Ideas* (Manchester University Press 1991)

Alan Grant (ed.), *Contemporary American Politics* (Dartmouth 1995)

Alan Grant and Edward Ashbee, *The 'Politics Today' Companion to American Government* (Manchester University Press 2002)

M.J. Heale, *The Making of American Politics* (Longman 1978)

Richard Hofstadter, *The American Political Tradition* (Cape 1967)

Anthony King (ed.), *The New American Political System*, Second Version (AEI Press 1990)

William M. Lunch, *The Nationalization of American Politics* (University of California 1987)

David McKay, David Houghton and Andrew Wroe, *Controversies in American Politics and Society* (Blackwells 2002)

Gillian Peele, Christopher Bailey, Bruce Cain and B. Guy Peters (eds), *Developments in American Politics* 4 (Palgrave 2002)

M.J.C. Vile, *Constitutionalism and the Separation of Powers* (Oxford University Press 1967)

Weblinks

National Archives Classroom: www.nara.gov/education/cc/main

National Constitution Center: www.constitutioncenter.org/

Congressional Research Service site on the US Constitution: www.access.gpo.gov/congress/senate/constitution/toc.html

US Constitution Resource Center Index: www.tcnnbp.com/index1.htm

Bureau of the Census: www.census.gov

Partnership for Trust in Government: www.trustingov.org

2 Making the laws

The American Congress

The role of the legislature

No other legislative assembly in the world probably fits the description of a 'law-making body' better than the United States Congress. In most democratic countries effective initiation of policies and laws has been taken over by the executive branch, and the legislature has generally become a body that reacts to and passes proposals put forward by the government. Nelson Polsby has described such bodies as 'arena legislatures' where parliaments become principally the forums for debate and approval of executive-inspired legislation. The US Congress, on the other hand, he calls a 'transformative legislature' enjoying an independent capacity, frequently exercised, to mould and transform proposals into law.[1] The Congress was given the function of law-making in the Constitution and, because of the separation of powers principle, it has to a large extent retained its powers over the initiation and passage of laws. Even in the United States, the President has played an increasing role in recommending and proposing legislation, but he still has to rely on friendly Congressmen to introduce his bills into Congress, and he is by no means certain of securing their passage. The legislature is seen as being constantly in a checking and balancing relationship with the President; there will always be friction and tension and occasionally direct conflict between the rival policies and interests of each branch. The Congress has, therefore, been called the most powerful legislature in the world; every year sees the introduction of thousands of proposals, but only a small minority ever became law by surviving the obstacle race of the legislative process. In the 106th Congress (1999–2000), for example, 10,840 bills and resolutions were introduced, many overlapping and on similar topics, but only 580 became public laws in the two-year period.[2]

What should the functions of a legislature be, and how far does the Congress successfully carry out these roles? It would appear that, apart from initiating and scrutinising legislation, there are a number of other things a responsible and representative legislative body should be doing. First, it should be acting as a check on the executive branch of government. This means that it should not only investigate carefully the President's requests for legislative action, but also should rigorously question and examine the administrative activities of government departments – what is known as its oversight function. It should keep a careful watch over the executive's requests for public money for the running of the departments. Congress has traditionally been the 'controller of the purse-strings' and the legislature's job is not only to approve taxation measures, but also to be vigilant against extravagance with the taxpayers' money. Last, as a representative body elected by the people, it should reflect the interests and aspirations of American society as a whole, while individual Congressmen should also be concerned with articulating the views of their own local constituencies.

Most Americans would accept that these are the major roles that they expect the Congress to perform, but there have been great differences of opinion as to how successfully they have been carried out. The American Congress has been the centre of great controversy and criticism, particularly in the last 30 or 40 years. Its supporters remind us that, despite the great increase in twentieth-century executive power, the Congress has remained a powerful body and that, more than any other assembly in the world, it has retained its central role in the legislative process. It is argued that it has managed to curtail executive power and maintain the balance in the constitutional system. Following the Vietnam War and the Watergate crisis of the 1970s Congress reasserted its authority and reformed its procedures so that it became increasingly independent, acting as an effective check on the President, whether Republican or Democrat. Ironically, as Allen Schick has pointed out, congressional independence has not been rewarded with acclaim; when it has acted as a check on the executive Congress has been castigated as an interloper, meddling or interfering and making life difficult for the President.[3] Proponents of Congress feel that it has a greater financial control over the executive branch than any other legislature in the world, and they believe that it has been sensitive to the climate of opinion in the country; given the demands of a heterogeneous society, the American Congress has been prepared to pass reform legislation, when it was convinced the public was behind such changes. It is a generally representative assembly that broadly reflects the wishes and views of the people. When Congress is divided on an issue and fails to act it is usually because the public it represents is also divided. Congress has focused on the important national issues of the day, while also allowing opportunities for members to raise matters of significance in their own local areas. Legislators have also increasingly provided a first-class service to their constituents, keeping in touch with the people they represent and helping them with a wide range of problems.

However, critics of the Congress have claimed that it has too often willingly given up its powers to the executive branch, especially in foreign affairs, and this, for example, led to America's disastrous involvement in the Vietnam War. They have argued that Congress has been prevented by its out-dated procedures from properly scrutinising legislation or the administrative activities of government departments, and that it has lost almost all control over government spending. Perhaps most serious is the claim that Congress simply has not been responsive to the needs of the majority of the American people, and that it does not pass measures quickly enough when they are required. Procedures in the Congress do give advantage to those people who wish to block legislation, and consequently it may take many years to pass a reform which many regard as urgent. Critics point, for example, to the failure of Congress to enact comprehensive regulation of handguns despite incidents such as the Columbine school massacre in Colorado in 1997 and widespread public support for such legislation. It is often argued, therefore, that Congress is too vulnerable to the pressures of rich interest groups, such as the National Rifle Association, and to the obstruction by minorities in the legislature. Congressmen have also been accused of being too timid in dealing with issues for fear of alienating constituents or of stimulating opposition which would mean that they would face a rigorous challenge in the next election. Parochial interests have often taken priority over the national interest and, even when the federal budget deficit was escalating, members would routinely support expensive 'pork-barrel' projects in their own districts or states, regardless of the impact on public expenditure. However, budget constraints in the 1990s did lead to a decline in the amount of substantive legislation dealing with the real problems the nation faces and an increase in what were known as commemorative acts. These provided special recognition of individuals, places, things or events and led to the designation, for example, of Tap Dance Day, Drinking Water Week and National Asparagus Month. In the 99th Congress no less than 46 per cent of all public laws passed were of this type.[4] The Republican-controlled Congress in 1995 introduced a ban on such bills, although some members have since tried to bypass this restriction by passing resolutions calling on the President to nominate such special occasions.

Claims of corruption and scandal have also frequently rocked Congress and there have been a number of well-publicised cases in recent years. Five Senators were accused of improperly intervening with the federal authorities on behalf of Charles Keating, the chairman of a savings and loan institution in financial trouble. Keating had provided campaign contributions to the members and in 1991 the Senate Ethics Committee criticised all five for poor judgement in the matter, while accusing Senator Alan Cranston of California of improper conduct.

In the House of Representatives there were the dramatic resignations of House Speaker Jim Wright and Democratic Majority Whip Tony Coelho, in June 1989. Wright finally stood down after the House Ethics Committee investigation of his affairs revealed that illegal gifts had been received by Wright from a Texas businessman and that he had received unusually high royalties for a book of his speeches in order to evade congressional limits on payments for speaking engagements. Coelho's problems centred around a Justice Department investigation into his investments and their relationship with insider trading. Although the two cases were unrelated they highlighted the question of ethical standards of legislators and led to demands for changes in the rules whereby Congressmen could supplement their salaries ($89,500 in 1989) by honoraria of up to 30 per cent of the salary for House members and 40 per cent for Senators. In 1987 members of Congress collected $10 million for making speeches and attending meetings or seminars, mostly organised by interest groups. In November 1989 the House of Representatives voted to ban members from taking any such honoraria after 1991 in return for a substantial pay increase to $125,000. The Senate at first would only reduce the ceiling on speaking fees in return for an increase in salaries, but in July 1991 it agreed to adopt a similar proposal to the House. By 2001 congressional salaries had been raised to $145,100, as a result of indexing for inflation.

In 1991 it was revealed that 325 current and former members of the House of Representatives had abused the privilege of having their own bank on Capitol Hill by routinely floating bad cheques and maintaining overdrafts without incurring any interest charges, a story that damaged many incumbents who were seeking re-election in 1992. In 1993 the powerful Chairman of the House Ways and Means Committee, Dan Rostenkowski (D. Illinois), was found guilty and jailed on corruption and embezzlement charges, among which was the conversion of thousands of dollars' worth of stamps into cash for his personal use. In 2002 James Traficant (D. Ohio) became only the second Congressman since the Civil War to be expelled from the House of Representatives after being convicted of racketeering, bribery and fraud. In the same year Senator Robert Torricelli of New Jersey was admonished by the Senate for accepting expensive gifts from a wealthy businessman and was forced to stand down as the Democratic candidate in the 2002 elections.

There is little doubt that increased media attention on Congress in recent years and the more open and adversarial nature of Congress has contributed to these exposures. As Christopher Bailey has pointed out, although there have been accusations of misconduct in the past, what was new was the extent to which such allegations served to focus concern on the performance of Congress. Bailey suggests that the escalating cost of campaigning has been a factor, and a number of allegations of unethical behaviour have involved campaign contributions. He also highlights the distinction between helping a constituent and exerting improper political influence on behalf of an individual. In the increasingly rancorous and partisan atmosphere in Congress, discussion about substantive issues has often taken second place to debate over ethics.[5] Not surprisingly, the overall impact of these cases damaged the reputation of Congress as an institution in the eyes of the public. Roger Davidson and Walter Oleszek point to the contrast between what they call 'the two Congresses'. Although the public have a generally negative view of Congress as a whole, individual legislators are often popular and almost all of those seeking re-election are victorious.[6]

In the 1994 mid-term elections the Republican Party's sweeping successes gave it control of both houses of Congress for the first time in 40 years. The Republicans argued that Democratic dominance of the legislature over such a long period had led to inefficiency and even corruption, as well as procedures that stifled open and democratic debate. The House Republicans' manifesto, the 'Contract with America', promised to make reforms in the way Congress did its business, as well as pledging radical changes in public policy. The preamble stated that the document was 'a detailed agenda for national renewal, a written commitment with no fine print'. The reforms, the Republicans argued, were necessary 'to restore the bonds of trust between the people and their elected representatives'.

Polls taken during 1995 did indicate a rise in public approval for Congress as an effective legislature, with the House succeeding in passing all but one of the main Contract bills but the budget crisis of 1995–96, which led to a partial shutdown of the federal government with departments running out of funds, changed the public mood dramatically. The majority blamed the Speaker, Newt Gingrich, and the Republicans for intransigence and believed the party's proposals to balance the budget were too extreme. President Clinton won the public relations battle with his congressional opponents by portraying himself as the defender of vital public services, particularly for the elderly and disadvantaged.

The attempt to show that the Republicans had swept away unethical practices in Congress was also undermined by allegations that Gingrich himself had been guilty of misconduct. After a long investigation which cast a shadow over the Speaker for most of the 104th Congress, the House Committee on Standards of Official Conduct (usually known as the Ethics Committee) eventually found that Gingrich had secured tax-exempt charitable donations to finance a college course he taught, knowing that its objectives were partisan and intended to aid the Republican cause. This offence was compounded by the fact that he provided misleading evidence to the committee. As a result, Gingrich was reprimanded and fined, and there was speculation as to whether he would be re-elected as Speaker at the beginning of the 105th Congress. In January 1997 Gingrich was re-elected by 216–205 votes; he failed, however, to secure an overall majority of the 435 members and four Republicans refused to support him.

The impact of the changes made by the Republicans in the 104th Congress will be examined later in this chapter; they affected not only the way the legislature works but also the distribution of power within Congress.

The membership of Congress

What sort of people become members of Congress? It is clear that Congress is not, and never has been, a true cross-section of the American people.

In terms of age, the members are generally older than the average age of the American population because of the constitutional restrictions (Senators have to be at least 30 and

House members at least 25), and because one can usually only obtain election after some considerable experience in politics or business. In January 2003 the average age of members of Congress was 55.5 years old, up from 53 a decade earlier. In the 1970s the trend had been towards younger legislators but this has been reversed since the 1984 elections with Congress slowly but steadily getting older. There has been a substantial increase in the number of women in Congress in recent years. The 2002 elections resulted in a record number of 59 female members or 14 per cent of the total membership in the House compared with 29 in 1992. There were also 14 women in the Senate as against only two a decade earlier. In the 108th Congress (2003–4) there were 37 blacks, 23 Hispanics and 3 Asians in the House but none in the Senate. Black members now constitute 8 per cent of the total in the lower house and the Congressional Black Caucus is an influential voting block in the House. There was a preponderance of Protestants with 265 members from the five main denominations, Methodist, Episcopal, Presbyterian, Baptist and Lutheran, and 38 non-denominational Protestants. There were also 149 Catholics (a proportional over-representation), 37 Jews and 17 Mormons.

The most obvious factor, as far as occupational backgrounds are concerned, has been the traditional predominance of the legal profession in Congress. In 1993 239 out of 535 members of Congress were lawyers. Law has traditionally been the main professional avenue to a political career because practice is financially rewarding, is compatible with holding public office, and because a legal background is regarded as advantageous to someone making the laws. However, in the 105th Congress the total number of lawyers declined to 225 and, in the House, the 172 lawyers were outnumbered, for the first time since records were kept, by the 181 members who gave business or banking as their occupation. This change reflects the changing composition of the House under Republican control. By 2003 the number of lawyers fell further, with 161 in the House and 165 coming from banking or business. The Senate, however, continued to be dominated by lawyers with 60 out of the 100 members having a legal background and 25 previously employed in banking or business. Thirty Senators and 145 House members gave public service or politics as their prior occupation. The other main occupational groups are educators (100), realtors/estate agents (33), farmers (31), doctors (19) and journalists (17).[7] There is a notable lack of people with manual working-class or trade union backgrounds even among the liberal members. The number of members who have served in the armed forces, 156, has continued to decline for over a decade, with only 37 having seen combat. Many Congressmen, particularly in the Senate, are very wealthy and more than a quarter are millionaires, some of them many times over.

Historically Congress drew its membership disproportionately from those with rural and small town backgrounds, contributing, some critics claimed, to a rather parochial perspective. Members tended to have served in state or local government in their own areas and, according to William M. Lunch, were often 'emissaries' from state and local party organisations receiving the party nomination as a reward for years of loyal service. In the 'New Washington' members are 'self starters' who have not relied upon the party organisation but have won the nomination through primary elections in which they were responsible for their campaigns. As a result when they are first elected to Congress they are typically much younger, they are more ideological in their outlooks and more concerned about influencing public policy. They are likely to be more cosmopolitan, better educated, well travelled and they do not use the district as an exclusive frame of reference. Today the national legislature, says Lunch, is 'dominated by political insurgents and independent entrepreneurs', making the working and style of Congress very different from that in 'Old Washington'.[8]

Although the average age of Congressmen has been rising there has also been a higher turnover of members with more members having relatively little experience in the legislature. In the 107th Congress almost two-thirds of House members, 65 per cent, were first elected in 1992 or in later years. In the Senate, although the average length of service of just over 11 years has not changed over the last decade, 45 members in 2001 had been in the chamber for six years or less. At the other extreme four of the six longest-serving Senators in American history were also in office: Strom Thurmond (R. South Carolina) aged 98 holding the record for the longest ever tenure at 46 years; Robert Byrd (D. West Virginia) 42 years; Edward Kennedy (D. Massachusetts) and Daniel Inouye (D. Hawaii), both with 38 years.

Most of the turnover of membership comes about as a result of decisions made by individual legislators to stand down. In some cases retirements are prompted by ill-health or old age; in others members may be motivated by the desire to make more money outside of politics, to spend more time with their families or move back full-time to their home state. Some may be standing down in order to run for another, often higher, office while others may have promised their constituents they would only serve a limited number of terms. In some case members decide that they have progressed as far in the congressional leadership hierarchy as they can and no longer find life in the legislature as rewarding or challenging. During the 1990s it also became quite common for retiring members to complain that they were disillusioned by Washington politics, particularly the partisan bickering and the need to be constantly raising funds to fight the next election.

Relatively few members leave Congress as a result of losing their seats at election time. Although some members' decisions to retire may be influenced by their anticipation of a tough re-election battle, by polls showing them heading for defeat or by a challenge from within their own party, these are the exceptions rather than the rule. The vast majority of legislators who wish to run again are re-elected and in most cases with large majorities and many times over. In most elections incumbent members, particularly in the House, are almost assured of victory unless they have been involved in a scandal, their constituency boundaries have been redrawn or they represent one of the declining number of marginal seats which are vulnerable to swings in voter sentiment. *A Congressional Quarterly* study in May 2002 showed that in 7,912 House election races between 1962 and 2000 when the sitting members were running for re-election, 93.3 per cent were won by incumbents and in only 6.7 per cent of cases did the member lose (see Table 2.1). In some years the proportion of successful incumbents has exceeded 98 per cent; in 2000 only nine of the 403 members seeking re-election were unsuccessful.[9]

There are some elections when a larger number of members lose their seats. In 1992 24 incumbents were defeated in the November general elections and another 19 lost to challengers within their own party in primaries. While the redrawing of district boundaries following the 1990 census played a part, many of those who lost were implicated in the House bank scandal referred to earlier in this chapter. 1992 was also the year when a record number of 65 House members decided not to seek re-election. In 1994 34 Democrats were defeated in the general election, victims of the big national swing to the Republicans which allowed them to take control of the House for the first time in 40 years.

Turnover in the Senate has been the result of both retirements and a higher percentage of incumbents being defeated than in the House. In 1996 a record number of 13 Senators stood down and 15 'freshmen' were elected to the 105th Congress. In 2000 six of the 29 Senate incumbents seeking re-election lost their seats.

Table 2.1 House incumbents and success in elections 1962–2000

Year	Incumbents winning	Incumbents losing
1962	368	34
1964	344	53
1966	362	49
1968	396	13
1970	379	22
1972	365	25
1974	343	48
1976	368	16
1978	358	24
1980	361	37
1982	354	39
1984	392	19
1986	385	9
1988	402	7
1990	390	16
1992	325	43
1994	349	38
1996	361	23
1998	395	7
2000	394	9

Source: *Vital Statistics on American Politics*, CQ Research; *Congressional Quarterly Weekly*, 18 May 2002, p. 1275.

Note: Total for 1962 to 2000: 7,921 races with incumbents winning 93.3% and losing 6.7%.

The powers of incumbency are formidable today and the variety of resources open to members but not to challengers has played a major role in the decline in competition. Pressure groups have increasingly contributed to the campaign funds of incumbent legislators, regardless of which party they represent, if they are thought to have supported the groups' interests while in office. In 2000 75 per cent of total contributions from political action committees (PACs) went to incumbents and 87 per cent of the money donated by PACs in elections where incumbents were seeking re-election. Challengers find it far more difficult to raise funds and the spiralling costs of elections create a severe disadvantage. During the last seven election cycles the average incumbent spent more than twice as much as his or her challenger. In 2000 the figures were $804,000 against $305,000.[10] Sometimes Congressmen have collected such a formidable war chest of financial contributions unspent from the last election that strong and credible challengers are deterred and the incumbent faces only a weak candidate or is unopposed.

Congressmen have better name recognition in their districts, can claim experience of Washington politics and may have an important position through seniority on a committee of importance to their constituents. Legislative leaders have recognised the importance of committee assignments to members and have increased the number of seats on key committees to accommodate more of their colleagues. For example, the House Transportation and Infrastructure Committee, which authorises billions of dollars for roads and public transport projects that can be directed to legislators' home districts, has been increased in size from 44 to 75 members in the last two decades.

Congressmen have large staffs both in the capital and in their districts who can help provide a constituency service for the voters. Another important advantage is the 'franking privilege'. This entitles House members to send free of charge six mass mailings a year to their constituents, as well as unlimited amounts of individually addressed first-class mail. Members use this opportunity to send newsletters to the electors and to publicise their activities in Washington on behalf of their constituency.

A key factor in the equation is the fact that the state legislatures are responsible for drawing the boundaries for congressional districts. A certain degree of gerrymandering under the guise of creating districts with equal numbers of electors as required by the *Baker* v. *Carr* (1962) decision[11] has taken place with the parties using their majorities at state level to design the balance of constituencies in their favour and in effect reducing the number of competitive seats. Most of the districts thus created give one party or another an overwhelming advantage. Most members win with lop-sided majorities and in some cases have no major party opposition. Of the 435 House seats, 324 or 74.5 per cent stayed in one party's hands throughout the five elections held between 1992 and 2000, despite the fact that this period included the momentous national victory for the Republicans in 1994. In the redistricting following the 2000 census the two main parties in most states agreed deals which protected incumbents as the top priority and made most seats even more solid partisan strongholds.[12]

While the advantages of incumbency apply equally to Senators (with even bigger office and staff budgets for those representing the larger states and more expensive campaigns involved) there are fewer safe seats in the Senate. Because the elections are statewide party competition is likely to be more intense over more heterogeneous areas that include both Democratic and Republican strongholds.

While it is often argued that long service in the legislature results in members being experienced and knowledgeable about the issues before Congress, critics have argued that the power of incumbents has led to the creation of a breed of professional politicians who are out of touch with the public they purportedly represent. Supporters of term limits argue that the democratic process has been hijacked and that voters are being deprived of real choice. This leads to low turnouts and lack of interest among the public. As we saw in Chapter 1, attempts to introduce a constitutional amendment providing term limits for Congress were unsuccessful in the mid-1990s. The term limits movement led by the group US Term Limits subsequently tried to persuade individual members to commit themselves to only serving a specific number of terms in Congress. There were relatively few 'self-pledgers' but those who did break their promise and ran for office again, such as George Nethercutt who had defeated House Speaker Tom Foley in his Washington district in 1994 with a commitment to serve only six years, were faced by concerted and well-financed, if not always successful, opposition in their elections by US Term Limits.

A bicameral legislature: the Senate and the House of Representatives

The Constitution established the bicameral legislature as one of the compromises necessary to secure the agreement of the 13 states. It was essential that, if the House of Representatives was to have its membership apportioned according to the size of a state's population, this should be balanced by having a second chamber, the Senate, which would represent all the states equally with two members each and this would protect the interests of the smaller states. The other aspect of the compromise was that the small Senate, with only 26 members when it was created, would act as a conservative check on a radical House, because it was to be indirectly elected by the state legislatures. This role has, of course, been modified considerably by the 1913 Constitutional Amendment

Table 2.2 The House and the Senate

The House	The Senate
Larger (435)	Smaller (100)
Short period of office (2 years)	Long period of office (6 years)
Elected by smaller constituencies	Elected by whole state
Special authority over tax bills and impeachment	Presidential appointments and trying impeachments. Ratifying foreign treaties
More formal	Less formal
Rules more rigid	Rules more flexible
Power less evenly distributed	Power more evenly distributed
Less prestige	More prestige
Members less publicly known	Members more widely known
Younger average age	Older average age
Easier qualifications (25 years and 7 years a citizen)	Stricter qualifications (30 years and 9 years a citizen)
Acts more quickly	Acts more slowly
Longer apprenticeship period	Shorter apprenticeship period

Source: Modified from Lewis A. Froman Jr, *The Congressional Process* (Little, Brown 1967), p. 7.

that converted the Senate into a directly elected chamber with each member being chosen in statewide popular elections.

The House of Representatives and the Senate are given equal powers over legislation because bills can be introduced in either house, and both houses must give their consent to a bill in exactly the same form before it is passed to the President. Each house is expected to participate in any declaration of war (really a formal power only, as war was never officially declared against North Vietnam) and both have to approve the nomination of the Vice-President if the Twenty-Fifth Amendment is used to fill the vacant post. However, each house was also given certain special constitutional functions which are its own particular powers. All taxation and financial measures must start their procedure in the House of Representatives (traditionally the lower or people's house) and the House also has the power to draw up the Articles of Impeachment against the President. The Senate, on the other hand, has the important power of approving most presidential appointments, such as Cabinet Secretaries, federal judges and ambassadors, and trying the impeachment of the President. It also has the power of ratifying foreign treaties which, although used to effect in the rejection of the Treaty of Versailles in 1919, was not so important in the twentieth century with the President's ability to make executive agreements with foreign heads of government, rather than formal treaties. However, the Senate ratification of the Panama Canal Treaties in 1978, changing the rights of control of the canal in a previous treaty, the Senate's approval of the INF treaty negotiated by Presidents Reagan and Gorbachev eliminating intermediate range nuclear missiles in 1988 and the rejection of the Comprehensive Nuclear Test Ban Treaty in 1999 by 51 votes to 48 all highlighted this power. The need for funding to carry out foreign policy, and thus the approval of both chambers, has in practice meant that the House is a significant partner in the making of foreign policy. Although the House of Representatives has had a longer history in representing the people, the Senate is known as the 'upper house', and in practice has greater prestige and status.

The Senate

Why should a chamber that is in some ways so clearly undemocratic, with two members for each state regardless of size, and procedures that allow small minorities to block the will of the majority, be so powerful a part of modern legislature? The Senate has, in the Constitution, stricter rules for qualification than the House; a Senator has to be at least 30 years old and must have been an American citizen for at least nine years, while entry to the House requires only that the individual is at least 25 years old and has been a citizen for seven years. As we have seen, this has led the Senate to have an average age several years higher than the House, and in this respect it is the senior of the two chambers.

Senators are also able to claim to speak for the whole state, and therefore they have more important and larger constituencies than Congressmen, who, except for those from the smaller states with only one member, represent only one district within a state. This role gives the Senator more political influence back home in his constituency, and the tradition of 'senatorial courtesy' means that he will be consulted on executive appointments to his state if he is of the same party as the President. In effect this means that the Senator can usually recommend to the President the name of somebody he would like to see fill, for example, a vacant post in the federal judiciary.

Senators are elected every six years and this means they have more time to establish themselves within the Senate and make their marks as legislators, and spend less time than members of the House in fighting re-election campaigns. The Senate, moreover, has increasingly provided the recruitment ground for more potential leaders and presidential candidates of the two parties than the House of Representatives, the most recent being Robert Dole, the Senate Majority Leader and the Republican presidential candidate in 1996, John McCain, a contender for the Republican nomination in 2000, and former Senator Bill Bradley who contested the 2000 Democratic primaries with Vice-President Al Gore, himself a former Senator. Senator Joe Lieberman became Gore's vice-presidential running-mate. Candidates have invariably been either Senators or Governors of states, but only a few, such as Richard Gephardt (Democrat) and Jack Kemp (Republican) in 1988, have been drawn from the House. However, despite the number of Senators who have tried to win the presidency successes have been elusive. The last sitting Senator to win the presidency was John F. Kennedy in 1960.

Because there are fewer Senators (100 as opposed to 435 in the House), the Senate is seen as a more exclusive chamber; each member is likely to be better known and to obtain more news coverage, and is able to acquire more power at an earlier stage. The difference in size goes a long way to explaining the differences in the procedures and operations of the two chambers.[13] There are fewer people to fill almost the same number of important positions, and therefore there is a more even distribution of power than in the House. Almost every Senator, except the freshman, is able to obtain some position which will give him some particular importance; there are jobs as committee chairmen, sub-committee chairmen, party leaders and whips, and on party policy and campaign committees, that all have to be filled.

Senate rules have always conferred greater power on individual members than in the House. Any Senator can generally offer any number of amendments to legislation, except appropriation bills, even if they are not germane or relevant to the bill before the chamber. Individual members can indefinitely prevent action on bills or executive branch nominations by using the system of 'holds' whereby they can indicate to leaders that they wish to delay consideration by the Senate under the cloak of anonymity. Passing reforms to Senate procedures requires a two-thirds majority and, without consensus, proposals have little chance of being implemented. The benefits of the existing rules to individual Senators outweigh the collective costs to the chamber in terms of institutional effectiveness.

Nelson Polsby's assessment, written almost four decades ago, remains true today: 'It is worthwhile to remember that there are only one hundred US Senators. Each one enjoys high status, great visibility, a large staff and substantial powers in his own right.'[14]

The larger number of committee assignments which Senators, with their more diverse constituencies, take on allows them to become more generalist than their House colleagues and to have influence on a wider number of issues. This also means considerably greater pressures on their time. Perhaps the most convincing evidence that the Senate is a more prestigious chamber than the House comes from the actions of politicians themselves. Members of the House often seek a seat in the Senate (for example, 40 Senators in the 104th Congress had previously served in the House) and see this as an avenue of advancement and promotion, whereas no Senator in modern times has given up his Senate seat to run for election to the House of Representatives.

What is distinctive about the workings of the Senate? The Senate has often been described as an 'exclusive club' with its small membership, its ornate chamber and long-standing traditions. Donald R. Matthews wrote in the 1970s about the norms or 'folkways' of Senate behaviour which led to Senators becoming socialised so that they were proud of the institution and showed respect and courtesy to each other.[15] Members were expected to serve an 'apprenticeship' by carrying out the least glamorous tasks when they first entered the chamber and to be 'work horses' rather than 'show horses'. While there was always the occasional maverick who did not follow the norms, a Senator earned respect and eventually influence by observing the folkways, being prepared to compromise and bargain on issues and by deferring to the desires of committees and their leaders in return for deference to his own committee's recommendations, a tradition known as 'reciprocity'. Over the last two decades the significance of these rules of behaviour has been much eroded. This has partly been as a result of aspiring presidential hopefuls in the Senate speaking out on a range of subjects beyond those of the committees on which they sit. New Senators were far more prepared to make speeches which would gain them television exposure and national recognition and on any issues they thought were important. The Senate debates have become more partisan and the traditional civilities often ignored. In many respects the Senate has become more like the House.

One of the Senate's traditional roles has been to protect minority interests, and the most extreme form of minority action blocking the will of the majority is the use of the 'filibuster'.[16] The Senate's rules are less formal and rigid than those of the House, and there is the tradition of extended or continuous debate in which Senators can speak for as long as they like on the floor of the chamber and can only be interrupted with their consent. There are no set limits on debates and it is difficult, if a minority is prepared to talk a bill out, to secure agreement on a cloture motion to end the debate and take a vote on the bill.[17] The filibuster device has often been attacked as undemocratic but its supporters claim it is an essential mechanism for protecting minority rights in a diverse society. It has been argued that, without such a method of defeating threats to the vital interests of minorities, states or regions, the Union's existence would be threatened. However, it is not just minorities but individuals who can effectively hold up the proceedings of the Senate. The record for the filibuster is held by Senator Strom Thurmond of South Carolina, who spoke for 24 hours and 18 minutes against the Civil Rights Act 1957; the longest group filibuster was by Southern Democrats against the Civil Rights Act 1964 and lasted 83 days!

Filibusters have been used more frequently and as a partisan tool; in the 1950s they averaged only one a year but this increased to 16.7 per Congress in the early 1980s and in recent Congresses they have averaged almost 30. Just under 30 per cent of major legislation in the late 1990s encountered some extended debate-related problems during the Senate's legislative process. The threat of filibuster can also become an effective veto power, especially if used when time is tight before a recess or at the end of a session. It may also be used to extract major concessions from the promoters of a bill. The political reality in the Senate is that 60 votes are needed rather than a simple majority of 51 for leaders to be sure that they will be able to pass legislation. As a result of such threats the Senate majority often has to make accommodations with the minority or factions within it. Therefore, despite increasing partisanship in the Senate, bipartisan coalitions are still more common than in the House. However, as Nicol Rae and Colton Campbell point out:

> The danger of a more partisan and ideological Senate . . . is that the authority of the chamber will be undermined as its rhetoric becomes more partisan. Failing the extraordinary situation of a Senate majority in excess of the sixty needed to impose cloture, the outcome of such partisan debate is likely to be endemic legislative grid-lock because of the nature of the Senate's rules. Eventually this is bound to have an adverse impact with the public as a whole. Indeed there is some evidence that this has already occurred. If a more partisan Senate is perceived to be less effective under the current Senate rules, then there may be pressure from the media and other shapers of American public opinion, such as parties and interest groups, to make major changes in Senate rules so as to make the Senate a majoritarian chamber on similar lines to the House of Representatives.[18]

When considering the House Republicans' 'Contract with America' bills, the Senate in many cases amended, diluted or blocked altogether some of the proposals, despite the party having a 53–47 majority in the upper chamber. Observers pointed out that the Senate was acting in exactly the way that the Founding Fathers had intended when they created a bicameral legislature. As James Thurber noted, in a comment echoing the words of George Washington:

> The Senate absorbs the populist feelings of the House of Representatives in the same way that you pour hot coffee out of the cup into the saucer to cool. It's deliberative. It's slow. It's politically more moderate.[19]

The House of Representatives

The House of Representatives has traditionally been organised in a more hierarchical way than the Senate, so that there is more clearly an elite who have worked their way to the top. This is partially the result of having fewer positions of leadership in proportion to the number of members, and in the early 1970s it caused considerable frustration among the junior and middle-ranking members of the House, who felt they could make little impact on decision-making until they had been in Congress a very long time. The centralisation of House leadership was modified by reforms made in the committee system in 1975 (see below, pages 42–3).

Congressmen in the House tend to become more specialised in particular fields than Senators as they have fewer standing committee assignments. House members are also likely to be more anonymous in Washington as they go about their work; they attract less public attention and even back in their own constituencies there will be many members of the electorate who will not even know their names. However, the televising of House debates has focused interest on House members and events in the chamber in a way that was very rare in the past.

The House has to have more rigid rules of procedure in order that an assembly of its size can deal with the legislative work. In contrast to the Senate, there are strict time limits on the length of debate and there are limitations on speeches, so that in some cases Congressmen may only speak for one minute each. Cloture requires only a simple majority, and therefore votes are taken and business dealt with quickly.

One of the most unusual aspects of the 104th Congress was the way in which the House of Representatives became the focus of public and media interest. Based on its 'Contract' manifesto, the Republican majority was able to set the political agenda for the nation in a way that only a newly elected President normally has the opportunity of doing. Indeed, the attention given to the swearing in of the Speaker and the new Congress in January 1995 was reminiscent of a presidential inauguration. For the first year of the 104th Congress, President Clinton and the Senate were principally concerned with reacting and responding to House initiatives. During their long years as the minority in the House, the Republicans had complained bitterly that the Democrats had imposed rules that prevented open debate and stopped them from introducing or voting on amendments to bills. By the 103rd Congress the Democrats had developed a repertoire of methods to expedite floor debate by limiting amendments that could be proposed, and 70 per cent of the rules governing debate were restrictive in this way. While ideological polarisation had intensified conflict, this resentment had contributed to the increasingly partisan and adversarial atmosphere in the House where there was little cooperation between the two sides. In a marathon session on the first day of the 104th Congress the House voted for sweeping changes in its rules and procedures, including those intended to allow more open debate (see below, pages 48–53).

The advantage of the larger states in the House of Representatives can be seen by the fact that often a state delegation can work together and manage to secure places for themselves in strategic positions on the most important standing committees. California, for example, now has 53 House members, while Wyoming has only one and cannot secure that sort of broad-based committee representation. However, the effectiveness of a state delegation will depend on its leadership and whether its members perceive common interests. Despite its size, California's delegation has often been divided on regional and ideological grounds and has not been able to maximise its potential influence. In recent decades caucuses of legislators representing regions or ethnic groups crossing state boundaries have become increasingly important. Taking House and Senate representation together, some states clearly have more political impact than others and this does not depend necessarily on size. A state's power in Congress is determined by the number of important committee and sub-committee chairmanships and elected leadership positions its members hold.

One of the most notable developments since the Republican takeover of both houses of Congress in 1995 has been the dominance of members from the Southern states in positions of power in both chambers. In the House, Speaker Newt Gingrich came from Georgia while Majority Leader Richard Armey and Majority Whip Tom DeLay were both from Texas. A Texan also chaired the Ways and Means Committee and a Louisiana member was Chairman of the Appropriations Committee. In the Senate Southerners held all the key Republican Party positions, following the retirement of Robert Dole and his replacement by Trent Lott of Mississippi as Majority Leader. Although this dominance was broken when Dennis Hastert of Illinois became Speaker in 1999, the Democrats took back control of the Senate in 2001 under the leadership of Tom Daschle of South Dakota and Trent Lott was forced to stand down as Republican leader in the Senate in December 2002, the power and importance of Southern members within the Republican Party in Congress is still evident.

Box 2.1 The congressional timetable

Each session of Congress commences in early January and, with recesses in the spring and summer, the legislature traditionally finished its business in early October. This allowed members to return to their constituencies and, every two years for House members, to campaign for re-election in early November. However, congressional adjournments in October have become the exception rather than the rule in the last decade or so; since 1991 Congress has only completed the session in October twice. A year-round Congress has become the norm with 'lame duck' sessions taking place after the November elections. 'Lame duck' sessions are so-named because the members of the current Congress, including those who are retiring or have been defeated, return to complete the legislative business rather than those who have just been elected.

The most frequent reason for the Congress having to stay until December has been the deadlocks over budget and spending bills, mostly resulting from the divided party control of the legislative and executive branches. President Clinton, for example, regularly dragged out negotiations on the 13 appropriations bills providing funding for government departments until late in the year so that he could put pressure on Congressmen wanting to leave the capital. There have also been crises and special situations such as the government shutdown of 1995, the impeachment of President Clinton in 1998 and the rewriting of the legislative agenda in 2001 after 11 September.

However, as *Congressional Quarterly Weekly* points out (31 August 2002, pp. 2233–34), another major factor has been the shorter working weeks which Congress has adopted in recent years. Congress now tends to meet from Tuesday to Thursday with some members not even arriving until the first votes on Tuesday nights. Legislators have increasingly demanded the right to spend more time in their districts and states, recognising that keeping in touch with their constituents and raising campaign funds are important tasks which will help their re-election efforts. For Senators fighting increasingly expensive and often competitive election races raising money is a particularly time-consuming business. Even members from the West Coast now expect to return home every weekend. This development has made scheduling meetings and expediting legislative business more difficult for the congressional leadership.

Congressional committees and their chairmen

Most of the important legislative work of Congress has traditionally been done by standing specialist committees that look at bills in their field and decide whether the full chamber should consider them. The committees, more often than not, decide the fate of a proposal, and therefore the composition of the membership is very important. The committees also investigate the work of the government departments and can call executive officials to appear before them; they often hold public hearings where witnesses will provide evidence and answer questions, and pressure groups and other interested bodies, as well as executive departments and agencies, usually send representatives to these meetings. The committee members merely question witnesses at these hearings and do not discuss the issues among themselves until a later occasion. Since 1973 committee meetings, including the markup sessions when bills are put together line by line, have generally been held in public. As Norman Ornstein has pointed out, these reforms dramatically changed the nature of committee business because members' actions and votes could be viewed by the press, their constituents and pressure groups.[20] Consequently the influence of chairmen was eroded and the ability of legislators to bargain over details was reduced. William Lunch commented that:

> The committee sessions that are now open are at the heart of the legislative process, and although subjecting them to public scrutiny has made available more public information, it has reduced the capacity of legislators to vote against the immediate interests of their constituents. As a result, the old system in which committee members 'made effective trade-offs and had effective discussions which produced effective legislation' has been rendered unworkable.[21]

Apart from the standing committees of the House and Senate, there are also a number of joint standing committees on which members from both chambers are represented, and special or select committees that investigate a particular problem over a shorter period. Examples of the most publicised select committees include the Senate committee chaired by Senator Sam Ervin on the Watergate events, which had daily television coverage, the Senate Committee on Intelligence which investigated the work of the Central Intelligence Agency (CIA), and the hearings on the Iran-Contra affair in 1988.

House committees are usually considerably larger than the corresponding Senate committees, and each one, with the exception of the Rules Committee where the majority party has a big advantage in seats, has the membership divided in proportion to the party strengths in the full house. Committee assignments are made by party committees in each chamber and then ratified by meetings of the full caucus. When deciding who shall represent the party on each committee, the leaders take into account the convention of seniority (that is, in this case, the length of service in the chamber), as well as the personal choices and constituency interests of members. They also wish to secure geographical balance and they realise that committee assignments are the main way in which they, as the elected party leaders, can influence the sort of decisions committees will make. Since the mid-1970s junior members have been less prepared, particularly in the House, meekly to accept whatever they were assigned, regardless of relevance to their constituency or personal interests.

Inevitably some committees are more popular with members than others, and some are regarded as having higher status. In both houses, committees dealing with taxation and government spending are highly prestigious. The House Ways and Means Committee and the Senate Finance Committee between them shape all taxation measures; their support is invaluable to a President contemplating tax changes or reforms. The Appropriations Committees allocate funds for government departments and for new and existing programmes. In the Senate, the Armed Services and Foreign Relations Committees have traditionally been influential bodies because of the Senate's special powers in foreign policy. In the House, the Rules Committee, which specifies the conditions under which bills are debated and amended, has a vital controlling voice over legislation, and therefore assignment to this small 16-member body is considered a valuable prize.

The committees of the Senate and the House were long recognised as the control centres of legislation, and therefore the committee chairmen or chairs have traditionally been

Table 2.3 Committees in the Senate and House, 108th Congress (2003–4)

Senate Committee	Chairman	State
Agriculture, Nutrition & Forestry	Thad Cochran	Mississippi
Appropriations	Ted Stevens	Alaska
Armed Services	John Warner	Virginia
Banking, Housing & Urban Affairs	Richard Shelby	Alabama
Budget	Don Nickles	Oklahoma
Commerce, Science & Transportation	John McCain	Arizona
Energy & Natural Resources	Pete Domenici	New Mexico
Environment & Public Works	James Inhofe	Oklahoma
Finance	Chuck Grassley	Iowa
Foreign Relations	Richard Lugar	Indiana
Governmental Affairs	Susan Collins	Maine
Health, Education, Labor and Pensions	Judd Gregg	New Hampshire
Indian Affairs	Ben Nighthorse Campbell	Colorado
Judiciary	Orrin Hatch	Utah
Rules and Administration	Trent Lott	Mississippi
Select Ethics	George Voinovich	Ohio
Select Intelligence	Pat Roberts	Kansas
Small Business and Entrepreneurship	Olympia Snowe	Maine
Special Aging	Larry Craig	Idaho
Veterans' Affairs	Arlen Specter	Pennsylvania

All Senate Chairmen are Republicans

House Committee	Chairman	State
Agriculture	Bob Goodlatte	Virginia
Appropriations	Bill Young	Florida
Armed Services	Duncan Hunter	California
Budget	Jim Nussle	Iowa
Energy and Commerce	W.J. Billy Tauzin	Louisiana
Education & the Workforce	John Boehner	Ohio
Government Reform	Tom Davis III	Virginia
House Administration	Robert Ney	Ohio
International Relations	Henry Hyde	Illinois
Judiciary	F. James Sensenbrenner	Wisconsin
Resources	Richard Pombo	Alaska
Rules	David Dreier	California
Science	Sherwood Boehlert	New York
Select Homeland Security	Christopher Cox	California
Small Business	Donald Manzullo	Illinois
Standards of Official Conduct	Joel Hefley	Colorado
Transportation & Infrastructure	Don Young	Alaska
Veterans' Affairs	Chris Smith	New Jersey
Ways & Means	Bill Thomas	California

All House Chairmen are Republicans

leaders in their own right. The party with the majority of seats in the chamber has the right to nominate all the committee chairmen. The sum of their powers once led Woodrow Wilson to describe American government as being 'government by the chairmen of standing committees'. Until the 1970s, the chairmen could exercise almost dictatorial powers over the running of their committees. The chairman could arrange the dates of meetings, decide the agendas, and control the resources and staff for the committee and its sub-committees. He was able to 'pigeonhole' bills to prevent legislation which he did not like from being discussed by his committee and he also wrote the report on bills which were sent to the full house. He could speak on the floor of the chamber on legislation from his committee, and he would be a leading member on any conference committee set up by both houses to hammer out a compromise version, if this was necessary. He could also appoint members of sub-committees and decide on the jurisdiction of these bodies.

These powers could be used responsibly but they were occasionally abused by autocratic chairmen. There were examples of chairmen calling meetings at very short notice, or when most members were away from Washington, in order to steam-roller a proposal through. Chairmen also sometimes rewarded their friends and penalised their opponents when assigning sub-committee appointments or funds for sub-committee work. Younger members, particularly in the House of Representatives, were often angry at their own impotence, but dared not challenge or antagonise the powerful chairmen. However, by the mid-1970s the pent-up frustration led to fundamental changes in the way the committee system operated. House committee chairmen were subdued by new procedural restrictions and forced to share power with their junior colleagues.

The most important development was the vast increase in the number of sub-committees and the expansion in their influence which decentralised much of the power of the full committees. Until the early 1970s, sub-committees (with the exception of those in the Appropriations Committees) did not play a dominant role in committees or in managing bills on the floor. However, between 1971 and 1975, the authority of committee chairmen was curbed in the House and that of sub-committee leaders strengthened. By the end of 1975, sub-committees were behaving more independently and their chairmen were playing a more active role on the floor of the House and sub-committee members were protected by a 'Bill of Rights' adopted by the House Democratic caucus.

Some observers believe that these reforms led to a shift from committee to sub-committee government, and there were fears that the decentralisation of power in the House had gone too far, creating further fragmentation and problems of leadership and coordination. As a result the number of sub-committees was reduced and their jurisdictions rationalised. In the House the 151 sub-committees in 1975 were cut to around 120 and the Senate, which had 140 such bodies operating in 1975, reduced the total to 87 in the 102nd Congress (1991–92). Ironically, the trend to decentralisation occurred at a time when House Democrats were trying to increase the powers of the Speaker, the Democratic Steering and Policy Committee, and the Democratic caucus in order to coordinate party policy on legislation and make themselves a more coherent body.

Selection of committee chairmen was traditionally a result of the 'seniority system'. This meant that the member of the majority party who had given the longest unbroken service to the committee automatically became the chairman with all the powers of that office. The justification for this system was that it prevented disputes about the chairmanship and rewarded experience of the committee's work. On the other hand, the seniority system did not take into account the individual expertise of members, the ability to have a good working relationship with other members, or loyalty to the party's general objectives and programme. The system rewarded those who stayed alive and could get re-elected. Consequently it was criticised for two main reasons. First, it resulted in most of the chairmen being much older than the average member, and some commentators dubbed it 'the senility system'. Second, the seniority system inevitably helped those members who were from one-party areas where, in practice, they faced little real competition at elections. This resulted, in the 1960s, in the Southern Democrats having control over not only a disproportionate number of chairmanships, but also most of the important and prestigious committees. The problem for the majority of liberal Democrats was that these Congressmen, although obtaining their positions by being Democrats, were out of sympathy with the party majority on important policies and usually cast their votes with the conservative Republicans. Therefore they used their positions to thwart the liberal legislation which was promoted and supported by the majority of their own party.

Reform of the seniority system was made a major objective of the liberal Democratic Study Group as well as pressure groups like Common Cause, and eventually the House Democrats decided, in 1973, to elect the chairmen by a party caucus (a meeting of all party members in the House) at the beginning of each session. The elections resulted in that year in the same people becoming chairmen who held the posts anyway through seniority. However, in 1975 the election of 75 new House Democrats, mostly young and liberal, led to a revolt that shook the seniority system to its foundations. The chairmen of each committee were subjected to the ordeal of interview by freshmen Democrats and the caucus voted 'Yes' or 'No' on each position, after the Democratic Steering and Policy Committee had given its recommendations. In the cases of three chairmen the caucus voted to replace them with other senior members of the committees. The effect of these elections was to remove three Southern Democrats in their seventies and eighties, men who had often been autocratic and unrepresentative chairmen, and to promote younger and more liberal Democrats. It also increased the powers of the Democratic caucus, and made the House more responsive to Northern liberal and urban opinion. In 1990 the Democratic Caucus voted to replace two elderly chairmen, while others beat off challenges to their positions. Two years later the Caucus removed 82-year-old Jamie Whitten, the Chairman of the powerful Appropriations Committee; Whitten had suffered a stroke but refused to stand down voluntarily and was replaced by William Natcher of Kentucky, the next in line (and 83 years old!). The Senate Democrats agreed in 1975 that they would select committee chairmen by secret ballot whenever one-fifth of the caucus requested it.

The expansion of sub-committees' responsibilities, the procedural constraints, and the crumbling of the seniority system combined to erode considerably the power and influence of the committee chairmen in Congress. What is more, the increasing role of party leaders and the stringent budget constraints of the 1990s limited the discretion of committees to pursue policies of their own choosing. The initiative for policy change shifted to party and budget leaders and away from committee and sub-committee chairmen who were accustomed to promoting and developing legislation.[22]

The elected party leaders

Traditionally, committee chairmen provided policy leadership in their own specialised areas, and party leaders were principally responsible for organisational matters such as scheduling bills, building coalitions and maintaining party harmony. The Constitution does mention the Speaker of the House specifically and he did have large personal authority, including the right to appoint members to committees. However, the allegedly 'dictatorial' methods of Speakers Reed and Cannon led to a revolt in 1910 and the stripping of the Speaker of many of his powers, including the chairmanship of the Rules Committee. The House reforms of the 1970s, while decentralising power away from the committee chairmen, also sought to strengthen the power of the Speaker and the party leadership. For example, the prerogative to nominate the majority party members on the Rules Committee gave him power over scheduling of legislation, while the right to refer bills to more than one committee (multiple referral) led the Speaker to become more involved in policy matters, as he often found it necessary to negotiate agreements between committee chairmen. In the post-reform Congress many of the most important bills were considered by more than one committee and the development of very large omnibus bills, covering many subjects and several thousand pages, helped to increase the role of party leaders. The introduction of summits between the White House and congressional representatives in order to break deadlocks over the federal budget gave party leaders more authority to try to reach agreement on behalf of their colleagues (although they still had to persuade legislators to go along with whatever was negotiated). On occasions party leaders also established a special task force of members to consider a particular issue and effectively bypassed the official committee structure.

Heightened partisanship, which was stimulated by divided party control of the executive and legislative branches and between the two houses (1981–87) increased members' expectations, particularly on the Democratic side, that their leaders would take a more proactive role in the legislative process and in relations with the President. As the ideological heterogeneity of the Democratic Party declined in the 1980s, and members elected from the South became more aligned with the rest of the congressional party, so did the fears that the exercise of strong leadership would pose a threat to individual policy or re-election goals. Democrats increasingly looked to their party leaders to speak effectively on their behalf in the media, to counter the impact of Republican Presidents.[23]

The main party leaders in the House of Representatives are:

1   The Speaker. The Speaker is formally elected at the beginning of each session, but the parties vote in blocs, and therefore the majority party is sure of having its nominee selected. In practice, therefore, he is chosen by the majority party caucus, and often the same person is selected without opposition until he decides to retire.[24] The Speaker is fulfilling two basic roles in the 'congressional game': he is at the same time 'referee' (or chairman of the House) and 'captain' of one of the teams (the party leader). As chairman, he presides over business, interprets the rules, and puts questions to the vote as well as assigning bills to the specialist committees. As party leader he is one of the major spokesmen for the party's policies, and influences the assignment of members to committees through his chairing of the party Steering Committee. He will only rarely take an active part in debate, although he can vote on every issue. The Speaker is usually able to combine satisfactorily these two potentially conflicting roles, and the element of discretion he has over procedural matters provides him with a possibly decisive influence over legislation. The Speaker is also constitutionally next in line for succession to the Presidency after the Vice-President.

Thomas 'Tip' O'Neill was Speaker from 1977 to 1987. His strong personality made him an influential leader on Capitol Hill, and the Carter administration's failure to establish good relations with the Democratic House Leader weakened the President's position with Congress. However, O'Neill was criticised during 1981 for his inability to hold the Democratic majority together in votes against President Reagan's tax and budget cuts. There had been some discontent with O'Neill's leadership but no formal challenges from among Democrats. His successor was Jim Wright of Texas who exploited the powers of his office and introduced an aggressive and highly partisan style of leadership. After only two and a half years leading the Democratic opposition to the Republican administration's policies Wright was forced to resign after an Ethics Committee investigation into his financial affairs (see above, page 28). He was replaced by Thomas Foley (Washington), a well-respected if somewhat less colourful figure in the House, who moved up from the position of Majority Floor Leader. The Speaker invariably has held this position before taking over the top post. Foley was the most prominent of the House Democrats defeated in the 1994 midterm elections, following which Newt Gingrich became the first Republican Speaker in 40 years. He became an extremely controversial leader and resigned in 1998 following the disappointing Republican performance in the midterm elections and criticism by party members. The Republican caucus supported Robert Livingston (R. Louisiana) to be his successor but he admitted to extra-marital affairs at a time when President Clinton was being impeached over the Monica Lewinsky scandal and he announced he would not become Speaker. The party then turned to the Chief Deputy Whip, Dennis Hastert (R. Illinois) and he was elected as Speaker in January 1999. Gingrich and Hastert are discussed in more detail below.

2 The Majority Floor Leader. The party caucus also elects an assistant to the Speaker who will undertake the role of leading the day-to-day strategy and efforts of his party on the floor of the House. He will negotiate with committee chairmen, the Rules Committee, and minority party leaders over the timetable. When Thomas Foley became Speaker in June 1989 the former presidential candidate Richard Gephardt of Missouri took over this role. The Republican Conference (the caucus of GOP members) elected Richard Armey of Texas as the Majority Leader in the 104th Congress. Armey, a strong conservative, was accused of being involved in a plot to depose Gingrich and only narrowly managed to secure re-election to his post in 1998. He announced during the 107th Congress that he would be retiring from the House at the end of 2002. Tom DeLay, also from Texas and the Majority Whip since 1995, was elected unopposed to replace Armey in the 108th Congress.

3 The Majority Whip. The majority party elects the position of Majority Whip whose main job is to inform the leadership of the voting dispositions of members of the party on bills coming up for decision in the House. To this end the Whip will negotiate with other members to persuade them to vote the way the leadership wants. He will provide information and act generally as a communication link between leaders and ordinary members; he is the 'eyes and ears' of the majority party leadership. The Whip, however, lacks the threat of disciplinary action that the British party whip relies on to secure compliance. By the late 1980s the Democratic whip system had expanded to include 102 members: the chief deputy whip, 15 deputies, 3 task force chairmen, 64 at-large whips and 18 regional zone whips. The size and representativeness of this group not only improved communications between the leadership and members but also provided, through the whips' task forces, opportunities for junior members to participate in the legislative process beyond their own committees. In the 104th Congress new Majority Whip, Tom DeLay, had a team of 55 members involved in securing the conversion of the 'Contract with America' into legislative enactments in the House. DeLay and his chief deputy, Dennis Hastert, met regularly with the full team and even more frequently with their 13 deputy whips. By 2001 the whip organisation had 67 members and DeLay was seen as the most important power-broker in the caucus, taking over from Armey as Majority Leader in 2003 and most likely to succeed Hastert when he retired.

4 Republican Party Committees. The Republican Conference has two main committees in the House: the Policy Committee and a new Steering Committee which replaced the Committee on Committees that had traditionally determined committee assignments for GOP members. The new committee, which also took over responsibility for proposing legislative priorities, gave the party leaders a stronger voice with the Speaker having five votes, the Majority Leader two, and four other elected positions one each, out of a total of 34 votes. The total membership was 29 in 2003 with four leading committee chairmen and members elected by the rank and file meeting alongside the leadership. The committee played the key role in the selection of committee chairmen in the 107th and 108th Congresses (see below, pages 54–5).

5 The Minority Party in the House. When they became the minority party in the 104th Congress, the Democrats elected Richard Gephardt as their Leader and David Bonior as Minority Whip. Bonior had been Majority Whip from 1991–95, while Gephardt had been Majority Leader under Tom Foley. Following the disappointing midterm election results for the Democrats in 2002, Gephardt stood down to be replaced by Nancy Pelosi, a liberal member from California who had succeeded Bonior as Whip and who became the first female leader of a congressional party. Pelosi defeated Harold E. Ford of Tennessee, the most conservative member of the Congressional Black Caucus and, at 32, the second youngest Democratic member elected to the 108th Congress, by 177 votes to 29. Steny Hoyer of Maryland took over as Minority Whip at the third attempt, having lost to Bonior in 1991 and Pelosi in 1999.

The leadership in the Senate is provided by the following positions:

1 The President of the Senate. In the Senate the chairman of the meetings is officially the Vice-President of the United States who is called the 'President of the Senate'. He fulfils only the 'referee' role of the Speaker and only votes in the event of a tie. The Constitution gives him this formal role, although he may not, in practice, attend Senate meetings very often; as he is elected at the same time as the President and is not a Senator, the President of the Senate may be a member of the party which is in a minority in the chamber.

2 The President Pro Tempore. The Senate majority party elects a senior member to be substitute chairman when the Vice-President is not present. He will, however, be able to be an active party member and can vote in all divisions; it is a formal position with little real power. Republicans gave this honour to Strom Thurmond, 94 years old at the time, who was re-elected in 1996 to his eighth term in the chamber and, as we have seen, is not only the oldest person ever to serve in the Senate but also has the longest tenure of any Senator in American history. Thurmond retired in January 2003, having recently celebrated his 100th birthday.

3 The Senate Majority Leader. The Senate Majority Leader holds the most powerful elected position in the upper house although the extent of his influence depends principally on his personality. Ability to persuade colleagues and to be a bargainer and broker of interests within the party are his main assets, and he has little patronage or disciplinary control over other independent-minded Senators. The Senate Majority Leader spends much of his time on the floor of the house, and one of his chief weapons in managing the Senate's business is the convention that he be recognised by the chair ahead of any other Senator. This allows him to control the day's proceedings by calling bills and resolutions for consideration and moving motions for recess. However, the Senate Majority Leader, who has always been institutionally weaker than the House Speaker, was not given any significant new powers to deal with the more active, assertive and less predictable membership that has been evident in recent decades. Barbara Sinclair has noted:

> As a result, the majority leader's control over the floor schedule is tenuous. A single senator can disrupt the work of the Senate by exercising the right of unlimited debate

or objecting to the unanimous consent requests through which the Senate does most of its work. Clearly a partisan minority of any size can bring legislative activity to a standstill.[25]

More recently Sinclair has commented:

> In the Senate unlike the House, a majority is not sufficient to act; to keep the Senate functioning requires super-majorities and this almost always requires the majority leader accommodate the minority to some extent. Yet, with the intensification of partisan differences, what his members see as central to the promotion of partisan interests is increasingly likely to be strongly opposed by the minority and thus to work against keeping the Senate functioning as a legislature. Furthermore, in the Senate, a cohesive, organised minority party has available formidable strategies for promoting its partisan interests. Majority party senators expect their leader to thwart such minority party efforts, but doing so is likely to interfere with keeping the Senate functioning.[26]

In order to progress legislation the Senate Leader will also have regular consultations with both the Speaker of the House and the President; the extent to which they work together is determined both by the partisan control of the institutions and the personal relationships that are developed.

In 1981 Senator Howard Baker became the new Republican Majority Leader and received almost universal praise for his ability in forging together a cohesive party group. Under Baker's leadership Senate Republicans showed unprecedented unity, with members voting 81 per cent of the time with their party on partisan divisions and 80 per cent with President Reagan on roll call votes in 1981. Baker retired from the Senate in 1985 and was replaced in the 99th Congress by Senator Robert Dole who beat four rivals to the Senate leadership. Dole stayed as Republican leader until June 1996 when, as the party's presidential candidate, he left the Senate to concentrate on his campaign. Dole was Majority Leader from 1985–87 and 1995–96 and, during his many years in the chamber, had developed a mastery of Senate procedure and earned a reputation as a pragmatic crafter of legislative deals. As a moderate conservative, Dole had often taken an independent line from the Reagan administration and he found that, during his time as leader, the party in both houses of Congress had become increasingly more conservative.

When Dole stood down, the Republican Conference elected Trent Lott of Mississippi as its new leader. Lott, a former Majority Whip, easily defeated his fellow Mississippian, Thad Cochran, for the top job. Having also been a former member of the House and a colleague of Gingrich, he was seen as well to the right politically of Dole and benefited from the strong support of the younger and more conservative members who had entered the Senate as a result of recent elections.

Lott was the Majority Leader at the beginning of the 107th Congress. Although the 2000 elections resulted in a 50–50 split between the parties the Republicans retained control by virtue of the fact that the presiding officer, the Vice-President Dick Cheney, was a Republican. The defection of Senator James Jeffords in May 2001 gave the Democrats a 50–49 advantage and Tom Daschle took over as Majority Leader, while Democrats took over the chairmanships of all the standing committees. With the Republicans regaining their majority as a result of the 2002 elections, Lott was due to resume as Majority Leader. However, he was forced to resign the leadership following criticism of a speech he had made at the 100th birthday celebration for Strom Thurmond in which he praised the retiring Senator's presidential campaign in 1948 when he had stood as a 'Dixiecrat' supporting racial segregation in the South. Lott's record on race relations issues came under intense media scrutiny and the Bush White House made it clear that it repudiated Lott's views. Despite attempts to apologise for his insensitivity Lott was obliged to bow to pressure from Senate Republicans and stand down in December 2002. Bill Frist of Tennessee was selected unopposed after the 51 Republican Senators held an unprecedented conference call during the congressional recess to find a replacement. Frist, the former Chairman of the National Republican Senatorial Committee was credited with having masterminded the party's successful campaign strategy in the 2002 elections and had the backing of President Bush. The President saw him as an attractive moderate conservative leader who would help to broaden the party's appeal after the damaging allegations of racism which led to Lott's downfall.

4 The Majority Whip. The Senate majority leader's closest assistant is the Majority Whip who, because of the smaller numbers involved in the Senate, has an easier job in keeping contact with other members and their voting dispositions than his counterpart in the House. Trent Lott became Majority Whip and Assistant Leader in January 1995 when he defeated Alan Simpson of Wyoming, who had been the Republican Whip for the last decade, by 27–26 votes in the Conference. His election had been interpreted as a message to Dole that the newer members wanted to see a more vigorous leadership pushing a right-wing agenda, similar to that in the House. When Lott took over the leadership in 1996, Don Nickles of Oklahoma became the Majority Whip. Nickles was forced to stand down at the end of the 107th Congress because of the term limit of six years imposed by the Republican conference in 1997 (see below, page 56). He was replaced by Mitch McConnell of Kentucky who was elected unopposed.

5 Other positions in the Senate. The Democratic Party in the Senate had to reconcile itself to its new minority status and find a new leader in January 1995. The retirement of George Mitchell and the defeat of his expected successor, Jim Sasser of Tennessee, in the 1994 election meant that Democrats turned to Tom Daschle of South Dakota who beat the more experienced Christopher Dodd of Connecticut by 24–23 votes. Wendell Ford of Kentucky became the Minority Whip to be replaced in 1999 by Harry Reid of Nevada.

Republican control of Congress

The Republican victory in 1994 led to significant changes in the working of Congress. For the Republicans in the House, control of the chamber for the first time in 40 years gave them the opportunity to establish a new form of party government with more centralised authority in the hands of the Speaker and the party leadership than had existed at any time since the early years of the century. Even in the Senate, where the party had been in control as recently as 1987, moves were made which would lead, albeit in less radical form, to more influence for party leaders over the notoriously decentralised and individualistic body.

The House of Representatives: changes in the 104th Congress

In examining the changes made in the House by the Republican majority it is important to place them in the context of the strengthened party leadership witnessed during the latter years of Democratic control and also the reforms made by the Republicans to their own rules while in opposition. Newt Gingrich's assertion of authority and the

Table 2.4 The elected leaders in the 108th Congress (2003–4)

The Senate

President of the Senate	Vice-President Dick Cheney	(R)
President Pro Tempore	Ted Stevens	(R Alaska)
Majority Leader	Bill Frist	(R Tennessee)
Majority Whip	Mitch McConnell	(R Kentucky)
Republican Conference Chairman	Rick Santorum	(R Pennsylvania)
Republican Policy Committee Chairman	Jon Kyl	(R Arizona)
Minority Leader	Tom Daschle	(D South Dakota)
Minority Whip	Harry Reid	(D Nevada)
Democratic Conference Secretary	Barbara Mikulski	(D Maryland)

The House

Speaker	Dennis Hastert	(R Illinois)
Majority Leader	Tom DeLay	(R Texas)
Majority Whip	Roy Blunt	(R Missouri)
Republican Conference Chairman	Deborah Pryce	(R Ohio)
Republican Policy Committee Chairman	Christopher Cox	(R California)
Minority Leader	Nancy Pelosi	(D California)
Minority Whip	Steny Hoyer	(D Maryland)
Democratic Caucus Chairman	Robert Menendez	(D New Jersey)

establishment of a dominant party leadership in the 104th Congress built on the foundations laid by these earlier developments.[27]

From the late 1940s until the mid-1980s the House Republicans had a very decentralised structure and their leader had little real power. However, in the late 1980s the House party made a number of changes which gave the Minority Leader, Robert Michel, more authority and adopted rules that mirrored those of the Democratic Caucus. At the same time a group of younger, conservative members formed the Conservative Opportunity Society and argued for a more aggressive approach as the opposition party in the House. They believed that the existing leadership was too prepared to compromise and do deals with the majority; they wanted to attack the Democrats to highlight the policy and ideological differences between the parties. Newt Gingrich who became Minority Whip in March 1989 was the effective leader of this faction and was primarily responsible for the attacks on Speaker Jim Wright which led to his enforced resignation.

The growing influence of the conservative activists led to limits being placed on the length of time ranking members (the chief spokesmen for the party on each committee) could hold their positions, and it was made clear to them that they were there to serve the Conference. When Michel announced his retirement in 1994, Gingrich was the undisputed choice to take over as leader and, when the party gained control in the elections of that year, he inevitably became the Speaker. Gingrich was also principally responsible for the House Republicans adopting the 'Contract with America' as their campaign manifesto. The document was designed to provide the party with a programme that united its candidates, clearly separated the Republicans from their Democratic opponents in the public mind and turned the mid-term elections into a national campaign rather than a series of local contests, which is the way congressional elections have traditionally been conducted. After the elections the Contract was transformed into an agenda for legislative action and the 224 candidates who were elected out of the 367 who signed it were under an obligation to support their commitment with their votes, thus creating a strong basis for party discipline in the House. The Contract included a promise to change the rules and procedures of the chamber.[28]

The Speaker and the party leadership

Greater party accountability for carrying out a manifesto required greater control by the party leadership. Gingrich moved quickly after the elections to establish his authority and, with President Clinton in a weak political position, he also saw the opportunity to use the Speaker's role to rival that of the presidency itself in articulating his vision of where the country should be going. Former presidential candidate and Senator, Eugene McCarthy, stated that, in this period, Gingrich seemed to see himself as 'a kind of Prime Minister' running 'a counter government'.[29]

Gingrich decided who the new committee chairmen would be on the basis of their ability and commitment to carrying out the party programme. Although he relied heavily on seniority, in some cases he bypassed the ranking members on committees from the previous Congress. His choices were made even before the Republican Committee on Committees was officially formed, and the Conference approved his nominations in December 1994 without dissent. A new Steering Committee, which gave the leadership more influence over assignments, replaced the Committee on Committees. In selecting members for committees Gingrich and his colleagues broke with convention and appointed junior legislators, and even freshmen, to important positions on committees such as Appropriations. Three freshmen even became chairmen of sub-committees. Gingrich had the loyalty of junior members; three-fifths of the Republican Conference had won their seats in the last two elections. As a gesture to those who criticised his new power, Gingrich accepted a call for an eight-year limit on anyone serving as Speaker, although the term limits did not apply to other leadership positions.

Committee and sub-committee chairmen

Gingrich did not inherit a group of entrenched and powerful committee chairmen and, to ensure that no independent fiefdoms developed in the future, a new rule was introduced limiting any individual to six years in any chairmanship. Despite some misgivings from senior Republicans who had waited many years to have the opportunity to chair a committee, term limits for chairmen were adopted by 355–74 in the House, with no Republican dissenters. Committee chairmen were also prevented from chairing sub-committees, although they did gain the power to nominate the chairmen of their sub-committees, with the Speaker's approval, and these bodies were brought more clearly under the aegis of their parent committees. For example, chairmen of standing committees were in future to control the appointment of sub-committee staff. These moves reversed the reforms of the mid-1970s that had decentralised power to sub-committees.

Committee structure and rules

Early in the transition period there were calls by some Republicans for a radical restructuring of the committee system. This opportunity was not taken and, in the event, the changes made were far less sweeping. There were two reasons for this: first, ranking members likely to succeed to chairmanships argued for the retention of particular committees and had to be placated; and, second, Gingrich saw the need to make immediate progress on his legislative agenda if the self-imposed 100-day limit for bringing bills to the floor for a vote was to be met.

Three committees traditionally tied to Democratic interests were scrapped; the District of Columbia and the Post Office and Civil Service Committees' business was transferred to a new Government Reform and Oversight Committee, while the work of the Merchant, Marine and Fisheries Committee was split between three other panels. Approximately one-fifth of the jurisdiction of the Energy and Commerce Committee (renamed the Commerce Committee) was distributed to other bodies. Several committees were renamed to symbolise their new Republican ethos; for example, Public Works and Transportation became Transportation and Infrastructure, but their jurisdictions remained basically unchanged. Pressure from Republican interests saved the Small Business and Veterans' Affairs Committees from abolition.

As we have seen, the Democrats had recognised the dangers of fragmentation in policy-making and had already reduced the number of sub-committees in recent years, but the Republicans wanted to go further. They abolished 25 sub-committees or 20 per cent of the total, although 13 of these came about as a result of the elimination of the three standing committees. With only a few exceptions, committees were not allowed to have more than five sub-committees and members could serve on a maximum of two main committees and four sub-committees. It was hoped that, as a result, there would be fewer scheduling clashes and better attendance would be encouraged.

Rule changes also affected the way committees worked. Among the most important was the abolition of proxy voting whereby a member could vote on behalf of an absent colleague. Chairmen had often used this practice to retain their party's majority and had been much criticised by Republicans when they were the minority. Although most committees had held their meetings in public since the 1970s, the rules had allowed them to close their sessions without explaining why. The new rules limited the circumstances in which a meeting may be held in closed session – for example, if national security might be otherwise threatened – and required a majority vote of the committee to take such a decision. In addition, radio and television coverage of all open meetings had to be allowed. In another move towards open and accountable government, committees were required to publish the names of members voting for and against all bills and amendments.

The practice of the Speaker sending a bill to more than one committee simultaneously for consideration, known as 'multiple referral', was also changed. New rules allowed him to send a bill to a second committee only after the first has finished its work or to refer different parts of a bill to separate committees.

In an effort to show the public that they were determined to cut out waste in Congress, the new majority voted to cut the staff assigned to committees by one-third. These reductions, as well as the displacement of personal staffs employed by defeated Democratic legislators, led to a large number of Democratic aides losing their jobs in 1995.

Floor procedures

As we have seen, the Republicans promised that they would allow freer debate and introduce less restrictive rules for proposing and voting on amendments. New procedures guaranteed the Minority Leader or his nominee the right to offer a 'motion to recommit', amending the bill under debate; a vote would then take place on sending the bill back to committee to make the revisions proposed.

A number of changes were also made to the way the House operates on the floor of the chamber. Automatic roll call votes were to be required on bills and conference committee reports that make appropriations and raise taxes as well as the annual budget resolution, thus allowing the public to find out exactly how their representatives voted on these key issues. Members were also no longer able to delete or amend speeches reported in the Congressional Record, except to correct grammatical or technical errors. Remarks inserted to revise or extend a speech were to appear in a different typeface in the record of the debate. Commemorative bills honouring individuals, places or events, which had been criticised as frivolous and a distraction from substantive business, were to be banned.

The most controversial change passed on the opening day session was the requirement that a supermajority of three-fifths of members voting would be required for the passage of any bill, amendment or conference report that contained an increase in income tax rates. Republicans supported this provision on the basis that it clearly demonstrated their belief that raising taxes should not be done lightly. However, many critics argued that the House was establishing an unwelcome precedent and that the measure moved in the direction of the Senate by allowing a minority of members to thwart the will of the majority. The new rule was eventually passed by 279–152.

Administration

Republicans claimed that, under the Democrats, the internal management of the House had become sloppy and bred corruption. The Speaker was given the right to nominate, and the House to elect, a new position of Chief Administrative Officer while the Inspector General was instructed to ensure that a complete audit of the financial records of the House was carried out. In July 1995 the resulting report by private auditors listed a catalogue of abuses and concluded that the institution was plagued by overspending, inadequate records and a lack of proper financial accountability. A list of recommendations for overhauling the system was submitted and the new Chief Administrative Officer was given the responsibility for implementing them while working with the House Oversight Committee.

Funding for 28 congressional caucuses, known as legislative service organisations, which received office space and budgets to operate on Capitol Hill, was abolished. This move caused an outcry among Democrats who claimed that these bodies performed important functions on behalf of the House, particularly those such as the Democratic Study Group which carried out research and analysis on legislative proposals. The Congressional Black Caucus and the Congressional Hispanic Caucus were particularly vocal in their opposition, claiming that the move was a Republican attempt to silence them. The majority argued that members were free to associate in such groups but that they should do so without public funding.

Impact of the House changes

In the 104th Congress Newt Gingrich called upon all the formal and informal powers at his disposal to assert strong party leadership in the House. He saw himself principally as a visionary, articulating ideas and values, as an agenda-setter and only secondarily as a political manager. In fact, he delegated most of the day-to-day responsibility for overseeing the implementation of the party programme to the Majority Floor Leader, Dick Armey. The leadership was intent on persuading, cajoling, and sometimes compelling, specific legislative outcomes from committees on a clear timetable, whereas committees had traditionally worked to their own schedules and usually determined their own policies. Chairmen had to acquiesce in intervention in their affairs in ways that their Democratic predecessors could neither have envisaged nor would have accepted only a year before.

The Speaker made extensive use of task forces of Republican loyalists on a wide range of issues, allowing him to ensure that committees pursued policies that were consistent with the leadership's wishes. While some chairmen did complain about their loss of independence, they were forced to go along with the new way of doing business or face losing their positions altogether. Most recognised that, at least in the first period of Republican control, the passing of the Contract legislation had to take priority and that the Conference demanded that they cooperate fully with the party leaders. In only a small minority of cases did committees report out bills that did not comply with the Contract or included significant amendments. The leadership did accept some changes but, on other occasions, used the Rules Committee to remove unwelcome amendments made by a committee.

However, after the winter 1995–96 budget crisis had weakened Gingrich's personal authority, Republican members increasingly began to criticise the centralisation of power within the leadership. There was also a recognition that, in bypassing committees which had subject expertise, the leadership had, on occasions, brought to the floor bills which then caused the party political trouble. During 1996, before the elections, committees became more active and helped initiate legislation which allowed the Republicans to claim that the 104th Congress had been productive. Many of the bills were compromise proposals that won both Senate support and President Clinton's backing.

In preparing for the 105th Congress the Republican Conference formally agreed to transfer more authority to committee chairmen to set the agendas in their areas and act as spokesmen for the party. Gingrich was also obliged to disband his small Speaker's Advisory Group and replace it with a broader and more representative body of around 20 members.[30]

The Hastert speakership and the return to 'regular order'

Although the party government system established by Gingrich to a large extent remained in place during the 105th Congress (1997–98) John E. Owens notes that the enduring forces of congressional politics – parochialism, constituency service, the permanent election campaign and decentralised and pluralistic legislative organisation – continued to reassert themselves. The House committees and their chairmen became more prominent and influential players constraining the power of the party leadership and offering alternative routes through which members could pursue their goals.[31] Owens argues that the post-Contract experience in the House demonstrates the limitations and obstacles to a party government strategy in a separated constitutional system which demands that power be shared and where the electoral connection between representatives and voters emphasises the importance of constituency interest.

The aggressive and centralised party leadership approach associated with Gingrich was tarnished by the Speaker's poor public image and the loss of Republican seats in the 1996 and 1998 congressional elections. Gingrich struggled to reconcile the demands of the conservative majority within the caucus for an ideological agenda with the moderates' insistence that such policies were damaging their electoral prospects and thus Republican hopes of retaining its majority status. They argued for compromise with the Clinton White House to produce centrist legislation which they thought would be attractive to voters. The conservatives' focus on Clinton's affair with Monica Lewinsky and their determination to pursue the impeachment of the President was blamed by most observers for the party's poor showing in the 1998 midterm elections when, for the first time since 1934, the President's party made gains in the House of Representatives.[32]

In the aftermath of the election Gingrich resigned. Robert Livingston, who had announced that he would challenge Gingrich, became the Speaker-elect and promised that he would revert to a more traditional style of leadership emphasising the mechanics of 'day-to-day governing' and advancing the party's legislative agenda in the House. Responsibility for producing the majority's legislation would return to the standing committees and most of the party task forces used by Gingrich to bypass or put pressure on the committees would be abolished. When Livingston resigned Dennis Hastert became Speaker and adopted this return to 'regular order'. He followed a more collegial style, broadening the leadership circle, deferring to committees and their chairmen and in personal terms took a much lower public profile to the extent that he was unknown to two-thirds of the electorate in July 2000.[33] Hastert relied on the skills he had developed in the Whip's office to build strong support within the Republican Conference and earned considerable praise from members for his personal style as a good listener and consensus-builder within the party. However, the partisan conflict of the Gingrich era continued and there was little or no attempt to seek the cooperation of the Democrats; in fact Hastert and the Minority Leader Richard Gephardt had a very poor working relationship and their mutual dislike was evident to all. Following the 2000 elections Hastert showed considerable acumen in balancing the political needs of his members and the legislative demands of the White House, enabling the President to enjoy a high success rate in his dealings with Congress and achieving a 91 per cent party unity score in 2001 (see Table 2.5). The importance of the House Republicans' loyal support to President Bush became even more crucial after May 2001 when the Senate once more came under Democratic control.

Despite the return to a more traditional balance and division of power between party leaders and committee chairmen not all aspects of the 'Republican Revolution' in the House have been reversed. Committee chairmen retained their authority over sub-committees and, most significantly, the term limits imposed on chairmen in 1995 have had a major impact in preventing the consolidation of power which many long-standing Democratic chairmen had established in the past. As a result of the six-year limit 13 chairmanships became available in January 2001. Speaker Hastert adopted a new process of selection to fill the vacancies, rejecting both the traditional seniority system and the approach used by Gingrich which led to the Speaker effectively choosing the chairmen himself. Instead the Republican Steering Committee, representing the House leadership

Table 2.5 Party scores in US Congress in 2001 and 2002 (%)

	2002		2001	
	Reps	*Dems*	*Reps*	*Dems*
Party support				
Senate	84	83	88	89
House	90	86	91	83
Opposition	*Reps*	*Dems*	*Reps*	*Dems*
Senate	12	15	10	10
House	7	10	6	14

Source: *Congressional Quarterly Weekly*, 14 December 2002, p. 3281.

Note: Party unity and opposition to party scores are composites of individual scores and show the percentage of time the average Democrat or Republican voted with or against his or her party majority in disagreement with the other party's majority.

and the ordinary members, interviewed 29 potential candidates for the 13 posts and, after a six-hour meeting, decided who should be proposed for confirmation by the full Republican Conference. In the event the Conference accepted all the nominees although it would have been possible for the membership to have rejected individuals as each post was voted on separately rather than as a slate which had been the practice in the past. Although Hastert had five votes on the committee he did not announce his preferences in advance and in some cases his choices were defeated. Overall, seniority did not prevail in a number of cases, with some moderates losing out to more conservative candidates and others being bypassed because they were perceived to lack the energy or ability to take on leadership roles. While some outgoing chairmen retired from the House (an unwelcome side effect of term limits for the leadership seeking to hold on to control of the chamber and fearful of losing the benefits of incumbency at the next election), others became chairmen of other committees or sub-committees; Henry Hyde, for example, was forced to give up the chairmanship of the Judiciary Committee, a post in which he gained national prominence during the impeachment of President Clinton in 1998, but he took over as Chairman of the International Relations Committee. In January 2003 the Steering Committee again ignored seniority in filling two of the four committee chairmanships to become vacant. The House Republican conference, in organising for the 108th Congress, decided to repeal the eight-year term limits for Speaker they had set in 1995 but retain the six-year limits for committee chairmen.

The 'Republican Revolution' had been the product of Gingrich's particular style of partisan leadership, of the pent-up frustration of Republican members who had been in opposition for so long and of the more sharply conservative beliefs of the majority of the Conference, bolstered by the influx of 73 freshmen or newcomers first elected to the House in 1994. The Republican takeover has left a significant institutional legacy even though some of the changes made to the way the House runs have not been permanent and the Democrats have no intention of keeping the term limits for committee chairmen when they are next in the majority. As Eric Schickler has pointed out:

> Since then [the Republican Revolution], many of the most fiery of the freshmen Republicans have left the House in defeat, have retired, or have run for other offices complaining about the difficulty of changing Washington. The remaining members of the class of 1994 appear to have become acclimated to congressional practices and are acting more like traditional law-makers, moving up on committee hierarchies and trying to direct federal projects back home. In the 107th Congress (2001–2), five members of the class of 1994 are deputy whips, eleven are sub-committee chairmen, and one is a full committee chair.[34]

The Senate

Unlike their colleagues in the House, Republican Senators had given no commitment to make procedural changes in their chamber. Far from feeling an oppressed minority, they had benefited from the opportunities that Senate rules give to the opposition. In the closing months of the 103rd Congress, for example, Republican Senators had blocked a number of important bills supported by President Clinton and the Democratic majority. However, the more conservative members of the Republican Conference quickly became frustrated as they saw the Contract bills that had passed the House slow to a crawl in their own chamber. They also felt that the minority of Republican moderates in the Senate had too much influence over legislation and that those who had acquired committee chairmanships through the seniority system were too often out of touch with the views of the conservative majority within the Conference. Traditionally committee members nominated their chairmen which they did on the basis of seniority in almost every case. The choice was then ratified by the Conference and subsequently by the full Senate. The position of chairmen and their relations with the party leadership and the Conference was highlighted by the Senate vote on a proposed balanced budget Constitutional Amendment (see Chapter 1). The failure of Mark Hatfield, the Chairman of the Appropriations Committee, to support the amendment meant that it fell one vote short of the necessary two-thirds majority. Although they failed to force Hatfield to resign from his chairmanship, conservative Senators persuaded the Majority Leader, Robert Dole, to set up a task force to examine rule changes in the selection of chairmen.

The task force, chaired by Connie Mack (R. Florida), made a number of recommendations, and the Conference passed a package of changes, to come into operation in January 1997, which were intended to strengthen the leadership and the party. These included a six-year term limit for party leaders (except the top leader) and committee chairmen, the adoption of a formal legislative agenda with positions on issues to be determined by a three-quarters majority in the Conference and the introduction of secret ballots when committee members vote for chairmen, thus allowing alternative candidates to be supported without fear of retribution if the effort failed. The full Conference would then vote on the committee's choice, also by secret ballot, and in the event of the proposed candidate being rejected, the Leader would then nominate a new chairman. Chairmen of major committees were also banned from chairing any other panel, either committee or sub-committee, with the exceptions of Appropriations, Ethics and Rules. These rule changes, combined with the influx of new members and retirements, led to nine new chairmen taking over in the 20 Senate standing committees in the 105th Congress. Power was also distributed more widely, with some first-term Senators being given the opportunity to become chairmen.

Although not as radical as those in the House, the changes did indicate that the Senate Republicans were prepared to take the first steps in securing greater accountability to the party and in strengthening their leader's ability to lead. As a result, Trent Lott was given somewhat greater authority than his predecessors but his tools for enforcing party regularity are still very limited and, given the need for moderate Republican Senators' support in future votes, he had to be very careful how he used them. Senator James Jeffords, a moderate Republican disillusioned by the conservative policy stances of President Bush and the party leaders in the Senate, defected in May 2001 to become an independent. This move not only handed control of the chamber to the Democrats but also demonstrated the problems faced by the leadership of an institution which displays both heightened partisanship alongside rampant individualism and independence among its members.

In June 2002 the Republican Conference approved a clarification of the rules on term limits for committee chairmen which had been introduced in 1997 in order to take account of the situation when the party was in the minority in the Senate. The compromise formula agreed lays down that Republicans can serve 12 years in the top position on a committee, six as ranking member (the senior spokesman for the minority party) and six as chairman. However, it places priority on the time spent as chairman and therefore anyone who has served as chairman for six years must relinquish the top slot regardless of whether he or she has served any time as ranking member. This meant that when the Republicans recaptured its majority status in 2003 six members could only serve a further two years as chairmen, taking account of the four years they had already served from 1997 to 2001.[35]

Factors influencing voting in Congress

Members of both houses have the opportunity of casting votes in committees and on the floor of their chambers on numerous bills and resolutions every year. As the Senate and the House of Representatives are elected by different constituencies and for different terms there can be a different party in control of each. From 1981–87 the Republicans controlled the Senate while the Democrats had a majority in the House of Representatives. From May 2001 the Democrats controlled the Senate, albeit by one vote, while the House had a narrow Republican majority. The Democrats have been in control of both houses of Congress for most of the period since 1933, with the exception of the years 1947–48, 1953–54 and, most recently, from 1995 to 2001 and since 2003. Differences between the chambers in political control have not been as common as those which have often existed between Congress and the presidency (see Chapter 3 for discussion of divided party government).

What then are the factors that influence the votes that Congressmen cast in the legislature? The process is a complex one, and there are many influences at work, some of which are more important than others on different issues and at different times.

Constituency interest

One common tie that unites almost all politicians is a desire to be re-elected to one's position for another term, and retaining the support of constituents is an important consideration for any legislator. In America, the Constitution lays down that Congressmen must be inhabitants of the state which they are representing. The 'locality' rule means that not only must a legislator have a residence in the area, but he will probably also have lived in the state for a considerable time, and many Congressmen actually have been born and bred in the constituency. There are exceptions and the rule can be interpreted liberally. In the 1960s Robert Kennedy became Senator for New York despite being labelled a 'carpetbagger'; he had residences in Massachusetts and Virginia. In 2000 the First Lady, Hillary Clinton, was elected to the Senate, again from New York, even though she had no previous connection with the state and had only recently purchased a property there.

Despite recent developments, the decentralisation of American parties means that the legislator owes his nomination and election much more to state and local party structures than to any national organisation, and he will listen closely to the views of party supporters at home. This pressure is increased for House members who face re-election every two years. What is more, election campaigns will often centre on local rather than national issues and voters often regard themselves as independent, voting 'split tickets' and not always remaining loyal to traditional party ties.

The Congressman cannot afford to lose contact with his constituency; he is allowed not only an office in Washington, DC but also offices and staff in his constituency so that local problems can be dealt with. It should be remembered that American legislators have far larger constituencies than their British counterparts. Whereas the 659 Members of Parliament at Westminster normally serve around 65,000–70,000 electors, the members of the House of Representatives have electoral districts with populations of approximately 625,000. The number of members in the House has remained constant at 435 since 1910, apart from a short period in the 1950s after the admission of Alaska and Hawaii to the Union, despite the huge increase in the population of the country, and therefore constituencies have become much larger in terms of the number of electors. In the Senate the two members from each state serve populations varying from Wyoming with just under half a million to California with almost 34 million in 2000. Even though some Congressmen have districts or states 3,000 miles from the federal capital, they make regular visits and use congressional adjournments for on-the-spot assessments of popular feeling, and the importance of the franking privilege in maintaining contact with the voters has already been noted. Some politicians pay for their own polls to be carried out to test opinion on sensitive issues coming before Congress. On most issues there is no clear-cut popular view and the Congressman is able to take into account other factors or use his own discretion, but sometimes letters, e-mails and phone calls to his office leave little doubt as to the public's feelings.

A Congressman is expected as a good representative to take up problems that constituents may be experiencing with the federal government. He becomes an intermediary between the ordinary citizen and the maze of 'red tape' and bureaucracy in Washington. Much of his time, and particularly that of his staff, is spent trying to sort out complaints or problems that require intervention to secure an expeditious and satisfactory response from the civil servants.

Another way the Congressman can show his advocacy of his constituents' causes is by using his influence on committees. He will attempt to secure a position on a committee that deals with the sort of issues in which his constituency has an interest. A legislator from the Midwest may well see the Agriculture Committee as his ideal assignment, while a Californian may attempt to obtain a place on the committee dealing with aeronautics and space projects. Congressmen will sometimes indulge in 'log-rolling', which means they will exchange favours and support each other's proposals. Legislators on some committees have the opportunity of passing 'pork-barrel' legislation; this allows them to obtain public works programmes, such as new highways or public buildings, in their own constituencies so that they can claim to have brought new jobs and prosperity to the area.

Morris Fiorina has argued that Congressmen tend to spend most of their time on matters that will help them get re-elected, such as casework and channelling federal funds and favours to their districts, and prefer to avoid policy areas that cause controversy back home, a factor which, as we have seen, has contributed to the decline in competitive elections in the House.[36]

Most Congressmen see themselves as combining the notion of a 'trustee' who votes as his conscience dictates, and the 'delegate' who follows the local views all the time.[37] In fact, many citizens do not know anything about their local representative and very few know his voting record on individual issues, although opponents in elections may well try to exploit positions taken by legislators on controversial issues. Therefore the Congressman is allowed a great deal of discretion in practice, but he must always remember 'the folks back home'.

Party membership

Political parties in the US Congress do not experience the same levels of cohesion and unity in voting as those in the British House of Commons. This is partly because legislators do not have to vote to support the continuing existence of the executive as they do in a parliamentary system. The separation of powers system prevents each vote on a bill being seen as a vote of confidence in the President, as he continues in office for a set term regardless of the fate of his proposed legislation. Therefore Democrats and Republicans can examine each bill, whether proposed by the executive or not, on its merits, and vote accordingly. Local views are expected to play an important part in the

Congressman's decisions, and party Whips do not expect to pressure members into voting against the expressed interests of their constituents. Whips and party leaders can only persuade, and they have virtually no disciplinary measures with which to threaten members into compliance. However, as we have seen, there have been attempts to make chairmen of committees and sub-committees more responsive to their parties with consideration being given to removing them from their posts.

Although party cohesion has traditionally been relatively weak in the American legislature, if there are no conflicting constituency interests Congressmen normally vote with the majority of their own party. Party membership is still the best single indicator of the way in which a legislator is likely to vote. Partisanship can be measured in two ways: the number of party votes, that is the percentage of roll call votes when the majority of one party opposes the majority of the other party, and the party unity scores which show the percentage of the time that members vote in agreement with the majority of their party on these party votes. The number of party votes increased dramatically in both chambers in the 1980s and 1990s, although there has been some decline in the House since the peak in 1995. Over the same period party unity scores have also increased noticeably and this is shown in Table 2.6. Partisanship increased with the more ideological politics of the 1980s, with Democrats after 1982 reacting against the Reagan agenda. In addition, political debate has been dominated by budget and deficit issues, which have also tended to polarise the parties. For example, President Clinton's budget package in 1993 was opposed unanimously by Republicans in both Houses because

Table 2.6 Party unity in Congress (%)

Year	Dems	Reps
1980	68	70
1981	69	76
1982	72	71
1983	76	74
1984	74	72
1985	79	75
1986	78	71
1987	81	74
1988	79	73
1989	81	73
1990	81	74
1991	81	78
1992	79	79
1993	85	84
1994	83	83
1995	80	91
1996	80	87
1997	82	88
1998	83	86
1999	84	86
2000	83	87
2001	85	90
2002	86	89

Source: *Congressional Quarterly Weekly*, 14 December 2002, p. 3281.

Note: Party unity is defined as being the average percentage Democratic and Republican Congressmen in both houses voted with the majority of their own party in party divisions.

they rejected tax increases and argued that it did not include sufficient spending cuts. The Republican takeover of Congress heightened partisanship even further.

Congressmen are now voting on average approximately eight or even nine times out of ten with their party when there is a party division. This average conceals great disparities in the levels of party loyalty of individuals; some Congressmen will vote with their own party majority well over 90 per cent of the time while some Southern Democrats have on occasions scored less than 20 per cent. House Republicans demonstrated unprecedented levels of party cohesion in 1995 with a 91 per cent party unity score for the year. A record 73 per cent of roll call votes in that year saw a partisan split with the majority of House Democrats voting against a majority of House Republicans.

Traditionally, many Southern Democrats have aligned with the majority of Republicans to form a 'conservative coalition' in Congress. In some periods the coalition played an important role, especially in providing Republican Presidents with support for legislation so that they were successful even when nominally the Democrats had majority control. For example, in 1981 a group of mainly Southern members formed the Conservative Democratic Forum and became known as the 'Boll Weevils'; they provided the vital votes which gave President Reagan victories in the House on his tax and spending cuts package in that year. However, in recent times there have been significantly fewer Democrats elected from the Southern states as conservative Republicans have made inroads there. In the 103rd Congress Southern Democrats numbered 85, or 62 per cent of the Southern delegation; by the time the 105th Congress met in January 1997 there were 55, or 40 per cent. Some Democratic legislators had defected to the GOP, but the Democrats who do win in the region have increasingly had to take account of the impact of demographic changes – and the allegiance of the growing number of black voters in particular – on their chances of renomination and re-election. As we have seen, the Democratic Party in Congress is less heterogeneous than in the past and an increasing number of Southern Democrats elected in the 1990s are black; of those returned in 1997, for example, 21 were from minority groups.

Republican cohesion in the House has generally been sufficient since 1995 for the leadership to win most key votes despite small overall majorities. Members of the 'Blue Dog Coalition', a group of mostly Southern fiscally conservative House Democrats, have often added to the size of Republican victories rather than being essential for their success.

As we have seen, the vast majority of House seats are 'safe' for one party. This has tended to reinforce the tendency towards partisanship in Congress. By voting with their party, members are usually reflecting the preferences of their local electorates. In both houses incumbents are concerned in particular not to alienate the ideological activists and highly partisan voters who are most likely to participate in the nominating primaries of both parties.

Principle or ideology

Many Congressmen consider themselves to be conservatives or liberals and this philosophy may provide them with the guidelines on which they will vote. This can lead to a consistency in decision-making over a vast array of otherwise unconnected legislation. A conservative may consistently vote against bills which tend to increase the federal government's role in the domestic field, but vote for those he regards as strengthening national defence. A liberal, on the other hand, may support programmes he perceives as regulating 'big business' but oppose those measures cutting foreign aid to developing nations. Often the principles will coincide with the views of the majority of his party, but, for liberal Republicans (who these days prefer to be known as 'moderates') or conservative Democrats, their philosophical commitment is often more important than party ties.

Identification with state, regional, ethnic and religious groups

On certain issues the most important influence on a Congressman may be his personal identification with particular groups in the population or within Congress. Occasionally all Congressmen in a state delegation will recognise a common interest and support a proposal which will entail voting across party lines. In some cases regional identity will lead a larger number of legislators to work together for mutual advantage. Southern members have done this for decades, but it appears to be an increasingly familiar phenomenon. For example, in debates on energy, the different interests of those Congressmen from oil- and gas-producing areas and those from regions where constituents are heavily dependent on cheap energy for heating (such as the North-East) have been clearly reflected in the voting on proposed legislation.

The caucus of black legislators has worked hard to support new civil rights and urban aid programmes; many see their role as promoting the interests of blacks across the country and not merely those within their constituencies. Jewish members have taken particular interest in American foreign policy in the Middle East and have strenuously backed continuing aid to Israel, while Catholic Congressmen have vigorously opposed the use of federal funds for abortion operations.

Committee decisions

The view of the standing committee that initially examined the proposal is an important influence on voting behaviour in the full chamber. If a bill had unanimous backing in the committee it is likely that it will pass without real opposition in the floor vote. A Congressman who has not been a member of the committee will rely, to a large extent, on what he has learnt about its details from colleagues who are members of his own state delegation or who feel philosophically as he does.

Pressure groups

Many pressure groups wishing to influence legislation employ fulltime lobbyists to see the legislator and persuade him to vote in a particular way; the professional persuaders usually know which Congressmen are likely to be favourable to their cause and who the waverers may be. They rarely waste their time contacting legislators they know will be in opposition to their group's objectives. Congressmen often acquire useful information and material for speeches on major bills from pressure groups, and, of course, at election times contributions from sympathetic groups to campaign funds are common. Very few Congressmen refuse to accept financial contributions from political action committees (PACs) which are frequently offered to incumbents defending their seats (see Chapter 5). Outright bribery in return for votes is probably rare but every Congressman has to ensure that his conduct, and that of his staff, is beyond public suspicion.

The White House

The President needs the support of Congress in order to govern effectively and therefore he will seek to influence congressional voting on a wide range of matters that are of considerable importance to him, including bills, budget resolutions, confirmation of nominees to the executive and judicial branches, ratification of foreign treaties and the sustaining of vetoes. Nelson Polsby has pointed out that electoral results are constantly reshaping the terrain over which presidential-congressional relations are battled out and these electoral results must be turned by acts of institutional leadership into legislative coalitions.[38] Thus, while a President can expect the help of party colleagues in the Congress who may see it as in their mutual interest to support him, he will probably have to appeal to other legislators as well. Republican Presidents have often sought support from a coalition of Republicans and conservative Southern Democrats, especially when faced with majorities for the Democratic Party in both houses.

The role of the President's Congressional Liaison staff is very important in carrying out the day-to-day discussions that take place between the two branches. The Office of Congressional Relations is usually made up of a small staff of experienced lobbyists who are each expected to get to know individually a number of legislators in the hope that a favourable climate and personal relationship will lead to support for the President. President Carter's early attempts at organising his staff on an issues basis rather than on this people-centred basis contributed to the poor relationship between the White House and Capitol Hill during his term of office.[39] Carter's problems also resulted from his failure to establish good personal relationship with the leaders of Congress and his dislike for politicking and bargaining. He also made the mistake of failing to involve Congress in the development of his legislative proposals and then overloading the legislature with a large number of issues with no clear indication of where his priorities lay. The failure of Congress to act upon many of these initiatives early on in his presidency resulted in his being perceived widely as a weak and ineffectual leader and this reputation handicapped him for the rest of his term.

President Reagan clearly learned the lessons of the Carter period. Despite the fact that like Carter he had run as an 'outsider' against the Washington establishment in the 1980 election, once elected he spent many of the early weeks of his presidency on Capitol Hill getting to know congressional leaders. He worked out a limited agenda of priorities that centred on budget and defence issues and agreed them with Republican leaders in Congress. The subsequent victories during 1981, particularly on his economic programme with reductions in federal spending and income tax cuts, established his reputation as a successful and strong President, an image that helped him in later years even when he was unable to obtain legislative support for his proposals.

The other major difference was that Ronald Reagan became his administration's own Chief Lobbyist and he obviously enjoyed meeting and talking to Congressmen. On many occasions Reagan saw personally or phoned members to persuade them to support him on issues that were of importance to the presidency. For example, in 1981 a Senate vote of 52–48 to approve the sale of advanced warning radar planes (AWACs) was seen as a test of the President's leadership in foreign policy. Reagan personally met 75 out of the 100 Senators, 44 of them alone, to press his case and at least seven of those committed to voting against the sale and a number of waverers came down on his side. President Clinton used similar tactics, phoning and meeting personally many Democratic members, including freshmen, before the vital House vote on his budget package in May 1993; he managed to persuade sufficient waverers to win the vote by 219–213. In November 1993 Clinton scored a major victory of vital importance to his presidency with the passage of the North American Free Trade Agreement (NAFTA) in the House of Representatives by 234–200 only days after defeat seemed probable. His party was split on the issue and 156 of 258 Democrats in the House voted against the agreement but, with Republican backing, Clinton was able to persuade sufficient members, in many cases with last-minute concessions and 'pork-barrel' projects for their districts, to win the vote.

In a 'honeymoon' period with Congress in 1981 President Reagan obtained an 82.4 per cent success rate on congressional votes. However, later Democratic victories in congressional elections, particularly in 1982 and 1986, resulted in a decline in Reagan's success rate, the low point being in 1987, the year the Iran-Contra scandal weakened his administration (see Table 2.7). In 1989 President Bush's score of 62.6 per cent was the lowest recorded for an elected President in his first year in office since *Congressional Quarterly* first analysed congressional voting in 1953, with only the unelected Gerald Ford faring worse in 1974. Despite the difficulties of his first period in office President Clinton achieved an 86.4 per cent success rate in both 1993 and 1994 when the Democrats controlled Congress. After the Republicans' victory in the 1994 midterm elections, Clinton was effectively marginalised and his success rate fell dramatically to 36.2 per cent, the lowest recorded for any President. However, Clinton's fortunes improved during the next year and, with both parties seeking compromise and legislative accomplishments before the 1996 elections, his success rate rose to 55.1 per cent, the highest one-year jump ever recorded. Weakened again by the Lewinsky scandal and the impeachment crisis, Clinton's success rate in 1999 slumped to 37.8 per cent. George W. Bush, benefiting from Republican control of both houses of Congress until May 2001 and from his soaring public approval ratings and desire for national unity following the terrorist attacks of 11 September, achieved an 87 per cent success rate in his first year in office. In 2002 his score rose to 87.8 per cent, the highest since Lyndon Johnson's 93 per cent in 1965.

Table 2.7 Presidential victories on congressional votes (%)

Kennedy		Reagan	
1961	81.0	1981	82.4
1962	85.4	1982	72.4
1963	87.1	1983	67.1
		1984	65.8
Johnson		1985	59.9
1964	88.0	1986	56.1
1965	93.0	1987	43.5
1966	79.0	1988	47.4
1967	79.0		
1968	75.0	*Bush*	
		1989	62.6
Nixon		1990	46.8
1969	74.0	1991	54.2
1970	77.0	1992	43.0
1971	75.0		
1972	66.0	*Clinton*	
1973	50.6	1993	86.4
1974	59.6	1994	86.4
		1995	36.2
Ford		1996	55.1
1974	58.2	1997	53.6
1975	61.0	1998	50.6
1976	53.8	1999	37.8
		2000	55.0
Carter			
1977	75.4	*Bush*	
1978	78.3	2001	87.0
1979	76.8	2002	87.8
1980	75.1		

Source: *Congressional Quarterly Weekly*, 14 December 2002, p. 3275.

Table 2.8 Congressional support for the President's position 2001–2 (%)

	2002		2001	
	Reps	*Dems*	*Reps*	*Dems*
Support for the President				
Senate	89	71	94	66
House	82	32	86	31
Opposition to the President				
Senate	5	26	4	32
House	15	64	12	67

Source: *Congressional Quarterly Weekly*, 14 December 2002, p. 3275.

Note: Percentages refer to the composite scores of all Republicans and Democrats in supporting the President's view on votes in Congress when he took a clear-cut position.

Congressional staff

As Congress has reasserted its power and attempted to compete with the vast civil service machine of the executive branch, so its own staff have increased very substantially. By 1999 there were 11,488 congressional staff working for individual legislators and committees. In addition, there are thousands of other officials who provide support to Congress through bodies such as the Congressional Research Service, the General Accounting Office and the Congressional Budget Office, giving a total of 23,648.[40]

Because of both the expanded workload and the increasingly technical nature of much of the legislation with which Congress deals, many of the staff employed are experts in particular fields. Congressmen, therefore, tend to become more dependent on the views of their advisers when they decide how to vote on a bill, particularly if it is in an area in which they have neither the time nor the interest to become involved themselves.

The political climate

Anthony King has argued that a significant influence in congressional voting (and in the relationship between Congress and the White House) is the difficult-to-define factor of political climate or mood. This is likely to involve the widespread feeling that some political force is all but irresistible and changes in the intellectual atmosphere where, for example, a cause may become hard to defend because people have, for whatever reason, become unreceptive to the theories and values underlying it. King gives as examples civil rights in the 1960s, the dissipation in the 1980s of the pro-Israeli atmosphere that had dominated American politics since 1948 and the Reagan budget and tax cuts of 1981.[41] In the 1990s, after years of evading the consequences of rising federal deficits, politicians of both parties began to recognise that the public expected them to take the problem seriously and came forward with ways to achieve a balanced budget. Following the 11 September 2001 atrocities, members felt compelled to support legislation to counter terrorism even if it involved measures that they would in more normal times have criticised as increasing the power of government too much and as posing a threat to individual freedom.

The legislative process in Congress

As only a small proportion of legislative proposals ever become law in America, the legislative process can be likened to an obstacle race with many runners or competitors falling at each of the hurdles, so that only a few actually finish the course. The filtering process that takes place means that it is often easier to prevent the passage of a bill than to ensure its success, and this is particularly true of controversial proposals or ones that directly affect the interests of important groups. It is worth considering the various stages of the legislative process, and particularly the vital points where a bill can be delayed or rejected.

1 Initiation. The inspiration or source of a bill can be individual members or their aides, pressure groups, the executive branch, or a committee in the Senate or House. Whatever the source, a Congressman must formally introduce the bill. A proposal can begin its life in either house or a joint resolution will allow concurrent consideration.

2 Committee investigation in the House. If a bill is first introduced into the House of Representatives it will be assigned to one of the standing committees by the Speaker. If the bill's contents overlap the jurisdiction of more than one committee, he can use his discretion to send it to the one most or least likely to be favourable, depending on his own view of the proposal. Bills may be referred to more than one committee for consideration. They are assigned to sub-committees, and those receiving approval go to the full committee for approval. If a bill is being seriously examined by the committee, there may be public hearings held to obtain evidence from interested parties. The committee stage is the main period when the bill's content will be shaped; it may be amended or combined with other bills in such a way that it is unrecognisable to the original proponents. On occasions a committee such as the Ways and Means Committee will write a bill itself, and, of course, this gives great power to the chairman. The committee decides whether to report the bill out to the full House, although on rare occasions a refusal to do so can be overruled by a 'discharge petition' passed by a majority of the chamber; in 2002, for example, members voted to consider and vote on the Shays-Meehan bill reforming campaign finance laws even though it was opposed by the Republican leadership. The committee chairman will usually write the report to the full House on the bill's contents or appoint another member to do so.

3 The Rules Committee. Once bills are approved by the standing committee, the Rules Committee establishes the order in which the full House will consider them and sets the terms of debate by issuing a 'rule' for each individual piece of legislation. The rules may limit debate and also determine whether amendments will be permitted. The Rules Committee in the 1960s was an independent and powerful body that was used by Republicans and their conservative Democratic allies to thwart liberal legislation, but it is now an arm of the majority leadership; its members are nominated by the Speaker who uses the committee to control and expedite floor action.

4 Discussion by the whole House and voting. The debate in the full House is for a limited period and a vote is easily obtained by the cloture rule. The vote can take a number of forms: a voice vote, a roll call with tellers or electronic voting with scores shown on a scoreboard. The roll call has been used to cause delay as each member is called in turn to announce his vote.

5 Procedure in the Senate. A bill passed in the House and introduced by a Senator is assigned to a committee by an official called the Parliamentarian, who is not a Senator.

The Vice-President can intervene and overrule him if he feels an inappropriate decision has been made.

The bill is usually considered by the Senate standing committee in the specialist area although the Senate Majority Leader has on occasions brought bills straight to the Senate floor, bypassing the committee stage if he feels that he lacks sufficient votes in the committee.[42] The bill is then assigned a place on the timetable by the majority party's Policy Committee. This body has the functions of the Rules Committee in the House. The main difference, however, is that the tradition of continuous debate without time limits allows a filibuster to be used by opponents to 'talk the bill out'. Failure to secure the necessary 60 votes on a cloture motion indicates that the bill will make no further progress for the time being.

6 Conference committees. If a bill has passed both houses but different amendments have been made which create two different versions, it is necessary for a conference committee, made up of members of the original Senate and House committees that considered the proposal, to meet and work out a compromise. The committee should be concerned only with resolving the areas of conflict, but in the past these bodies were often accused of rewriting whole bills. As a result of committee reforms in the 1970s, these conference committees are now open to the public, thus preventing secret deals by members, and junior members as well as senior Congressmen have been allowed to take part in conference committees. The House and Senate then have to approve the revised version of the bill without further amendment before it goes to the White House.

Conference committees have normally comprised 5–12 members from each house but, with the development of multiple referrals and omnibus and mega-bills, large conferences became common. In 1981 a record number of over 250 conferees met on the omnibus reconciliation bill to resolve over 300 matters of disagreement between the two chambers. On occasions there would also be sub-conferences established to work out agreements in specialist areas, while general conferees coordinate their activities.[43]

7 Presidential action. The President has three alternatives open to him when he receives a bill that has passed Congress during a session. He can sign the bill, passing it into law with his approval. He can allow it to become law after ten working days without signing it, thus showing some reservations about its contents, or he can veto it. The President may veto only a whole bill and not specific items or sections within it, and therefore Congress sometimes exploits the inflexible veto weapon by including provisions it feels the President dare not veto, even though he may disagree with much of the content. As we have seen in Chapter 1, the attempt by the 104th Congress to give the President a line item veto over appropriations bills was declared unconstitutional by the Supreme Court in 1998.

If the President does veto a bill he must write a message to Congress explaining his reasons, and they can attempt to override his decision by obtaining a two-thirds majority in both houses. A President will obviously weigh his chances of sustaining the veto when he makes his decision and sometimes he will threaten the use of the veto as a tactic to try to force Congress to make changes he wants in a bill. President Clinton was particularly effective in using his power as a negotiating tool, managing to persuade the Republican majority in Congress to increase funding for his priority programmes in appropriations bills or face a presidential veto.[44] On occasions the President will decide to go ahead on principle even though he knows Congress will probably override his veto. President Ford, for example, vetoed 48 bills but on 12 occasions his veto was overridden by the large Democratic majorities in Congress. A President requires a minimum of 34 allies in Congress, a third of the Senate, to defeat an attempt to override his veto. President Bush,

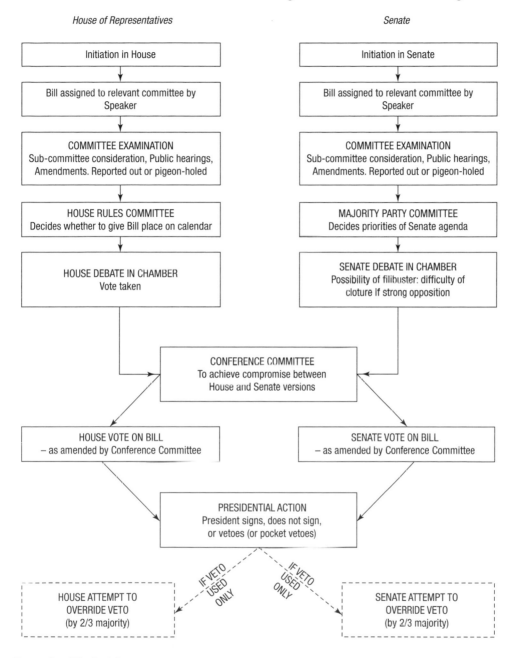

Figure 2.1 The legislative process in Congress

supported by Senate Republicans, sustained all but one of the 36 vetoes he used during his term in office (1989–93).

President Clinton vetoed a total of 37 bills during his two terms in office. All of the vetoes were used against bills passed by the Republican-controlled Congress between 1995 and 2000 and the legislature only managed to override the veto twice, one of these restoring military construction spending which Clinton had struck out using his short-

Table 2.9 Presidential vetoes 1933–2002

	Regular vetoes	Pocket vetoes	Total vetoes	Vetoes overridden
F.D. Roosevelt (1933–45)	372	263	635	9
H. Truman (1945–53)	180	70	250	12
D. Eisenhower (1953–61)	73	108	181	2
J. Kennedy (1961–63)	12	9	21	–
L. Johnson (1963–69)	16	14	30	–
R. Nixon (1969–74)	26	17	43	7
G. Ford (1974–77)	48	18	66	12
J. Carter (1977–81)	13	18	31	2
R. Reagan (1981–89)	39	39	78	9
G. Bush (1989–93)	27	17	44	1
B. Clinton (1993–2000)	37	0	37	2
G.W. Bush (2001–)	0	0	0	0

lived line-item veto. President George W. Bush was criticised by some conservatives for not using his veto power at all in his first 18 months in office, arguing that he was weakening his credibility with Congress. They were upset that he had not vetoed the campaign finance reform legislation passed by Congress in 2002 and which Bush signed into law reluctantly despite misgivings about the constitutionality of some of its provisions.[45] Historically overrides of presidential vetoes have been infrequent, with only 106 of the 2,561 vetoes issued between 1789 and 2000 being overridden.

If a President receives the bill less than ten days before Congress adjourns, the bill dies if he does not sign it. In using the 'pocket veto' he does not have to explain his reasons for not signing it, and Congress does not have the chance to override a pocket veto. This device is important as Congress finishes consideration of many bills in a rush at the end of a session. Clinton became the first President since Franklin Pierce (1853–57) to serve a full term without using the pocket veto.

Financial control by Congress

Even when a bill has passed the difficult legislative process, there is still a major problem to be surmounted: this is to obtain approval for funds so that the intention of the legislature can be implemented by government departments. The specialist committees of the House and Senate can authorise the amount of money to be spent on a purpose defined in a bill, that is 'what ought to be spent'. Within that framework, the Appropriations Committees of the two houses decide what will actually be spent. Therefore separate bills have to pass the Congress, appropriating money for particular legislation already on the statute book.[46]

The Appropriations Committees are the biggest standing committees in their respective houses and are divided into a large number of sub-committees which specialise in particular aspects of expenditure such as defence, agriculture and welfare. The Appropriations sub-committees are very important power centres because their decisions on levels of expenditure are usually accepted by the full committee and eventually by the whole house.

The President's budget, which includes requests for money to cover the ongoing administration of departments, is also examined by the Appropriations sub-committees on a piecemeal basis. Traditionally Congress never debated the full implications of the whole budget on the floor of either house; parts were approved or modified, taking each separately. The President cannot necessarily expect that his requests will be granted in

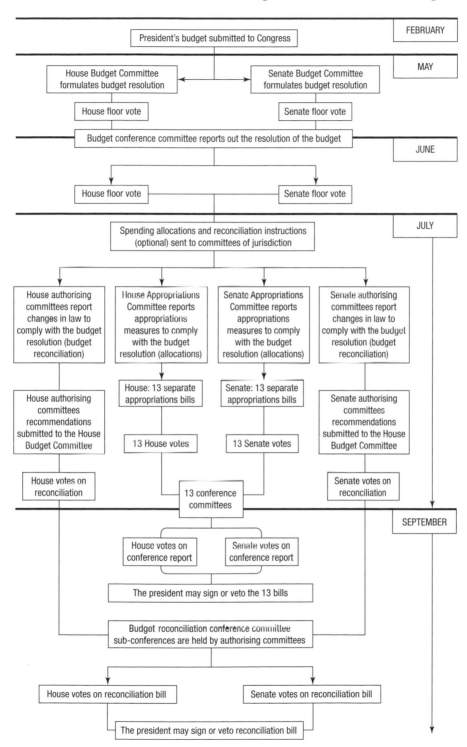

Figure 2.2   The budget process in Congress

Source: House Budget Committee.

full. After hearings, the sub-committee may well vote substantially less than has been asked for in the departmental submission. However, it is impossible for the Congressmen, even with a substantial staff, to scrutinise properly all the detailed work of the government and assess the justification of expenditure. Congress has to pass 13 separate appropriations bills each year to fund the running of the federal government. If the President and Congress fail to agree these by the 1 October start of the new financial year Congress may pass a continuing resolution which is a stopgap measure to keep government departments running at the existing funding levels until the appropriations bills have been approved.

The congressional system of approving expenditure came in for a great deal of criticism in the early 1970s as President Nixon accused the specialist committees and the Appropriations Committees of approving and appropriating funds without regard for the total levels of government expenditure. He claimed this extravagance was creating large deficits and thus fuelling inflation in the country at large. The criticism was to a large degree justified, as the congressional committees that decide how much revenue is to be raised (House Ways and Means and Senate Finance Committees) had almost no idea of what total level of appropriations they were supposed to finance until the fiscal year was almost over. In other words, the piecemeal consideration did not allow any congressional body to consider general economic strategy.

President Nixon's answer to the problem was to impound millions of dollars of appropriated funds for particular bills he felt were unnecessary. He refused to spend the money to avoid the building up of even bigger budget deficits. Congress passed a law severely restricting the President's right to impoundment; the Impoundment Control Act 1974 provides that the President must spend appropriated funds unless both chambers consent to impoundment within 45 days of a presidential request. However, the controversy also resulted in the establishment of Budget Committees in the House and the Senate. These committees are supposed to provide an overall view of the financial situation that had been lacking in the appropriations procedure. The committees have a Congressional Budget Office whose economists and other specialist staff are supposed to analyse tax and spending options in all areas as well as forecasting expenditure trends. The reports from the Office have certainly led to Congressmen being better informed on the consequences of their actions.

The Budget Committees fix the targets of either overall surplus or deficit by 15 April of each year and also set the spending totals and subtotals for different areas of expenditure. Between May and September the normal appropriations process takes place, and then a second look is taken at the spending totals in the light of developments. If the sum of individual appropriations made exceeds the total, Congress can choose to cut appropriations, raise taxation, or go further into deficit. This process is known as reconciliation and is completed with the passing of a second budget resolution.

The reforms were heralded as another example of Congress modernising its procedures to redress the balance in its relations with the executive branch. Critics argued that the Budget Committees were given insufficient power to enforce their spending guidelines and the jurisdictions of the Appropriations and taxation committees were left largely intact. The House Budget Committee is also weakened by having a rotating membership; no one, including the chairman, can serve more than six consecutive years. The committees' limited success was in forcing members to consider trade-offs and the setting of spending priorities.

The budget reforms of the 1970s, while improving some procedures, did not succeed in forcing Congress to make hard choices in balancing spending and revenue. As the federal budget deficit increased in size in the 1980s, Congress voted, with President

Reagan's support, to approve the Balanced Budget and Emergency Deficit Reduction Act (known after its sponsors as Gramm-Rudman-Hollings). This landmark legislation set a series of targets for reducing the deficit to zero by 1991. The original version of the legislation had given the Comptroller General of the General Accounting Office the final say over the allocation of cuts but in 1986 the Supreme Court decided that this would violate the separation of powers principle because the Comptroller General is an officer of Congress. Congress then approved a process whereby the legislature itself would pass a resolution in both houses and send it to the President to order spending cuts. As amended in 1987, the Act gave the President's Budget Director the final say in choosing the economic projections that would determine the size of the overall spending reductions. Social Security and interest on the national debt were to be excluded but cuts to meet the targets for deficit reduction would come equally from defence and domestic programmes.

Even the sponsors of the legislation admitted it was a 'bad idea whose time had come' but argued that the threat of automatic cuts would provide an incentive for Congress (and the President) to face the difficult choices avoided in the past and that the overriding need to reduce the deficit justified the extreme action. Although the legislation helped to stabilise the deficit at about $150 billion for three years, it failed in its stated aim of a balanced budget. When it appeared that the targets for deficit reduction would not be met, Congress adjusted them upwards. Programmes were taken 'off budget' and spending was moved from one financial year to another to make the figures look better than they were in reality.

The budget process became more centralised and in 1990 direct negotiations took place between congressional leaders and the White House; committee hearings were effectively a sideshow while the real decisions were made in these private discussions. Congress was then presented with a budget package and, although it at first rejected the deal agreed by President Bush and its own leaders, the proposals were soon adopted after some adjustments were made and more of the tax increases were shifted from the poorer to the wealthier taxpayers. The abandonment of his 1988 election pledge, 'Read my lips, no new taxes', damaged President Bush politically, particularly as he vacillated and changed his mind several times while the negotiations were going on.[47]

The 1990 budget summit effectively, if not formally, repealed the Gramm-Rudman-Hollings legislation. The focus of the agreement, formalised in the Budget Enforcement Act, was to control increases in spending. Any new spending in three separate categories of discretionary expenditure – defence, international and domestic programmes – would have to be offset by decreases elsewhere within a category. Failure to make decisions as to where reductions would be made would lead to across-the-board sequestration within the affected categories. The deficit targets for the 1990s were also revised drastically upwards to recognise the reality of the budgetary situation, made worse by recession. The President was given authority to adjust the targets in the light of changing economic circumstances. The new procedures gave the President more budgetary power and, by locking in spending totals for five years, deprived the Budget Committees of their main functions.[48]

President Clinton therefore came to office in 1993 with an accelerating financial crisis, and his first budget included a major deficit reduction package. He was forced to drastically dilute proposals made during his election campaign to stimulate the economy by increased public spending on infrastructure projects and, after months of wrangling with Democrats in Congress over the detail of tax increases and spending cuts, the budget was passed by a mere two votes in the House and with the aid of Vice-President Gore's casting vote in the Senate. The plan to cut the deficit by a total of $496 billion over five years was unanimously opposed by Republicans in Congress on the basis that it relied too heavily on tax increases and insufficiently on reductions in expenditure.

As we saw in Chapter 1, the period of Clinton's first administration saw a recovery from recession and a marked reduction in the federal deficit in 1996 due to increased economic growth. The Republican majority in the 104th Congress had eventually forced Clinton to accept the need for future plans that would bring the budget into balance by the year 2002; the bitter budget crisis of the winter of 1995–96 centred on the differences between the rival alternative proposals and projections submitted by the President and congressional leaders, Republicans being convinced that the goal could only be achieved by tackling the escalating costs of entitlement programmes such as Medicare. In 1997 the two branches agreed a bipartisan plan to balance the budget. However, Clinton continued to oppose the passage of a balanced budget constitutional amendment, one of the central planks of the 'Contract with America', arguing that it was an unnecessarily rigid constraint on economic policy-making, particularly in a time of recession.

Recent attempts to reform the budgetary process, such as the introduction of a two-year budget cycle which would give Congress more time for the oversight and reauthorisation of programmes, failed to muster the necessary majorities in Congress, with members being particularly concerned not to hand more power over the budget to the executive branch.[49]

Chapter summary

- The US Congress has often been called 'the most powerful legislative body in the world' because it has retained its independence from the executive branch. As a result of the separation of powers Congress retains its central role in the legislative process.
- Congress has often been criticised for the way it has carried out its functions and its reputation with the public has occasionally been damaged by incidents of scandal or corruption. Voters generally have a more favourable view of their own individual legislators than the institution as a whole.
- Membership of Congress is still overwhelmingly white, male, middle-aged and made up of people from professional and business backgrounds, many of whom are very wealthy. However, there has been a notable increase in the number of women and members from minority racial and ethnic groups, particularly since 1992.
- Incumbent or sitting members of Congress are overwhelmingly successful in their campaigns for re-election, particularly in the House of Representatives. There are very few competitive or electorally marginal seats in the House.
- The House and Senate are given equal powers over legislation but each chamber has some exclusive constitutional roles. The Senate's power to approve presidential appointments is one particularly significant example.
- The culture and procedures of the two chambers are different and can be explained principally by the difference in the size of their respective memberships. The opportunity for filibuster in the Senate gives a minority of Senators the power to block legislation which the majority, possibly in both houses, would wish to pass. In certain respects, such as the heightened partisanship witnessed in recent times, the two houses have become more alike.
- The standing committees of the House and Senate have long been recognised as the important control centres of the legislative process and their chairmen have played key leadership roles in their specialist policy areas.
- The two parties elect their own leaderships in each chamber. The powers of party leaders have grown in the post-reform Congress since the 1970s.

- The Republican takeover of both house of Congress in 1995 led to some major changes in rules and procedures, particularly in the House. Party leaders were strengthened in relation to committee chairmen. Following Newt Gingrich's replacement as Speaker in 1998 by Dennis Hastert there has been in many respects a 'return to regular order'. However, the term limits for committee chairmen, which were introduced in 1995, remain and have had a significant impact by preventing the consolidation of power in the hands of a few leading committee members.

- Members of Congress are influenced by many factors when deciding how to cast their votes in the legislature. Consideration of their own constituency's interest is very important, as is the view of the party's leadership. Other factors include the ideology of the member, his or her identification with state, regional, ethnic or religious groups and the views of colleagues on the standing committee which considered the bill in detail. Members will also consider representations made by lobbyists for pressure groups, the attitude of the President and the advice of congressional staff. They will also be influenced by the political climate at the time.

- The legislative process can be likened to an obstacle race where very few of the bills that are introduced will survive the course and become law. There are many points in the process in both houses, not to mention the possibility of a presidential veto, where a proposal may be modified, delayed or rejected altogether.

Box 2.2 Congressional oversight

One of the major roles of Congress, carried out through its committees, is that of oversight of the executive branch. The legislature has the responsibility to monitor and investigate the activities of executive agencies and personnel, including the President. Congress had been criticised for neglecting this function as executive power grew during the twentieth century, but the reassertion of congressional authority in the 1970s saw a number of developments to improve legislative capacity in this area. These included the establishment of the Congressional Budget Office, increased staffing for committees and the use of legislative vetoes in new laws to limit executive discretion. The growing interest by Congress in this work led some critics to accuse it of 'micro-management' and excessive interference in the implementation of policy.

Congressional oversight can be interpreted as either an ongoing activity where members are continuously reviewing executive behaviour to ascertain whether instances of mal-administration have taken place or as a response to complaints received about government wrong-doing. Generally members of Congress have many pressures on their time and they will tend to react to demands for investigation of alleged maladministration rather than actively seek out instances of such behaviour themselves. Committee hearings and scrutiny will only take place when legislators feel that the problem is sufficiently serious to justify the time and cost involved and when they deem it politically profitable to do so.

Congressional oversight is a legitimate and important method of ensuring executive accountability but, with the existence of divided party control of the two branches, the majority in Congress has more of an incentive to harass and embarrass the President and his administration. The most publicly visible instances of oversight since the 1970s were when Democratic Congresses acted to confront Republican Presidents: the Watergate affair and the impeachment hearings of Richard Nixon; the inquiries into maladministration in the Department of Housing and Urban Development (HUD) and the Environmental Protection Agency (EPA) in the 1980s; and the Iran-Contra hearings of 1987.

The decline of cooperation and collegiality and the rise of partisan tensions in Congress has been exacerbated by what many see as the use of legislative oversight for blatantly party political ends. It is therefore not surprising that, with the Republicans in control of Congress, a number of committees launched investigations into alleged wrong-doing by President Clinton, his wife Hillary and the White House staff. These included allegations that the Clintons acted improperly over property transactions in Arkansas when Bill Clinton was Governor (the Whitewater affair), charges that officials responsible for organising White House travel were dismissed to give the business to associates of the Clintons ('Travelgate') and, following the 1996 elections, accusations that the Clinton campaign had raised large illegal contributions from foreign businessmen in exchange for influence over government policies that affected them. This culminated in the attempt to impeach and remove President Clinton from office following the publication of the report of the Independent Counsel, Kenneth Starr in 1998. The process in 1998–99 was intensely partisan in nature with Republicans overwhelmingly supporting impeachment in the House and the subsequent attempt to convict in the Senate and almost all Democrats opposed. A handful of members crossed party lines on these votes.

Chapter 3 examines the impeachment process and the role of the Independent Counsel in more detail. For an analysis of the oversight function see Peter Falconer, 'Congressional Oversight: The Development of Legislative Review' in Alan Grant (ed.), *Contemporary American Politics*, Dartmouth, 1995.

Think points

- What are the key similarities and differences in the powers and working of the House of Representatives and the Senate today?
- Who has power over the legislative process in Congress?
- Why have congressional politics become increasingly partisan in nature and what impact has this had on the working of the legislature?

Some further reading

Ross K. Baker, *House and Senate* (Norton 1989)

Colton C. Campbell and Nicol C. Rae (eds), *The Contentious Senate* (Rowman and Littlefield 2001)

Roger H. Davidson (ed.), *The Postreform Congress* (St Martin's Press 1992)

Roger H. Davidson and Walter J. Oleszek, *Congress and its Members* (Congressional Quarterly Press 2000)

Lawrence C. Dodd and Bruce I. Oppenheimer, *Congress Reconsidered* (Congressional Quarterly Press 2001)

Lawrence C. Evans and Walter J. Oleszek, *Congress Under Fire: Reform Politics and the Republican Majority* (Houghton Mifflin 1997)

Morris P. Fiorina, *Congress: Keystone of the Washington Establishment* (Yale University Press 1989)

Michael Foley and John Owens, *Congress and the Presidency: Institutional Politics in a Separated System* (Manchester University Press 1996)

Charles O. Jones, *Separate But Equal Branches: Congress and the Presidency* (Chatham House 1995)

Anthony King (ed.), *Both Ends of the Avenue* (American Enterprise Institute 1983)

John E. Owens, 'Congress after the "Revolution": The Continuing Problems of Governance in a Partisan Era', in *American Politics: 2000 and Beyond*, Alan Grant (ed.) (Ashgate 2000)

Eric Schickler, 'Congress', in *Developments in American Politics 4*, Gillian Peele, Christopher J. Bailey, Bruce Cain and B. Guy Peters (eds) (Palgrave 2002)

Steven Smith, *The American Congress* (Houghton Mifflin 1995)
James A. Thurber and Roger H. Davidson (eds), *Remaking Congress: Change and Stability in the 1990s* (Congressional Quarterly Press 1995)

Weblinks

The House of Representatives: www.house.gov
The Senate: www.senate.gov
Roll Call (a newspaper about congressional politics): www.rollcall.com
Library of Congress (on legislation and congressional votes): www.thomas.loc.gov
Project Vote Smart (explains current legislation and its progress in Congress): www.vote-smart.org

3 Law execution
The President and administration

> I do solemnly swear that I will faithfully execute the office of President of the United States and will to the best of my ability preserve, protect and defend the Constitution of the United States.

With these words each of America's 43 Presidents has been sworn into office. However, America's Chief Executive takes over an office that has developed substantially since George Washington took the same oath more than two centuries ago. The Founding Fathers could hardly have conceived that the office, which was intended to avoid the tyrannies connected with hereditary monarchy, would eventually have the formidable array of powers that any modern President inherits.

The President's central position in American government is based on the fact that he is the only nationally elected politician who can claim to speak for the United States as a whole. Both in foreign policy and in domestic affairs, the President can claim to be representing the national interest as he sees it. When he meets a foreign head of state or takes an initiative on education policy, he speaks for America. In contrast, the Congress can be seen, in many respects, as 535 local politicians who represent parochial interests. In a government system that exhibits the separation of powers, a dispersion of authority and fragmentation of influence, the President has a major role in providing some form of unity and coordination.

The perception of many people is that the President is all-powerful and that the 'presidential system' inevitably leads to the Chief Executive getting his own way. In practice the position is far more complex. The checks and balances principle inherent in the American Constitution often leads to frustration for the President. The reality of presidential power is therefore something of a paradox; he is very powerful in some areas and almost powerless in others, and the effectiveness of the President will often depend upon factors over which he has no control. The problem for the President therefore is to ensure that his constitutional powers actually work for him. A President must not only use executive authority constructively and wisely in the interest of the United States, but also within the limits of the constitutional system.

The different roles of the President

The presidency of the United States is one office held by one individual, but in fact the Constitution sets out a number of roles for him that can, analytically at least, be seen as distinctive. However, the Constitution has surprisingly little to say about the powers of the President, and this silence in many areas has allowed the holders of the office to 'fill in the details' by extending presidential action in ways not necessarily foreseen by the

Founding Fathers. In addition to the constitutional roles which are set out, there have evolved some political roles which are equally important for an understanding of the modern presidency.

1 The Head of State. All nations have a head of state who welcomes foreign dignatories, represents the state abroad and attends ceremonial functions. In this respect, the President takes on a similar role to the British monarch. The President provides a focal point for the loyalty of a very diverse society; a symbol of America that children are from their earliest experiences taught to respect. Problems do arise from this attempt to unite in one office the position of head of state and the political roles of a head of government. It is sometimes argued that the President is too busy with the administration of the country to be concerned with taking part in university graduation days, greeting astronauts after a space flight, or playing the first ball of the American baseball season. The popularity, status and publicity attached to these time-consuming duties can be utilised by the President to help him carry out his political functions. It is also true that the President's family and the Vice-President take some of the responsibilities in this area from his shoulders. A more serious criticism is the difficulty of a President's fulfilling the roles of both national unifier and leader of a partisan government with controversial policies. This problem was seen in its most extreme form when, with the Watergate crisis hanging over President Nixon in 1974, the constitutional system provided no focus for national loyalty and unity. On the other hand, President Reagan demonstrated that it is possible to perform both these roles successfully. Paradoxically Reagan was the most ideologically committed President in the post-war era and yet he was able to maintain a distance between himself and 'politics'. Philip John Davies points out that:

> In part, this detachment has been the result of his impressive skill in the ceremonial role of the presidency . . . [it] is almost always fulfilled with an air of nationalistic pride that enhanced the Presidential stature as a common man's head of state.[1]

Washington journalist David Broder comments on Reagan's performance in this role:

> When it comes to a patriotic occasion, a memorial service or a religious observance, his words, his bearing, his expressions and gestures speak eloquently for the American people and nation.[2]

President Clinton learned to play this role effectively, as was evident in the aftermath of the terrorist bombing of the federal building in Oklahoma City in 1995, and this helped to improve his overall standing with the public. President George W. Bush's reputation with the public was enhanced very considerably by his newly found eloquence in speaking for a nation in shock, following the attacks on New York and Washington, DC on 11 September 2001. On the other hand, the scandals afflicting the Clinton presidency, and in particular the liaison with Monica Lewinsky, brought discredit to Clinton himself and, many believed, tarnished the dignity of the presidential office.

2 Chief Executive. The role of head of the executive branch of the federal system is clearly stated in the Constitution by the phrases 'The executive power shall be vested in a President of the United States' and 'He shall take care the laws be faithfully executed'. The President is thus responsible for the carrying out of policies and laws passed by the Congress; the Founding Fathers decided to have one man accountable for this operation although they recognised that he would need help. Government departments, such as

State and Treasury, were quickly established, but under the control of the President. Today the President is responsible for 15 departments, numerous federal agencies and commissions, and approximately 2.8 million civil servants. The President has a major role in attempting to coordinate the many semi-autonomous parts of the government machine, and in bringing some coherence to policy-making and execution. He is also responsible for formulating and presenting to Congress the federal budget which sets out the spending requirements for various parts of the executive branch. The Chief Executive can also determine how the laws are administered by appointing, subject to Senate approval, the top officials, Cabinet Secretaries and agency directors who will make up his government. The President may also issue, under the authority of statutes passed by Congress, executive orders which are rules having the force of law relating to the running of the federal government. Recent Presidents have issued approximately 40–50 such orders annually.

3 Chief Legislator. The President is, of course, not part of the legislative branch, but this has not prevented Presidents from playing an increasingly important role in the legislative process. In the nineteenth century they tended to see their role as executing laws which Congress initiated and passed, but today a Chief Executive is expected to have a programme or package of measures which he will encourage the legislature to pass. Some of the most important pieces of national legislation to reach the statute book since the First World War were initiated by the White House. The Constitution says: 'He shall from time to time give the Congress information of the State of the Union and recommend to their consideration such measures as he shall judge necessary and expedient.' The President may also call emergency sessions of Congress, but he lacks the powers of dissolving the assembly and calling elections. The White House tries to influence the legislative process by the initiation of bills, by building coalitions and persuading legislators to support or oppose measures and, in the final analysis, by the use of the veto power. (See Chapter 2 and Table 2.9 on presidential vetoes.) The President is therefore a major, if not *the* major, participant in the legislative process.

4 Chief Diplomat. The President is the Chief Diplomat for the United States, even though the Founding Fathers intended that Congress should participate in the foreign policy-making process. Congress officially declares war and the Senate can ratify treaties as well as approve the appointment of the Secretary of State and ambassadors. The President's primacy in foreign policy developed in the nineteenth century, and in 1936 the Supreme Court confirmed that the executive branch alone has the right to negotiate with foreign states. The President should keep Congress informed of international developments, for example, by 'State of the World' messages or by officials appearing before congressional committees, but there is little doubt that the President, in practice, is in charge of both policy making and execution in this field, although he must obtain the necessary financial support from Congress to carry out his objectives effectively.

5 Commander-in-Chief of the Armed Forces. Allied to the role of Chief Diplomat is that of Commander-in-Chief, because it is only by the ability to use effectively the might of America's armed forces, often known as his 'war powers', that foreign policy can be credible. The role of Commander-in-Chief gives the President extensive powers in wartime, and it has been used to justify action which would have been regarded as dictatorial if carried out in peacetime. Lincoln argued that he had the right to do anything necessary to ensure the survival of the Republic, and Roosevelt took over private companies and set up emergency boards during the Second World War. The President can also make tactical decisions on the deployment of troops and the running of a war. Truman, for example, determined to use the atomic bomb on Hiroshima in 1945 to hasten the surrender of Japan, while Lyndon Johnson decided to bomb Hanoi and Haiphong in North Vietnam. The nuclear age has made the President's power in this field both more formidable and more onerous a responsibility.

The command of the armed forces by an elected President shows the Framers' belief that civil control over the military generals was necessary for a free society to continue. The most dramatic example of this supremacy in modern times was the dismissal of General Douglas MacArthur by President Truman in April 1951. MacArthur was a national hero in his own right, but had consistently refused to follow presidential instructions on how the Korean War should be conducted, and publicly criticised the President.

6 Head of Party. The five roles described above can be said to comprise the constitutional responsibilities of the President. The Founding Fathers hoped that the President would be free from the divisive influences of parties and factions, but it was inevitable that rival groups would wish to control the executive branch, and even in Washington's term of office parties began to develop. The presidency became the major prize in the federal system and provided the most important reason why state parties combined. Patronage, in the way of jobs and favours that any President can bestow, has also helped to keep the loose American party system together.

The President can use his party identification to advantage in securing support from Congressmen for his legislative proposals, and parties have therefore helped to bridge the separation of powers, although political scientists have noted that Congressmen today do not see the same advantages of helping a President of their own party as in the past. This has come about as a result of the increasingly independent campaigns that both candidates for Congress and the presidency run, the declining influence of party organisations over the nomination process which is carried out mainly through primary elections and the phenomenon of split-ticket voting which has reduced the natural interdependence of the President and legislators of his own party. The President exercises great influence over the party's national organisation and can play a major role in determining who his successor as the party's standard-bearer will be. He provides one of the major parties with national leadership while the absence of a 'leader of the opposition' weakens the other party. On the other hand, the President's party identification can make it more difficult for him to obtain consensus on policies and carry out his role as national leader.

Austin Ranney has noted that most Presidents have not been strongly partisan in their approach to governing as they have often needed support in Congress from the opposing party (particularly in the case of Republican Presidents) and because of the increasing anti-party tone of American political culture with the weakening of party identification and growth in the number of independents, the decline in importance of party organisation in presidential elections and an anti-politician and anti-party bias among network television broadcasters. Most Americans expect him to be a 'President of all the people'.[3]

7 Other roles. Clinton Rossiter has described other extra-constitutional roles for the President; as 'Voice of the People' – the national voice in American affairs; as 'Protector of the Peace' – intervening in natural disasters, race riots and other emergencies with the full force of the federal government; and as 'World Leader' because the President has become the head of a Super-Power and can be seen as a spokesman for the Western world.[4] Rossiter also calls him the 'Manager of the Prosperity' to describe the Chief Executive's responsibility for the general management of the United States' economy. The

President has a number of ways he can help maintain economic stability, and since the Depression of the 1930s it has been expected that the President use techniques such as changes in the tax structure, administration of the federal budget and public works programmes to avoid the extremes of large-scale unemployment and rampant inflation. Even Republican Presidents, pledged to the maintenance of a free enterprise economy, have intervened extensively.

It is misleading to think of these different roles as being self-sufficient. They are over-lapping and make up the presidential office as a whole. Sometimes the President's performance in one area will help him achieve success in another; at other times presidential roles may conflict and collide with one another. Only one thing is certain: the burdens placed upon a President make total success an impossibility. The President must attempt to use his constitutional and political powers to maximise advantages where he can, and minimise the risks of failures and mistakes.

The growth of the presidential office

Why did the presidency grow during the twentieth century in power and importance compared with the somewhat more passive executive office of the previous century? There have been a number of factors leading to this phenomenon:

The growth in 'big government'

Twentieth-century experience of wars and economic crises led to a world-wide develop-ment of strengthened executives and declining legislatures. The United States was no exception to this general pattern. The increasing involvement of the President in the nation's economic and social affairs as 'Chief Legislator' and 'Manager of the Prosperity' inevitably led to a growth in the size of government itself. The bureaucracy that has expanded since the 1930s is more difficult for Congress to control, but at the same time has not necessarily increased the power of the President personally. Frustration with the departmental organisation has led to Presidents developing their own 'mini-bureau-cracies' in the White House, in order to surround themselves with advisers they have felt they could trust. The main objection to this trend has been that, unlike Cabinet Secretaries and other senior departmental officials, these close aides are neither approved by nor controlled by Congress. President Nixon claimed that the doctrine of 'executive privilege', first forcefully asserted by Grover Cleveland in 1885, prevented these people being interrogated by legislative committees. It has been accepted that the President has a right to confidential advice from his closest counsellors, and that effective government and national security could be threatened if these officials were forced to divulge the views expressed within the White House. However, the courts did not allow such arguments to interfere with the criminal investigations arising from the Watergate revelations, and presidential aides did eventually appear before the Senate select committee. In May 1998 a federal judge also rejected President Clinton's claim that his senior advisers should not have to testify before a grand jury investigating the Lewinsky affair. Two months later the Supreme Court decided in an unprecedented move that even the President's secret service bodyguards should face questioning on what they knew about the liaison. The justices also ruled in a separate case that Clinton confidantes who were also White House lawyers and paid for by public funds must testify before the grand jury, if requested, and that their relationship with the President was not protected by client–attorney privilege of confidentiality.

The importance of foreign policy

Until the twentieth century, the United States generally followed a policy of isolationism and therefore the President's roles as Chief Diplomat and Commander-in-Chief, while not unimportant, were obviously limited in scope. With the development of America's world power and responsibilities, the two roles have grown dramatically, while the ability of Congress to supervise and participate in foreign policy has declined. 'Summit diplomacy' these days requires top level meetings between heads of governments such as those held between Presidents Reagan and Gorbachev and it has been recognised that the President must have a degree of flexibility and manoeuvre when negotiating with the former Soviet Union or other major powers. The President's ability to take initiatives, such as President Nixon's visit to China in 1972, which opened a dialogue with the communist regime for the first time, provides him with opportunities to transform international relations and gain personal status and publicity. In an emergency the President is able to act quickly, decisively and, if necessary, in secret. The Cuban Crisis of 1962 provides a good example of the sort of situation where only the President and his close advisers could make decisions; Congress is, by its nature, too cumbersome and deliberative to deal with such crises. Clinton Rossiter has written:

> Secrecy, dispatch, unity, continuity and access to information – the ingredients of successful diplomacy – are the properties of his [the President's] office, and Congress . . . possesses none of these.[5]

In addition, Congress cannot provide coherence in the making of foreign policy; jurisdiction over foreign affairs is shared by dozens of committees and sub-committees. The presence of different ethnic groups within the American population and their influence within Congress can also be said to have imposed distortions on US foreign policy, for example, in the Middle East, which the executive branch has to attempt to counter.[6]

The President's degree of personal involvement in foreign policy will depend upon his own interests and experience; he may well depend heavily on the advice and recommendations of his Secretary of State, as Gerald Ford tended to when he assumed office in August 1974. Patriotic support for presidential action when dealing with foreign powers has often led to a bipartisan approach, and the President can therefore expect more general support in Congress and among the public on foreign policy than he receives on domestic issues. This led some political scientists to assert that there were 'two presidencies'.[7] However, despite the fact that since the Vietnam War Congress has involved itself much more in the details of foreign and defence policy, it has also allowed the President to avoid the formal treaty-making provision in the Constitution by the use of executive agreements. These do not require the two-thirds ratification of the Senate, and with the failure of the proposed Bricker amendment in 1954 which would have required such approval, executive agreements have become a major tool of presidential foreign policy. For example, during Ronald Reagan's two terms in office (1981–89) there were 2,840 such agreements covering areas such as military commitments, overseas aid and trade, while only 125 formal treaties were signed in the same period. The main distinction between the two methods seems to have been the preparedness of Presidents to submit them for Senate approval.

The use of American military power by the President on his own initiative was demonstrated by President Reagan's decisions to invade Grenada in 1983 and launch a bomb strike against Libya in 1986. In June 1993 President Clinton ordered a missile attack on Baghdad and Saddam Hussein's intelligence headquarters after it was claimed that evidence showed that Iraq had planned the assassination of former President George Bush while on a visit to liberated Kuwait. In October 1994 Clinton used US forces to secure the restoration to office of President Aristide in Haiti. In 1998 Clinton ordered air attacks on Iraq in response to violations of the agreement that brought an end to the 1991 Gulf War and in 2001 George W. Bush did the same in response to Iraqi targeting of Western planes in the 'no-fly' zones. None of these actions had long-term implications for US military involvement of the sort Congress had in mind when passing the War Powers Resolution of 1973 which limited presidential power in this area (see below, page 86 for details). The executive branch has grown in strength as America's international commitments and military power have increased.

Personalities and the conception of the office

The presidential office has grown partly as a result of the precedents set by various Presidents during the nation's history. Sometimes the requirements of the time, particularly wars and economic crises, have necessitated strong action by the chief executive, while more peaceful and tranquil periods, such as the 1920s under Calvin Coolidge, have not demanded dynamic presidential initiatives. Conservatives have tended to see less of a role for the federal government than liberals, and therefore conservative Presidents, such as William Howard Taft (1909–13), have had a fundamentally different conception of the President's role from Franklin Roosevelt (1933–45) or Lyndon Johnson (1963–69). The influence of the personalities of the individuals holding the office must also be taken into account. James D. Barber, in a controversial book *The Presidential Character*, classified the Presidents of the twentieth century according to the energy they put into the job (passive or active) and their feelings about their presidential experience (negative or positive).[8] On this basis, for example, Dwight D. Eisenhower was categorised as 'passive-negative' while Richard Nixon was 'active-negative', John F. Kennedy 'active-positive' and Ronald Reagan 'passive-positive'. He argued that these factors served as the principal determinants of their performance in office, a view which has been much criticised by other political scientists who denied that Presidents could shape the national agenda after their own image and likeness.[9]

With the increasing complexity of government and the industrial society within which it operates, Presidents now tend to be activists rather than non-activists in their conception of the presidential office. This applies to conservative Presidents as well as liberals. President Reagan, while renowned for not working as long hours as many of his predecessors, took a very active leadership role in attempting to reduce the role of the federal government in the nation's affairs. Another conservative, Richard Nixon, expressed this view in 1968:

> The days of the passive presidency belong to a simpler past. The next President must take an activist view of his office . . . he must lead.[10]

The inertia of Congress and the erosion of the balance

The growth of the executive branch as a result of war and the Depression led to the Congress recognising in the post-Watergate period that there was a need to reassert its authority. During the previous 40 years Congress had surrendered much of its own influence, by granting the President wide discretionary powers within statutes in the domestic field, and allowing him to make executive agreements and military interventions abroad. For the major part of this period the Democratic party controlled both the Congress and the presidency, and legislators tended to trust 'their' Presidents – Roosevelt, Truman, Kennedy and Johnson – to do whatever was right for the country. Only with the frustrations of the Vietnam War, which it originally supported, did the Democratic Congress start to criticise the Democratic President, Lyndon Johnson, on a broad basis. American liberals have traditionally supported a strong presidency as the most likely method of securing what they see as much-needed reforms; it was therefore something of a conversion when liberals in Congress started to argue for a strengthening of congressional power in the 1970s against the 'Imperial Presidency'. One writer has described this liberal support for the presidency as follows:

> The presidency, in the liberals' view, is uniquely equipped to authorize and give legitimacy to political and social programs which are of urgent importance but which can be counted on to meet opposition or be hamstrung if left to the inherently obstructionist procedures of the national legislature.[11]

The Supreme Court has also tended to support, by its decisions since 1937, the right of Congress to grant the executive branch large areas of discretionary power. Before that time, statutes such as the National Industrial Recovery Act, a major piece of New Deal legislation giving the President broad powers, were declared 'unconstitutional'.

The mass media

The mass media can concentrate on one national political office more easily than on the many faces of Congress, and therefore everything the President does is news. The cameras and reporters will record him meeting foreign heads of state, electioneering for his party, signing a bill into law, and even his vacations become major news stories. The President's family also have to learn to live with endless intrusions into their private lives and they may become national celebrities in their own right. The Kennedys, for example, became a form of royal family for the American media.

The President is able to use the media to advantage in publicising and mobilising support for his policies. President Reagan used his experience and skill in this area with nationally televised appeals for public support in securing the passage of his economic measures through Congress in 1981. Franklin D. Roosevelt was the first President to utilise the media in this way. He recognised the importance of radio and initiated the 'fireside chats' which took him into millions of American homes.

Presidential press conferences have been held, since 1945, in a large hall in the White House where hundreds of correspondents can attend. John F. Kennedy initiated the 'live' press conference where the full session is seen on television without editing. The President is fully briefed by his advisers on likely questions, but he does have the opportunity to explain and justify policies, not only to the reporters present, but to the nation as well. Until the 1970s Presidents were holding on average two press conferences a month but President Nixon made only 37 appearances in over five years. His relations with the press, which were never very good, deteriorated during the Watergate period, and his press conferences became very rare. Jimmy Carter was keen to have an 'open' administration and intended to have regular informal briefings with reporters as well as the normal conferences. Carter also became the first President to participate in a radio 'phone-in' programme when he answered questions from ordinary citizens on the air. President

Reagan held only 44 press conferences during his two terms in office and was criticised for not allowing the press accessibility and for being too protected by staff who prevented journalists asking him direct questions. However, Reagan was able to use the media through 'photo opportunities' and also became known as the 'Great Communicator' because of his mastery of the prepared and recorded television address to the nation. Reagan frequently used his televised appearances to 'go public' by appealing for support for specific policies and putting constituency pressure on legislators before major votes in Congress. Such an outsider strategy can be seen as an alternative way of trying to persuade Congress without directly negotiating and bargaining with members of the legislature.

James P. Pfiffner points out that George Bush did not go public to the same extent:

> As President, Bush approached politics much more as the insider he had been for most of his career. His experience and personal style lent themselves much more to bargaining than going public. Bush's television presence and speaking abilities were not as suited to public appeals as were Reagan's, which was reflected in Bush's decision to hold ninety-one press conferences but only five television addresses in his first three years in office.[12]

President Clinton continued the use of a successful campaign technique when he came to office in 1993 by holding televised 'town meetings', where ordinary citizens could question him on matters of concern to them. This was in addition to regular press conferences with the White House press corps who, early on, felt they were being bypassed with these meetings. All Presidents have therefore been able to use the media to increase both their public visibility and their status.

In contrast to the institution set up in 1787 by the Founding Fathers, the US President today is stronger *vis-à-vis* Congress, is more involved in national policy-making, is in charge of a greatly enlarged bureaucratic machine, and is one of the world's major statesmen. The President is also elected in a more democratic fashion and is the leader of a political party; due to the modern methods of mass media and technology, he is also the subject of far more national attention and scrutiny.

The limits of presidential power

It has been made clear from the examination of the checks and balances of the American Constitution in Chapter 1 that the President does not exercise unbridled power. It is worth considering the institutional and political checks on the chief executive to obtain a balanced picture of the presidential office.

Political culture

As we saw in Chapter 1, the political culture of the United States, that is, people's widely shared beliefs and values about government and its relationship with them as citizens, has as one of its major characteristics a distrust and suspicion of all forms of authority. The separation of powers principle, the checks and balances and the federal division of powers have institutionalised these concerns into a fragmented and decentralised political system where power is shared among many leaders. As David Mervin has pointed out, Presidents in particular need to be aware of these sentiments, even as they are expected to provide strong and effective leadership for the nation; the anti-leadership system rooted in the American political culture continues to constrain Presidents to this day.[13]

Congress

The President may have increased his influence in relation to the legislature during the twentieth century, but this does not alter the fact that no President can govern effectively for very long without congressional support. It is required for the passage of any legislative proposals and for the appropriations to fund the executive branch. We have seen in the chapter on Congress that a President may find that his own party is in a minority in the legislature, and even when there is a majority in both houses, the President is by no means assured of success. Tables 2.7 and 2.8 illustrate this fact. A liberal Democratic President such as John F. Kennedy was constantly frustrated by opposition from a coalition of Republican conservatives and Democratic Southerners. Two years after taking office, Kennedy made this observation on the role of Congress as a check on the presidency:

> The fact is that I think the Congress looks more powerful sitting here than it did when I was in Congress . . . when you are in Congress, you are one of a hundred in the Senate or one of 435 in the House, so that power is divided. But from here I look at a Congress and I look at the collective power of the Congress . . . and it is a substantial power.[14]

Since Kennedy's time, reforms within Congress in the 1970s tended to fragment power even further and made the job of Presidents even more difficult. In addition to trying to secure the support of party leaders and committee chairmen for presidential initiatives, negotiating and bargaining with groups of members and even individual legislators has now become the norm (see Chapter 2). Heightened partisanship, the increased use of the filibuster in the Senate, combined with divided control of the two branches for much of the time, has further complicated the President's task.

Congress has the right to question executive branch officials through its committees and now has the staff support and expertise to provide it with the capability of more adequately scrutinising the administration and carry out oversight investigations.

The President is also bound to consider whether the people he nominates to executive positions are acceptable to the Senate. The condition of Senate approval acts as a check on the President's freedom of choice, although he usually secures the ratification of his nominees. In rejecting by 53 votes to 47 the nomination by President Bush of former Senator John Tower as Defence Secretary in March 1989, the Senate used its power to withhold consent from a Cabinet nominee for the first time in 30 years and only the ninth time in American history. The Senate was concerned at allegations about Tower's private life, including claims that he had developed business links with defence contractors in the period since leaving his position in Geneva in charge of strategic arms talks. The rejection of Tower was seen as throwing doubt on Bush's judgement in persevering with the nomination long after it was clear that it faced strong opposition and it also abruptly ended the new President's 'honeymoon' period with Congress. President Clinton was forced to withdraw the nomination of Zoe Baird for the post of Attorney-General in his new administration after it was revealed that she had employed two illegal immigrants and failed to pay social security taxes for them. In 2001 George W. Bush's choice for Labor Secretary, Linda Chavez, also had to stand down after it was alleged that she had employed an illegal immigrant as a cleaner.

The Senate has in recent years taken a tougher line on the many sub-cabinet level appointees the President makes. It has been concerned about potential conflicts of interest but has also rejected nominees because of their political views, particularly if they were regarded as extreme or out of sympathy with the objectives of the agency to which they were being appointed. The Reagan White House, for example, withdrew the nomination of Ernest Lefever as Assistant Secretary of State for Human Rights after the Senate Foreign Relations Committee had rejected him by 13 votes to 4. In June 1993 President Clinton withdrew the nomination of personal friend and black lawyer Lani Guinier as Assistant Attorney General for Civil Rights, following criticism by members of the Senate Judiciary Committee, including liberal Democrats such as its Chairman Joseph Biden, of controversial articles on voting rights that she had written for a law review. Guinier's nomination was withdrawn before the official hearings by the committee had begun and this action led to strong complaints about the President's handling of the affair by civil rights groups, the Congressional Black Caucus and the media.

The national legislature also made frequent use of the device known as the 'congressional veto'. Between 1932 and 1985 over 200 pieces of legislation included some review of executive action by Congress. Whereas many legislative vetoes applied to the delegated rule-making powers of federal agencies and were seen by Congressmen as a way of checking the unelected bureaucracy, some applied to the President himself in major areas of policy. In June 1983, in a major separation of powers case, the Supreme Court decided that the congressional veto was unconstitutional. The Court said that when Congress delegated to the executive branch the authority to issue regulations or make certain kinds of decisions it 'must abide by its delegation of authority until that delegation is legislatively altered or revoked'.[15] In March 1987 in the case of *Alaskan Airlines* v. *Brock*, the Supreme Court unanimously ruled that unconstitutional legislative veto provisions do not invalidate the laws in which they appear, provided that they were not critical to the congressional decision to pass those laws in the first place. Although the Supreme Court decision has reduced the effectiveness of the legislative veto, executive agencies have continued to respect the restrictions imposed because they have not been willing to risk congressional anger by doing something that the legislature has clearly opposed. Prominent examples of the principle of the congressional veto are those included within the Impoundment Control Act of 1974, and the 1976 Arms Export Control Act which requires the President to submit to Congress major military contracts with foreign governments; if both houses vetoed the proposal it could not go ahead.

While the President has the powers of Commander-in-Chief of the armed forces, Congress has the constitutional power of declaring war. Over two centuries the United States has been engaged in over 130 significant military conflicts, whereas Congress has only formally declared war on five occasions, and in four of these cases the declarations simply recognised that hostilities had broken out. Following the Vietnam War, Congress passed the War Powers Resolution of 1973 over President Nixon's veto in an attempt to limit the President's ability to act unilaterally in this area. The resolution requires that the President consult with Congress before introducing armed forces into situations where hostilities are imminent. It also requires the President to report his actions to Congress. If, after 60 days, Congress has neither declared war nor given a time extension the President must withdraw the troops. Presidents have consistently argued that this resolution unconstitutionally impinges upon their powers as Commander-in-Chief and it has had little effect in practice. Presidents have still taken military action with little or no reference to the legislature when a brief display of force was thought to be necessary. Congress did invoke the resolution in 1983 when it authorised US marines who were in Lebanon as part of a multinational peacekeeping force to remain there for up to eighteen months.

Following the Iraqi invasion of Kuwait in 1990 President Bush moved a large American force to Saudi Arabia. Bush did not report to Congress the deployment of troops to the Gulf and Congress made no attempt to invoke the War Powers Resolution. In early 1991 the President asked Congress for authorisation to use force to implement UN resolutions calling for unconditional Iraqi withdrawal from Kuwait. The House of Representatives agreed by 250–183 to his request while the Senate voted 52–47, but this was not a formal declaration of war. Opinion was divided as to whether the President required authorisation for such a major military involvement. Some argued that the request effectively recognised that the President did not have the authority to wage war himself; others said that he wanted political rather than constitutional backing. However, failure to secure such support from Congress would certainly have provoked a constitutional confrontation.[16] Les Aspin, the then Chairman of the House Armed Services Committee, is reported to have told advisers that if Bush had not sought approval he would have led the move to impeach the President.[17]

Following the terrorist attacks of 11 September 2001 Congress gave the President authority to use military force against all those involved. The House voted 420–1 in favour of the resolution while the Senate supported it by 98–0, reflecting the public's outrage at the attacks and backing for the President in retaliating against those responsible. This vote led to the military operation in Afghanistan to overthrow the Taliban regime which had supported Osama bin Laden's al-Qaeda network. In October 2002 Congress voted to give the President broad authority to launch a preemptive strike on Iraq 'as he determines to be necessary and appropriate'. This followed the President's claims that Saddam Hussein's regime was stockpiling weapons of mass destruction against United Nations' resolutions and was a threat to the national security of the United States as well as the world more generally. The House vote was 296–133 and the Senate 77–33 in favour, even though the resolution contained no provision for congressional review or an expiry date and did not place any constraint on the military action President Bush could order. It merely required the President to inform Congress once action begins and report on military operations at least once every 60 days. Despite the minority in Congress warning that the legislature was giving the President a 'blank cheque' in allowing him to decide whether or not to go to war and was akin to the Gulf of Tonkin resolution which led to the United States becoming embroiled in Vietnam, the post-11 September political environment provided considerable bipartisan support for action against Iraq.

Congress still retains a number of important powers in relation to foreign policy. It insists that it be presented with the texts of all executive agreements in order to avoid secret arrangements between the President and foreign states which lead to commitments of American troops and money. Congress has also shown its willingness to refuse funds for a foreign policy with which it disagrees. In 1973 an Act was passed banning the bombing of Cambodia after 15 August 1973 and in 1975 the Ford administration was denied further finances to help the crumbling regime in South Vietnam. President Reagan also had considerable difficulties persuading Congress to provide financial support for his policies of assisting the governments of El Salvador and the Contra rebels in Nicaragua. The Iran-Contra affair, which resulted from an attempt to provide funding for the Contras despite the lack of congressional approval, allowed members of Congress to become even more involved in foreign policy matters. In 1987 Speaker Jim Wright took the initiative away from the White House and even appeared to negotiate with Nicaraguan President Daniel Ortega who had been refused access to the Reagan administration for over two years. Wright's intervention led to intense criticism that he was infringing the

President's prerogatives in diplomatic relations and even Wright himself later conceded he may have inadvertently overstepped his role.[18]

President Clinton was forced to take account of the Republican majority in the 104th Congress in making foreign and national security policy. Conservatives and, in particular Jesse Helms, the new Chairman of the Senate Foreign Relations Committee, had strong views on issues such as the role of United Nations peacekeeping forces and relations with Cuba which conflicted with those of the administration. It is also true that the growing importance of trade issues to America's post-Cold War agenda has increased congressional assertiveness, particularly as they affect the national economy as well as jobs and prosperity in members' constituencies. In 1998 Congress voted to deny President Clinton renewal of 'fast-track' authority over negotiating trade agreements.

Michael Foley argues that the reassertion of Congress in the 1970s created an apparently transformed institution interested not only in the development of high strategic policy, but also in the implementation of policy itself. However, its strategy is to challenge the executive branch but not to succeed to the point of having to assume responsibility itself for policy measures. He concludes: 'Congressional participation in American foreign policy is not dissimilar to taking a bus ride. Congress gets on and off at its pleasure.'[19] John Dumbrell argues that, even though policy-making in foreign affairs has become more decentralised in the post-Cold War era, Congress has not really come close to actually seizing the initiative, even after the Republicans took control in 1995. Indeed, faced with a highly assertive Congress in domestic policy, Clinton concentrated more of his time and attention on international issues than in the first two years of his presidency. Therefore, he concludes, Presidents retain their power to define foreign policy issues, particularly in the areas of military engagement and war powers.[20]

Box 3.1 Impeaching the President

The Constitution states that a President 'shall be removed from Office on Impeachment for, and conviction of, Treason, Bribery, or other high Crimes and Misdemeanors' (Article II Section 4). The implication of the word 'other' is that the Founding Fathers intended that offences meriting removal from office should be comparable to treason and bribery. The primary purpose of the provision is to remove a President who has used his office to undermine the Constitution or whose continuance in office poses a threat to the American public, and thus impeachable offences would be high matters of state rather than petty crimes. Article I Section 3 says that in cases of impeachment the penalty handed down by the Senate, in the event of it convicting a President by a two-thirds majority, shall be restricted to his removal from office and disqualification from holding other public office in the federal government but that, once convicted, he may be subject to trial and punishment in the courts according to the law.

In 1868 Abraham Lincoln's successor, President Andrew Johnson, was in dispute with both radical and conservative Republicans over the treatment of the South in the aftermath of the Civil War. When the President dismissed the Secretary of War the House of Representatives accused him of abusing his office under the Tenure of Office Act, which banned the sacking of officials appointed with congressional advice and approval, and voted by 126–47 to impeach him. After 37 days the Senate passed a motion to convict him by 35–19, one short of the necessary two-thirds majority. In 1974, following the Watergate scandal which included the White House's complicity in a cover-up of its connection to a break-in at the Democratic Party headquarters, the House of Representatives passed articles of impeachment against President Richard Nixon. The motion was supported by many

Republicans as well as Democrats and, when it became clear to the President that he lacked sufficient support in the Senate to survive a trial, Nixon become the first President to resign his office.

Despite the many other scandals that afflicted the Clinton presidency the impeachment crisis in 1998–99 was caused by Clinton's sexual affair with a young White House intern, Monica Lewinsky. The President denied his involvement in any such activities in a deposition in a civil sexual harassment case brought by Paula Jones which was later thrown out by the court, but his alleged attempt to get Ms Lewinsky to lie was sufficient for Independent Counsel Kenneth Starr to investigate and later propose impeachment charges to the House of Representatives. The alleged impeachment offences were in essence that the President had lied under oath, that he had urged Lewinsky and his secretary Betty Currie to also lie under oath about the relationship, and that he tried to obstruct justice by getting his secretary to hide evidence and by attempting to find Ms Lewinsky a job to encourage her silence.

The main case made for impeachment and removing the President from office was therefore not that he had a sexual relationship with a junior staff member in the White House (reckless though that might have been) but that his misconduct constituted "an ongoing sense of deliberate and direct assaults by Mr Clinton upon the justice system of the United States". Those opposed to impeachment argued that Clinton's actions did not constitute impeachable offences against the Constitution or the polity that the framers had intended. Although Clinton lied under oath it was to prevent personal embarrassment rather than to undermine the Constitution. It was suggested that the evidence to support the other charges was either ambiguous or unconvincing. Opponents also argued that an impeachment trial would be disruptive and damaging to the country and that a censure of the President by Congress would be sufficient punishment (even though there is no constitutional provision for such an action).

The House of Representatives voted on 19 December 1998, mainly on party lines, to support two of the four articles of impeachment proposed by the Judiciary Committee. The House then appointed 13 managers, Republican members led by Henry Hyde, to prosecute the trial in the Senate. The trial opened on 13 January 1999 with the Chief Justice of the Supreme Court, William Rehnquist, presiding. Senators were not allowed to make speeches; their role as jurors in the case was to listen to the cases made by lawyers representing the House managers and the White House, submit written questions to the Chief Justice and then cast their vote in a roll call in the chamber. The final vote was taken on 12 February; both articles failed to receive the two-thirds majority necessary for conviction and removal from office. Article I relating to perjury was defeated by 55–45, with nine Republicans voting to acquit and Article II charging obstruction of justice was defeated 50–50, with five Republicans helping to produce a tied vote. Clinton therefore survived the impeachment process but his reputation was severely tarnished.

Box 3.2 The demise of the independent counsel

In 1978 Congress passed the Ethics in Government Act and, as part of the reforms resulting from the Watergate scandal, the new law allowed for the creation of independent counsels. Its purpose was to avoid the appearance of a conflict of interest when the Justice Department, headed by the Attorney-General, was faced with investigating allegations of wrong-doing by senior members of the executive branch of which it is a part. Congress was aware of the sensitivities surrounding such appointments and required that the statute be reauthorised every five years. This it did in 1983 and 1987 and, although it was allowed to lapse in 1992 at the end of the Bush administration, it was revived in 1994 with the support of President

Clinton. Republicans were initially unenthusiastic about the law because their Presidents and executive members had been the subject of investigations during the 1980s.

The very independence of the lawyers appointed to become independent counsels gave rise to serious questions concerning their position in the constitutional system. Two of the central issues regarding the independent counsel law were those relating to the separation of powers and to the accountability of the office. Some critics argued that Congress gave the supervision of independent counsels, once they had been appointed by the Attorney-General, to a three-member panel of judges and this offended the separation of powers principle. They contended that prosecution of cases of wrong-doing is the responsibility of the executive branch whose role is to make sure the laws are faithfully executed. In terms of accountability, independent counsels enjoyed wide discretion and could expand their investigative enquiries with relative ease, having little or no regard for the cost to the taxpayer or how people unrelated to the original issue under scrutiny could find themselves facing charges and huge legal bills in order to defend themselves.

Twenty investigations by independent counsels between 1978 and 1999 cost a combined total of $148.5 million. In 11 of the 15 enquiries which had been completed by June 1999 when the law expired no charges were filed at all. Most of the convictions were of people subordinate or peripheral to the stated targets of the investigations.

Although there were high profile investigations in the past, such as those into the Iran-Contra affair and the Housing and Urban Development Department during the Reagan administration, the 1990s saw five Clinton Cabinet Secretaries being subject to separate enquiries and, of course, the President himself coming under the scrutiny of Kenneth Starr. He was appointed to investigate the Whitewater affair, a complicated set of land investments involving Clinton when he was Governor of Arkansas. This enquiry expanded to cover a range of allegations concerning the Clinton White House and eventually ten convictions resulted, including those of close associates of the President. However, it was the controversial widening of the scope of the investigation to include the President's sexual liaison with Monica Lewinsky and the subsequent report which led to the impeachment trial that highlighted the role of the independent counsel and led to its eventual demise. Following the strong criticisms of the way Starr conducted the enquiry at a cost of approximately $50 million there was bipartisan support for allowing the statute to lapse. Ironically, Starr himself argued against the law being renewed, saying that it had led investigations to become embroiled in party politics. 'The mechanism intended to enhance confidence in law enforcement thus had the effect of weakening it', he told the Senate Governmental Affairs Committee.

Janet Reno, the Attorney-General, revived a system which was similar to that in place before the 1978 Act. Serious allegations against a senior member of the executive branch would in future be investigated by a special counsel appointed by the Attorney-General and recruited from outside the Justice Department. New guidelines concerning the appointment and oversight of such counsels were issued and it was made clear that they could only be dismissed by the Attorney-General for 'good cause'.

The Supreme Court

The Supreme Court has the power to declare that a President has acted 'unconstitutionally' and this can severely damage his status as well as negate the particular activity. President Truman ordered the seizure and operation of the steel industry by government in his capacity as Commander-in-Chief when he regarded an industrial dispute as a threat to the war effort in Korea. The Court decided, however, in *Youngstown Sheet and Tube Company* v. *Sawyer* in 1952, that the President's powers did not allow this and that he was therefore acting *ultra vires*.[21]

The Court can also define the limits of the President's powers. As we have seen, this has been done with regard to executive privilege and, in the 1997 case of *Clinton* v. *Jones* the Justices unanimously ruled that the President can, despite the responsibilities and burdens of his office, be subject to civil litigation. They determined that the President had to be subject to the law as any other citizen would be and denied Clinton's request that the case, brought by Paula Jones who alleged that he had sexually harassed her while he was Governor of Arkansas, should be delayed until he had left office. The President's lawyers had argued that it was against the national interest for a President to be distracted by such concerns and that a decision to go ahead with the case could encourage other mischievous and politically motivated litigation.

Constitutional amendments

The Twenty-Second Amendment limits any individual to two four-years terms as President, unless a Vice-President succeeds to the office in the second half of a term. Critics of the amendment argued that this could seriously impede the bargaining powers of the President in his second terms and reduce him to being a 'lame duck President', and that it was a denial of the democratic wishes of the electorate if they wanted to re-elect a popular President. The change was made after Roosevelt had been elected in four consecutive elections and seemed to be building a large personal power.

The Twenty-Fifth Amendment could be used to remove from office a man who was physically or mentally unfit to continue, and it is worth remembering that the Tenth Amendment provides for the reserved powers of the states. The fact that America has a federal system with 50 states that have a large degree of autonomy over their own affairs is, in itself, a check on the federal government, and thus on the President. Several Supreme Court cases in the 1990s reasserted the rights of the states and placed limits on national authority (see Chapter 8).

The mass media

The media may have played a part in strengthening the presidency during the twentieth century, but it is also true that the 'freedom of the press' has been a major check on presidential power. As a result of the Vietnam War and Watergate, the press in America has taken an increasingly critical attitude towards the executive branch. The major liberal newspapers such as the *New York Times* led the way, but investigative journalism has become a major feature of the American press. The role of the *Washington Post* in revealing the true proportions of the Watergate affair made celebrities of its reporters, Carl Bernstein and Bob Woodward.[22] The prestige and influence of some television news personalities rivals and indeed exceeds that of many top politicians; they are seen and listened to every night by millions of Americans. Both Lyndon Johnson and Richard Nixon felt that they were dealt with unfairly by the media, and former Vice-President Spiro Agnew specifically attacked the press and television for being irresponsible.

Both President Clinton and his wife Hillary believed that they had been subjected to a barrage of unfair press attacks. Conservative critics countered by arguing that the scandals which came to light during Clinton's first term were not given the same degree of scrutiny or treated as seriously by the media as they would have been if a Republican had been in the White House because of liberal bias among journalists.

However, the abrasive criticism of the executive branch by the mass media is an essential part of a free society, and Presidents have to learn to accept it even when they feel it is unfair or ill-informed. The media have been helped in investigating government by the Freedom of Information Act, given teeth in 1974, which opens up many federal files to public scrutiny.

Even though Presidents have used the media to 'go public', developments in the 1990s can be said to have reduced the effectiveness of following an outsider strategy. The major television networks now face strong competition from a range of alternative sources of news and entertainment; the advent of cable channels, 24-hour news networks, specialist programming and the Internet mean that less than half the country now relies upon the national networks for their news coverage. This fragmentation of the media makes it harder for the President to communicate and get his message across to the public; they are just more difficult to reach. In 1995 President Clinton was even refused free air time by most of the networks for nationwide televised addresses which his predecessors had expected and been granted.[23]

Pressure groups

Any President operates as part of a political, economic and social system in which considerable power rests in the hands of private groups. Pressure groups are considered fully in Chapter 5, but it is important to note that business executives, trade union leaders, farmers and professional bodies all have considerable influence on how policy decisions are made and executed. The President must take account of these countervailing forces, particularly in the domestic field, when he is exercising the powers of his office. Even in foreign policy pressure groups have become more numerous and diverse and arguably more influential in the period since the end of the Cold War.

Public opinion

The modern President can find out from opinion polls how the public feels about particular policies, or about his administration in general. Public support is important to the success of a President and, if the indications are that a President is losing popularity, the opposition in Congress, the media and within the administration itself will use their checking mechanisms more extensively. The Gallup Poll has for many years regularly asked a sample of Americans, 'Do you approve or disapprove of the way [the incumbent] is handling his job as President?' The levels of support can fluctuate and the volatility of public opinion can be demonstrated by the responses recorded during President Carter's years in office. His approval rating was 75 per cent in March 1977, declined to 39 per cent in April 1978 and rose again after the Camp David summit on the Middle East to 56 per cent in September 1978. By July 1979 public approval of Carter had slumped to 28 per cent but rallied dramatically to 61 per cent after the seizure of the US hostages in Iran. However, with the failure to secure the release of the hostages Carter's previous unpopularity reasserted itself and in July 1980 only 21 per cent approved of his performance as President, the lowest ever recorded by Gallup Polls. President Reagan on the other hand left office in 1989 with his approval rating at 64 per cent, a similar level to that early on in his first term. Reagan had two relatively brief periods when the polls showed downturns in his support, in 1982–83 when the economic recession bit deeply and unemployment rose and immediately after the Iran-Contra affair. Gallup recorded 63 per cent approval in late October 1986 before exposure of Iran-Contra, a decline to 40 per cent in late February 1987 when the Tower Commission issued its critical report on the affair, a recovery to 53 per cent by June and by December 1987 support levels again above 60 per cent, following the successful summit meeting between President Reagan and Mikhail Gorbachev. Reagan's underlying popularity with the electorate (three-quarters of those polled still held a high opinion of him personally and felt he was honest even at the height of the Iran-Contra affair) allowed him to survive and recover from short-term crises.

Following the Gulf War, in early 1991, President Bush enjoyed the highest approval rating, 89 per cent, ever recorded for a President. However, in the run-up to the 1992 presidential election his popularity slumped dramatically as Americans turned their attention to domestic issues and particularly the problems of the economy in recession. The deadlock with the Democrat-controlled Congress became more evident as legislators reacted to the weakness of the President and partisan differences became more strident as the election period approached.

The high approval ratings which President Clinton continued to enjoy for his job performance, even at the height of the Lewinsky scandal, showed a surprising willingness by the public to separate their disapproval of his personal behaviour from their judgement as to his effectiveness as President. His continuing popularity, while not deterring Republican opponents from pursuing their attempts to impeach and remove him from office, probably saved Clinton his position. It is likely that far more Democrats in Congress would have turned against him if the polls had indicated that the majority of the public wanted him to go.

Public opinion can therefore be a constraint as well as a source of support, because the President will be influenced by his anticipation of the next election, if he is eligible to run again, and also by the effects which public reaction will have on other actors in the political system.

Party opposition

In America's two-party system the President can expect criticism within and outside Congress from the opposition party. The television networks are obliged to allow opposition replies or rebuttals to presidential addresses to the nation. However, unlike Britain where there is a clear Leader of the Opposition and a Shadow Cabinet, the 'out' party not holding the presidency lacks a focus and at different times a number of congressional leaders or state Governors may take on this responsibility. The President may also find vocal opposition to his policies from factions within his own party or indeed from the congressional leaderships of his own party. Opposition from within the party to a presidential incumbent seeking another term in office can not only considerably reduce the chances of re-election but also weaken the President's position politically in the final year of his first term, as Presidents Ford, Carter and Bush discovered.

The bureaucracy

Presidents have consistently found that the bureaucracy they formally control has expanded, but that their real powers to get things done have not. This may be due to inefficiency on the part of civil servants, or it may be the result of deliberate obstructionism or noncompliance by department heads, bureau chiefs or permanent officials. There are many semi-autonomous agencies over which the President has little or no control, and Presidents and their aides have frequently been frustrated to find that decisions taken by the White House have not been implemented by the appropriate department six months or a year later.

The burdens of office

The size and intractability of many of the problems that Presidents have to deal with, the workload and the limitations of time at their disposal also provide major constraints on presidential power. Each new President who takes office finds a period of optimism and good will on behalf of the public and the media. However, in the past public expectations have often been too great and hopes have been disappointed, with the consequent erosion of popular support.

Box 3.3 Presidential power and the 11 September attacks

While Congress has traditionally kept a close watch on any attempts by Presidents to broaden executive powers, the legislature has also been reluctant to do anything that might be said to undermine the President at a time of national crisis. In the immediate aftermath of the terrorist attacks of 11 September 2001 Congress backed the President with two tools that he had stated he needed to launch a 'war against terrorism'. First, it passed an emergency appropriations measure which gave the President unprecedented authority to spend $20 billion to recover from and retaliate against the attacks. Congress added a further $20 billion with the proviso that it would have primary responsibility for allocating the money. Second, it supported a resolution authorising the use of military force against all those involved in the attacks with only one dissenting vote in the two chambers. George W. Bush therefore had authority to launch an offensive against the al-Qaeda organisation and the Taliban regime in Afghanistan which supported it.

Bush invoked the National Emergencies Act of 1976 on 14 September, principally to suspend most personnel regulations governing the armed forces and issued an executive order on 24 September freezing the assets in the US of 27 individuals and organisations suspected of having links with Islamic terrorist groups. The President also set up a White House Office of Homeland Security and appointed the former Governor of Pennsylvania, Tom Ridge, to be its Director. Ridge, as a presidential adviser, was refused permission by the White House to testify before congressional committees in support of budget requests for homeland security.

By the end of 2001 Congress had passed legislation federalising airport security, increased defence spending and passed an anti-terrorism law, the USA Patriot Act. This law gave the government broad new powers to root out terrorists in the United States by making more effective use of intelligence information and allowing the federal authorities to hold suspected persons for questioning more easily. Inevitably civil libertarians were concerned at this growth in government, the threat to individual freedom posed and the way the Justice Department might use these powers. Congress did insist that the most controversial elements of the legislation would expire in 2005 and would then be reviewed, but legislators did not want to be held to blame for not giving the executive sufficient powers to protect Americans from further terrorist attacks and the Act had broad bipartisan support. Subsequently the Justice Department and Attorney-General John Ashcroft were criticised for refusing to give information to Congress on how the new powers were being used.

In 2002 Congress voted to give the President broad power to launch military action against Iraq if he decided that it was necessary and appropriate in the war on terrorism. Congress supported by large majorities in both houses Bush's demand that Saddam Hussein should disarm and rid Iraq of its 'weapons of mass destruction'. At the end of the year the legislature supported legislation establishing a new federal Department of Homeland Security and gave Bush the authority to conduct the largest government reorganisation in half a century with little congressional interference. Bush had originally opposed the idea of creating a new department which had been promoted by Democratic Senator Joseph Lieberman and others but changed his mind after the disclosure of mistakes within the Immigration and

Naturalization Service in March 2002. Bush demanded 'managerial flexibility' in organising the new department, which was interpreted by trade unions as meaning that the President wanted to ban staff from union membership. After five months during which the Democrats took up the union case they eventually gave in after the midterm elections and Congress passed the law giving the President what he wanted.

Therefore, Congress passed a welter of new laws, many giving the President and the executive branch broad authority, with a speed unimaginable in normal times. However, members recognised that '9/11' had changed the political landscape dramatically. While other areas of domestic policy were still subject to partisan debate and the usual uncertainties of the legislative process, measures seen as necessary for the war on terrorism and to protect national security were passed expeditiously and with bipartisan support.

The public rallied behind the President following the terrorist attacks, with Gallup recording a 90 per cent approval rating for Bush, the highest ever recorded for any President on 21–22 September. Bush's poll ratings continued to remain high during 2002 with 60 per cent or more regularly approving of his performance in office. After an initially hesitant start the crisis seemed to give Bush a new belief in himself and he appeared to most Americans to be a strong and courageous leader when the country needed one. Politically, the events of '9/11' provided the Democrats with a dilemma as to how far to oppose a popular President, particularly on national security and foreign policy issues. The Democrats were split on whether to support Bush's policy in relation to Iraq, a factor which harmed the party in the 2002 midterm elections when the President used his public support to help Republican candidates to regain control of both houses of Congress.

Dimensions of presidential power

Many Americans realised for the first time in 1974 the tremendous accretion of power in the hands of the President. The separation of powers principle was incorporated within the Constitution to prevent a concentration of power in one part of the government. The Watergate scandal and the revelations of abuses of power by the executive branch reminded the nation of the message spelt out at Philadelphia. A system that places the responsibilities we have described in the hands of one man must offer temptations for abuse. Arthur Schlesinger Jr argued that the concept of the constitutional presidency had given way by the 1970s to an 'Imperial Presidency' – a revolutionary use of power quite different from that envisaged by the Founding Fathers.[24] However, it would be a serious error to assume that the growth of executive power happened suddenly during Richard Nixon's administration. The history of the executive branch has been one of aggrandisement as people have turned to presidential initiatives to get things done, and the President has filled the power vacuum left by the inertia or inaction of Congress, the states, or private enterprise. The growth of the presidency has not been at a consistent pace – there were reactions to Lincoln's temporary autocracy and to governmental control in the First World War. The major expansion has undoubtedly taken place since the 1930s and the excesses of the Nixon presidency came as a culmination of 40 years of executive development. Expectations of the presidency increased during this period without an equivalent increase in his constitutional authority.

We have already seen how Congress in the 1970s introduced new laws and reformed its procedures in order to reassert its position *vis-à-vis* the presidency. By the end of that decade many observers were sounding new alarms about the modern-day version of congressional government. It became clear that when a President is unable to exercise authority and leadership it is difficult if not impossible for anyone else to do so with anything like the necessary drive and purpose. The presidency seemed perilously weakened and political scientists were talking about the 'Impaired' or 'Imperilled Presidency' rather than the 'Imperial Presidency'. After Nixon had resigned in disgrace, his appointed Vice-President, Gerald Ford, was left with little political power and only his veto as leverage against an increasingly assertive Congress. Jimmy Carter, despite the existence of a Democratic Party majority in both houses of Congress, appeared just as debilitated and there was an increasing feeling that perhaps the job of the presidency had become too big for one person to handle.

President Reagan's achievement was therefore to demonstrate that the presidency was manageable and that a popular President who knew what he wanted to do and had clear priorities could not only influence the national policy agenda but win support in Congress for his programme.

> Whether or not people believed in Ronald Reagan's policy priorities, many supported his view that the country needed a strong President who would strengthen the presidency and make the office a more vital centre of national policy than it had been in the years immediately following the Watergate scandals.[25]

Reagan's period in office has therefore been described by some writers as the 'Resurgent Presidency' and, despite criticisms of his management of the executive branch, which involved considerable delegation of authority to subordinates, and of his mastery of detail, as we have seen, Reagan left office in January 1989 with a 64 per cent public approval rate and became the first President since Eisenhower to serve two full terms in the White House.

President Bush faced large Democratic majorities in both houses of Congress during his term of office, 1989–93. Although he is credited with successes in foreign policy, and particularly his handling of the Gulf War crisis, his lack of clear or consistent objectives in domestic policy, coupled with a generally hostile legislature, resulted in considerable public concern at the inability of divided party government to deal effectively with urgent and important problems at home. Bush made extensive use of his veto power to block Democratic initiatives in Congress while it in turn failed to act on the administration's programme or made major amendments to the President's proposals.

Bill Clinton's campaign for the presidency centred on the need for change and an end to deadlock in Washington. He offered the hope that a Democrat in the White House could make the power of the presidency work more effectively in cooperation with his party's majority in Congress.

However, despite what appeared to be a high success rate in congressional votes (see again Table 2.7), Clinton's first two years in the White House were disappointing and demonstrated the difficulties and frustrations which a modern President can face even when his own party controls the legislature. As a candidate who had won only 43 per cent of the popular vote in 1992, Clinton lacked any clear electoral mandate and could not rely on the backing from party members in Congress, grateful for helping them win their own elections. He made a faltering start in office with early problems over appointments to important positions within the administration and an ineffective and inexperienced team within the White House. There was confusion over policy priorities and he demonstrated a shaky grasp of foreign policy issues. His first budget deeply divided the Democratic Party in Congress, being passed by the slimmest of margins, and the legislature failed to act on the centrepiece of his policy agenda, health care reform. In 1994 a number of other important bills were blocked by a united Republican opposition, particularly in the

Senate where the filibuster was used. Clinton was attacked for having abandoned his promise to govern as 'a new kind of Democrat' and his public approval ratings sank precipitously. Angry voters reacted by forcing him to work with a Republican-controlled Congress from 1995 and, at the beginning of the 104th Congress, an increasingly marginalised Clinton felt obliged, somewhat pathetically, to assert at a press conference that the President was still relevant in American government.

In his later years in office Clinton managed to adjust his style and leadership approach to accommodate the new political situation. He used the veto power and threats of using it as well as executive orders to promote his policy priorities. He spent more time on foreign policy issues and cut back his domestic programme to focus on smaller scale and more achievable goals. He adopted a 'triangulation' strategy whereby he placed himself ideologically in the centre ground, taking stances on policy questions between the conservative Republican majority in Congress and the liberal-dominated Democratic minority. This enabled him to cultivate an image with the public of a moderate and reasonable leader who would oppose extremism from the right while distancing himself from the more contentious policies of his congressional party. Throughout his presidency Clinton adopted a 'campaigning to govern' strategy. This made full use of the President's excellent communications skills in appealing to the electorate directly while maintaining a constant eye on public opinion through polling and focus groups and tailoring his policies and messages accordingly. In short, Clinton continued to use the techniques which had successfully propelled him into the White House while actually doing the job of running the country.

When George W. Bush entered the White House many observers pointed out that the circumstances in which he took office were likely to reinforce the weakened state of the presidency. He was the first President since 1888 to have won a majority in the Electoral College, which determines the election, while at the same gaining a smaller share of the national popular vote than his main rival. Even his Electoral College victory was disputed because of the prolonged legal challenges to the outcome in Florida, the state whose 25 votes gave Bush his narrow victory (see Chapter 7). As a result of the battles in the state and federal courts which culminated in the US Supreme Court's 5–4 decision effectively ending Gore's challenge, the outcome of the election remained in the balance five weeks after polling day. These circumstances led many Americans to question the very legitimacy of Bush's victory. What is more, the delay meant that Bush had much shorter time than is normal to implement the transition from one administration to another. This is a period when much work needs to be done: for example, appointing Cabinet Secretaries and other key staff, organising the White House Office, establishing relationships with leaders on Capitol Hill and determining budgetary and legislative priorities.[26]

Although on the face of it Bush's Republican Party had secured control of both houses of Congress in reality the 2000 elections, both presidential and congressional, had shown not only that the country was divided politically but that the parties were almost equally balanced. The Republicans had a small but shrinking majority in the House and the Senate was tied 50–50. Republican control at the beginning of 2001 came about as a result of the party holding the vice-presidency but this was lost in May with the defection of a Republican Senator. Therefore the new President lacked a strong mandate and for many observers the outlook for a Bush presidency was anything but bright. Indeed, David Broder went so far as to argue that Bush was in the weakest position of anyone elected to the presidency in modern times.[27]

This brief survey of the presidency since the 1970s demonstrates the pitfalls of making broad generalisations about presidential power. Each President comes to the office in different circumstances and the political environment in which he seeks to provide leadership is in a state of constant flux. Among the most important factors affecting presidential power are the following:

1 Personal and political background. Presidents arrive at the White House with substantially different personalities, experience and political backgrounds. Some have been elected in landslide victories (Johnson 1964, Nixon 1972 and Reagan 1984), while others have had only marginal victories or gained less than half the popular vote (Nixon 1968, Carter 1976, Clinton 1992 and Bush 2000). Some have been elected to replace a President of the other party and are expected to make a change of direction (Carter 1976, Reagan 1980, Clinton 1992 and Bush 2000), while others have been re-elected for a second term (Nixon 1972, Reagan 1984 and Clinton 1996). Former Vice-Presidents have been elected as the heir-apparent (Bush 1988) or have replaced a President who died in office (Johnson 1963). We have even seen a non-elected Vice-President move into the Oval Office (Ford 1974). Some Presidents have won election 'running against Washington' (Carter 1976, Reagan 1980) while others have emphasised their experience as 'insiders' (Bush 1988). These differences can lead to a President adopting alternative strategies and approaches to governing and help explain their performances in office. Charles O. Jones, writing in his 1994 book *The Presidency in a Separated System*, sets out the advantages and disadvantages which each of ten post-war Presidents faced when they assumed office either for the first time or as a result of re-election.[28] It is evident that in only a small minority of cases does a President come to the White House with the ideal political conditions of having achieved a landslide personal victory with a clear programme for which there appears to be an electoral mandate and accompanied by a substantial majority for his own party in both houses of Congress. Jones concludes that there are five governing strategies Presidents may follow:

- *Assertive*: With a strongly positive balance upon entering office, the President is aggressive in promoting policy proposals from the start (Johnson 1963 and 1964, Reagan 1980).
- *Compensatory*: With significant disadvantages, and particularly lacking an electoral edge, the President devises supplementary means for authenticating his leadership (Truman 1948, Kennedy 1960, Nixon 1968, Carter 1976, Clinton 1992).
- *Custodial*: In assuming the office of a strong predecessor, the President takes custody of an agenda already in place (Truman 1945).
- *Guardian*: Typically associated with re-elections; the strongest advantage, a landslide victory, is not bolstered by congressional majorities. The President uses his electoral reaffirmation to protect or guard what has been done (Eisenhower 1956, Nixon 1972, Reagan 1984, Bush 1988).
- *Restorative*: Due to the stark and positive contrast with his predecessor the new President at entry adopts a strategy of restoring the status of the office (Eisenhower 1952, Ford 1974).

Jones argues that in most cases the early behaviour of the new President and his administration has generally followed the strategy that might have been predicted as a result of the circumstances in which they took office. The exceptions such as Truman (1948), Nixon (1972) and Carter (1976) tended to follow more assertive strategies than the conditions seemed to warrant. This would also appear true of George W. Bush. Most observers expected that, given the circumstances in which he took office, his campaign talk of 'compassionate conservatism' and the need for bipartisanship because of the even balance of power in Congress, he would follow a moderate, compensatory strategy. In practice, Bush adopted an assertive strategy, promoting a distinctly conservative agenda which included a $1.6 trillion tax cut over ten years, as if he had been given a clear mandate from the people. The Bush team believed that if they adopted an approach based too much on compromise and trying to obtain consensus with the Democrats it would lend credence to those who were seeking to cast doubt on the legitimacy of the Bush presidency. At least until the Jeffords defection in May 2001 Bush decided to rely principally upon Republican unity and cohesion in Congress to push forward his conservative priorities.

As David Mervin has argued:

> Statecraft, or governance, requires that American Presidents demonstrate the capacity to overcome the difficulties posed by a notoriously intractable political system in order to translate policy goals into policy realities. Different Presidents approach these obligations with different strategies or leadership styles derived from their personal characteristics, their view of the world and their previous experience.[29]

2 *The nature of the times.* The ethos of the period in which the President is in office can also make a difference. President-led governmental action has been more acceptable at some times than others. Crises such as the Great Depression of the 1930s or the attacks of 11 September 2001 which led to the declaration of a 'war on terror' tend to lead to the public and Congress supporting the exercise of presidential power to protect America (see Box 3.3).

On the other hand, the post-Vietnam and Watergate era of the 1970s was a bad time to be President; Ford and Carter faced particular difficulties in making the institutional powers of the office work for them as Congress became more assertive in reining in presidential power.

3 *Fluctuations within the presidential term.* All Presidents have ups and downs in their status and influence during their terms in office. As we have seen, public approval ratings fluctuate and popular and media perceptions of presidential performance can change quite dramatically. As Charles O. Jones has pointed out, Johnson and Nixon are dramatic examples of how political and policy conditions can be transformed within a presidential term.[30] Both were elected with landslide victories and yet, within a few years, Johnson was so unpopular that he decided not to seek a further term while Nixon was forced to resign in disgrace. More recently, and less dramatically, Bill Clinton recovered from the repudiation of 1994; he enjoyed high approval ratings, increased his influence over the legislature and coasted to re-election in 1996.

4 *Different policy areas.* Presidential power will also vary in different policy areas. In general terms Presidents have traditionally been able to exercise more independent authority and found it easier to mobilise congressional and public support on foreign and national security issues than in areas of domestic and economic policy where they commonly have to share power – particularly in the legislative process – with other political actors and there is less likely to be deference to presidential goals. However, we have seen that, in more recent times, congressional assertiveness even on aspects of foreign and defence policy has become commonplace.

5 *Unified and divided party government.* Presidents are obliged to work within a constitutional structure where they share powers with Congress and the balance of forces

within the legislature, between the parties and ideologically, is something over which they have no control once the elections have taken place. This fact of life determines the political parameters within which the President has to operate. We have seen that, in modern times, even when a President has served at a time when his own party holds majorities in both houses of Congress (Carter and Clinton 1993–95), this has not guaranteed successful performance in office, however that may be interpreted or measured. More commonly, recent Presidents have had to face either one or both houses controlled by the other party and have had to work within a system of divided party government.

Divided party government can certainly not be described as an aberration; in the period since 1968 it has become the norm with 13 out of 18 presidential and mid-term elections between 1968 and 2002 leading to such a balance of control. Although quite common in the nineteenth century, divided control was a rarity in the first half of the twentieth century when 22 out of 26 national elections resulted in unified control, with the Republicans dominating the first quarter of the century and the Democrats the second quarter.[31] Where divided control did occur it was a result of mid-term losses in the legislature by the party in the White House. In more recent times divided control may happen in presidential election years, such as 1988, or in mid-term as in 1994. What is more, divided control may lead to the President's party having a majority in one house but not the other, as in the Reagan years between 1981 and 1987 (see Table 3.1).

Such election results arising from a decline in partisan attachment and split-ticket voting (see Chapter 6) may indicate a wish among a substantial proportion of the electorate to prevent one party monopolising power and to create a form of coalition government which reinforces the checks and balances in the constitutional system. It may also reflect the impact of incumbency and the voters' perceptions of the strengths and weaknesses of the parties in dealing with different policy areas. Whatever the reasons for the phenomenon, divided party control sets even greater challenges for the modern President seeking to fashion effective leadership.

Some political scientists have seen divided party control as a major problem in governing the United States. Not only does it obscure accountability and confuse the electorate as to who is responsible for what, but it can also makes the fragmented constitutional system almost unworkable. James Sundquist has argued that institutional rivalries are reinforced by clashing partisan interests so that each branch of government has an electoral incentive to work for the failure of the branch held by the other party.[32] This heightened conflict results in immobility and stalemate as well as a failure to deal with important problems such as the federal deficit. President George Bush's term (1989–93) is often seen as an example of this form of deadlocked government. Certainly the increased use of the presidential veto is closely correlated with divided party control and the trend towards more adversarial and confrontational politics has coincided with the frequency of split control of the two branches.

However, an alternative view has been put forward by David Mayhew who carried out an extensive study of legislation passed in the period 1946–90.[33] He concluded that the historical record indicates that periods of divided party control can be just as productive in terms of legislative output as eras of unified control. Although there may be periods of stalemate, both parties may demonstrate a willingness to compromise, each seeking to gain credit from the voters by finding solutions to problems. The final year of the 104th Congress, when Clinton and the Democrats in Congress reached accommodation with the Republican majority, may be seen in this light. Both sides wanted to go into the 1996 election campaign being able to show the electorate some legislative achievements and major new laws were passed on, among other things, welfare reform and health. Of

Table 3.1 Split party control of the presidency and Congress

President and year	Type of split control		Time split control occurred	
	Both houses	One house	Presidential Election	Midterm
Buchanan (D) 1858	...	x (H)	...	x
Grant (R) 1874	...	x (H)	...	x
Hayes (R) 1876	...	x (H)	x	...
Hayes (R) 1878	x	...	...	x
Garfield (R) 1880	...	x (S)[a]	x	...
Arthur (R) 1882	...	x (H)	...	x
Cleveland (D) 1884	...	x (S)	x	...
Cleveland (D) 1886	...	x (S)	...	x
Harrison (R) 1890	...	x (H)	...	x
Cleveland (D) 1894	x	...	...	x
Taft (R) 1910	...	x (H)	...	x
Wilson (D) 1918	x	...	...	x
Hoover (R) 1930	...	x (H)[b]	...	x
Truman (D) 1946	x	...	...	x
Eisenhower (R) 1954	x	...	...	x
Eisenhower (R) 1956	x	...	x	...
Eisenhower (R) 1958	x	...	...	x
Nixon (R) 1968	x	...	x	...
Nixon (R) 1970	x	...	...	x
Nixon (R) 1972	x	...	x	...
Ford (R) 1974	x	...	...	x
Reagan (R) 1980	...	x (H)	x	...
Reagan (R) 1982	...	x (H)	...	x
Reagan (R) 1984	...	x (H)	x	...
Reagan (R) 1986	x	...	...	x
Bush (R) 1988	x	...	x	...
Bush (R) 1990	x	...	...	x
Clinton (D) 1994	x	...	...	x
Clinton (D) 1996	x	...	x	...
Clinton (D) 1998	x	...	...	x
Bush (R) 2001	...	x (S)	c	...

Source: Adapted from Charles O. Jones, *The Presidency in a Separated System* (Brookings Institution 1994), p. 13; data in Harold W. Stanley and Richard G. Niemi, *Vital Statistics on American Politics* 3rd edition (CQ Press 1992), Table 3–17.

Notes
a Following the 1880 elections the Senate was split evenly: 37 Democrats, 37 Republicans, two independents. After much manoeuvring and two Republican resignations, the Democrats appointed the officers and the Republicans organised the committees.
b The Republicans, in fact, won a majority of House seats (218–216), but by the time the Congress first met, a sufficient number had died to permit the Democrats to organise the House.
c The Senate was tied 50–50 as a result of the 2000 elections but the Republicans retained control by virtue of Vice-President Cheney being a member of the party. The defection of a Republican Senator in May 2001 to become an independent gave the Democrats a 50–49 majority.

course, whether a President and congressional leaders are willing and able to compromise depends upon the personalities and the issues involved as well as the particular political circumstances at the time.

Personal and institutional perspectives on the presidency

Richard Neustadt in his influential book *Presidential Power* argues that, in the complex system within which he has to operate, the President's success or failure in achieving his goals depends ultimately on his ability to persuade other political actors to go along with his wishes. The President's problem is to get his constitutional authority to work for him.

> The essence of a President's persuasive task is to convince such men [bureaucrats, Congressmen etc.] that what the White House wants of them is what they ought to do for their own sake and on their own authority.[34]

The President has to be aware of the likely resistance to every step he takes, and he will find that giving orders will not necessarily result in their implementation. President Truman is quoted as saying:

> I sit here all day trying to persuade people to do things that they ought to have the sense to do without my persuading them. . . . That's all the powers of the President amount to.[35]

Neustadt concludes that presidential power can only be effective if the President builds up his prestige with the 'Washington Community' and with the public at large; a President can maximise his power by the choices and decisions that he has made in the past. Tim Hames has pointed out that this conception of the presidency is a highly personal one:

> The powers are personal, the office is personal, success or failure is personal; the repercussions that flow from the personal actions of a single individual in the White House shape the wider system. Private political skills explain the extent and nature of the executive's impact on public policy.[36]

Whereas Neustadt's study tended to focus on the skills and performance of the occupant of the White House and was centred on the presidency, Charles O. Jones has argued that this emphasis can lead to a seriously distorted picture of how the national government works. He argues:

> The plain fact is that the United States does not have a presidential system. It has a separated system.[37]

Instead of a presidency-centred, party government perspective, Jones proposes a separationist, diffused responsibility perspective where the President and Congress are genuinely equal branches of government. He sees policy-making in a separated system as being commonly characterised by 'multiple participation, mixed representation, variable institutional and partisan interaction, and diffused responsibility'.[38]

We may conclude that any proper evaluation of presidential power must take account of the constitutional system and political environment within which the President operates and the wide range of variables that affect the exercise of that power. As Jonathan Herbert has noted:

Presidential scholars largely agree that the institution they study has been weakened over the last three decades. However, the experiences of Clinton and Bush suggest that the presidency remains a force for change in the political system under the right conditions. . . . While presidential power is a long way from its peak in the 1960s, given the appropriate confluence of historical circumstance and strategic skills the office remains influential.[39]

Sources of presidential support

The Executive Office of the President

As the President's responsibilities grew it became increasingly difficult for him to do the job efficiently with the support of only a few clerks and secretaries. A committee of scholars reported in 1937 that 'the President needs help', and in 1939 President Roosevelt established the Executive Office of the President. As Rossiter has written:

> It converts the presidency into an instrument of twentieth-century government; it gives the incumbent a sporting chance to stand the strain and fulfil the constitutional mandate as a one-man branch of our three-part government.[40]

James Pfiffner notes that:

> The steady growth of the presidential apparatus since then has been a response not only to the expansion in the size and scope of the federal government, but also to the feeling by presidents that they need more control of the government to fulfil their promises and control their political fortunes.[41]

In addition the development of the 'Public Presidency' has also led to a huge expansion in the number of staff dealing with the media and communications.

The Executive Office of the President (EOP) is the umbrella under which exist a dozen or so key agencies which serve the President directly. It is his personal bureaucracy whose function is to provide the President with advice and information on top-level matters and future planning. Its job is essentially to make sure the presidency works. Presidents have expanded the organisation since the 1930s, creating new councils or offices as new problems emerged, and abolishing or reconstituting others. Staff numbers increased to well over 5,000 under Johnson and Nixon but, since the mid-1970s and criticisms of the growth of an 'Imperial Presidency', there has been a substantial reduction and the EOP has had less than 2,000 officials. For example, during the Clinton years the number of staff stabilised at around 1,500. The main components are as follows:

1 The White House Office. The President's closest aides and staff are located in the White House Office. During the Nixon presidency the size of the Office grew dramatically with well over 500 personnel. In 1995 there were 400 staff working in the White House Office. In practice only a few dozen senior advisers will see the President on a regular basis. The President will have 'special assistants' on foreign and domestic affairs, speech writers, liaison officers with Congress and the departments as well as an appointments secretary and a press secretary.

The most senior aides may see their roles as protecting the President from being burdened by subordinate matters. The White House Office also works to ensure that urgent and priority matters reach the President's desk quickly. Advisers on specialist areas of policy also review the information provided by bureaucrats and experts within the President's political perspective. The other main role of the White House Office is to try to secure compliance by departments with presidential policies, and so obtain some presidential control over the federal administration.

The President's assistants obtain their very real authority from their closeness to the President and the trust which he places in them. By deciding whom the President should see or which issues are priority ones, these aides have a large degree of discretionary power. The danger is that the President becomes remote from the realities of the political world and is over-protected by his staff. He may also surround himself with 'yes-men' who tell him what they think he wants to hear, and thus prevent him making balanced judgements.

Some Presidents, such as Kennedy and Carter, tried to oversee the management of the White House Office themselves but it is now generally accepted that the appointment of a Chief of Staff is essential for the effective administration of the modern presidency. The Chief of Staff plays key roles which include imposing order on the White House by coordinating the flow of paper, acting as an arbiter between other advisers and regulating access to the President. Cabinet Secretaries have often had to have their meetings with the President 'cleared' by the Chief of Staff, which has occasionally caused tension and bad feeling. James Pfiffner argues that one of his most important roles is to be an 'honest broker' who will accurately represent the views of other White House staff and Cabinet Secretaries to the President. If he is not perceived to fulfil this function fairly powerful people in the administration will try to find alternative ways of ensuring their views reach the President and order will be undermined. Pfiffner concludes that experience has demonstrated that when a President opts for a Chief of Staff who plays a domineering role there will be trouble and the official will leave under a cloud. However, a Chief of Staff in the facilitating tradition can relieve the President of much 'administrivia' but the President has the responsibility to monitor the system to ensure that it is not over-protective.[42]

In President Reagan's first term three top aides were regarded as having the greatest access to the President and thus considerable power within the federal government. Edwin Meese, as Counsellor to the President, supervised the Cabinet and White House policy advisers and was the first White House aide ever to hold Cabinet rank. James Baker, as Chief of Staff, was in charge of relations with Congress, lobbying, press conferences, political liaison and personnel and also served, with Meese, on the National Security Council. Michael Deaver was Deputy Chief of Staff and concerned with the President's daily schedule, the travel office, visitors to the White House and Mrs Reagan's staff. Meese and Deaver had both served Reagan when he was Governor of California, while Baker had managed George Bush's campaign against Reagan in the 1980 presidential primaries. This 'troika' appeared generally to work well in Reagan's first term. All three had to be involved in any important decision.

However, after the 1984 election Meese and Baker moved to Cabinet positions and Deaver went into private business. Donald Regan, who had been Treasury Secretary, took over as Chief of Staff and appeared to have a greater concentration of power in his hands than any recent predecessor; not surprisingly, during 1985 his position attracted a great deal of public attention and criticism as a number of other officials such as Robert McFarlane, the National Security Adviser, left the White House, having been denied direct access to the President. Regan's autocratic style was blamed for many of the problems afflicting the Reagan White House in his second term and in February 1987 he was forced to resign after scathing criticisms of his mishandling of the Iran-Contra affair by the Tower Commission. Former Senate Leader Howard Baker took over as Chief of Staff for the remainder of the second term in a move that was universally welcomed, and particularly on Capitol Hill.

President Bush surprised most observers when he selected the Governor of New Hampshire, John Sununu, as his Chief of Staff in 1989. Sununu's abrasive and autocratic approach soon made him extremely unpopular with the press, legislators and many within the Bush administration, but his loyalty to the President made him valuable to Bush himself. However, following allegations that he had misused government transport for personal trips, Sununu became a political liability and Bush reluctantly replaced him in December 1991.

President Clinton, like other Democratic Presidents, was not enthusiastic about appointing a Chief of Staff and his personal style of leadership worked against the delegation of authority to any one individual. However, Thomas 'Mack' McLarty, an old school friend, was appointed to the post, although he played a fairly low-key role compared with his predecessors. He was severely criticised in the first few months of the administration for having failed to establish an effective management structure. The White House Office appeared disorganised and verging on chaos at times. A number of serious mistakes and poor staff work over appointments damaged the new President's credibility. McLarty was eventually replaced for the remainder of Clinton's first term by Leon Panetta, a very experienced Washington insider, who transferred from the position of Director of the Office of Management and Budget to which he had been appointed in 1993. Although Panetta tightened up the management of the White House he could not force Clinton into adopting a traditional Chief of Staff system. Clinton's Chief of Staff also had to negotiate with two other power centres in the White House in addition to the President. The First Lady, Hillary Clinton, played an important and unique role in policy development within the administration and Vice-President Al Gore also had a more influential position than previous holders of the office.

Clinton was also criticised for appointing too many young and inexperienced aides, straight from his election campaign and totally new to Washington politics, to important positions within the White House. However, one of them, George Stephanopolous, who had been in effective charge of the 1992 campaign, remained as a key policy adviser during Clinton's first term even though he lost his original position as Communications Director.

George W. Bush appointed an experienced Washington insider, Andrew Card, as his Chief of Staff. Card had served Bush's father as Secretary of Transportation. Bush's Vice-President, Dick Cheney, who himself had served as Chief of Staff under President Ford and as Defense Secretary under President Bush Senior, played a central role in the administration, liaising with Congress, and meeting regularly with Bush in private. Bush also relied heavily on the advice of his political strategist, Karl Rove, and communications adviser, Karen Hughes, both of whom had worked for the President when he had been Governor of Texas. The departure of Hughes in June 2002, following a decision to move her family who had been unhappy living in Washington back to Texas, was seen as a serious loss for the President, with Card describing her as 'irreplaceable' because of the trust Bush placed in her advice.

2 The Office of Management and Budget. President Nixon reconstituted the Bureau of the Budget into the Office of Management and Budget in 1970, intending that the new body should become a major managerial instrument for the President. The main function of the OMB, which had 542 officials working for it in 1995, is the preparation of the federal budget which will be submitted to Congress, and all appropriations requests from departments or agencies must be approved by the office. The OMB therefore attempts to resolve conflicts within the executive branch over the relative shares of the fiscal 'cake' and it is the main method by which the President can exercise control over the levels of federal government spending. The Director of the Office is one of the President's principal economic advisers and his is one of the few Executive Office positions that require Senate approval. The OMB also acts as a mechanism by which the President can coordinate governmental activities and ensure, in his role as manager of the executive branch, that programmes are being carried out as efficiently as possible. Early in his first term President Reagan required that all departments and agencies systematically obtain clearance through OMB for any changes in federal regulations, thus seeking to establish tighter presidential control over the executive branch and ensure that department and agency policies were consistent with the White House perspective.

President Reagan's Budget Director, David Stockman, became prominent in the administration during 1981 as he had the responsibility for drawing up the list of expenditure cuts which would apply to all the domestic departments of the federal government. Inevitably this led to conflicts with individual Cabinet Secretaries. Stockman, who was the youngest as well as one of the most influential of Reagan's senior staff, resigned in July 1985 after disagreements about policy on reducing the federal budget deficit. President Clinton's choice of OMB Director, Leon Panetta, had previously served as the Chairman of the House Budget Committee. Panetta's close links with congressional Democrats were seen as being important in winning legislative support for a difficult deficit reduction package in 1993. When Panetta moved to become White House Chief of Staff, he was replaced by his deputy, Alice Rivlin, who switched from the legislative to executive branch, having previously served as Director of the Congressional Budget Office. Bush appointed Mitchell Daniels Jr as his OMB Director in 2001.

3 The National Security Council. The objective of this body, established in 1947, is to advise the President on domestic, foreign and military matters relating to national security. It consists of the President, Vice-President and Secretaries of State and Defense, although other officials such as the Joint Chiefs of Staff and the Director of the Central Intelligence Agency may be asked to attend. President Eisenhower met regularly with the NSC and developed a committee structure beneath it. Other Presidents, such as John F. Kennedy, preferred more informal consultations with members of the Council, often on an individual basis.

The Kennedy and Johnson administrations saw the rise to prominence of the President's National Security Assistant or Adviser, with influence and visibility that often rivalled that of the Secretary of State. Dr Henry Kissinger was initially President Nixon's National Security Adviser and kept this role when he became Secretary of State. President Carter, on the other hand, returned to the separation of the two roles and chose Dr Zbigniew Brzezinski – a Warsaw-born academic – to advise on national security matters. Conflicts between Brzezinski and the Secretary of State, first Cyrus Vance and then Edmund Muskie, over policy issues and influence with the President in decision-making seriously damaged the credibility of the Carter administration both in diplomatic circles and in the media.

Under President Reagan the role of National Security Adviser was deliberately down-graded and direct access to the President was often denied. George Shultz, as Secretary of State, did not have the competition for the President's ear on foreign policy matters that his recent predecessors had had. Ironically, he was unaware of the activities being carried out by the NSC staff which became known as the Iran-Contra affair. It was revealed that NSC officials including its head, John Poindexter, and Lieutenant-Colonel Oliver North, had been involved in clandestine operations to help the Nicaraguan opposition in order to bypass a ban on government funding of the Contras passed by Congress. The Tower Commission was of the view that there was nothing fundamentally wrong with the NSC system which had operated for over 40 years but that it required presidential leadership to make it work. However, in the Iran-Contra affair the NSC had moved away from its analytical and advisory functions to become the initiator and executor of counter-policies to those officially being carried out by the State Department.

One of the members of the Tower Commission, Brent Scowcroft, a former NSC adviser for President Ford, took over the post again in the Bush administration, thus re-establishing the credibility and status of the NSC within the administration. Clinton's first term NSC adviser, Anthony Lake, played a relatively low profile role in the administration before being nominated in 1997 to become Director of the Central Intelligence Agency (CIA). However, Lake withdrew from consideration after Senate criticism of his performance at the NSC and his suitability for the new post. In 2001 President Bush appointed Condoleezza Rice, an academic and expert on Russian politics, as his National Security Adviser, making her the most influential black woman in American politics (see Box 1.1).

4 The Council of Economic Advisers. We have seen that economic policy has become increasingly important as one of the President's responsibilities, but few Presidents have been economic experts, and therefore since 1946 there has been a three-man panel of professional economists who are appointed with the consent of the Senate to offer advice on the major decisions facing the President. These economists are usually from the universities, but incoming Presidents select professors who have a similar political outlook to their own. However, differences over policy do develop and in July 1984 Martin Feldstein, Chairman of Reagan's Council, resigned after much-publicised warnings about the need to increase taxes in order to reduce the federal government's deficit were rejected by the President. The Council has a purely advisory role, unlike the OMB, whose functions are administrative, but it prepares on the President's behalf an annual economic report for presentation to Congress; this sets out the administration's view of economic trends for the next year.

The other major advisory bodies to the President in the Executive Office are shown in Figure 3.1. The President may reorganise the structure when he comes into office to suit his own needs. Some offices therefore demonstrate continuity across administrations while others reflect the interests or priorities of individual Presidents. For example, George W. Bush established an Office of Faith-Based and Community Initiatives to develop proposals to carry out his election pledge to involve religious and voluntary organisations in the implementation of social policy.

The Cabinet

In deciding upon a single man rather than a collective executive the Founding Fathers ensured that the American Cabinet would become a subordinate advisory body to the President rather than the main organ of executive decision-making. The Constitution does not mention the Cabinet by name at all, and its existence rests purely on convention. The document merely says that the President may require the advice in writing of the Principal Officer in each department about their respective duties. Unlike the British Cabinet, American departmental secretaries are the President's subordinates and are not colleagues

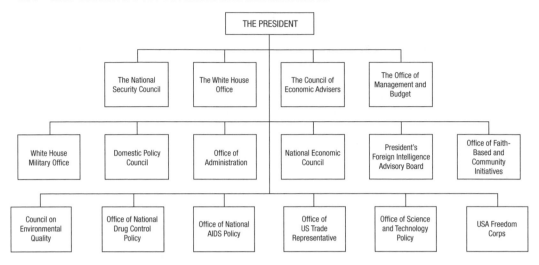

Figure 3.1 Organisation of the Executive Office of the President under Bush (2002)
Source: http:// www.whitehouse.gov/government/eop/html, accessed 10 September 2002.

with whom he has worked for many years in the legislature. The concept of collective responsibility does not exist; Cabinet members owe their loyalty to the President individually. Moreover, being a Cabinet Secretary is not necessarily seen as the pinnacle of a political career as it is in the British system.

1 Appointment of the Cabinet. The selection of the heads of the executive departments is one of the first actions a President-elect takes before his inauguration, and it therefore receives great public attention as the choices give an early indication of the style and tone of the new administration. In many respects the President has a very wide choice of people to fill the top posts in his government. The individuals do not necessarily have to be in the same party as himself and there is no need for the appointees to have held any political post before. Many Cabinet Secretaries are selected for their specialist expertise or administrative capabilities and may well have previously worked in industry, commerce or the academic world.

As we have seen, Senate approval of Cabinet appointments is normally given after committee hearings but President Bush suffered a severe setback when John Tower became the first Cabinet nominee to be rejected since the Senate rejected Lewis Strauss as Eisenhower's Commerce Secretary in 1959. However, controversial appointments can lead to lengthy Senate Committee hearings and close questioning of the candidate's qualifications and views. President Reagan's nomination of Edwin Meese as Attorney-General in January 1984 was stalled by prolonged investigations into his financial dealings when White House counsellor. Over a year later Meese was approved by a 63–31 vote in the Senate. George W. Bush's nomination of John Ashcroft, a former conservative Republican Senator, as Attorney-General was particularly controversial and strongly opposed by liberals who objected to his views on abortion and gun control and accused him of being insensitive on racial issues. Ashcroft was eventually approved by the Senate by a vote of 58–42 after five weeks of heated debate.

However, there are some limitations on presidential choice. First, many members of Congress are not prepared to give up their seats and seniority in the legislature to take a temporary job in the executive branch, although President Clinton was able to persuade a number of senior members of Congress to join his Cabinet in 1993: Les Aspin, the Chairman of the Armed Services Committee in the House of Representatives, became Defense Secretary; Mike Espy was appointed as Agriculture Secretary; Lloyd Bentsen, the Chairman of the Senate Finance Committee, became Treasury Secretary and, as we have seen, Leon Panetta took over at OMB. Prominent business executives will often not be prepared to make the financial sacrifices to take a position in Washington. The President will also be concerned with the loyalty of Secretaries to himself and his programmes, as his choice will have a crucial effect on how far he can influence future policy in the particular department. The President may also feel that it is necessary to reward prominent state politicians who helped him in the election campaign, and he must try to achieve some sort of geographical balance and representation of various regions within the Cabinet. The Agriculture Department, for example, is often headed by a Midwesterner, while the Interior Department with its interest in the management of large areas of federally owned land normally has its Secretary from the Western states.

President Nixon's first Cabinet in 1969 was all-male, all-white and all-Protestant, and made up primarily of self-made businessmen. President Ford, on the other hand, tried to achieve more social balance, appointing a woman (Carla Hills, Secretary of Housing and Urban Development), a black (William T. Coleman at the Transportation Department) and two Jews (Henry Kissinger and Edward H. Levi at State and Justice) to his Cabinet. In 1988 President Reagan appointed Lauro Cavazos as Secretary of Education who became the nation's first Hispanic Cabinet member and he continued in this position in the Bush Cabinet. President Clinton came to office in 1993 with a pledge to appoint an administration that 'looked like America' and was committed to reflect this diversity by selecting more women and members from minority groups to Cabinet positions. The President's wife, Hillary Clinton, was believed to have had considerable influence on a number of appointments. Finding suitably qualified candidates for Cabinet, sub-Cabinet and other high-level posts led to considerable delays in the appointment process, particularly in the Justice Department where Janet Reno was not confirmed as Attorney-General until mid-March. Clinton's first-term Cabinet included four blacks, two Hispanics and three women; for his second term Clinton nominated three black members, one Hispanic and four women. He also appointed a Republican, former Senator William Cohen, as his Defense Secretary in an attempt to broaden support for his administration following the 1996 elections. Among the female members appointed in 1997 was Madeleine Albright who, by becoming the new Secretary of State in succession to Warren Christopher, took over the most senior position in American government ever held by a woman. She had served as US Ambassador to the United Nations during Clinton's first term (see Box 1.1).

George W. Bush's Cabinet also showed diversity with four women and representation of minorities, including the appointment of Colin Powell, the black former Chairman of the Joint Chiefs of Staff of the armed forces, as Secretary of State. One Democrat, Congressman Norman Mineta, was chosen as Secretary of Transportation.

2 The Use of the Cabinet. Each President can use the Cabinet as he likes; he can call it frequently in formal meetings, such as Dwight Eisenhower favoured, or he can have only irregular meetings, work with fuzzy lines of responsibility, and deal with department heads on an individual basis as John F. Kennedy preferred. Kennedy felt that full meetings tended to be a waste of time which could be better used by members in their own departments. President Clinton who, unlike his recent predecessors, had not promised to run a cabinet-style government, called only seven meetings in 1993.

President Eisenhower formalised the meetings for the first time with the introduction of agendas, papers for discussion and minutes. He felt that such institutionalisation would result in less wasteful debate and better-prepared meetings. It was hoped that Cabinet sessions would serve as useful sounding-boards for new ideas, so that the views of other departments could be heard before a policy was embarked upon, and the result would be greater administrative coherence in the diffuse system of federal government. However, the Cabinet does not really work as a team, and it is weak in terms of well-informed discussion of policy alternatives for the administration as a whole. Presidents have preferred to work through bodies such as the White House Office and the Office of Management and Budget for advice and policy coordination, and therefore the influence of the Cabinet has been eroded. Most recent Presidents have promised to reverse this trend by strengthening the role of Cabinet Secretaries as advisers, by having regular full meetings of the Cabinet as well as establishing sub-committees or councils of the Cabinet to confer on issues that cross departmental lines, look at long-term problems or produce option papers for the President. President Reagan, in particular, declared that his Cabinet would be his inner circle of advisers and likened the Cabinet to a board of directors. In the early days of his administration the Cabinet met weekly and debated issues around the table. Reagan also emphasised the importance of delegation to Cabinet Secretaries and he stated in an interview:

> When I've heard enough of the debate to satisfy my needs about knowing, then I make a decision. I believe in this because it is really the only way to execute a job this big. The trap you could fall into would be trying to keep your finger on every single detail.[43]

However, by the second year of his administration Reagan was following the familiar tendency of his predecessors by strengthening and relying more upon the White House Staff and policy advisers in the Executive Office of the President and less on Cabinet Secretaries. As Hugh Heclo has pointed out: 'It is significant that no President has ever left office extolling the virtues of cabinet government.'[44]

In April 1985 Reagan announced a new streamlined system with the replacement of eight Cabinet Councils by two new bodies. The Economic Policy Council, the Domestic Policy Council and the National Security Council were to be the primary channels for advising him on policy matters. President Reagan's Cabinet Council system was an attempt to reinforce White House policy management and to help insulate Cabinet Secretaries from the permanent bureaucracies and from congressional committees. As Edwin Meese, the man who devised the system, put it:

> The difference in this presidency is that Reagan has used his system so that the Cabinet members all feel closer to him than they do to their departments. And he gives them a lot of opportunity to remember that.[45]

It is also interesting to note that during the Reagan administration there was far greater interchange of personnel than ever before between the Executive Office of the President and the Cabinet departments. In 1983 William Clark moved from NSC to the Interior Department and Elizabeth Dole moved from the White House Office to become Transportation Secretary. At the beginning of his second term Reagan appointed Edwin Meese as Attorney-General; John Herrington, Assistant to the President for Personnel, became Energy Secretary, while William Brock, US Trade Representative, took over at the Labor Department. Meanwhile James Baker, the White House Chief of Staff and Treasury Secretary Donald Regan swapped jobs in the new administration.

Whereas under Clinton the influence of the Cabinet as an institution was minimal, George W. Bush expressed a desire to move to a business model of governing whereby he would act as the chief executive officer (CEO) and delegate more responsibility to department heads. However, Jonathan Herbert points out that Cabinet Secretaries have not found their prerogatives entirely restored under Bush and the President has repeatedly overruled decisions made by individual department heads, often at the cost of public embarrassment.[46]

3 Cabinet Secretaries and their departments. Each member of the Cabinet is responsible to the President for his department's affairs; there is no collective responsibility with other Cabinet members for government policy. The Secretaries may be rivals for the President's attention and for available funds, and occasionally disputes between department heads break out into public conflict. The President may have to intervene in order to maintain the appearance of a harmonious administration, as President Ford did in 1976 when he dismissed Defense Secretary James Schlesinger after a long feud with Henry Kissinger over détente policies with the Soviet Union. After giving his Cabinet Secretaries a great deal of autonomy in his first year in office President Carter became increasingly concerned about the loyalty and discipline of some members and, in an unprecedented purge in July 1979, he dismissed five department heads from their offices. However, instead of projecting an image of decisive leadership by this action Carter merely increased the scepticism about his own ability and judgement.

Sometimes the President will have to replace a Cabinet Secretary midway through the term if it becomes evident that he is failing to do the job effectively or has lost the confidence of Congress, departmental officials or important interest groups. It soon became clear that Les Aspin, Clinton's first Defense Secretary, was unsuited to running a huge executive department such as the Pentagon. His wide knowledge of security matters gained as a congressional committee chairman did not qualify him to be an effective manager and he was replaced by William Perry, a defence technocrat who had been his deputy. In December 2002 President Bush dismissed the Treasury Secretary Paul O'Neill who had made a number of outspoken comments which had embarrassed the White House and alienated Wall Street. He had also come into conflict with the President's economic adviser, Larry Lindsay who similarly lost his job at the same time.

A department head is often chosen for his ability in a particular policy area and there are few interdepartmental moves during a presidential term such as one sees with British Cabinet 'reshuffles'. However, James Baker moved from the Treasury Department in 1989 to become President Bush's Secretary of State, while Elizabeth Dole who had served as Reagan's Secretary of Transportation 1983–87 became Secretary of Labor in the Bush Cabinet. Frederico Peña, who served as Clinton's Transportation Secretary during his first term, was nominated to take over as Energy Secretary in 1997 in order to ensure continued Hispanic representation in the Cabinet.

The problem for the individual Cabinet Secretary is that he is subject to a number of different pressures and often conflicting claims. He is appointed by the President and owes a responsibility to him for executing the administration's policies. He also has a responsibility to his department which has its own traditions and interests; his civil servants will expect him to represent their views at the highest level. The President's rapport with the Cabinet Secretary often declines as the latter seems increasingly to be an advocate of the department and the pressure group clientele with which it has relations.

Tension also builds between the Cabinet member and the White House assistants, who see him as obstructing presidential objectives and question his loyalty. The department head also has to take into account congressional demands; he owes confirmation of his appointment to the Senate, and he will be expected to appear before congressional committees to justify and 'sell' his department's policies as well as secure funds for its programmes. Richard Fenno has written:

> For his part, the President's influence over the Cabinet member becomes splintered and eroded as the member responds to political forces not presidential in origin or direction. From the beginnings of his involvement in the appointment process, the President's power is subject to the pervasive limitations of the pluralistic system in which he seeks to furnish political leadership.[47]

The Vice-President

'My country has in its wisdom contrived for me the most insignificant office that ever the invention of man contrived or his imagination conceived.' These are the words of John Adams, the first Vice-President of the United States, but they could have been uttered with equal feeling by most of his successors. The Vice-President has a very limited number of constitutional roles, but one of them – to succeed to the presidency in the event of death, resignation or removal from office – can be of vital significance. The Vice-President is literally 'a heart-beat away from the presidency' and his main role is to wait in the wings to be called upon to take over the duties of the Chief Executive. As eight Presidents have died in office, four having been assassinated, and one has been forced to resign, there is a real possibility that such a call might come.

The Vice-President must have the same formal qualifications as the President, that is to be over 35 years old, a natural-born American citizen, and have been a resident of the country for 14 years. The voters choose, at election time, between rival teams of presidential and vice-presidential candidates and there is no opportunity to 'split the ticket'. Therefore the presidential candidates of each party have traditionally been concerned with achieving a balance in the team to make it as attractive as possible to various regions of the country, different ethnic and religious groups, and factions within the parties. John Kennedy, for example, as a Northern Catholic with strong liberal support, saw Lyndon Johnson, a Protestant from Texas who could win the votes of Southern conservatives, as an ideal choice for the vice-presidency in 1960. As the presidential candidate has often made his choice in the emotional aftermath of his own nomination and in something of a hurry, the scrutiny of an individual's suitability for the office has sometimes been cursory and inadequate. In 1968 Richard Nixon selected Spiro T. Agnew as his running mate to appeal to conservative Southerners, but the former Governor of Maryland was forced to resign from the vice-presidency in 1973 after he was charged with tax evasion and other offences. In 1972 Thomas Eagleton was chosen by Democrat George McGovern without the presidential candidate knowing that the Missouri Senator had undergone electric shock treatment for depression. When Eagleton's medical history was revealed, he resigned from the ticket and the first-ever special convention was called to choose a new vice-presidential candidate. In 1988 George Bush's selection of Senator Dan Quayle of Indiana was followed by a furore over allegations that he had evaded military service in Vietnam. Although he stayed on the ticket Quayle turned out to be an embarrassment to the campaign while adding nothing to its attractiveness to the voters. On the other hand Bill Clinton's selection of Senator Al Gore, a well-respected moderate

Box 3.4 President George W. Bush's Cabinet, 2001

The Cabinet includes the Vice-President and, by law, the heads of the 14 executive departments. Cabinet rank has also been accorded to certain other officials, including certain members heading organisations within the Executive Office of the President.

Department	Secretary	Background
Agriculture	Ann Veneman	51, A lawyer and former Deputy Secretary in the Department under Bush Sr.
Commerce	Don Evans	54, Chairman of a Texas oil company and Chairman and fund-raiser of Bush campaign.
Defense	Donald Rumsfeld	68, Defense Secretary and White House Chief-of Staff under Ford; Ambassador to NATO under Nixon.
Education	Rod Paige	67, Superintendent for Houston, Texas public schools; former Dean of College of Education, Texas Southern University.
Energy	Spencer Abraham	48, Former Deputy Chief-of-Staff to Vice-President Dan Quayle; lost re-election bid for his Senate seat from Michigan in 2000.
Environmental Protection Agency	Christine Todd Whitman	54, Republican Governor of New Jersey 1993 to 2001.
Health and Human Services	Tommy Thompson	59, Republican Governor of Wisconsin for four terms, gaining a reputation for welfare reform.
Housing and Urban Development	Mel Martinez	54, Chairman of Orange County, Florida, Board of Commissioners and Co-Chairman of Bush campaign in Florida; former refugee from Cuba.
Interior	Gale Norton	46, Attorney-General of Colorado for eight years; previously held posts in the Interior and Agriculture Departments.
Justice	John Ashcroft	58, Missouri Governor for eight years; lost Senate seat in the 2000 election.
Labor	Elaine Chao	47, Born in Taiwan; former Deputy Secretary of Transportation under Bush Sr; wife of Republican Senator Mitch McConnell; fellow at Heritage Foundation.

State	Colin Powell	63, Former general and Reagan's National Security Adviser; Chairman of Joint Chiefs of Staff under Bush Sr and Clinton.
Transportation	Norman Mineta	69, Commerce Secretary from July 2000 under Clinton; a Japanese-American and first Cabinet member of Asian descent; Democratic Congressman from California for 21 years.
Treasury	Paul O'Neill	65, Chairman of aluminium company for ten years; served Ford as Deputy Budget Director. Dismissed December 2002.
Veterans Affairs	Anthony Principi	56, Deputy Secretary under Bush Sr; held legal posts in Navy; won Bronze Star in Vietnam.

Other Members of the Cabinet:

Vice-President	Dick Cheney
President's Chief-of-Staff	Andrew Card, Jr
Office of Homeland Security	Tom Ridge
Office of Management and Budget	Mitchell Daniels, Jr
Office of National Drug Control Policy	John Walters
United States Trade Representative	Robert Zoellick

from Tennessee, was widely applauded by the party and the media; he undoubtedly added to the appeal of the Democratic ticket in the 1992 election. In 2000 Bush's selection of Dick Cheney, a highly regarded Defense Secretary in the administration of the candidate's father and a 'safe pair of hands', was seen as providing the ticket with much-needed expertise in foreign and security policy that Bush himself lacked.

The Twenty-Fifth Amendment provides for the President to nominate an individual to fill the office of Vice-President if it becomes vacant between elections. In this way, Gerald Ford became the first non-elected Vice-President to succeed to the presidency in 1974.[48]

The Vice-President is a reserve to the President. He must be ready to take over the responsibilities of the office if the Chief Executive dies or if he is unable to carry out his duties as a result of illness. In the 1950s Richard Nixon acted on behalf of Dwight Eisenhower when the President suffered from a serious heart condition. The Vice-President will also be expected to take on some of the ceremonial duties and represent the United States on formal occasions, such as the funerals of foreign leaders.

The other constitutional duty of the Vice-President is to chair meetings of the Senate and vote in the event of a tie. On occasions this can be of crucial significance; in June 1993 Vice-President Gore used his casting vote to secure the passage in the Senate of the President's budget bill after a number of Democrats defected because of the political unpopularity in their home states of some of the tax increases and spending cuts within the package. Between January and May 2001 the Republicans controlled the Senate, which was evenly balanced in party support, by virtue of the fact that Dick Cheney was a Republican. Most holders of the office have attended as 'President of the Senate' only infrequently as, not being members of the Senate, they can rarely exert political influence but are merely 'referees' who interpret the rules. This can occasionally lead to controversy; Vice-President Rockefeller was involved in a major row in 1975 when his procedural decision led to a reform of the filibuster, thus angering many Senate conservatives.

Although he has his own staff and office in Washington, the degree to which the Vice-President will actually be involved in the administration will depend on the President. Some Vice-Presidents have felt shunned and even humiliated by the President's close advisers. Harry Truman was not told about America's development of the atomic bomb until he stepped into the Oval Office, and relations between Kennedy's staff and Lyndon Johnson were notoriously cool. However, there has been a tendency in recent times to give the Vice-President more to do; he is a member of the Cabinet and the National Security Council; he may chair a presidential commission, as Vice-President Rockefeller did with the investigation into the CIA; he may become a 'roving ambassador' for the United States abroad, as Hubert Humphrey did by travelling around the world, explaining America's foreign policy. Vice-President Mondale's first major responsibility in 1977 was to undertake a tour of major European capitals on behalf of the President. Vice-President Agnew saw his most important role as being that of political mouthpiece for the administration and projecting its image around the United States. He became a controversial political figure with his scathing attacks on anti-Vietnam War demonstrators and the mass media. A great deal of his time was spent at fund-raising dinners and events for the Republican Party.

Vice-President Bush was given responsibility for reviewing federal regulations and made head of the Reagan administration's crisis management team. Bush was seen as an effective and influential Vice-President. He had an office in the White House, access to policy papers and played a prominent role in the National Security Council. Bush's experience in foreign affairs was of particular value to Reagan and in 1983 he won widespread acclaim for his role in helping persuade America's NATO allies to go ahead with the deployment of Cruise and Pershing missiles and for reassuring them that the administration was serious about arms control. However, loyalty to the President can also lead critics to question, as with Bush, whether the Vice-President has a clear political identity of his own, particularly when he becomes a presidential candidate himself.

Al Gore fought the 1992 election campaign very much as part of the Clinton-Gore team and became a prominent member of the Clinton administration. He was involved in the making of key policy decisions and was given specific responsibility for reviewing the operation of the federal bureaucracy (see below, page 122). Gore's relationship with Clinton suffered in 1998 when the Vice-President publicly criticised the President's behaviour in the Lewinsky affair, although he did loyally stand by him. The relationship deteriorated further during and after the 2000 presidential election when Clinton felt Gore had marginalised him and made insufficient use of his campaigning skills. Clinton also believed Gore had squandered his opportunity of succeeding him and continuing Democratic control of the White House. Gore, on the other hand, blamed his defeat partly at least on negative voter reaction to the scandals of the Clinton years.

As we have seen, Vice-President Cheney has played a particularly prominent role in the Bush administration and has established himself as a key member of the President's inner circle of advisers.

Although in the past many able politicians found frustration and disillusionment in waiting on the side-lines of the Washington political scene, it does appear that it is possible for the modern Vice-President to play a meaningful role and hold an influential

---

Box 3.5 Presidential succession

When President Ronald Reagan was shot in an assassination attempt in 1981 Vice-President George Bush was hurriedly recalled to the White House. In trying to prevent any public panic the Secretary of State, Alexander Haig, stepped before the cameras to announce: 'As of now, I am in control here, pending return of the Vice-President.' Later Haig was criticised for this assertion of authority. Under the Presidential Succession Act of 1947 the following is the order in which individuals become Chief Executive.

The Vice-President

Speaker of the House of Representatives

President pro tempore of the Senate

Secretary of State

Secretary of the Treasury

Other Cabinet Secretaries based on the year in which the department was established.

---

position within the administration; certainly they can help take some of the burdens of office from the shoulders of the President. It is also worth remembering that, of the 43 American Presidents, 14 had previously served as Vice-President, although George Bush became the first sitting Vice-President since 1836 to have been elected to the presidency.

Organisation of the executive branch

A major characteristic of the American executive branch is the way in which power is distributed among a bewildering proliferation of departments, agencies and bureaux that have developed as new problems and programmes have emerged. The Hoover Commission of the 1950s recommended a streamlining of the executive branch, and Presidents have struggled to reorganise and simplify the structure. Unlike a British Prime Minister, who can reorganise the departmental structure of government as he wishes, the President is unable to do likewise without the support of Congress even though he is nominally in charge of the executive branch in which the departments are located. The President can reorganise part of the administration if Congress does not veto the plan within 60 days, but opposition to reform has often come from vested interests within the bureaucracy, from pressure groups who are comfortable with the existing arrangements and from Congress, which hesitates about strengthening further the President's authority. The problem for all Presidents remains: to coordinate and direct the activities of the diffuse and unwieldy administrative machine.

The main elements within the federal administration are:

The executive departments

By the end of 2002 there were 15 departments headed by Cabinet Secretaries – in 1789 there had been three (see Table 3.2). The largest is the Defense Department which has approximately 647,000 civilian employees. Within some departments there are bureaux

Table 3.2 The executive departments in order of formation

State	1789
Treasury	1789
Interior	1849
Justice	1870
Agriculture	1889
Commerce	1913
Labor	1913
Defense	1947
Health and Human Services	1953
Housing and Urban Development	1965
Transportation	1966
Energy	1977
Education	1979
Veterans' Affairs	1989
Homeland Security	2002

Notes:
1 The Post Office was a Cabinet department 1872–1970, when it was replaced by the US Postal Service, an independent agency.
2 The Department of Commerce and Labor was created in 1903 and became two separate departments in 1913.
3 Department of War (the Army) created in 1789 and Department of Navy (1798) was consolidated with the Air Force in Defense Department in 1947.
4 Department of Health and Human Services was formerly Department of Health, Education and Welfare 1953 to 1979.

which can act almost independently of the control of the Secretary; there are, for example, the Federal Bureau of Investigation within the Department of Justice, the Food and Drugs Administration which is part of Health and Human Services and the Bureau of Indian Affairs within the Interior Department. B. Guy Peters even describes American Cabinet departments as:

> largely holding companies for a number of agencies within them. . . . These agencies have a legal life of their own, most having been formed by an Act of Congress or by an Executive Order, and have their own budgets and personnel allocations.[49]

During President Carter's term of office two new federal departments were created. In 1977 the Energy Department took over responsibilities that had previously been scattered throughout many departments and agencies. The Education Department was established in 1979 by splitting off functions from the giant Department of Health, Education and Welfare which was renamed the Department of Health and Human Services. Ronald Reagan had promised during his election campaign that he would abolish these two departments as he believed they extended federal government intervention into areas best left to the private sector or to state governments and that essential federal responsibilities could be devolved to other departments or agencies. However, suggestions to downgrade the status of the Education Department to an agency or foundation and to merge the Energy and Commerce Departments found no favour with Congressmen. In October 1988 President Reagan agreed to the elevation of the long-established Veterans' Administration to a Cabinet-level Department of Veterans' Affairs, thus making it the fourteenth federal department. President Clinton had wanted to raise the status of the Environmental Protection Agency and make it a full Cabinet department but, with disputes over appropriate departmental jurisdictions and a climate of budget cuts, Congress failed to support the change in 1994. However, the Director of the EPA is a member of the Cabinet. Sometimes members of Congress itself may seek to initiate changes in structure, but conservative attempts to abolish the Commerce and Energy Departments during the 104th Congress were unsuccessful.

In June 2002 President Bush announced his plan to establish a new Department of Homeland Security which would bring together the work of 22 separate federal agencies with powers to coordinate counter-terrorism programmes in the biggest reorganisation of the federal government for over half a century. With 170,000 officials it would become the second biggest department. The new organisation would include the Coast Guard, the Customs Service, the Immigration and Naturalization Service, the Border Patrol, the Secret Service, the Federal Emergency Management Agency and the recently created Transportation Security Administration, as well as absorbing selected functions from other Cabinet departments. The FBI and the Central Intelligence Agency (CIA) would not be substantially affected. Civil libertarians were concerned about the size and scope of the new department's powers but most observers felt that the United States needed a better coordinated response to the threat of terrorism within the nation's borders. Congress passed the necessary legislation in November 2002.

The executive agencies

A large number of agencies exist under presidential authority which are almost indistinguishable from departments, except that they do not have the status of having Cabinet Secretaries. They are headed by Directors appointed by the President and confirmed by the Senate and examples include the General Services Administration and the National Aeronautics and Space Administration (NASA).

Independent regulatory commissions

There are many commissions which have been established to regulate particular areas of economic activity that remain in private ownership. They are 'independent' in the sense that the President does not directly control their activities and their functions are administered by boards with usually five to seven members each. The President does appoint the members with the approval of the Senate, and although the requirements of staggered terms and bipartisan composition are intended to prevent presidential control, in practice any individual President can select a majority on most of the Commissions during his term of office. Both the President and the Senate are interested in the political views of appointees, and pressure groups affected by the Commission will try to influence the selection as well. A Supreme Court decision in 1953 laid down that a President cannot, however, dismiss a Commissioner in the way he can other executive appointees (see Table 3.3).

The Commissions, which became known as 'the headless fourth branch of government', have a wide variety of powers including the granting of licences, authorising airline routes, approving the opening of natural gas pipelines, and regulating fares and rates on the railroads. Their functions, therefore, are quasi-legislative, quasi-executive and quasi-judicial, and do not fall easily within any of the three branches of government. These bodies have been subject to severe criticism from all sides of the political spectrum; the main charge has been that they are neither 'independent' nor 'regulatory' because they have become the captives of the industries which they are supposed to be controlling. Informal influences behind the scenes and interchangeability of personnel between the

Table 3.3 Major independent regulatory commissions

Commission	Established jurisdiction
Consumer Product Safety Commission Five members with seven-year terms	Investigation of products' safety. Consumer protection
Federal Communications Commission Five members with seven-year terms	Television and radio stations licences. Telephones and telegraphs
Federal Election Commission Six members with six-year terms	Public funding of presidential elections. Election regulations
Federal Reserve Board Seven members with fourteen-year terms	Monetary policy-interest rates
Federal Trade Commission Five members with seven-year terms	Unfair competition, price fixing, advertising
Inter-State Commerce Commission Five members with five-year terms (from 1 Jan. 1986)	Railroads, buses, freight, oil pipelines
Nuclear Regulatory Commission Five members with five-year terms	Nuclear power
Securities and Exchange Commission Five members with five-year terms	Registration of brokers and regulation of Stock Exchange

Commissions and private corporations have led many consumer advocates to argue that the boards do more to protect the industries than they do to help the public. Since 1975 politicians of both parties have supported deregulation to relax or repeal rules that have inhibited competition or kept prices artificially high.

One of the most significant agencies is the Federal Reserve Board which controls monetary policy, a vital element in economic decision-making. Presidents have to learn to live with 'the Fed', knowing that, even though they do not directly control it, the Board will have important effects on the success of their economic strategies. Dr Arthur Burns, who was Chairman from 1970 to 1978, was well known for his conservative monetarist views, and disagreements with President Carter's economic advisers led to the President not renewing his appointment. His successor, Paul Volcker, became a target for many politicians who criticised the 'tight money' policies of the Fed which led to high interest rates. Alan Greenspan, the most recent Chairman of the Fed, gained a reputation in the 1990s as the architect of America's continuing prosperity by overseeing an effective monetary policy which produced a period of low inflation and strong economic growth.

The federal civil service

In 2000 there were approximately 2.8 million Americans working for the federal government as non-military employees and around 1.6 million uniformed personnel in the armed services. At the beginning of the twentieth century there were less than 250,000 federal civil servants but the New Deal and the Second World War led to a vast increase in those working for the government. However, despite the growth of federal government responsibilities, regulations and expenditure the number of federal civil servants remained stable over recent decades and actually declined in the 1990s. This is particularly remarkable, given the huge increases in the US population which we noted in Chapter 1. Two points are worth emphasising. First, the nature of employment has changed in the federal bureaucracy and there are now far more professional and technical staff and fewer lower grade and manual workers, with the civil service more concerned with planning, analysing, regulating and dispensing funds than actually carrying out direct services to the public. Second, the number of state and local government employees increased considerably as grants-in-aid programmes led to programmes being administered at a lower level but in large part financed by the federal government. Therefore federal civilian employees constitute only 10.4 per cent of the total public sector workforce, compared with 17 per cent in 1990 (2.8 million out of 20.2 million).[51]

It should also be remembered that only a small minority of the federal civil servants work in the capital, Washington, DC; the others are based in federal offices and bureaux all over the United States. There is therefore a considerable degree of administrative decentralisation in America. 'Civil servants' include a vast range of jobs from senior advisers to Cabinet Secretaries to the most junior clerical posts. There are also thousands of specialists such as statisticians, economists, architects and engineers who work for the departments.

The development of the civil service

Employment by the federal government in the early days of the Republic was normally based on patronage; Presidents felt that they should reward those people who had helped them win the election and that they needed to have officials whom they trusted in key positions in the administration. Jefferson appointed supporters to government positions, but Andrew Jackson later was to institutionalise the 'spoils system' on a broad basis. He felt that a rotation of office would prevent corruption and allow the dismissal of the lazy or incompetent. After the Civil War, the federal government grew and the need for more permanent and specialised staff became apparent; in addition, the morality of the patronage system was increasingly questioned. It was not, however, until President Garfield was assassinated by a disappointed office-seeker in 1881 that Congress was persuaded to pass a reform. The 1883 Pendleton Act established a classified Civil Service – permanent officials to be appointed on merit – and the setting up of a bipartisan Civil Service Commission to administer the system. Initially, only 10 per cent of federal posts were classified and the rest remained patronage jobs, but gradually the situation was reversed so that the Commission became responsible for the appointment of approximately 90 per cent of civil servants while organisations like the FBI also appoint on a 'merit' basis through examinations and tests, leaving only a few thousand appointments to be made by the President. In 1993 Congress passed legislation to repeal the 1940 Hatch Act provisions that imposed restrictions on the political activity of civil servants; new rules permitted federal employees to run for local office and participate in party campaigns outside of office hours.

The permanent civil servants

Most civil servants are placed on one of the General Schedule grades (GS1 to GS18), according to an evaluation of the job within a unified grading system. Competitive public examinations are held at a number of centres throughout the country, and successful applicants are offered a vacancy when one occurs within a department or agency. The tests themselves tend to emphasise practical ability required in the job rather than more academic skills.

Civil Service positions became much sought after in the 1970s because they not only provided good job security, pensions and health schemes, but higher average salaries than those obtainable in private companies. However, by 1980 concern was being expressed that a pay freeze on senior administrators' salaries which Congress had imposed five years before was having the effect of draining the service of its most talented and experienced officials, many of whom were seeking early retirement or posts in private industry.

Public criticism of both the cost and the efficiency of the federal bureaucracy led Jimmy Carter to promise in his 1976 election campaign that he would reorganise the bloated Civil Service machine. He ordered the Office of Management and Budget, and his newly appointed Civil Service Commission Chairman, Alan Campbell, to put forward plans for reform. The main problems were seen to be complacency caused by high salaries and automatic pay increases, and the difficulty of dismissing, transferring or penalising employees whose work was unsatisfactory. The Civil Service Reform Act of 1978 was the first major overhaul of the civil service for almost a century. The Civil Service Commission was abolished and a new Office of Personnel Management was established to act as the President's personnel arm handling recruitment, pay, examinations and job classifications while a Merit Systems Protection Board would review appeals against dismissal and hold investigations into alleged corruption or waste. The new law allowed some flexibility for the dismissal of employees for incompetence, although not as much as Carter had wanted, and also allowed a new system of merit pay increases for middle managers rather than automatic rises. The most significant change was the establishment of an elite corps of some 8,000 managers at the top of the bureaucracy, known as the Senior Executive Service (SES), of whom a proportion would be political appointees. They had less job security and could be transferred more easily from one department to another, but in return they were able to earn substantial bonuses for exceptional performances. Over 90 per cent of those eligible agreed to join the SES.

The idea of introducing incentives such as those in the private sector was widely supported at the time, but Congress later restricted the number and size of the bonuses for fear that too many civil servants were being awarded them – a move which not surprisingly caused an outcry among the SES.

The Reagan administration used the provisions of the 1978 Act to give itself greater control of the federal bureaucracy and to weaken the scope for independence of action by the permanent civil service. It used its powers through the Office of Personnel Management to promote those who were sympathetic to the administration's goals and to reassign or downgrade civil servants who were unsupportive or ineffectual. Thus, 2,326 senior executives were reassigned in 1982 and 1983, while others left the civil service to avoid adverse moves.[52] Concern was expressed about the increasing politicisation of the senior levels of the civil service, both in terms of its effect on the morale of bureaucrats and the long-term effectiveness of a neutral and competent government machine. For conservative Republicans the federal bureaucracy was seen as largely unsympathetic to their policy objectives. Therefore considerable efforts were made, particularly in the Reagan years, to control it through the appointments process, to restrict it through the OMB's oversight of regulatory activity and to bypass it as far as policy initiatives were concerned.[53]

In 1993 Congress passed the Government Performance and Results Act with the intention of linking the performance of departments in achieving their goals with the budgetary process and allocation of resources. Federal agencies were involved in selecting performance indicators which would best allow evaluation of their success or failure in meeting their objectives. Congress could then decide whether public money had been spent effectively, assess the quality of management in organisations and the extent to which they should be rewarded or punished in the fixing of future budgets.

The Clinton administration's major initiative on civil service reform was the establishment of a National Performance Review under the auspices of Vice-President Gore. Inspired by the widely publicised book, *Reinventing Government*, the Gore Commission's survey of the federal government's operations found that huge potential savings in money and staffing could be made by reorganising agencies, reducing costly regulatory activity and reforming procurement policy.[54] Its recommendations were based on the adoption of a model of government service which moved away from the traditional bureaucratic approach, based on hierarchical and highly rule-bound organisations, to a system of more entrepreneurial management. This involves the decentralisation of authority and decision-making, a greater involvement of employees in their organisations, more emphasis on the 'customers' and the quality of services and greater use of contracting out to other providers.

There was a general welcome given to the idea of streamlining the federal bureaucracy in an era when 'big government' has become unpopular, although it was also widely recognised that implementing the proposals could be problematic given the resistance to radical change within the system. Congressional opposition to proposed cuts which might affect their constituencies or reduce the availability of pork-barrel projects, as well as legislators' wishes to scrutinise the details of administration of the executive branch through oversight activities, tend to work against the spirit of the entrepreneurial model. The process of changing the bureaucracy was seen as a long-term one and has been going on since the mid-1990s. It appears that, despite some failures, some public bodies involved in the reinventing reforms have been able to change themselves quite radically. B. Guy Peters concludes that the American public bureaucracy has been transformed substantially by the Gore Commission and its ideas. One in six of the civil service posts available at the start of the reform process have disappeared, the style of management has altered and the rules that bound the hands of managers have been relaxed to a large extent.[55]

The new Bush administration came to office without any major new initiatives for reforming the bureaucracy. Rather its declared intentions were to reduce the size of government and rely more heavily than in the past on contracting out functions to the private sector, both of which have become well-established conservative priorities in the United States as well as elsewhere.

Political appointees

When President Bush took office in January 2001 he had the opportunity to change over 4,000 top positions in the federal government. Presidents have the power to appoint several hundred executive schedule or 'Schedule C' posts when they form their administration, as well as the political appointees within the SES mentioned above. A study by the General Accounting Office in 1993 showed that in 1991 there were 2,436 political appointees who did not require Senate confirmation, an increase of 414 since 1981. Of these, approximately one-quarter were Schedule C posts and three-quarters were non-career SES personnel. There were 600 or so top-level political appointees who did require Senate approval.[56] Below the rank of Cabinet Secretary there are Under-Secretaries, Deputy Under-Secretaries, Assistant Secretaries and Office Directors. These important positions are the ones likely to be filled by presidential selection, although there may be permanent civil servants serving alongside such appointees in top grades. The President-elect himself delegates authority to his close advisers to make appointments for most of the vacancies, although he may personally interview and sift through the candidates for the top 75 to 100 jobs. The transition period between the November election and the inauguration of the new President in January is filled with frantic activity as the President-elect and his senior advisers go through dossiers and files on potential recruits. Unlike Jimmy Carter, who allowed his Cabinet Officers the power to appoint subordinates them-selves, the Reagan White House exerted control of the appointment process. Michael Turner points out that:

> In consequence, whereas the Carter administration came to be characterised by incoherence and contradiction, the Reagan team maintained a high degree of unity of purpose and commitment to the President's goals.[57]

Cabinet members were consulted about sub-Cabinet posts but they did not have a free hand and many radical right conservatives were placed in these strategically important positions. It was intended that:

> the Reagan Revolution would be effected by a corps of dedicated political appointees willing to assert presidential goals and push for their adherence in the face of anticipated reluctance from a federal bureaucracy committed to the continuance of threatened services and programmes.[58]

Many of the temporary appointees come to Washington for short-term contracts with the government and will expect to return to private business, law practice or a university after the presidential term ends. The Carter administration laid down the rule that these government officials, however, must promise not to take a job in a private company related to their department's affairs until two years after they have resigned from the admin-istration. The 1978 Ethics in Government Act requires public disclosure of appointees' personal finances and was designed to prevent corruption by exposing potential conflicts of interest among high-level officials. However, President Reagan also found that the disclosure provisions acted as a significant deterrent in the recruitment of prominent people to senior posts in his administration and this was one factor contributing to delays in appointing staff to important positions. Other factors such as the need for background checks by the FBI and congressional hearings have led all recent administrations experi-encing delays in filling political posts. James P. Pfiffner's analysis of the appointment process showed that by the end of April 1993 President Clinton had nominated only 177 out of the top 625 appointments and, of these, just 51 had been confirmed by the Senate.[59] George W. Bush's administration had hundreds of unfilled positions six months after taking office and less than half of those whose names had been submitted by the President had been considered by the Senate.[60]

There are relatively few political appointees in each department but as most of these posts are at the senior levels they have a decisive effect on the President's chances of controlling government activities. Some of the appointees will take jobs in the regional offices of departments, exercising considerable influence on how federal policies are carried out in their areas.

The advantages and disadvantages of the recruitment system

The American method of staffing the administration is based on the unique traditions of the presidency: positions of party patronage existing alongside a large permanent bureau-cracy appointed on the basis of competitive examinations. This piecemeal evolution has, of course, led to problems, but at the same time the system of recruitment has proved to be functional within the diffuse executive branch.

The President is able to receive political advice from people he trusts and who are committed to the administration's programmes. He is able to influence policy-making and execution by appointing senior advisers and some 'middle management' positions in each department. The system combines the experience and continuity of the permanent civil service with the new ideas and fresh approach of temporary appointees. It can be argued that such a system prevents complacency and institutional conservatism from developing within the bureaucracy. Government can benefit from the expertise of the short-term officials who bring to their work valuable insight gained from experience in private industry or the academic world. The President also has the opportunity of rewarding the men and women who worked for his election, and although patronage has diminished considerably, it is still a factor in attracting talented people to support presidential campaigns.

On the other hand, it can be argued that the system of recruitment causes friction between the permanent civil servants and the 'outsiders' who are immediately placed in senior positions while knowing little or nothing about the practical workings of the department. There is the problem of dislocation when there is a change of President; for several months during the transition period effective decision-making is halted as the upper echelons of one administration hand over power to the new officials. Some critics feel there are dangers inherent in a system that allows the President to hear advice principally from those people who owe their jobs to him and who think politically along the same lines. There is also occasionally difficulty in attracting high-calibre staff to work in temporary positions that offer no form of job security and which may require a drop in salary. What is more, the turnover of political appointees is high. Senate hearings in May 1993 revealed that in the past decade 31 per cent of such officials left after only 18 months and 50 per cent had resigned within 27 months. It is clear that many of the people appointed see the post as a way of obtaining good experience before moving on to more senior and lucrative jobs, mostly outside government; Senator John Glenn, the Chairman of the Governmental Affairs Committee at the time, described this as 'résumé enhancement'.[61] Finally, there are the possibilities of corruption which inevitably exist where temporary appointees have contact with former business associates, and where interchange of personnel between government and private organisations is common.

The power of the bureaucracy

The senior civil servants in the federal government have a considerable amount of power: they cannot be seen merely as neutral administrators of policies laid down by elected politicians. Bureaucrats themselves have an essential role in the policy-making process, weighing alternatives, taking initiatives and recommending courses of action to Cabinet Secretaries. Their knowledge, expertise and skills mean that political leaders are dependent upon them in many areas.

As government intervention expanded (for example in the New Deal period and the 1960s and 1970s), new bureaucracies were created to take on new tasks such as the protection of the environment, the guarantee of civil rights, the improvement of public safety and the protection of the consumer. The legislation establishing these new agencies with regulatory and promotional functions was usually written in broad and general terms allowing the bureaucrats considerable discretion and power to interpret the laws, although in some more recent statutes legal challenges to the decisions of the agency experts have been allowed. This ability to make discretionary decisions also increased bureaucratic power. The growth of the President's personal staff in the Executive Office of the President has to a large extent been driven by the desire to oversee and control the power of the federal bureaucracy.

Observers of American politics have noted the way parts of the federal bureaucracy also draw support from associated clienteles or interest groups as well as congressional committees involved in funding the agencies. Often known as 'iron triangles', this type of close relationship was seen as creating 'policy sub-governments' and criticised as working against the public interest and blurring accountability. Other writers have pointed out that in Washington today there are 'issue networks',[62] more complex relationships that involve not only bureaucrats, Congressmen and interest groups but also lawyers, journalists, state governments, professors and other experts. The common denominator is the specialised knowledge about public policy alternatives related to specific issue areas. William Lunch has commented that the new networks allow for a wider variety of views than the largely closed sub governments, but at a cost.

> Since the policy debates are frequently abstruse and obscured in a cloud of statistics, academic articles, think tank reports, and congressional hearings, which are very meaningful to the experts but virtually impenetrable to most citizens, the capacity of the voters to follow and pass judgement on policy questions is reduced.[63]

Chapter summary

- The separation of powers and the checks and balances in the American Constitution ensure that the presidency is not the all-powerful office sometimes depicted in the media.
- The President has a number of constitutional and political roles. Clinton Rossiter described the former as: Head of State, Chief Executive, Chief Legislator, Chief Diplomat and Commander-in-Chief of the Armed Forces. The latter include: Head of Party, 'Voice of the People', 'Protector of the Peace', 'Manager of the Prosperity' and World Leader.
- The presidential office grew in importance in the twentieth century for a number of reasons. The growth of 'big government', whereby the federal government played an extended role in the economic and social affairs of the nation, was a key factor. The US became first a 'great power' and then a 'super power' and, as it is acknowledged that the President has the main constitutional authority in foreign policy, this was also very significant. Presidents were increasingly expected to play an active rather than passive role in the legislative process and Congress was willing to grant the President wide discretionary authority at home and support his policies abroad, particularly at the height of the Cold War. The development of the media, particularly television, allowed the public to focus on the presidency, and Presidents in turn had to learn how to communicate effectively with the electorate by way of the media.
- The limits on presidential power include a political culture that has as one of its characteristic features a distrust of government and an array of congressional checks on his authority, including the power to approve presidential appointments, the laws he wishes to see enacted and the budget for the executive departments. Constitutional amendments, particularly the Twenty-Second, and the judgments of the Supreme Court in cases involving the powers of the presidency have also acted as constraints. Media scrutiny, pressure group campaigns, criticism from within his own party and

from the opposing party and the difficulty in ensuring bureaucratic compliance with presidential wishes act as further checks. If opinion polls indicate public support for the President or his policies is slipping these can also help mobilise opposition to presidential action.

- Each President comes to office in different circumstances and the political environment is forever changing, making it difficult to generalise about the exercise of presidential power. Among the factors affecting presidential power are the personal and political/electoral background of each new President and the strategies for governing they choose to adopt, the nature of the times, the fluctuations that take place within a presidential term, the different areas of policy in which the President is seeking to provide leadership and whether or not the President's party controls one or both houses of Congress.
- The President draws support from the Executive Office of the President (which includes the White House Office, the National Security Council and the Office of Management and Budget) the Cabinet, which is made up principally of department heads, and the Vice-President.
- The executive branch consists of 15 federal government departments and a large number of executive agencies. There are also independent regulatory commissions that are not under the direct control of the President.
- The federal civil service comprises around 2.8 million officials. All but a few thousand are permanent and are appointed through a competitive and non-political selection process to serve whichever administration is in power. However, Presidents retain the right to appoint key positions in the senior management of each department on a party political and patronage basis. These appointments help the President secure some control over the federal bureaucracy.

Think points

- Does the United States have a *presidential* system of government?
- To what extent are personality and style important factors in explaining the successes and failures of American Presidents?
- Has divided party control of the presidency and Congress led to a 'deadlock of democracy'?
- To what extent does the President in practice control the executive branch of government?

Some further reading

James D. Barber, *The Presidential Character; Predicting Performance in the White House* (Prentice-Hall 1985)
Gary C. Cox and Samuel S. Kernell, *The Politics of Divided Government* (Westview Press 1991)
Morris Fiorina, *Divided Government* (Macmillan 1992)
Fred Greenstein (ed.), *Leadership in the Modern Presidency* (Harvard University Press 1988)
Tim Hames, 'Presidential Power and the Clinton Presidency', in *American Politics: 2000 and Beyond*, Alan Grant (ed.) (Ashgate 2000)
Jonathan Herbert, 'The Presidency', in *Developments in American Politics 4*, Gillian Peele, Christopher Bailey, Bruce Cain and B. Guy Peters (eds) (Palgrave 2002)
Charles O. Jones, *The Presidency in a Separated System* (Brookings Institution 1994)
Charles O. Jones, *Passages to the Presidency: From Campaigning to Governing* (Bookings Institution 1998)

Samuel Kernell, *Going Public: New Strategies in Presidential Leadership* (CQ Press 1997)
Louis W. Koenig, *The Chief Executive* (Harcourt Brace Jovanovich 1990)
David Mervin, *Ronald Reagan and the American Presidency* (Longman 1990)
David Mervin, *The President of the United States* (Harvester-Wheatsheaf 1993)
Richard Neustadt, *Presidential Power* (John Wiley 1980)
Richard Neustadt, *Presidential Power and the Modern Presidents: The Politics of Leadership from Roosevelt to Reagan* (Free Press 1990)
B. Guy Peters, 'Federal Bureaucracy and Public Management', in *Developments in American Politics 4*, Gillian Peele, Christopher Bailey, Bruce Cain and B. Guy Peters (eds) (Palgrave 2002)
James P. Pfiffner and Roger H. Davidson (eds), *Understanding the Presidency* (Longman 2000)
Richard Rose, *The Post-Modern President* (Chatham House 1988)
Norman Thomas and Joseph Pika, *The Politics of the Presidency* (CQ Press 1997)
James A. Thurber (ed.), *Divided Democracy* (Congressional Quarterly Press 1991)

Weblinks

The President: www.whitehouse.gov
The White House Historical Association: www.white-hous006ehistory.org
National Archives and Records Administration (presidential documents and links to presidential library sites): www.nara.gov/nara/president
Library of Congress: www.lcweb.loc.gov/global/executive/fed.html

4 Law adjudication

The Supreme Court and the judiciary

On 24 July 1974, the Supreme Court of the United States announced one of its most historic and fateful decisions: it declared in a unanimous judgment that the President, Richard M. Nixon, must release tape-recordings of conversations which would reveal his involvement in the Watergate cover-up. After spending a day debating whether to obey the highest court in the land, Nixon capitulated and admitted:

> Those arguing my case, as well as those passing judgment on the case, did so with information that was incomplete and in some respects erroneous.[1]

On 9 August Nixon, faced with certain conviction in a Senate impeachment trial, became the first President to resign the office of Chief Executive.

The case of *United States* v. *Richard M. Nixon* grew out of the Watergate scandal – the creation of the 'plumbers' unit in 1971, the break-in at the Democratic National Headquarters in 1972, and the perjury, obstruction of justice and conspiracy within the Nixon administration that followed in order to conceal from the American people the fact that the President himself was a party to the cover-up operation. The case was examined by the Supreme Court because the federal District Court's subpoena on the President to produce 64 taped conversations was resisted by Nixon on the grounds of 'executive privilege'. The public importance of the issue meant that the Supreme Court undertook consideration of the case and bypassed the US Court of Appeals. The Supreme Court came to the conclusion that the President had the right to confidential advice and discussions with his assistants, particularly on diplomatic and security matters. However, this right could not be extended to a general claim of 'executive privilege' to deny the production of relevant evidence in a criminal proceeding, as this was central to the administration of justice. Chief Justice Warren Burger wrote:

> The impediment that an absolute, unqualified privilege would place in the way of the primary constitutional duty of the Judicial Branch to do justice in criminal prosecutions would plainly conflict with the functions of the courts under Article III [of the Constitution].

He continued:

> A President's acknowledged need for confidentiality in the communications of his office is general in nature, whereas the constitutional need for the production of relevant evidence in a criminal proceeding is specific and central to the fair adjudication of a particular criminal case in the administration of justice. Without access

to specific facts a criminal prosecution may be totally frustrated. The President's broad interest in confidentiality of communications will not be vitiated by disclosure of a limited number of conversations preliminarily shown to have some bearing on a pending criminal case.[2]

The Supreme Court's involvement in the downfall of President Nixon is an impressive illustration of its role in the American political system. It acted as the highest court of appeal to determine what the Constitution and the law meant when the ruling of a lower court was challenged. It was involved in the process of law adjudication, and its role as the final arbiter of the Constitution is essential as parts of the written document are ambiguous and require interpretation. In this particular case, the doctrine of 'executive privilege' is not even mentioned specifically in the Constitution, and the Supreme Court had to decide whether the independence of the executive branch, implied by the separation of powers principle, extended to an absolute privilege of confidentiality of presidential communications.

The compliance by the President with the Supreme Court's decision on the release of the subpoenaed tapes demonstrated the unique position which the Court had achieved. The executive and legislative branches of government accept the decisions of the Supreme Court even though it has no direct way of enforcing its decisions on the other institutions. The Court has consistently found support in the popular belief that the judiciary stands apart from the elected institutions and defends the fundamental law of the Constitution, and the level of respect and confidence in the Court's integrity has been an important factor in this development.

The Nixon case confirmed once again the importance of the separation of powers doctrine and the role of an independent judicial branch in preventing an arbitrary abuse of power by the executive authority. The Supreme Court's decision effectively led to the resignation of a President who had lost the confidence of the people, but it was the culmination of a number of searching investigations by the judicial system. The District Court of John Sirica in Washington DC played a particularly crucial role in revealing the extent of the Watergate affair, and the lengthy legal procedures that went on for a couple of years after the original break-in showed the tenacity and effectiveness of the judicial process. The independence of the Supreme Court was also demonstrated by the fact that three of the eight justices who voted against the President in the case (Justice Rehnquist played no part in the discussions) were, in fact, appointed by Richard Nixon himself.

A quarter of a century later the Supreme Court's intervention in the case of *Bush* v. *Gore* (2000) effectively determined the disputed result of the closest and most hotly contested presidential election in American history. In deciding that George W. Bush had won Florida's 25 electors and therefore a majority in the Electoral College the Court entered the 'political thicket' of electoral politics which had it has generally sought to avoid (see Box 4. 2 on pages 159–60). Although the case was one of the most controversial the Court had ever heard and it deeply divided the justices as well as the country, its decision was accepted by all sides and George W. Bush was inaugurated as the forty-third President of the United States on the day designated by the Constitution in January 2001.

It would be wrong, however, to conclude that the Supreme Court has always enjoyed so well-established a position. The Constitution of 1787 had relatively little to say about the judiciary; judicial power was vested in one Supreme Court 'and in such inferior Courts as the Congress may from time to time ordain and establish'. The judges would hold their positions during 'good behaviour' and could be removed only by congressional impeachment. Congress could also control the Supreme Court's jurisdiction over appeals from lower courts. It was not clear exactly how important the Supreme Court would be; the Constitution did not lay down many specific powers, but neither did it actually deny or prevent the Court from assuming a central role. In many respects the judiciary could be seen as the weakest institution established by the Founding Fathers with its dependence on the elected branches for nominating and confirming judges and for funding its operations. Only the Supreme Court itself has its existence guaranteed by the Constitution.

Undoubtedly the major figure in ensuring the establishment of the Court's preeminence in judicial matters was John Marshall, who was Chief Justice of the Supreme Court between 1801 and 1835. He was a Federalist and he believed that the Union could only survive with a strong national government; under his auspices, the Court became a major influence in American politics and there was a considerable expansion of the federal government's power *vis-à-vis* the states. In these important formative years in the Court's history, three vital developments took place. First, the danger of the President or Congress dominating and undermining the Court was avoided and the independence of the judiciary from the other branches was established. When Jefferson became President and found the courts manned by Federalist supporters it was felt that impeachment could be used to remove the incompetent or politically objectionable judges. However, the Senate failed to muster the necessary two-thirds majority to dismiss Samuel Chase from the Supreme Court. If this had been successful, Marshall himself would probably have faced impeachment and the future independence of the Court would have been severely jeopardised.

The second major achievement of the Marshall Court was the development of the role of 'judicial review'. This convention has led the Supreme Court to declare null and void as 'unconstitutional' any statute or action of the federal or state governments which it believes to conflict with the supreme law of the Constitution. The right of interpreting what the Constitution means has given considerable weight to the Court's opinions. The precedent for this role was set in the case of *Marbury* v. *Madison* (1803).

The Federalist President John Adams appointed a large number of his party supporters to new judicial positions just before he left office himself in March 1801. The new President, Thomas Jefferson, was angry at this blatant act of packing the judiciary, and when it was discovered that some of the commissions had not been delivered he ordered his Secretary of State, James Madison, to stop the appointments. One of the aggrieved appointees, a man named William Marbury, decided to seek redress in the courts. He claimed that the Judiciary Act of 1789 gave the Supreme Court the authority to issue a writ ordering a government official to carry out his duty; he wanted the Court to tell Madison that he should secure Marbury his rightful appointment. The case placed the Supreme Court in a serious predicament. If the Court ordered the executive branch to give Marbury his job, it was likely that the President would refuse and the Supreme Court's prestige and future influence would be endangered. On the other hand, if the Court supported Jefferson and Madison it would vindicate the argument of their party that the judiciary had no power over the executive branch, as well as being politically distasteful to the Federalist majority in the Court.

Marshall's decision, in February 1803, was a landmark in constitutional history because it declared that, although Marbury had a grievance and was entitled to his commission, the Supreme Court had no power to deal with his problem. Marshall argued that section 13 of the Judiciary Act purported to give the Court original jurisdiction in this area, but that this conflicted with Article III of the Constitution, which limits the Supreme Court's original, as opposed to appellate, authority to cases in which an Ambassador, foreign Minister or state was involved as a party to a dispute. The Judiciary Act, in seeming to grant this power to the Supreme Court, was therefore unconstitutional, and the Supreme Court could not uphold an unconstitutional law. Marshall's skill had allowed him to deal with a very difficult situation, and in extricating himself he took the opportunity to set forth the doctrine of judicial review.

In the case of *Fletcher* v. *Peck* (1810), the Court for the first time declared a state law unconstitutional and although it was not until the Dred Scott case in 1857 that another congressional statute was nullified by the judges, the principle of judicial review was established as a vital part of the constitutional system despite the lack of specific authorisation in the Constitution.

The Marshall Court laid the basis for the modern Supreme Court's position by claiming and securing the principle of judicial sovereignty. This has led other institutions, including the state supreme courts, to accept its decisions as binding on them. In *Martin* v. *Hunter's Lessee* (1816), the Supreme Court's right to reverse the verdicts of state courts was accepted. Within a few years of Roger B. Taney's succeeding Marshall as Chief Justice, it was widely agreed that the Court was independent of the other branches of government, it had the power to declare actions of those branches 'unconstitutional', and its decisions were binding on both federal and state institutions.

The structure of the American judiciary

Law adjudication in the United States is carried out by two parallel systems of courts which consider a wide range of civil and criminal cases. There are 50 state systems which have been established by individual state constitutions and decide actions and settle disputes concerning their own laws. The nature of federalism has allowed differences to exist in the working and in the terminology used in the court system; for example, in about three-quarters of the states, judges are elected by a variety of methods, while in the remainder they are appointed. The vast majority of cases are settled in state municipal or justice courts in towns and cities all over the country. However, there is a right of appeal to the state appeals courts, and in a small minority of cases the state supreme court will make the final decision. Usually these are issues which require the highest court in the state to interpret the constitution of the state or involve basic constitutional rights.

There is also the federal judicial system which, as the nation has expanded and the amount of legislation passed by Congress has increased, has become relatively more important. The 'supremacy clause' of the Constitution (Article VI paragraph 2) makes it clear that the federal Constitution, and laws and treaties made under it, are supreme over state constitutions and laws, and therefore federal judicial decisions can also have a broad impact on decisions of the state courts. Federal laws also pre-empt or take precedence over state laws where there is concurrent jurisdiction and both levels of government have passed statutes in the same policy area (see Chapter 8).

There are three tiers within the federal court system.[3] District courts have been established by Congress in each state to examine federal cases. The number of courts and judges may be increased when Congress feels that a growth in population or caseload justifies this. There is at least one court in each state, depending upon population, giving 94 courts in total. Most cases are examined and settled at this level but they can be reviewed by one of the US Courts of Appeals, which are set up in 12 circuits, with six to 28 judges on each circuit. The jurisdiction of a Court of Appeals therefore extends over the boundaries of states, as the number of appeal cases does not justify one circuit for each state. As the number of cases considered by the Supreme Court has declined (see below, page 133), the importance of the Courts of Appeals has grown; their decisions in

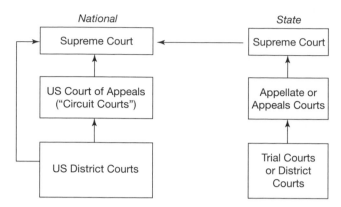

Figure 4.1 The structure of the American judicial system

practice determine matters to the extent that they have been described as the 'regional supreme courts'.[4] The number of cases filed with the appeals courts rose from 50,224 in 1993 to 57,464 in 2001.

Both in 1984 and 1990 Congress approved the creation of an additional 85 district and appeal court posts, bringing the total by 1999 to 844. This increase in the size of the federal judiciary was necessary because of the substantial growth in the workload of the courts. The caseload of the district courts rose by 42 per cent in the 1980s, a result of population growth, an increasingly litigious society, new federal laws and regulations and anti-crime drives, particularly against drugs.

The Supreme Court of the United States is almost completely an appellate (or appeal) court. It has original jurisdiction (that is, cases which go directly to it for consideration) only over very specialised issues mentioned in the Constitution.[5] Most of its caseload is drawn from cases that have been considered by the US Court of Appeals or from state courts where some important constitutional principle is involved. The majority of the cases appealed to the Supreme Court come from petitioners who feel they have suffered a violation of constitutional rights, but the Court turns down around 95 per cent of such applications on the grounds that no substantial constitutional question is at stake. The Court may call for a case from the lower courts for its consideration, if four out of nine Supreme Court justices feel that it is sufficiently important. Judges at district or appeal court levels may announce their views as to the constitutionality of a law in cases before them but, of course, it is the Supreme Court's opinion that is final and binding.

Each year the Supreme Court's session in Washington DC extends from October to June. The groundwork for the approximately 8–9,000 appeals which are filed annually with the Supreme Court is prepared by law clerks who help the justices by presenting the facts and issues in the cases so that decisions can normally be reached speedily and efficiently. The clerks play key roles in deciding which cases should be admitted to the Court's docket and in writing the first drafts of the justices' opinions. Law clerks are mostly one- or two-year appointees from the cream of the law school graduates; they have an important role in expediting the business of the Court, although some critics have suggested that the Supreme Court justices delegate too much power to relatively inexperienced people.

The Supreme Court agrees to hear less than 2 per cent of the cases filed each year. In 2001, for example, it rejected 9,039 cases and let the rulings of the lower courts stand. The vast majority of cases will be settled by examining the written evidence and records of previous hearings, but the Court does hear oral evidence in a certain number of cases each year. In the 1980s the Court would have a docket of up to 150 a year but, in the 1990s, Chief Justice Rehnquist reduced the caseload by over a third. For example, in 1995 the Supreme Court gave full review to only 79 cases, in 1996 to 86 and in 1997 to 93.[6] On these occasions lawyers have thirty minutes to argue their case, and can be interrupted for questioning during this time by the justices. The Court hears oral arguments beginning in early October and finishing in late April. All cases will be decided and the Court's opinion announced before the summer recess begins in late June or early July.

The Court normally meets on Fridays in secret conference to discuss pending cases and applications for *certiorari* (that is, those cases to be 'made certain'). The judges speak in order of seniority and then vote in the reverse order. Compromises may be made behind the scenes as different opinions are exchanged and discussed on the arguments and technical aspects of the law. A unanimous decision on the case tends to strengthen the impact of the Court and create an impression of unity. Chief Justice Marshall established the custom that, where there was general agreement, one justice's opinion should stand for the decision of the whole Court. On the other hand, where there is disagreement there will be a majority opinion which is the official decision of the Court and dissenting minority opinions. The Chief Justice decides who will write the Court's decision if he is in the majority; if not, it is left to the most senior ranking member of the majority to assign the writing of the Court's view. The opinions are often a result of a number of compromises so that a majority of judges are prepared to sign the final statement; it is not unusual for it to have undergone ten drafts in a justice's chambers and 17 or 18 more drafts before it satisfies everyone. Each justice writes about ten majority opinions a year and nearly as many dissenting and concurring views.

The views of the minority of dissenting justices are of considerable interest: at some time in the future their views may become the majority decision because, apart from a constitutional amendment, the only method of changing the Supreme Court's inter-pretation is for the Court itself collectively to change its mind. It is reluctant to make too frequent reversals on major constitutional issues but it may do so if conditions in society change or if the composition or personal views of the justices are modified.

The announcement of a Court decision, which has often laid down new rules and interpretations, is awaited expectantly not only by the plaintiffs in the particular case but by lawyers, judges, politicians, pressure groups and the mass media all over the country. The reverberations from the magnificent Grecian-style building in the nation's capital may well have a profound and fundamental effect on the lives of the American people.

The appointment of the federal judiciary

District and circuit judges

All federal judges are appointed by the President with the approval of the Senate. In practice, the President is advised by the Department of Justice and the Deputy Attorney-General's office whom he should recommend for appointment to the district and appeals courts. District judges are usually selected from among local lawyers and judges who have worked in the state judicial system. When a position becomes available, members of the local community often put forward names and the Justice Department's job is to vet nominations to ensure that anyone the President eventually recommends is suitable for the position. The Federal Bureau of Investigation will check the candidate's personal background for honesty and integrity, while the American Bar Association, the legal profession's organisation, has traditionally rated the nominee's training, legal qualifications and experience for the job. The ABA's 15-member committee's involvement in the procedure has acted as a check on the appointment of unqualified individuals to positions in the federal judiciary.

In 1989 the ABA was involved in two controversies relating to its advisory role on judicial appointments. In a case in June 1989 brought by two public interest pressure groups the Supreme Court decided that the ABA committee could continue to conduct its business in secret; it had been argued that because the committee was an advisory one to government it should, under a 1972 statute, hold open meetings and keep a public record of its decisions. The ABA was also accused by some conservatives of being biased in its evaluation process. Attorney-General Richard Thornburgh and ABA President Robert Rowen told Senators in June 1989 that the ABA had agreed to leave out of its judicial evaluation any consideration of political philosophy; it would confine its scrutiny to candidates' professional qualifications, competence, integrity and temperament.[7] This suspicion of the ABA by conservatives was demonstrated once again when the new administration of George W. Bush decided to exclude the organisation altogether from the selection process, saying that no interest group should have a privileged role in the selection of judges. However, the Democratic Party in control of the Senate said it would not act to confirm presidential nominees until it had received the views of the ABA, meaning that the evaluations would begin after the nominations had been sent to the Senate rather than before.

There is no doubt that party politics and political views intrude heavily on the appointment process. Most judges are selected by the President from within his own political party, and although all Chief Executives maintain that they are picking the best people for the job, the records indicate that partisan affiliation is a major factor in selection. For example, 94.1 per cent of Jimmy Carter's appointees to the district courts were Democrats while of Ronald Reagan's appointments, 95.9 per cent in his first term and 90.7 per cent in his second term were Republicans. Presidents have always rewarded party supporters in the states with patronage in this fashion; the posts are desirable because federal judges enjoy high public esteem, and although the salary levels have been criticised as inadequate by judges and lawyers, they generally have security for life. The President decides which particular party supporters to honour by consulting the Senator from the state to which the judge is to be appointed, if there is a member of his own party holding one of the state's two Senate seats. The convention of 'senatorial courtesy', referred to in the chapter on Congress, arises from the Senate's right of advice and consent over presidential appointments. If there is no Senator of the same party, the President may consult other senior party notables such as the Governor or State Chairman, but he is likely to have more flexibility in such a situation. This is also true of appeals court judgeships because the circuits overlap state boundaries.

The Senate Judiciary Committee holds hearings on appointments, but if the convention of courtesy had been observed, and there were no obvious objections to the candidate's suitability, these and the vote in the full Senate were in the past usually little more than a formality. Hearings were often so brief that one judge, an Eisenhower appointee, missed his because he was late reaching Capitol Hill. 'I walked into the committee room with my knees shaking,' he recalls, 'but the Chairman just gave me a big smile and said, "Hi, we already confirmed ya"'.[8] However, in March 1980 the Senate Judiciary Committee rejected Charles Winberry Jr, Carter's nominee for a judgeship in North Carolina, by a 9–6 vote. It was the first time since 1938 that the Committee had rejected a presidential nomination for a district judge; since then a further eight nominees have been turned down by the Judiciary Committee.

The experience of the 1980s showed that the Senate Judiciary Committee was taking its role of scrutinising nominees far more seriously and was no longer a rubber stamp. The Reagan years were marked by the President's commitment to appoint conservative judges and after the Democrats regained control of the Senate in 1986 they determined to play a more meaningful role in the nominating process. As Democratic Senator Patrick J. Leahy commented: 'I think the Judiciary Committee finally re-discovered the advice and consent clause of the Constitution.'[9] The Democratic majority on the Committee did not use their power to reject a Republican President's nominees unless they regarded an individual's views as extreme and unacceptable. The Committee insisted on more time to conduct investigations before having to vote on them. However, even with this more rigorous oversight President Reagan lost only two nominees at committee level and two on the floor of the Senate. He was successful in winning the confirmation of 95 per cent of his district court and 87 per cent of his appeal court nominees.

During his eight years in office President Reagan had a considerable impact on the federal judiciary. He was able to appoint 48.9 per cent of the 556 full-time district court judges and 48.1 per cent of the 160 appeal court judges serving in November 1989. What is more, the Reagan administration made it clear from the beginning that it intended to make ideology and judicial philosophy the key factors in determining whom to nominate. Whereas this was not unusual in itself, Sheldon Goldman of the University of Massachusetts says that the Reagan administration:

> represents the most systematic, most coordinated effort at the use of the appointment power to maximize the President's agenda and to maximize the President's influence on the appointment process.[10]

Reagan was looking for judges committed to 'judicial restraint' who would tend to defer to the legislative body and not intrude upon the functions of the other branches of government, as opposed to 'judicial activists' who it was claimed tend to substitute their beliefs for the intent of the legislators who wrote the law.

This emphasis on ideological qualifications goes a long way in explaining the relatively small number of minority group and women appointees during the Reagan years compared with Jimmy Carter's term of office. Carter had deliberately sought to increase the representation of these groups on the federal bench; among his 262 appointees there were 40 women, 38 blacks and 16 Hispanics. Of Reagan's 360 appointees there were only 30 women, 7 blacks and 14 Hispanics; while administration officials argued that there were relatively few qualified lawyers in these groups, it is clear that even fewer of them would pass the political qualification test. During his term in office George Bush appointed 185 district and circuit judges, almost a quarter of the total. Bush pleased conservatives by continuing the Reagan approach to judicial appointments; their main criticism was that delays in filling vacancies meant that when Bush left office in 1993 President Clinton had the immediate opportunity to fill over 100 judicial positions with Democratic nominees.

President Clinton won confirmation for 307 district court and 65 appeal court judges during his two terms in office. He doubled the number of black judges on the district courts and almost doubled the number of women. However, his success rate was much lower than Reagan's, with 80.6 per cent of his district court and only 61 per cent of his appeals court nominees being approved by the Senate. Thus, after eight years of

Democratic administration, Republican appointees still dominated the Courts of Appeals, with seven having Republican majorities, three where Democrats were in the majority and two that were evenly split.[11]

Most of Clinton's nominees were moderates in line with his 'New Democrat' ideology and he tried to avoid too many conflicts with the Senate after the Republicans took control in 1995 by dropping some of the more controversial liberal nominees and consulting with the Chairman of the Judiciary Committee, Orrin Hatch, before sending nominations to Capitol Hill. Clinton, on occasions, also made deals with individual Republican Senators whereby the President agreed to nominate conservative judges favoured by the legislators in return for their support for his own choices in their states. Such agreements were criticised by many Democrats and liberal pressure groups who believed that Clinton had not fought hard enough to win the confirmation of his own nominees and that he had missed the chance to reshape the federal judiciary as a lasting legacy of Democratic control of the White House.[12]

However, Clinton also suffered from the heightened partisanship in Congress which had a major impact on the judicial appointment process in the 1990s. Many Republican Senators were still bitter about the way Democrats had rejected Robert Bork as a Supreme Court nominee in 1987 (see below, page 141) and sought to win favour with conservative activists and pressure groups hostile to activist judges. They were determined to use their majority on the Judiciary Committee and, if necessary, in the full Senate to block Clinton nominees whom the Senators regarded as too liberal or activist from their past experience or pronouncements. Their main strategy for achieving this was to delay consideration of the nominees, sometimes for many months and in a few cases for several years. Although the White House is not obliged to consult Senators from the opposing party, they can obstruct nominations of which they do not approve. Senators are routinely asked their opinion on judges named to fill vacancies in their home state by filling in a form. To be considered by the Judiciary Committee a nominee must obtain a positive 'blue slip' from both home state Senators. Clinton's second term saw a slowdown in the number of appointments confirmed; 36 in 1997, 64 in 1998, 35 in 1999 and 37 in 2000.[13] This pattern of confirmations did not keep pace with the number of judges retiring and in January 1998 Chief Justice William Rehnquist criticised the Senate for its slowness, complaining that one in ten judicial posts were vacant at a time of increasing workloads, putting the courts under considerable pressure and delaying the hearing of cases. While delays in considering appointments became the norm only one Clinton nominee was actually defeated. In October 1999 a black Missouri judge, Ronnie White, was refused a seat on the district court by the full Senate in 54–45 vote. This prompted angry and bitter exchanges with Clinton accusing the Republicans of racism; they in turn denied any bigotry and claimed White was an extreme liberal.

The rancour between the parties continued after George W. Bush became President. In his first two years in office the Senate confirmed only 80 of the 131 judicial nominees sent for consideration, while a further 18 were awaiting floor votes having been approved by the Judiciary Committee This was partially the result of the unusual circumstances in 2001, with the change of party control of the Senate in May and the impact of 11 September on the chamber's agenda and priorities. However, it was also clear that many Democratic members were intent on avenging what they saw as the obstructionism of the Republicans during the Clinton years. Some Senators stated that they were not prepared to vote for the confirmation of conservative judges, making consideration of ideology a more significant factor than qualifications in the process. Rather than simply delay consideration of nominees the Democrats in control of the committee after May 2001 were prepared to hold hearings and then reject individuals in Judiciary Committee votes. In March 2002 the Senate Judiciary Committee voted on party lines by 10–9 to reject Bush's nomination of Charles Pickering Sr from Mississippi to the fifth circuit of the US Court of Appeals. Similarly in September of that year Priscilla Owen was rejected for a seat on the same court. Pickering's record on civil rights led to heated arguments in the committee, while Democrats objected to Owen's anti-abortion views and accused her of being unsympathetic to trade unions and employees' rights. Bush asked the Senate to reconsider these two as well as 28 other candidates for the judiciary whose nominations had been blocked once the Republicans took over control of the chamber again in January 2003. Pickering's case aroused considerable controversy because he had been sponsored by Mississippi Senator Trent Lott who had been forced to resign as Republican leader in the Senate following comments he had made in support of racial segregation (see Chapter 2).

In October 2002 President Bush proposed new rules for Senate consideration of judicial nominees whereby a clear timetable would be established so that all those proposed by the White House would be assured of a committee hearing and vote in the full Senate. The Judiciary Committee would lose its power to reject nominees and no matter how it voted there would be a floor vote in the full chamber. However, as changes to Senate rules require a two-thirds majority it was extremely unlikely that such proposals would be adopted even after the Republicans regained control of the Senate following the 2002 elections.

Therefore the success rate for presidential nominations to the judiciary in the first two years of their terms has declined noticeably in recent years. Whereas Presidents from Carter to Clinton in his first term saw over 90 per cent of their nominees confirmed, Clinton in his second term managed to secure the appointments of only 70 per cent and George W. Bush a mere 62 per cent of those they submitted to the Senate.[14] Appointment to the federal judiciary, even at the district level, has therefore become a high profile issue in American politics, with the tensions of divided party control of the presidency and Senate magnifying its importance.

As we have seen, federal judges can be removed from office by congressional impeachment procedures: the House votes for impeachment and conviction in a Senate trial by a two-thirds majority for 'treason, bribery or high crimes and misdemeanours'. A separate provision says federal judges hold office 'during good behaviour'. In the last two decades there have been three cases of incumbent federal judges being impeached and removed from office (Walter L. Nixon Jr of Mississippi, Harry E. Claiborne of Nevada and Alcee L. Hastings Jr of Florida). Claiborne became the first sitting judge to serve a prison sentence after being convicted for tax evasion and the Senate removed him from office in 1986. The other two were removed in 1988. Despite this record Hastings was elected as a Democratic member to the House of Representatives in 1992. The long and difficult process of removing judges who have been convicted of crimes before the courts has given rise to debate about whether there should be alternatives to the process. The most common suggestion has been to authorise the federal judiciary to discipline its own members, as many state courts do. Others have argued that a constitutional amendment is required to automatically remove judges upon conviction of a felony.

Supreme Court justices

Every American President has attempted to extend his political influence by his appointments to the Supreme Court. There are nine justices (one Chief Justice and eight Associate

Justices) and they are appointed for life or until they decide to retire. In the event of a justice retiring or dying in office the President has the right to nominate his successor, therefore the number of such opportunities in any four- or eight-year period can vary considerably. Uppermost in the President's mind when he is choosing an appointee will be the political views of the candidate. It is likely that he will seek to fill the post with a judge who has a similar political disposition to himself. If he is fortunate enough to be able to appoint a number of justices he may be able to mould the Court so that it reflects his views or general outlook. Some Presidents have succeeded in changing the political balance of the Court and thus in influencing the American political system long after they themselves have left the executive office. Franklin Roosevelt managed to do this, primarily because of his long period as President, and one of his appointees, William O. Douglas, who became a justice in 1939, was still a member of the Supreme Court 30 years after Roosevelt's death.

The Supreme Court is not merely the puppet of the executive branch and, as we have seen, judicial independence was established early in the Court's history. The life term, with no requirement for reappointments, the large salary, and effective guarantee of full pay on retirement, as well as the knowledge that removal can only be achieved by impeachment, have a wonderfully liberating effect on Supreme Court justices. Although it can be argued that life terms could lead to out-of-touch and arrogant judges, it is generally accepted that it is a necessary prerequisite for the maintenance of judicial independence. They have nothing either to gain or to fear from the executive and legislative branches. Occasionally a President has appointed someone to the Supreme Court only to find that, once in office, the justice has acted politically in his decisions in a way very different from that originally expected. President Eisenhower selected the Republican Governor of California, Earl Warren, as Chief Justice only to find that his appointee led the Court to a new activist and liberal period of decision-making. A conservative himself, Eisenhower reportedly felt this to have been his worst mistake while being President. When making decisions on controversial issues, Supreme Court justices do not always act kindly towards the President who appointed them. We have seen that the appointees of President Nixon voted against him in *United States* v. *Richard M. Nixon*, and President Truman experienced a similar rebuttal when two of his appointees declared that he had acted unconstitutionally in *Youngstown Sheet and Tube Company* v. *Sawyer* (1952).

A President will be provided by his Attorney-General with a short-list of possible candidates for the vacancy in the Supreme Court from whom he will select his nominee. The Department of Justice will have provided an analysis of the alternatives, and reports on the characters of the people concerned. The ABA will also have rated the candidates on the basis of their qualifications for membership of the highest court in the land. There are four grades ('exceptionally well qualified', 'well qualified' 'qualified' and 'not qualified') and a high rating will help a candidate's chances of selection, although a low grade will not necessarily disqualify him. Richard Nixon was so annoyed about leaks of ABA ratings, which are supposed to be confidential, that, when a candidate being seriously considered was rumoured to have been given an unfavourable grade by the ABA, the administration threatened not to consult the organisation in future. The controversy over allegations of bias in the ABA's Standing Committee on the Federal Judiciary reached new heights in 1987 when the ABA's evaluation of Robert Bork who had been a Yale University law professor, US Solicitor-General and a judge on the US Court of Appeals for the District of Columbia suggested it was interested not only in qualifications and ability but in philosophy, particularly in relation to his strict interpretation of the Constitution. Although a majority found Bork 'well qualified' to serve on the Supreme

Court, four of the 15 members found him 'not qualified', the first time in 15 years that the ABA Committee had not awarded a Supreme Court nominee its unanimous support.[15] Presidents have not always promoted judges from the lower federal courts and, although nominees will probably have had a legal training, they do not necessarily have to be practising judges. Politicians – legislators, Governors and, in the case of William Howard Taft, even a former President – have been appointed to the Supreme Court. However, recent nominees have been drawn from the US Courts of Appeals (see Table 4.1).

Table 4.1 The composition of the Supreme Court 2003

	Birth date	State of origin	Party	Previous position	Date appointed	Appointed by
William Rehnquist	1923	Ariz.	Rep.	Ass. Attorney-Gen.	1971	Nixon
John Paul Stevens	1920	Ill.	Rep.	US Court of Appeals	1975	Ford
Sandra Day O'Connor	1930	Ariz.	Rep.	Ariz. Appeals Court	1981	Reagan
Antonin Scalia	1936	NJ	Rep.	US Court of Appeals	1986	Reagan
Anthony Kennedy	1936	Cal.	Rep.	US Court of Appeals	1988	Reagan
David Souter	1940	NH	Rep.	US Court of Appeals	1990	Bush
Clarence Thomas	1948	Ga.	Rep.	US Court of Appeals	1991	Bush
Ruth Bader Ginsburg	1933	NY	Dem.	US Court of Appeals	1993	Clinton
Stephen Breyer	1938	Cal.	Dem.	US Court of Appeals	1994	Clinton

The President's nominee will therefore be chosen with all these factors in mind: ability, experience, honesty, political views, and possibly the need to reward allies from the last election campaign. Acceptability to the Senate is also an important checking mechanism on presidential choice. The Senate Judiciary Committee, and indeed all Senators, will be very interested in the qualifications and political outlook of the nominee. The Senate takes its role of advice and consent for Supreme Court justices very seriously and, of course, it is a matter of concern to the whole nation and not just to one state. There may well be a long and thorough investigation and interrogation of the nominee at public hearings. Pressure groups may actively campaign for and against the selection, and the President's friends and enemies will be lobbying strongly behind the scenes. The Senate has refused approval to 29 (or about 20 per cent) of the nominations sent to it in the period to 2002.

Richard Hodder-Williams has pointed out that all nominations are made within two contexts. The 'White House context' is created exclusively by the President himself and reflects the goals and strategies to be achieved by nominating particular individuals. These may include the hope that the nominee will advance certain policies on the Court or that the nomination – of a woman or a member of a minority group, for example – will have symbolic significance. The 'Washington context' is essentially outside the President's control and means that he has to take account of the balance of political forces in the Senate. The 'law of anticipated reactions' may prevent the President from submitting the name of his ideal choice because ignoring such reactions may lead to the failure of the nomination.[16] Sometimes Presidents wishing to avoid a battle with the Senate will value 'confirmability' above other factors.

When Richard Nixon became President in 1969 he entered the office pledged to use his appointment power to influence a change in the political balance of the Court, if the opportunity should present itself. Conservative Americans, angered by the judicial activism and liberal policies of the Warren Court, wanted to see the future appointment of 'strict constructionists'. These would be conservative judges who would, as far as possible, interpret the Constitution and the law with the intent of the Founding Fathers and law-makers in mind, but not break into new areas which were the prerogative of Congress. Nixon, in a campaign speech in November 1968, stated:

> They would see themselves as caretakers of the Constitution and servants of the people, not super-legislators with a free hand to impose their social and political viewpoints upon the American people.

The new President had an early opportunity to fulfil the promise as two liberal justices retired. Earl Warren left the position of Chief Justice vacant and Nixon selected a conservative 'law and order' judge from Minnesota, Warren Burger, to replace him. Although his appointment was approved by the Senate without problems Nixon had much greater difficulties in filling the other vacancy, left when Abraham Fortas (a Johnson appointee) resigned after criticism of his freelance activities as a legal adviser. The President wanted to select a Southern conservative to the Court, partly as a reward to his political supporters in the region for backing him in the 1968 presidential election. They, in turn, wanted a justice who would help moderate the Warren Court's liberal stance on civil rights and segregation. However, the majority in the Senate, made up of Democratic and Republican liberals from the Northern states, had no intention of approving anyone who had the slightest taint of racial discrimination in his past record, and most of these Senators were suspicious of Southern conservatives on this basis. Unfortunately for President Nixon, the Justice Department did not adequately screen the first of his appointees to the vacant post; Clement Haynsworth, from South Carolina, was rejected by the Senate after it had been revealed that he had tried some cases where he had a conflict of interest. Nixon's second nominee for the vacancy, Harrold Carswell, was rejected 51–45 by the Senate in April 1970. He was charged with showing racial bias in the Florida courts and with having a mediocre record as a judge, having been frequently overruled by higher state courts. Nixon was unable to count on solid support from Senate Republicans and, in the Haynsworth case, even Minority Leader Hugh Scott voted against confirmation. Having accused the Senate of bias against the South, Nixon then nominated Harry Blackmun, a moderate federal appeals court judge from Minnesota. The vacancy was thus filled at the third attempt, and the episode demonstrated that no President is assured of obtaining the support and consent of the Senate on Supreme Court appointments. In 1971 two other liberals from the Warren Court, Justices Harlan and Black, retired and Richard Nixon had the chance to appoint two more conservative replacements. Lewis Powell Jr, a Virginia lawyer, and William F. Rehnquist, the Assistant Attorney-General, both secured confirmation by the Senate. Therefore by the end of his first term in the presidency, Richard Nixon had been able to shape the political composition of the Court by naming four out of the nine justices. If he had remained in office for a full second term, he would have had the opportunity of choosing the successor to William Douglas, the most outspoken liberal in the Court, and of appointing an actual numerical majority. Gerald Ford's choice of John Paul Stevens, from Illinois, received the unanimous support of the Senate in December 1975 in an unusual demonstration of political consensus.

President Carter became the first President to serve a full term in office who did not have the opportunity of appointing a Supreme Court justice as no vacancies occurred during his term. Ronald Reagan had the opportunity of filling three vacancies on the Supreme Court during his eight years in office. In 1981 he appointed Sandra Day O'Connor, an Arizona appeals court judge, as the first woman Supreme Court justice on the retirement of Potter Stewart. In 1986 Reagan named William Rehnquist, the most conservative judge on the Court, as the new Chief Justice in place of Warren Burger who stood down to preside over arrangements for the celebration of the bicentennial of the Constitution, and appointed Antonin Scalia, the first Italian-American ever to sit on the Court, in Rehnquist's position. Rehnquist was approved 65–33 votes in the Senate after a protracted debate on the nomination. The third vacancy came about as a result of the retirement of Lewis Powell, a Nixon appointee who had often joined liberals and had been the swing vote on the Court on a number of key issues. It was recognised that the filling of this vacancy would be extremely significant to the future political balance of the Court. Apart from Powell, other Republican nominees, Blackmun and Stevens, had during the 1980s moved increasingly to support the liberal judges on the Court, while Byron White, a Kennedy appointee, had moved to the right.

Reagan's first nominee, Robert Bork, was, as we have seen, in most respects well qualified to become a Supreme Court justice. However, his personality and judicial philosophy aroused considerable opposition from liberal Senators and with the Democrats back in control of the Senate in 1987 and the Iran-Contra issue eroding Reagan's political influence, Bork's nomination was lost after the most bitter and public campaign ever seen involving a judicial appointee. Civil rights groups were successful in their lobbying against the nomination and despite an unprecedented appearance on his behalf before the Judiciary Committee by former President Gerald Ford, Bork was rejected in October 1987 by a Senate vote of 58–42, the most decisive defeat ever suffered by a nominee in American history. Reagan's second choice, Douglas Ginsberg, was forced to withdraw only days after his nomination when it was revealed that he had taken drugs when he was a college student. The President then turned to Anthony Kennedy, a Californian appeals judge, who was confirmed by the Senate 97–0 in February 1988. Ronald Reagan was therefore able to shift the political balance of the Supreme Court decisively to the right before he left office.

In July 1990 George Bush was presented with his first opportunity to nominate a Supreme Court justice when one of the remaining liberals on the Court, William Brennan, announced his retirement. Brennan, who was 84 years old and had been appointed by President Eisenhower in 1956, had been one of the most influential members of the Supreme Court during his 34 years of service. In nominating David Souter, a former New Hampshire state supreme court judge and recently appointed member of the federal appeals court, President Bush was able to appoint an uncontroversial conservative to fill the vacancy without a bitterly contested confirmation process in the Senate, which was controlled by the Democrats. With the resignation of Thurgood Marshall in 1991 Bush was able to make a second nomination to the Court and he selected black conservative judge Clarence Thomas to fill the vacancy. Thomas was opposed by a number of pressure groups and given a lukewarm 'qualified' rating by the ABA (with two of the 15 committee members declaring him 'not qualified'). Despite the frustration of Democratic Senators at Thomas's refusal to answer controversial questions at the Senate Judiciary Committee hearings, his eventual approval did not seem in doubt until allegations of sexual harassment surfaced late in the process. Anita Hill, a law professor and former colleague of Thomas, testified before the committee, whose televised proceedings became the focus of huge public interest. Thomas was confirmed in October 1991 by a narrow 52–48 margin, after doubt had been cast on his character and following concerted lobbying by women's groups against his nomination. What is more, the process of selection and approval of justices itself was criticised as demeaning to the dignity and stature of the Supreme Court. *Time* magazine described the Thomas hearings as an 'ugly circus'.[17]

The Chairman of the Senate Judiciary Committee, Joseph Biden, called for more consultation between the White House and the Senate before nominations are submitted in order to try to avoid confrontation between the two branches. He also criticised extremist lobbying campaigns on appointments but defended the Senate's right to review a nominee's ideology as well as his or her character.[18]

In 1993 Byron White's retirement gave President Clinton the first opportunity a Democratic President had had since 1967 to nominate a Supreme Court justice. After raising expectations that he was planning to propose his recently appointed Interior Secretary, Bruce Babbitt, a former Governor and presidential candidate, Clinton eventually decided to nominate District of Columbia Appeals Court judge Ruth Bader Ginsburg to the post. She was widely perceived to be a well-qualified moderate and her nomination was approved 96–3 in the Senate in August 1993. With the retirement of Harry Blackmun, Clinton was able to appoint Stephen Breyer, another moderate whose nomination also aroused no controversy, in 1994.

During the 2000 presidential campaign the parties and both conservative and liberal pressure groups were very aware that the successful candidate would quite possibly have the opportunity to select one if not more new justices to the Supreme Court. There had not been a new appointment in six years and several of the justices were elderly or suffering ill health; John Paul Stevens was 80 in 2000, William Rehnquist was 75 and Sandra Day O'Connor was 70. The importance of such a vacancy was also highlighted by the fact that in the previous session of the Court many decisions were very close, with 21 out of 74 being determined in whole or part by a single vote. Bush's victory meant that the conservatives on the Court would more than likely find their position con-solidated or strengthened, a situation made more likely by the Republicans' success in regaining control of the Senate in the 2002 elections. By the beginning of the 108th Congress in January 2003 there had still been no new appointments to the Supreme Court, making it the longest period without a change in its membership since the early nineteenth century.

The Supreme Court and the role of government

The Supreme Court has had a great influence on the development of American federalism. It was not clear at the beginning of the nineteenth century whether the structure of government initiated in 1787 would lead to a strong national government, or whether the powers of the states and the loyalties of peoples to their local areas would stand in the way of such a development. John Marshall, as Chief Justice, used his position to interpret the Constitution in favour of the federal government when there were jurisdictional conflicts with the states. A written constitution and a division of powers between tiers of government require interpretation and this was one of the main factors behind the Supreme Court's importance. The Civil War altered the balance of power in favour of the national government, but in the latter part of the nineteenth century conservative judges emphasised other sections of the Constitution to restrict federal and even state govern-ments' intervention in economic and social affairs, in line with the generally accepted *laissez-faire* economic philosophy of the time. However, after 1937 and the 'New Deal' legislation in response to the Depression, the Court began to allow federal government influence in those areas previously seen as reserved to the states or those where govern-ment intervention of all kinds had been prohibited. In the economic and social fields, the Court has broadly interpreted three main sections of the Constitution and has thus enlarged the permissible areas of federal involvement in the life of the nation.

Box 4.1 President Roosevelt and the Court-packing plan

In the late nineteenth and early twentieth centuries the Supreme Court regularly struck down federal and state laws which sought to regulate economic activities as being in conflict with the Constitution's guarantees of liberty in the Fifth and Fourteenth Amendments. When Franklin D. Roosevelt was elected President during the Great Depression in the 1930s with promises to use the power of the federal government to create a 'New Deal' and alleviate the economic and social crisis, he and his Democratic Party which controlled Congress were on a collision course with the Court. Two major pieces of New Deal legislation passed in 1933 (the National Industrial Recovery Act and the Agriculture Adjustment Act) were declared unconstitutional.

Roosevelt came up with a novel scheme to confront this problem. He proposed a bill in 1937 which would give him the power to appoint a new justice for every member of the Court who was over 70 years old, ostensibly to help the ageing judges with their workload. As there were six members of the current Court who were over 70 Roosevelt would have an immediate opportunity to choose six new judges sympathetic to the New Deal who could help him overcome the resistance of the Supreme Court to his policies.

Even many of the President's own supporters were critical of the plan, seeing it as a crude attempt to threaten the independence of the judiciary and violate the separation of powers. In the event, before Congress voted on the legislation, the Court reversed one of its earlier decisions and allowed a minimum wage law to stand. The judgment indicated that the power of Congress in relation to the general welfare of the country could take precedence over economic liberty, thus opening the way to widespread federal government intervention in the American economy in the years since 1937.

---

1 The 'implied powers' clause. Article I Section 8 of the Constitution sets out the enumerated powers within which Congress can legislate; these are specific areas such as defence, trade and the postal services. However, at the end of this section the Constitution states that 'Congress shall have the power to make all laws which shall be necessary and proper for carrying into execution the foregoing powers'. The Court interpreted the 'necessary and proper' clause to mean that Congress can legislate on additional matters to those set out in the enumerated powers as long as these are important for carrying out the listed functions. Therefore in *McCulloch* v. *Maryland* (1819) it was argued that the enumerated power of coining money gave the federal government the implied power to set up a bank for the United States, even though banking is not specifically mentioned in Article 1 Section 8.

2 The 'inter-state commerce' clause. One of the constitutional enumerated powers of Congress is 'to regulate commerce . . . among the several states', whereas commercial activity within the boundaries of one state was subject only to state regulatory action. But what does 'commerce' include? Should the phrase be narrowly or broadly construed? The Supreme Court, in effect, interpreted this section of the Constitution to allow federal government regulations of almost any activity that crosses state boundaries. In *Gibbons* v. *Ogden* (1824) ferries between New York and New Jersey were judged to be involved in commerce and subject to federal taxes. In the twentieth century the amount of inter-state, as opposed to intra-state, commerce increased substantially, and if a company is involved in trading both within and outside a state it is subject first and foremost to federal laws if there is a conflict with a state regulatory law, because of the 'supremacy clause' of the Constitution. It was not until the 1990s that the Rehnquist Court started to set limits on what Congress could legislate upon based on the commerce clause and, in particular, restricting its jurisdiction on law and order matters (see Chapter 8).

3 The 'general welfare' clause. Congress was also given another general enabling clause which allows for a broad judicial interpretation. This is the power to 'lay and collect taxes . . . to provide for the common defence and general welfare of the United States'. The term 'general welfare' obviously requires definition and clarification. In the 1930s the Supreme Court first decided that the Social Security Act was unconstitutional because it attempted to allow federal regulation in an area reserved to the states. The Court then reversed its view and decided that it was permissible because it could be seen as a 'taxing act for the general welfare', rather than as a regulatory act.

On the other hand, the Supreme Court, at other times, has used the Tenth Amendment specifically to prevent federal action in areas reserved to the states in the Constitution. The Court has also used the 'due process' section of the Fourteenth Amendment to protect industry and banking from state government regulation in such economic matters as wages and hours of work for employees. The Amendment says: 'No state shall deprive any person of life, liberty or property without due process of law.'

It is clear that the Supreme Court has chosen at various times in its history to place emphasis on one phrase or section of the Constitution rather than another in order to justify its decisions, and retain a flexibility which can keep it in line with public opinion.

Judicial activism and the Warren Court

After the Second World War, the question of the federal government's powers in economic matters was no longer the central issue taking up the Supreme Court's time, mainly because Roosevelt's appointees and the new liberal majority in the Court made it clear by their decisions that they would not stand in the way of an expanded federal role. New issues were taken up by the Court, particularly after Earl Warren became Chief Justice. The Supreme Court examined questions which became very controversial but which had previously been dormant in American politics. Other institutions – the presidency, Congress and state legislatures – would not act as they were too sensitive and difficult for elected politicians to handle. The Warren Court symbolised 'judicial activism' that was both applauded and condemned with tremendous emotional energy on both sides. It made a vast impact on many areas of American life where appointed judges were prepared to take up causes that were electorally unpopular. Often the issues went to the very heart of democracy – the rights of individuals, the rule of law, equal representation, and equality before the law. The Court was frequently in the position of defending minority rights against the views of a majority of the people. Many argued that the Warren Court was usurping the role of the elected legislature by making new laws and taking up new issues. Earl Warren himself admitted that the Court 'makes law' when it interprets the Constitution, but that it is not trying to take over the role of Congress. If Congress passes an act, then the judiciary has to interpret the statute; if Congress does not like the interpretation then it can pass a new law or amend the old one. However, if no statute exists in a particular area, the Court has to look at the broad language of the Constitution and see what rights exist from that document.[19]

Archibald Cox, the man Richard Nixon dismissed as Watergate special prosecutor and a distinguished legal authority, has written:

The appointment of Earl Warren as Chief Justice of the United States in 1953 marked the opening of a new period in our constitutional development. In the next fifteen years the Supreme Court rewrote, with profound social consequences, major constitutional doctrines governing race relations, the administration of criminal justice and the operation of the political process. The extent and rapidity of the changes raise grave questions concerning the proper role of the Supreme Court in our national development – questions concerning the nature and function of constitutional adjudication.[20]

Martin Shapiro argued that:

the Warren Court took a fairly clear direction: to serve the value of equality and to incorporate that value more deeply in the Constitution. Although the structure was never completed, the blueprint was clear. . . . The Warren Court was attempting to change the Constitution and impose its own will on that of other governmental bodies, particularly state legislatures. It was pretty clear that by the late 1960s nobody in the Warren-Brennan majority really cared much about anything but the policy outcomes of the cases.[21]

We shall examine four issue areas in which the decisions of the Warren Court between 1953 and 1969 had major social and political impact and where substantial constitutional questions were raised.

1 Segregation and race relations. Since the Civil War, equal rights for black Americans had been, in many respects, a hollow promise. In some areas, particularly in the Southern states, segregation of public facilities was practised and even written into and institutionalised in the state laws. Blacks and whites went to separate schools, ate at separate lunch counters and had separate compartments on buses and trains. In other areas where there was no legal segregation, separation of the races took place in practice because of residential living patterns. The Supreme Court had decided in the case of *Plessy* v. *Ferguson* (1896) that, as long as they were substantially equal, separate facilities were constitutional and permissible. For the next 60 years neither Congress nor the presidency wished to step into this political minefield and intervene in such a controversial area.

The Warren Court was prepared to re-examine the principle and decided in the landmark case of *Brown* v. *Board of Education, Topeka (Kansas)* (1954) that separate facilities for blacks and whites were inherently unequal under the Fourteenth Amendment. The relevant section of the Amendment says that: 'No state shall . . . deny to any person within its jurisdiction the equal protection of the laws.' In this case, Oliver Brown wanted to send his daughter Linda to the school nearest his home. However, because the family was black, Linda had to travel across town to school and was not allowed to attend the all-white school a few blocks away from her home. Backed by the National Association for the Advancement of Colored People (NAACP), Mr Brown took his case to the Court, and it decided that 'equal protection' was being denied. The Court argued that the doctrine of 'separate but equal' had no part to play in state-financed schools and that separation 'generates a feeling of inferiority as to their status', thus retarding black children's educational development. The Court argued that states and school districts should desegregate their schools with 'all deliberate speed'. The *Brown* case was a momentous decision but it did not result in an immediate end to segregation. Direct intervention by the President with federal troops to enforce desegregation, for example, in Little Rock, Arkansas, and the Civil Rights Act of 1964, followed in the dispute between the federal government and stubborn state authorities. Fifteen years after the *Brown* decision, the Court, impatient at local resistance, said that authorities were obliged to desegregate their schools 'at once' (*Alexander* v. *Holmes County Board of Education*, 1969).

Opponents of the desegregation decision argued against the Court on a number of grounds. They felt that the Court had accepted 'pseudoscientific' evidence, such as psychological data and statistics on educational achievement, without allowing any challenge to the validity of this material. It was also argued that such information was not relevant to the Court's role of interpreting the constitutional document. Others pointed to the Tenth Amendment and argued that, as education is among the reserved powers of the states, the federal authorities had no constitutional right to intervene in the running of the schools.

However, the Court's decision and the fact that it was supported by all the Supreme Court justices, not only established the new principle but provided a firm commitment on behalf of the judiciary to the protection of minority rights.

2 Equal representation and reapportionment. Each state's legislature in the United States has the right to determine boundaries for all elections within its jurisdiction. These include, as well as local government elections, contests for both houses of the state legislature itself and for the House of Representatives. In the early 1960s, most state legislatures tended to under-represent the increasingly urban electorate and proportionally over-represent the rural areas with declining populations. This was a result of the failure to reapportion seats in the legislature on a regular basis to take into account shifts in population within and between states. There was often an unwillingness on the part of the dominant elites in these legislatures, many of whom came from rural areas, to make changes which would threaten their hold on the levers of power. Consequently, there were glaring inequalities in the size of electoral districts, with some highly populated towns and cities having fewer representatives than sparsely peopled country areas.

The Supreme Court had been asked to investigate whether such a situation was constitutional, but in the case of *Colegrove* v. *Green* (1946) it declined to do so on the grounds that it wished to avoid entering what it called 'the political thicket', full of party political controversies. By the 1960s demographic changes in America made the problem even more urgent, and in 1962 the Warren Court reversed the 1946 decision and examined the vexed question of reapportionment. The Supreme Court took a major initiative in the case of *Baker* v. *Carr* (1962). It said that the state of Tennessee, which had not reapportioned its legislature since 1901, was acting unconstitutionally and denying 'equal protection' to its urban citizens as required by the Fourteenth Amendment. A series of related cases followed and all ended with the same conclusion: states must provide electoral districts that are fair and equal and provide, as far as possible, a 'one person, one vote' system. The state of Georgia tried to argue that, even if its lower chamber was based on this principle, the upper house could be based on unequal districts to protect the rights of minorities, just as the US Senate was designed to do at the national level. In *Reynolds* v. *Sims* (1964) the Court dismissed the 'federal analogy' on the grounds that the political subdivisions of a state had never been independent units but were simply subordinate administrative areas within the unitary structure of the state.

The Supreme Court argued that the federal courts would have to supervise the states to ensure compliance with the 'equal protection' clause, and the state legislature would be obliged to submit its reapportionment plans to the judges to see whether they were within the guidelines laid down. A major furore developed as many conservatives argued that this was again an example of interference with states' rights and angrily protested that the Constitution does not lay down anywhere that a 'one person, one vote' principle must be used in voting.

Earl Warren said that he regarded this area of decision-making as the most important single area examined by the Supreme Court in his 16 years as Chief Justice. Not only was it one that was central to democracy; he felt that if everyone had fair representation in the elected branches of government then most problems could be resolved by the political process rather than being the subject of judicial decision making.[22]

3 The rights of the accused. Important steps were also taken during the 1960s in protecting the rights of accused persons. The Bill of Rights includes specific mention of individual rights in criminal cases, because it was recognised that these were an essential defence against a tyrannical government. The Fifth and Sixth Amendments are particularly relevant here.

> No person shall . . . be compelled in any criminal case to be a witness against himself, nor be deprived of life, liberty and property without due process of law. (The Fifth Amendment)

> In all criminal prosecutions, the accused shall . . . have the assistance of counsel for his defense. (The Sixth Amendment)

The basic rights 'to remain silent' and to legal counsel were extended to the states by a number of Supreme Court decisions which selectively incorporated these principles into the 'due process' clause of the Fourteenth Amendment.

In the case of *Gideon* v. *Wainwright* (1963), the Court decided that a man convicted of a felony in Florida had been denied his rights as no legal counsel had been provided by the state for his assistance. Gideon had been found guilty in his trial, having been unable to afford to hire a lawyer to help defend him. Although government provision of legal advice to the poor had been accepted in federal cases, the *Gideon* episode led to the widespread development of public defender systems in the states. The principle involved in *Gideon* v. *Wainwright* was that the poor should not be disadvantaged in criminal cases because of their financial status, and most people accepted this as a fair and reasonable argument, even if they did not welcome the extra burden on the taxpayer.

However, the next year saw a more controversial extension of the rights of the accused. The Supreme Court ruled in *Escobedo* v. *Illinois* (1964) that a citizen had the right to counsel *before* a trial, and that he should be provided with legal advice, if necessary by the state, when general interrogation of a suspect becomes an accusation of a criminal charge. Furthermore, any information gained by the police without a counsel being present was not admissible as evidence in court. In *Miranda* v. *Arizona* (1966) the Court further limited the admissibility of confessions as evidence. To ensure voluntary confessions by defendants, the police were to be obliged to warn the suspect of his rights to remain silent and to legal counsel. In the event of a citizen's waiving these rights, it was the responsibility of the police to show that he understood what he was doing.

The introduction of these procedural safeguards by the Court was greeted with great hostility by state governments, politicians and police forces across the country. It was argued that the police were being expected to fight crime with one arm tied behind their backs, and that the guilty would go free on technicalities in court. Opponents of the

Warren Court argued that it was more concerned with protecting the criminal than with protecting society from the criminal. It should be remembered, however, that the main motivation of the Court was to prevent innocent people accused of crimes from being denied their rights, and from being overwhelmed by the physical and psychological pressures of their position.

4 Religion and the state. The First Amendment to the Constitution states that 'Congress shall make no law respecting an establishment of religion, or prohibiting the free exercise thereof'. The Supreme Court, under Earl Warren, supervised how the states acted in this field by ruling against policies that seemed to represent the establishment or support of a religion by any government or public body. In doing so, the Court ran into a great deal of hostility from ordinary Americans who saw such prohibition as an interference with the free exercise of their religion. The Court's decisions could be seen, depending upon one's point of view, as upholding the 'establishment clause' and protecting minorities who do not wish to see their tax dollars supporting churches or religions, or as an unwarranted interference in the rights of the majority within a state freely to practise their faith.

In *Engel* v. *Vitale* (1962), the Supreme Court declared unconstitutional a non-denominational prayer that had been written by the New York State Regents for use in the schools, on the grounds that it was intended to promote religious views. In the next year, the Court went further in *School District, Abington* v. *Schempp* (1963) and declared that Bible reading in public state-supported schools was unconstitutional if it was intended as worship or as a method of advancing religious beliefs. The Bible could, however, be used in an objective study of religions. Many American Christians were incensed at what they saw as the Court's support for the arguments put forward by atheists and humanists. An Alabama Congressman, George Andrews, declared: 'The Court has put the Negroes in the schools and now they've driven God out.'

The Court argued that, although the state cannot deny anyone the right to practise his religion, it cannot conversely, through majority rule, impose any set of beliefs on all its citizens. Free exercise of religion does not mean, therefore, that people may use the machinery of the state (such as government or school buildings) or tax moneys from all citizens to further or practise their beliefs.

The Burger Court 1969–86

The activism of the Warren Court led to accusations that the judges were ignoring the Constitution and substituting their own liberal views when interpreting the law. We have seen how Republican Presidents were determined to use their appointment powers to alter the political balance of the nation's highest judicial body. Under Warren Burger (1969–86) the Court moved to the right and in the 1980s there was more emphasis on judicial restraint and the other political branches of government being left to assume the leadership responsibility for major initiatives and social policies. 'Federal judges – who have no constituency – have a duty to respect legitimate policy choices made by those who do', the Court declared in a 1984 case involving interpretation of the 1984 Clean Air Act and this fairly summed up the philosophy of the Court. It also based its rulings on narrow statutory or constitutional grounds and avoided making judgments of general application. The Burger Court did not reverse the major decisions of the Warren Court, as some liberals had feared in the early 1970s. It could not, and would not have wished to turn the clock back to the situation before *Brown* v. *Board of Education, Baker* v. *Carr* and *Gideon* v. *Wainwright*. It did, however, on occasions, modify and narrow inter-pretations in areas where the Warren Court had taken a pioneering role. Martin Shapiro concludes:

> the Burger Court spent its early years largely in marginal readjustments of Warren Court policies . . . In grappling with the record of the early Burger Court most commentators concluded that it was an activist Court but one that tended to use balancing doctrines to reach ad hoc policy judgments in particular cases rather than announcing major new constitutional rights, except in the abortion and death penalty areas.[23]

The Burger Court was a period of considerable stability in terms of its membership and, after the initial Nixon appointees of the early 1970s, only two new members – John Paul Stevens and Sandra Day O'Connor – were appointed in the next 15 years. Like previous Supreme Courts, the Burger Court was not divided into rigid conservative and liberal blocs. There were changing alliances and majorities among its members and a shifting middle ground with various justices holding a pivotal position at various times. The political climate also changed in the United States so that judges who may have been regarded as conservatives when appointed in the early 1970s, such as Lewis Powell, Harry Blackmun and John Paul Stevens, were increasingly seen in the 1980s as moderates or even liberals on some issues. The Burger Court was often described as factionalised and criticised for lack of leadership and it was certainly true that commentators who wanted to sum up the Court's philosophy in a simple or clear-cut way were frustrated. Consistent trends were hard to establish and predictions of the outcomes of particular cases were more and more difficult to make. However, despite its generally conservative reputation, the Burger Court more often than not frustrated the Reagan administration when it called for major changes in areas such as civil rights, abortion and school prayer. Attorney-General Robert Jackman wrote in 1940, a year before he was appointed to the Court, that:

> The Supreme Court is almost never really a contemporary institution – the Judiciary is . . . the check of a preceding generation on the present one.

The Burger Court, appointed largely by earlier Presidents, upheld policies adopted by earlier administrations and laws passed by previous Congresses. In doing so justices often invoked Supreme Court decisions of the 1960s and 1970s as the basis for their actions. The Burger Court generally continued the Warren Court's tradition of enlarging the Constitution's protection for individual rights, while taking a decidedly more conservative view in criminal law cases where it favoured the arguments of the police and prosecutors three or four times as often as those of defendants. It also moved away from the liberal position on reapportionment as well as on civil rights and affirmative action issues. It is notable, however, that the Burger Court was responsible for one of the most controversial and, for conservatives, most objectionable decisions in the Supreme Court's history when it struck down state laws banning abortion in *Roe* v. *Wade* in 1973. The majority based its decision on the individual's right to privacy which, although not specifically mentioned or enumerated in the Constitution, could its supporters argued, be implied by other parts of the document. To its opponents, Roe was the epitome of liberal judicial activism which had been characteristic of the Warren Court.

The Rehnquist Court since 1986

After William Rehnquist became Chief Justice in 1986 President Reagan had the opportunity to replace Lewis Powell with a more conservative judge, Anthony Kennedy. Bush's appointment of two conservatives, Souter and Thomas, to replace two liberals, Brennan and Marshall, shifted the balance of the Court even further to the right. Indeed, the 1990–91 term, before Thomas joined the Court, was marked by 'a surge in conservative activism' where the Court had policy objectives, particularly in the area of criminal law, and where it was more likely to depart from precedent in its rulings. At times the Court went beyond the questions immediately before it and addressed constitutional issues that dissenters said did not need to be tackled. Some commentators argued that this was precisely the kind of judicial activism for which conservatives used to criticise the Warren and Burger Courts.[24]

During the 1991–92 term a group of moderate conservatives, O'Connor, Kennedy and Souter, were seen as significant in resisting a trend further to the right and, in a number of cases, they parted from the more conservatives justices, Rehnquist, Scalia and Thomas. However, by the 1994–95 session, O'Connor and Kennedy were voting more consistently with the other conservatives, providing a five-member bloc that formed a majority in the most important cases that year, while Souter adopted a more moderate liberal stance on many issues. The conservatives were increasingly assertive both in setting out their views and in questioning recent practices in a number of controversial areas, such as the proper balance between federal and state governments and race issues. Stevens and Souter were often to be found voting with the two Clinton appointees, Ginsburg and Breyer.[25]

Although labels and categories of judges can be criticised for over-simplification and majorities and minorities within the Court vary according to the types of cases being considered, it is possible to view the Supreme Court today as comprising three main groupings. As Robert McKeever has pointed out, by the standards of the 1960s none of the current justices would qualify as liberals. The four justices, Stevens, Souter, Ginsburg and Breyer can best be described as 'moderate liberals'; O'Connor and Kennedy are 'moderate conservatives' and Rehnquist, Scalia and Thomas may be called 'radical conservatives'.[26] Therefore the Rehnquist Court, while decidedly more conservative than the Warren and Burger Courts, does not have a consistent majority for the more far-reaching conservative positions favoured by some justices and by most ideological conservative activists in the country and in Congress. In practice the more centrist judges, Kennedy and in particular O'Connor, have exercised considerable influence on the direction the Court has taken on many key issues and have acted as a restraint on their more radical colleagues.

Major decisions of the Burger and Rehnquist Courts

We shall now consider some of the most significant judgments made in a number of policy areas by the Supreme Court in the years since the retirement of Earl Warren.

1 Segregation and race relations. Whereas the Warren Court had made separation of the races sanctioned by law (*de iure* segregation) unconstitutional, the Burger Court had to wrestle with the more difficult problem of how to deal with *de facto* segregation. In many Northern cities, for example, schools were segregated in practice principally as a result of residential patterns with blacks and whites living in different areas and whites moving increasingly to the suburbs. If children continued to go to the nearest neighbourhood schools segregation would remain in place. The Court took the view that where *de facto* segregation resulted from discriminatory decisions by public bodies then it was illegal. The Court accepted in *Swann* v. *Charlotte Mecklenberg Board of Education* (1971) that bussing children was a proper means of dealing with schools that are segregated as a result of official bias, and in 1976 it broadened the ban on segregated schools to include private as well as state-financed institutions. On the other hand, the Court turned down plans to solve city school segregation by bussing children between city centres and suburbs in a number of judgments between 1974 and 1977. These were based on the grounds that no clear intention to discriminate had been proven.

In its first attempt to influence the Court on the issue of school bussing for desegregation the Reagan administration in 1983 sought to persuade the Court to use a Nashville case as the vehicle for reconsidering its support for the practice. However, the justices refused to do so, leaving intact a lower court decision that required more bussing of Nashville pupils.

The Court also had to consider how far affirmative action programmes which were intended to help minority groups achieve equal opportunities in education, jobs and housing after centuries of discrimination, were constitutional. It struggled to produce a clear and consistent policy on affirmative action. Justices had to examine the meaning of the 'equal protection' clause of the Fourteenth Amendment and how far to adopt 'strict scrutiny' in reviewing such programmes; that is, how far they serve a compelling governmental goal and whether they are virtually indispensable in achieving that goal. Conservatives argued that programmes which favoured minorities should be subject to the same strict scrutiny test as those that used to favour whites. Liberals wanted to adopt a more lenient set of criteria for review.[27]

In 1977 the Supreme Court considered the case of *Regents of the University of California* v. *Allan Bakke*. Bakke claimed that he had been discriminated against because, as a white male, he was unable to obtain one of 16 quota places set aside out of a 100 at Davis Medical School for ethnic minorities, despite the fact that he had achieved higher test scores than some of the students accepted for these places. He believed that he was a victim of 'reverse discrimination' and the case had broad implications for the future enrolment policies in American higher education and 'affirmative action' programmes designed to help minorities. In an important judgment in June 1978 the Supreme Court found that Bakke had been illegally discriminated against because he was white and ordered the medical school to admit him. The Court's decision, by a 5–4 majority, yielded six separate opinions. It ruled that an institution could take race into account in future admissions selection, but that this was not to be the sole determining factor. Justice Powell in the leading opinion said that the state had a substantial interest in a properly devised admissions programme 'involving the competitive consideration of race and ethnic origin'.

When dealing with job discrimination the Court decided in June 1977 that seniority systems used within many companies were not necessarily illegal even if their effect was to favour white males over others in bidding for promotions, protection from redundancies and other benefits of years in the job. This weakened the basis for further 'past discrimination' suits which had been pressed by minority ethnic groups in recent years. The Rehnquist Court gave five important rulings in the 1988–89 session that demonstrated the new conservative majority. All five decisions were settled by a 5–4 majority and narrowed the options and redress available to minorities and women facing employment discrimination. For example, in *Wards Cove Packing Co. Inc* v. *Antonio* the Court held that the burden is on plaintiffs to prove that an employer has no business necessity for practices with discriminating effects, whereas previously the employer had to prove the practice was necessary. In *City of Richmond* v. *Croson* the Court invalidated the practice of cities setting aside a certain number of contracts for minority-owned businesses. The majority also stated that all state and local government affirmative action programmes must be subjected to strict scrutiny. In another case involving firemen in Birmingham, Alabama the Court changed procedures to allow challenges by white workers to affirmative action programmes.

Congress subsequently passed the 1991 Civil Rights Act to reverse the results of the Rehnquist Court decisions on employment discrimination. The conservative majority on the Court made it increasingly clear that they were uncomfortable with government classifications based on race. They argued that at the heart of the Constitution's guarantee of equal protection lies the requirement that the government must treat citizens as individuals, not simply as components of a racial, religious, sexual or national class. Thus in the 1994–95 session, in the case of *Adarand* v. *Peña*, the Court set in motion a rolling back of federal affirmative action by insisting that federal, as well as state, programmes must be reviewed using strict scrutiny criteria. Clarence Thomas, the black conservative justice who became increasingly vocal during this session, declared that 'It never ceases to amaze me that the courts are so willing to assume that anything predominantly black must be inferior'.

The conservatives' 'colour-blind' ideal was also exemplified by their striking down of 'majority-minority' congressional districts. Following the 1990 census which reapportioned the 435 congressional seats, many states redrew their district lines under the provisions of the 1965 Voting Rights Act which requires them to safeguard the influence of minority voters. A number of states, either on their own initiative or under pressure from the Justice Department, created districts in which minorities made up the majority of electors. In so doing, the boundaries were often drawn so that the constituencies lacked geographical compactness or community of interest. In *Voinovich* v. *Quilter* (1993), the Court accepted the right of states to concentrate racial minorities in certain voting districts in order to secure minority representation. However, in another case in the same year, *Shaw* v. *Reno*, the Justices warned that race-conscious redistricting could sometimes constitute unfair discrimination against white voters and, while it did not strike down the North Carolina districts in question, it cast doubt on 'bizarrely shaped' constituencies and said that they must be closely scrutinised. In 1995, in *Miller* v. *Johnson*, the Court went further and rejected Georgia's redistricting map, and in 1996 it decided by 5–4 to strike down three disputed districts in Texas (*Bush* v. *Vera*) and others in North Carolina (*Shaw* v. *Hunt*), where a group of white voters were continuing with a challenge to their state's congressional map. In the *Miller* case Justice Kennedy endorsed the goal of ridding America of racial discrimination but warned, 'The end is neither assured nor well-served by carving the electorate into racial blocs', while Justice O'Connor spoke disparagingly of 'apartheid'.

The Court concluded that, in balancing the requirements of the Voting Rights Act and the constitutional provision of equal protection, states should avoid making race the predominant factor in redistricting; to do so overstepped the line and became racial gerrymandering. On the other hand, the justices did not rule out race-conscious redistricting altogether, but said that the states had to present a compelling justification for such action. The problem has since been that, after a decade of rulings on the issue, states such as North Carolina are still uncertain as to how to draw district boundaries that satisfy the Voting Rights Act by providing opportunities for minorities to get elected to Congress while at the same time complying with the Court's criteria.[28]

2 Equal representation and reapportionment. In 1983 the Court reaffirmed the importance of the 'one person, one vote' principle in drawing the boundaries for congressional
districts. It rejected a New Jersey plan in which the difference between the largest and
smallest constituencies was less than 1 per cent, a mere 3,674 electors. However, despite
the strict application of the principle, states have been allowed more flexibility in drawing
the districts for their own legislatures. The Burger Court in practice showed greater
deference to the states responsible for reapportionment by placing the burden of proof to
those challenging inequalities of electors between districts.

3 The rights of the accused and law and order issues. In this area more than any other
the Burger Court followed a more conservative approach than the Warren Court, and
under William Rehnquist this tendency has been even more marked.

In *Harris* v. *New York* (1971), the Justices decided that confessions extracted in
violation of the rule set out in *Miranda* v. *Arizona* could be used for the limited purpose
of helping jurors decide whether the defendant was lying on the witness stand. It also
ruled that the right of counsel does not apply to a confrontation between suspect and
victim, arranged by the police prior to the lodging of formal charges.

In 1984 the Court approved the first exception since 1966 to the rule set out in *Miranda*
v. *Arizona* that suspects must be advised of their rights before they may be questioned. The
Court held that in some situations considerations of public safety may require that a police
officer question a suspect first – for example, about the whereabouts of a weapon – and
only then inform him of his constitutional rights. However, later that year the Court
reaffirmed that the *Miranda* warnings of the rights to remain silent and to the aid of a
lawyer apply to questioning of all persons in custody regardless of the seriousness of
their alleged offence. Although people may be questioned briefly, for example, over a traffic
violation without being informed of these rights, once arrested this must be done
immediately.

Also in 1984 the Court approved a relaxation of the controversial 'exclusionary rule',
first enunciated 70 years before, which bans the use of illegally obtained evidence in court.
The Reagan administration backed the arguments of state prosecutors that it was time to
relax major Warren Court rulings denying prosecutors the use of certain evidence. The
Court approved two major exceptions to the exclusionary rule: the first provided that
such evidence may be used if it is clear that it would have inevitably been discovered for
reasons independent of improper police conduct and later in the term the justices gave
prosecutors what they had been wanting for almost two decades, a 'good faith' exception
to the rule. They determined that, when police conduct a search based on a warrant, only
to find out later that the warrant was in some way defective, the evidence obtained may
still be used in court. The Burger Court's approach was well demonstrated by the fact
that in the 1982–83 session it resolved nine cases in which searches by law enforcement
agencies were challenged as unconstitutional. In seven the Court upheld the search or
arrest at issue and in an eighth upheld the police practice in general while finding that in
the particular case the suspect's rights had been infringed.

In the 1972 case of *Thurman* v. *Georgia* the Supreme Court struck down by a 5–4
majority all existing state death penalty laws. Whereas two of the judges were opposed
to capital punishment in principle and regarded it as unconstitutional under the Eighth
Amendment's ban on 'cruel and unusual punishments', others in the majority were
convinced by arguments that its implementation in the states was in many respects
arbitrary and unfair. Four years later in *Gregg* v. *Georgia* (1976) states were given back
their discretion as to whether to impose the death penalty after many had reformed their

procedures. The *Gregg* ruling by the Court accepted the constitutionality of these revised laws, opening the way to its use in 38 states that have since adopted the penalty. Since 1976 the Court has generally restricted challenges to the practice and restricted the grounds for appeal.

However, despite its reputation for taking a harder line on law and order questions, the Burger Court also extended the right of counsel for poor defendants to include those facing minor as well as serious criminal charges and in 1981 limited the right of police to question a suspect before his lawyer arrives. In 1983 it struck down as unconstitutionally vague a California law that permitted police to arrest anyone on suspicion of a crime who did not provide them with reliable identification, saying that the law left the police too much discretion. In the same session the Court also held that it was unconstitutionally cruel and unusual punishment for South Dakota to jail for life, without possibility of parole, a man convicted of seven relatively minor and non-violent crimes.

The Rehnquist Court decided in 1989 that the government may seize a criminal defendant's assets that might have been used to pay attorneys' fees. Following congressional legislation to allow forfeiture of assets from organised crime and drug-trafficking the Court rejected arguments that defendants' rights to due process and a choice of lawyer would be violated by such a seizure. In the same year the Court decided by 5–4 that the constitutional ban on 'cruel and unusual punishments' does not forbid the execution of youths who commit crimes at 16 or 17 years of age; nor does it automatically prohibit capital punishment for people who are mentally retarded, decisions which not surprisingly aroused considerable criticism.

In another case in 1989 the Court decided that the police need not use 'the exact form' of the *Miranda* warnings to inform arrested suspects of their rights but, in the case of *Dickerson* v. *United States* (2000), a 7–2 majority strongly affirmed the constitutional requirement set out in *Miranda*. It struck down a federal law that made police failure to administer such warnings as only one factor to be considered by the courts when determining the validity of a confession. Several justices, including Chief Justice Rehnquist who had been publicly sceptical about *Miranda*, joined the majority in what was to many observers the most surprising decision of the session. The Court held that *Miranda* had provided a 'constitutional rule' that could only be overridden by the Court and not by Congress.

In 1991 the Court decided in *Arizona* v. *Fulimante* by 5–4 that a coerced confession used at a trial does not automatically taint a conviction (reversing a 1967 decision) and by 6–3 that the impact of a crime on victims and their families could be taken into account in sentencing a person convicted of murder. In *Harmelin* v. *Michigan* it ruled by 5–4 that a state may require life in prison without parole for a first-time drug offence without violating the Constitution's ban on 'cruel and unusual punishments'. However, Justices did agree in the 1993 case of *Helling* v. *McKinney* that an inmate in a Nevada state prison who was forced to share a cell with a heavy smoker was exposed to an unreasonable health risk and that his Eighth Amendment rights had been infringed.

By 2000 the death penalty issue had again become controversial, with DNA tests throwing doubt on the convictions of some of those on Death Row. Governor George Ryan of Illinois, who had been in favour of the death penalty, ordered a moratorium on further executions in his state, while Justice O'Connor expressed her concern that some innocent people were being executed. Polls indicated that public support for capital punishment, which stood at 80 per cent in 1994, had fallen to 65 per cent by 2001. In June 2002 the Supreme Court made two significant rulings on the implementation of the death penalty. In the first it made the execution of mentally retarded prisoners unconstitutional on Eighth Amendment grounds, reversing the 1989 decision referred to above. The majority argued that changing public views on the issue made such punishment unacceptable. In the second case the Court argued that juries and not judges must decide if defendants should receive the death penalty. The justices decided by 7–2 that a death penalty imposed by a judge was unconstitutional because it deprived the accused of his right to a trial by a jury of his peers, as required by the Sixth Amendment. Nine states of the 38 that allow the death penalty were affected by the ruling and were forced to review the way their laws operated.

4 Religion and the state. The relationship between church and state again became a prominent issue in American politics in the 1980s. President Reagan on many occasions expressed his view that the saying of prayers in America's public schools should be permitted and he backed a proposed constitutional amendment that would have reversed the Supreme Court decisions of the 1960s. The Supreme Court dealt with a number of cases in this area which have fallen into four main categories: so-called 'parochaid' cases which involve the question of public money supporting private parochial or religious schools, those relating to school prayer, cases which had at issue the use of public buildings by religious groups and those concerning other aspects of the free exercise of religious beliefs.

Generally the Burger Court maintained the view of its predecessor that the Constitution requires a 'high wall' of separation between church and state and that government should demonstrate a neutrality to religion, neither promoting nor hindering a particular faith or faith generally. On religious issues the Rehnquist Court could be said to be divided between 'separationists' who continued to assert the views of the Warren and Burger Courts and those 'accommodationists' who advocated some relaxation of the rules to allow more flexibility in relations between church and state.

In the case of public funding to religious organisations, the Burger Court set out a three-part test in the case of *Lemon* v. *Kurtzman* (1971); it must have a secular purpose, it must have a primary effect of neither advancing nor inhibiting religion and it must not foster too close a relationship between government and religious institutions. The Court reviewed at least a dozen different forms of aid to parochial schools and in only one or two cases did it find such support from the public purse permissible. For example, in 1985 the Court ruled that it was unconstitutional for New York City and Grand Rapids, Michigan to pay teachers who went into private parochial schools to teach remedial classes or provide counselling services, on the basis that such arrangements fostered 'an excessive entanglement between church and state'. One of the exceptions which the Court allowed in the 1982–83 session was a Minnesota law which provided for a state tax credit for tuition fees, transport and textbooks for parents of children at *both* private and public schools. In a major departure from previous practice, the Rehnquist Court allowed the provision by a public authority of a sign-language interpreter for a deaf student who was attending a religious school (*Zobrest* v. *Catalina Foothills School District* 1993). Since then the Court has been more sympathetic to such arrangements. In *Agostini* v. *Felton* (1997) it reversed its 1985 decision and allowed federally funded school teachers to provide remedial classes for students in church-run schools. In 2000 the Court held in *Mitchell* v. *Helms* that federal education programmes could provide materials such as library books and computers to a religious school if the same aid is available to all qualifying schools. The most important issue was neutrality and the government could neither favour nor disfavour religion in providing such material support. In 2002 the Court ruled by 5–4 that vouchers paid for by public taxation which allowed children from poor homes to attend private schools were permissable even if they could be used in religious schools. The case involved 4,500 children in an Ohio school district who could attend 41 church schools as well as other private institutions. The justices argued that vouchers did not amount to the sponsoring of indoctrination as parents had a choice as to whether they sent their children to religious schools. This case was also seen as a victory for President Bush who had made school vouchers a central plank of his education policy in the 2000 campaign.

In 1985 the Court declared unconstitutional an Alabama law authorising a moment of silence for meditation or voluntary prayer in public schools. Advocates of school prayer felt that the concept of silent prayer might have been more acceptable to the Court than the recital of prayers by a class, which the previous year the Court had reaffirmed as unconstitutional, but the justices still insisted that it infringed their neutrality rule. In 1993 the Court decided that prayers may be said at high school graduation ceremonies if they were organised and led by the students, rather than a member of the clergy, which they had ruled impermissable the previous year. However, in *Santa Fe Independent School District* v. *Jane Doe* (2000) the justices prohibited student-led prayer at public football games as unacceptably coercive.

The Court ruled in 1981 that Missouri State University had violated the freedom of religion of its students by denying the use of its campus buildings to student religious groups when allowing such use by other student groups. Other decisions have also widened public access by church groups in the use of school buildings for meetings outside school hours. For example, in 2001 in *Good News Club* v. *Milford Central School* the Court held that public elementary schools, like their high school counterparts, cannot deny religious groups access to school facilities after hours that are available to other groups.

With regard to the free exercise of religion, one of the most controversial areas has been how much latitude a government has to regulate activities central to a religious group's beliefs. For many years the Court made it difficult for government to do so by requiring that it prove a 'compelling state interest' for such a restriction. The standard was later reduced to allow regulation if the government can show that the rule serves a broader purpose and is neutral with regard to religion. In *Employment Division* v. *Smith* (1990) the Court determined that it was not a violation of the Constitution when a criminal law that applies to all people incidentally infringes upon the free expression of religion of some. In this case two workers were dismissed for using an illegal drug that is part of a sacrificial practice of some Indian tribes. The case established the neutrality test. In 1993 Congress attempted to reverse this doctrine by passing the Religious Freedom Restoration Act but the Court declared this statute unconstitutional in *City of Boerne* v. *Flores* (1997) (see Chapter 8).

However, the Court has also made decisions which strongly support the freedom of people to practise their religion even if they offend the majority of the public. In 1993 the Justices ruled unanimously that a Florida city had acted unconstitutionally in banning animal sacrifices because it was a direct attack on the religious practices and free exercise of religion by adherents of Santeria, most of whom were Cuban immigrants. Anthony Kennedy wrote for the Court:

> Legislators may not devise mechanisms, overt or disguised, designed to persecute or oppress a religion or its practices.[29]

5 *First Amendment freedoms.* The Supreme Court under both Burger and Rehnquist has generally given considerable protection to the right of free expression and has not hesitated to strike down laws which appear to unduly infringe upon the First Amendment rights of individuals and groups. For example, the justices rejected a federal law which banned editorial comment on public broadcasting television channels as an infringement of freedom of speech of broadcasters and also struck down a $1,000 limit on the independent expenditures by pressure group political action committees in presidential election campaigns. Justice Rehnquist writing for the Court wrote that this was 'like allowing a speaker in a public hall to express his views while denying him the use of an amplifying system'. In 1996 a 7–2 majority in *Colorado Republican Federal Campaign Committee* v. *FEC* ruled that political parties could spend as much money as they wished in congressional races, so long as they acted without coordinating their contributions with candidates' campaigns, thus giving them the same rights as pressure groups in making independent expenditures. In 2001 the Court held in *Legal Services Corporation* v. *Velazquez* that a regulation which prohibited lawyers working for the Legal Service Corporation, a government agency, from challenging welfare payments on behalf of poor clients violated the free speech guarantee, as well as denying the clients full legal representation.

In two controversial 5–4 decisions in 1989 and 1990 the Court supported the right of a member of the Revolutionary Communist Youth Brigade to burn the American flag, saying that the action was protected under the First Amendment's freedom of speech provision. The judges struck down as unconstitutional federal and state laws prohibiting desecration of the flag. The Supreme Court also decided unanimously that a 1988 federal law banning so-called dial-a-porn telephone messages was drawn too widely and also violated the First Amendment.

In 1997 the Court struck down a central part of the 1996 telecommunications legislation which banned the use of the Internet or online services to disseminate indecent or patently offensive material which might be seen by minors. In *Reno* v. *ACLU* the civil liberties group argued that such restrictions were an unconstitutional infringement of the First Amendment. In 2000 another part of the same legislation was invalidated. The requirement that cable television operators completely scramble signals from adult entertainment channels to prevent children from viewing was judged to be too restrictive and alternative methods to block the signal to households that requested it was held by the Court to be accomplishing the same goal but without interfering with the First Amendment guarantee of free expression.

The Supreme Court also considered in 2000 the case of *Boy Scouts of America* v. *Dale* which involved a scout organisation which removed a homosexual scoutmaster. The New Jersey Supreme Court decided that this action was contrary to the state's law which prohibited discrimination on the grounds of sexual orientation. The US Supreme Court, however, reversed the judgment, arguing that forcing the organisation to retain a scoutmaster whose behaviour conflicted with its moral values unduly infringed the Boy Scouts' freedom of association.

6 *Abortion and privacy cases.* The constitutional right to privacy was first cited in the case of *Griswold* v. *Connecticut* (1965) when the Supreme Court struck down a state law which prohibited the use of contraception. The majority argued that specific guarantees in the Bill of Rights such as the Fourth Amendment's protection against 'unreasonable searches and seizures' demonstrated a concern with privacy and that 'zones of privacy' had been created by the Constitution even though no such specific words were used. In

the landmark case of *Roe* v. *Wade* (1973) the Court by 7–2 voted to find a new right to abortion based on this.[30] Regulation of abortion had up to this time been left to the states and a wide variety of laws existed in different parts of the country. Henceforth governments could not prevent a woman from having an abortion in the first three months (or trimester) of her pregnancy; in the second trimester the state may regulate abortion 'to the extent that the regulation reasonably relates to the preservation and protection of maternal health', for example, by licensing physicians or abortion clinics. In the final three months when the foetus could survive outside the womb the state may ban abortion except when it is necessary to preserve the health or life of the mother.

The judicial arguments over abortion have taken place against a background of bitter disagreement between 'pro-life' and 'pro-choice' advocates. Fundamentalist positions leave little or no room for compromise between those who feel most strongly on the issue, making it one of the most divisive in American politics.

The *Roe* decision left the states with certain regulatory powers and those in which there was strong pro-life sentiment passed statutes designed to deter and discourage women from exercising their constitutional right to an abortion. The Supreme Court struck down state laws or city ordinances which required certain information to be given to a woman considering an abortion that was clearly designed to discourage her from going ahead with the procedure (*Akron* v. *Akron Center for Reproductive Health*, 1983). Similar regulations were rejected in 1986 in *Thornburgh* v. *American College of Obstetricians*. However, Justice O'Connor stated that the resolution of this case did not require a full reconsideration of *Roe*.

In 1989 the Supreme Court upheld a Missouri law in *Webster* v. *Reproductive Health Services* that banned the use of state facilities and prohibited state employees from performing abortions on the ground that it 'leaves a pregnant woman with the same choices as if the state had chosen not to operate any public hospitals at all'. In *Rust* v. *Sullivan* (1991) the Court upheld federal regulations barring workers at publicly funded clinics from counselling pregnant women about abortion (rules that were reversed by the new Clinton administration in 1993).

In the 1992 case of *Planned Parenthood of Southeastern Pennsylvania* v. *Casey* Justices took the middle way on the abortion issue by upholding restrictions (waiting periods and parental notification requirements) by the state of Pennsylvania as legal, while at the same time affirming a woman's right to have an abortion. These decisions stopped short of reversing the *Roe* v. *Wade* decision and three of the Reagan/Bush appointees, O'Connor, Kennedy and Souter, issued a joint opinion stating that, whether the original *Roe* decision had been correct or not, it had become an established precedent which was worthy of respect. Together with the two pro-choice justices, Stevens and Blackmun (the author of the *Roe* decision), these justices reaffirmed the right to abortion by a 5–4 vote. The *Casey* decision eliminated the rigid trimester framework set out in *Roe* but banned 'undue burdens' on a woman's decision to terminate her pregnancy. In the case of *Stenberg* v. *Carhart* (2000) the Court used this argument in striking down a Nebraska law which banned late-term or 'partial birth' abortions because it did not include an exception to protect the health of the mother and because the language defining the procedure was too broad.

Another area where the right to privacy has been asserted is the issue of gay rights. In the mid-1980s about half of the states had laws which prohibited sodomy. In Georgia a man was arrested for engaging in consensual homosexual activity in the privacy of his home. In the case of *Bowers* v. *Hardwick* (1986) the Supreme Court for the first time addressed the issue but by 5–4 refused to support the case that such activity, even in private, was a protected right. It therefore left the states to decide whether such behaviour was permitted or not.

On the other hand, the Court did strike down an amendment to the Colorado state constitution, passed by voter initiative, which prohibited legislation banning discrimination against homosexuals in employment, public accommodations and health services. In *Romer* v. *Evans* (1996) the Court by 6–3 ruled that the amendment was unconstitutional because it singled out homosexuals as the one group which could not seek government protection from discriminatory practices and policies. This was clearly in conflict with the equal protection clause of the Fourteenth Amendment to the US Constitution.

7 Government relations cases. The Supreme Court throughout its history has had to settle conflicts arising from the constitutional division of powers established by the Founding Fathers, both between institutions at national level (separation of powers cases) and between the national and state governments (federalism cases). It has also had to interpret the extent to which individual governmental institutions have particular powers and they way they may exercise them.

In the earlier chapters of this text we have already discussed those affecting Congress and the presidency. For example, the cases considered by the Burger and Rehnquist Courts include those involving:

(a) the unconstitutionality of the 'congressional veto' (*Immigration and Naturalization Service* v. *Chadha*, 1983);
(b) the unconstitutionality of the 'line-item veto' (*Clinton* v. *New York City*, 1998);
(c) the issue of executive privilege in cases involving Presidents Nixon and Clinton;
(d) the question of presidential immunity to civil actions (*Clinton* v. *Jones*, 1997);
(e) the unconstitutionality of legislative term limits for Congress set by state governments (*Thornton* v. *Arkansas*, 1995).

In Chapter 8 we shall consider the Supreme Court's renewed interest in the 1990s in federalism and the acceptable limits of federal government power in relation to the states. Indeed, the willingness of the Rehnquist Court to limit the power of Congress to legislate, using the 'inter-state commerce clause' as its basis for its intervention, has been one of the most distinctive features of its jurisprudence.

Box 4.2 *Bush* v. *Gore* (2000)

The closeness of the 2000 presidential election meant that whichever candidate, George W. Bush or Al Gore, won the 25 Electoral College votes of Florida would become the next President of the United States. The day after the election the Florida Division of Elections reported that Bush had received a mere 1,784 votes more than his rival from a total of more than 5.8 million ballots cast. After a machine recount showed Bush still leading but by a reduced margin, Gore sought manual recounts of ballots in those counties which he thought might provide the additional votes he needed to win a majority in the state as a whole. There followed five weeks of challenges and counter-challenges by the two sides in the Florida state and federal courts. Bush's lawyers argued that no manual recounts were necessary and those which the Florida courts had agreed could go ahead were chosen to favour Gore. They also contended that the Florida Supreme Court's decision to alter the deadline by which results had to be certified in order for the recounts to take place was an unconstitutional interference with the right of the Florida legislature to select the state's electors and the manner in which they are appointed, under Article II of the US Constitution.

The judicial process culminated in the US Supreme Court's ruling on 12 December by 7–2 that the way the manual recount of votes in Florida was taking place violated the Constitution, and by 5–4 that it was too late to improve the procedure in order to comply with the deadline for states choosing electors for the Electoral College. The decision prevented any further action in Florida and confirmed the vote total certified on 26 November which showed Bush beating Gore by a total of 537 votes in the state. Gore formally conceded the election to Bush the next day.

In its decision the 7–2 majority found that the 8 December plan ordered by the Florida Supreme Court requiring a hand count of all the state's 'undervotes' violated the 'equal protection' clause of the Fourteenth Amendment. Florida voters were not being treated equally because different standards were being applied in different areas to evaluate ballots where the voting machines could not discern a vote. The Florida Supreme Court had instructed the county canvassing boards responsible for the count to try and discern the 'intent' of voters on ballots where the hole indicating candidate preference for President had not been completely punched through, but it had offered no uniform standard by which the boards should evaluate each ballot.

The *Bush* v. *Gore* case was the first time that the nation's highest court had taken a role in settling the winner of a presidential election; although state courts are often asked to settle disputed elections, the US Supreme Court had until 2000 avoided becoming involved in such a highly charged political issue. The fact that the decision to prevent further recounts was settled by the narrowest of majorities and that the most conservative justices supported the view which led to the election of the Republican candidate suggested to many that the Court was voting on political rather than strictly legal lines. Some critics pointed out that the majority's willingness to overturn the Florida court's decision was strangely inconsistent with its decisions on other recent federalism cases where it had asserted the rights of the states. On the other hand, other commentators argued that the case was so significant that the Supreme Court could not realistically have refused to hear it. Given the length of the delay in determining the presidential election result, the Court was acting as the final umpire in ensuring that the rules of the game were being applied fairly and at the same time providing the country with a sense of closure by resolving the issue once and for all.

The political nature of the Supreme Court

Robert McCloskey has pointed out that the Supreme Court is neither completely a judicial body nor completely a policy-making and political body; it has managed to blend both in a complex mixture.[31] It has been apparent that politics play a crucial role in the appointment, working and decision-making of the American Supreme Court and many of its judgments have had broad policy implications. What is more the federal judiciary has been forced to become involved in detailed regulation by devising remedial actions, drawing up electoral boundaries and supervising the actions of other government bodies in order to ensure that the rights it has asserted are actually granted in practice. However, the Court is limited in a number of important ways. It does depend in the main on the executive branch to enforce the law it has interpreted. The Court can also only wait and react to cases that are brought into the judicial system. Unlike the President and Congress, the Supreme Court cannot, by itself, initiate policy-making. Therefore the Court may find itself dealing with such matters as family or lifestyle issues because cases on these matters are brought before them and they are too significant to be refused judgment. This may be so, even at a time when the conservative majority tries to disclaim such an intrusive role in everyday life.[32]

Finally, the justices are aware that they are appointed to their positions and must use their powers sparingly, so that wherever possible direct confrontation is avoided with the democratically elected branches of government. The judges are part of the society within which they are working and they are subject to many of the same influences and prejudices as elected politicians, but the Court's high standing with the public would be threatened if it resisted for long periods clear trends in public opinion. Who the Court's friends and enemies are depends upon the nature of its decisions at any one time; it has been attacked in turn by conservative and liberal politicians. Its decisions have often been controversial and it has been in the centre of the political arena precisely because the questions it examines are in important areas of vital interest to society and democracy. Professor Archibald Cox explains why the Court has managed to command general support for its judgments as follows:

> The Court must know us better than we know ourselves . . . the roots of its decisions must already be in the nation. The aspirations voiced by the Court must be those the community is willing not only to avow but in the end to live by, for the power of the constitutional decisions rests upon the accuracy of the Court's perception of this kind of common will and upon the Court's ability, by expressing its perception, ultimately to command a consensus.[33]

Richard Hodder-Williams has argued that the legitimacy of the Court, in the sense that people accept its judgments as authoritative and its role as proper, has been threatened by three factors in recent times: the division in partisan support in the executive and legislative branches preventing a dominant political consensus in Washington on the right judgments of the Court; the increasingly open way that interest groups use litigation as part of their overall political strategy and embroil the Court in the most contested controversies of the day; and the extent to which the Reagan administration set out publicly to influence the judicial branch as a whole and the Court's jurisprudence in particular. He concludes:

> These developments appeared to pose a very real threat to the mythic role of the Supreme Court as the impartial guardian of the Constitution and thus offered a real challenge to its legitimacy.[34]

Many critics argued that the Supreme Court's unprecedented intervention in resolving the contested 2000 presidential election damaged its credibility in terms of fulfilling this historic role. Justice John Paul Stevens, a member of the minority in the case of *Bush* v. *Gore*, argued that:

> Although we may never know with complete certainty the identity of the winner of this year's presidential election, the identity of the loser is perfectly clear. It is the Nation's confidence in the judge as the impartial guardian of the rule of law.[35]

Despite these difficulties and that of finding consensus in a society that is deeply divided on many of the issues that come before it today, the role of the Supreme Court is to maintain the Constitution as a living document by interpreting it in the light of the needs of a complex modern industrialised society. The Founding Fathers could not have predicted, for example, that one day the Fourth Amendment's prohibition of 'unreasonable searches and seizures' would be used to prevent, in most cases, the police invading the privacy of the individual by the use of electronic bugging devices on telephones (*Katz* v. *United States*, 1967).

The Supreme Court is, by its nature, the one institution set up at the Philadelphia Convention that can take the long term into account as it has no elections or constituents to worry about, and for similar reasons it can protect minority rights from the prospect of a 'tyranny of the majority'.

Chapter summary

- The Supreme Court's pre-eminence in judicial matters was secured during the period when John Marshall was the Chief Justice (1801–35). In the case of *Marbury* v. *Madison* (1803) the Supreme Court's power of judicial review was first established, whereby the Court could declare null and void any statute or action by government that it believed to be in conflict with the supreme law of the US Constitution.

- The Supreme Court is at the apex of the federal judicial system which comprises district courts, each based within one state, and regional appeals courts. The Supreme Court hears only a small percentage of the approximately 9,000 appeals that are filed each year.

- All federal judges are nominated by the President and have to be confirmed by the Senate. The convention of senatorial courtesy is important for the appointment of district court judges who hear cases in one state. The process of selecting and approving judges has been increasingly affected by partisan politics and disputes between the elected branches, particularly in periods of divided party control. This has led to delays in appointments being confirmed and posts remaining unfilled for long periods.

- The appointment of Supreme Court justices has always been a highly political matter, with Presidents seeking to extend their influence over the political system long after they have left office themselves through their selection of judges to the highest court. Presidents who have had the opportunity to make several appointments have been able to change the political balance among the justices, thus affecting the types of judicial decisions on important matters of public policy. With a number of elderly justices on the Supreme Court, George W. Bush appeared likely to have the opportunity to fill one or more of the positions during his term.

- During the period 1953–69 when Earl Warren was the Chief Justice the Supreme Court earned a reputation for liberal judicial activism. It was prepared to take up issues that the elected branches of government found too sensitive or politically unpopular to handle. These included the rights of accused persons, reapportionment of electoral districts, church–state relations, First Amendment rights and, most notably, race relations. The Court's impact on American society is nowhere better demonstrated than by its decision in *Brown* v. *Board of Education* (1954) when it declared that racial segregation was unconstitutional because it conflicted with the 'equal protection' clause of the Fourteenth Amendment.

- Appointments of Supreme Court justices by Republican Presidents from the 1970s onwards led to a gradual shift in the balance of power within the Court with the conservative judges becoming a majority. The Rehnquist Court since 1986 has reflected this change in composition by the nature of its decisions. However, the most conservative justices (Rehnquist himself, Scalia and Thomas) cannot always rely upon the support of O'Connor and Kennedy to form a majority. Therefore, for example, in recent years a 5–4 majority has reaffirmed the right to an abortion first established in *Roe* v. *Wade* some 30 years earlier.

Think points

• What is judicial review and why has it been so important in America's constitutional and political development?
• Why have the appointments to the federal judiciary become so politically contentious?
• Is the Supreme Court principally a judicial or a political body?
• As an appointed and non-elected body does the Supreme Court exercise too much power?

Some further reading

Henry J. Abraham and Barbara A. Parry, *Freedom and the Court* (Oxford University Press 1998)

Lawrence Baum, *The Supreme Court* (Congressional Quarterly Press 1995)

Martin Belsky (ed.), *The Rehnquist Court: A Retrospective* (Oxford University Press 2001)

Edward Lazarus, *Closed Chambers* (Times Books 1998)

Robert McKeever, *Raw Judicial Power? The Supreme Court and American Society* (Manchester University Press 1993)

Robert McKeever, *The United States Supreme Court: A Political and Legal Analysis* (Manchester University Press 1997)

Robert McKeever, 'In Search of a Role: The Supreme Court in a Post-Civil Rights Era', in *American Politics: 2000 and Beyond*, Alan Grant (ed.) (Ashgate 2000)

David M. O'Brien, *Storm Center: The Supreme Court in American Politics* (Norton 1993)

David G. Savage, *Turning Right: the Making of the Rehnquist Supreme Court* (Wiley 1993)

Elder Witt, *The Supreme Court at Work* (Congressional Quarterly Press 1990)

Bob Woodward and Scott Armstrong, *The Brethren – Inside the Supreme Court* (Secker and Warburg 1980)

Tinsley Yarbrough, *The Rehnquist Court and the Constitution* (Oxford University Press 2001)

Weblinks

The Supreme Court: www.supremecourtus.gov
The Federal Judiciary: www.uscourts.gov
Findlaw (text of Supreme Court rulings): www.findlaw.com
Oyez Oyez Oyez (Northwestern University site on the Supreme Court): www.oyez.nwu.edu
Cornell Legal Information Institute (Cornell University): www.supct.law.cornell.edu/supct

5 Pressure group politics

We have observed already that politics in the United States can be seen as a continuous process of different groups competing to persuade the formal institutions to reflect their interests and objectives in the official policies of the nation, state or locality.[1] Having examined the working of the three branches of the federal government, it is now time to consider how these groups operate, what contribution they make to the political process, and how the political system provides checks on their power.

Pressure groups and political parties are often described as 'informal' political institutions, because although they are not mentioned in the Constitution as official bodies, an understanding of their role in the system is essential for a proper appreciation of policy-making. Indeed, in our consideration of the formal institutions the importance of these bodies should already have been clear. Pressure groups are organised attempts to influence government policy rather than institutions which try to control the government and enter candidates in elections for office. In this respect they are different from parties, which are examined in the next chapter. Pressure groups should also be distinguished from the many social groups that exist to promote objectives that have no political content – sports clubs, operatic societies, rotary clubs, parent-teacher associations and private charities are formed by groups of people who have similar interests, but their common activities do not normally involve government or attempts to influence its policy. On the other hand, if there is the danger of a major highway being built across the sports club's field, or if the government proposes to change the tax status of a charity, then even these groups may enter the political arena.

Pressure groups have an important role in the political system; they are conveyors of demands from the ordinary American citizens to the decision-makers, intermediaries that can provide both ideas and reactions to government policies. In a democratic system, the importance of such bodies in the two-way process of political communication can hardly be overemphasised.

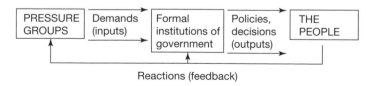

Figure 5.1 Pressure groups in the political system

The American system and pressure group activity

It has often been said that the American political system is particularly open to pressure group influence, and even in the early nineteenth century Alexis De Tocqueville commented:

> Better use has been made of association and this powerful instrument of action has been applied to more varied aims in America than anywhere else in the world.[2]

What was evident to a European visitor to the United States in those days has continued to be a factor of major political importance as a result of a number of social, cultural and institutional influences.

1 The diversity of American society. In Chapter 1 it was emphasised that America is a country of rich social diversity. The many ethnic and national backgrounds of its people, the different interests of its regions and the complexity of its economy have all contributed to making the United States a country ripe for the development of competing pressure groups. Since De Tocqueville wrote his major works, America has had widespread and heterogeneous immigration, a tremendous growth in its territory, and the movement from a fairly simple agrarian society to a vastly more complicated industrial and technological nation. With greater division of labour and economic specialisation, and with increasing government intervention which has accompanied industrialisation, the number and variety of groups affected by public policy who wish to protect their interests have grown dramatically. Groups formed to represent both the recipients and the providers of public services in areas such as health and welfare have a strong interest in the continuance and possible expansion of those services.

2 The political culture. The American political culture has encouraged the growth of pressure groups as legitimate methods of free expression in a democracy. The constitutional guarantees of free speech and press and, most particularly, freedom of assembly are of vital importance to the development of such associations, and in states which do not allow these rights pressure groups have been effectively curtailed. The acceptance by Americans of pressure groups is based on the belief that private groups have a right to be heard as long as they work within the law and the constitutional system. There is little support for the view that such groups are inimical to the public interest and are destructive of national unity, an approach which finds support in many countries where pressure groups are discouraged or work only under severe social and legal constraints.

3 The decentralised nature of American government. The organisation of the formal governmental institutions also provides many opportunities for pressure groups to exert influence in the policy-making process. Pressure groups inevitably seek contacts with those decision-makers who have the power to affect their particular interests, and the decentralised and diffuse nature of American government has led to there being many 'access points' which are open to these organisations. The separation of powers means that the legislature, executive and judiciary, as well as bodies such as independent regulatory commissions, can all have a crucial role in particular areas of policy. The federal structure entails possible approaches to the national or state authorities, or to a variety of local government bodies. The multiplicity of official positions at various levels in America has resulted in there being more 'access points' than in other political systems, but they are not all of equal importance to pressure groups. Those interested in defence or foreign policy will obviously see that most decisions in these areas are made in Washington, and therefore they will concentrate on the Defense and State Departments and on Congressmen who have seats on the relevant House and Senate committees. On the other hand, groups interested in education will find that access to local authorities, such as school boards, will probably be as important, and in some cases more so, than contacts in the state capital or in Washington. Changes in Congress in the 1970s and 1980s made the legislative process both more open and more complex. The opening up of committee sessions to public scrutiny and the televising of both chambers means that groups can monitor the activities of legislators more closely. At the same time decentralisation of authority to sub-committees and overlapping jurisdiction on matters such as environmental or foreign and trade policy within congressional committees (as well as executive departments and agencies) has provided more access points for groups to approach. However, it has also made the task of influencing policy more complicated and uncertain in terms of outcome achieved, as they have to spread their efforts across a number of decision makers.

4 *The weakness of party.* One other side-effect of the separation of powers system and localised politics is that party cohesion among Congressmen and state legislators has tended to be weaker than in centralised parliamentary systems, although we have seen in Chapter 2 that partisan voting has increased in recent times. Legislators in America are able to take independent stands on policy issues, knowing that their votes will not affect the existence or future of the executive, and this freedom means that they are more useful to pressure groups. Parties cannot dictate to legislators how they must vote on major issues: neither can pressure groups, but they do have the opportunity of influencing the direction of those votes.

Many of the thousands of official decision-makers are elected and this provides further opportunities for pressure groups. Candidates for office, including those for positions such as sheriffs and coroners which are appointed in most countries, need financial resources to fight elections. Political parties face legal limitations on how much they can spend in direct support of their candidates and pressure groups can fill the gap in financing campaigns. The use of primary elections to nominate candidates for office has also taken power away from the party leaders and activists and broadened participation to a wider electorate. The need for candidate-centred organisations to obtain finance and the relatively small percentage of the electorate who use their votes in primary elections gives well-organised single-issue pressure groups a good opportunity to make their presence felt.

In many US elections voter turnout is low; in the midterm congressional races, for example, under 40 per cent of those eligible bother to go to the polls and the key to success is motivating core groups of party supporters to vote. Pressure groups can play a vital role through their 'get out the vote' efforts; this can include advertising and contacting members and activists directly to encourage them to cast their ballots. In close races these efforts can make all the difference between victory and defeat; elected members will be left in no doubt that they owe a debt of gratitude to a particular pressure group when they come to use their votes in Congress on policy matters of importance to the group.

5 *Direct democracy.* Although there is no provision in the federal Constitution for the people to vote directly on policy issues, 24 states allow proposed state laws to be placed on the ballot by citizen petition and then enacted or rejected by the electorate. The initiative process has been used more widely and on a greater range of issues in recent times. In addition referendums which allow state laws passed by the legislature to be

referred to the voters before coming into effect are also used in many states; for example, many state constitutions require tax increases to obtain voter approval and all states except Alabama demand that amendments to the constitution be submitted to the electorate in a referendum.

In 2000, 72 initiatives and 133 referendums featured on the ballot papers in 42 states. They included controversial issues such as gun control, gay marriages, the legalisation of marijuana for medical use, school choice, campaign finance controls and genetically modified food. The use of direct democracy at state and local levels allows pressure groups to organise and finance campaigns to influence public opinion and persuade ordinary citizens rather than elected representatives to make decisions the groups support. Critics of the use of initiatives and referendums argue that the process has often been hijacked by wealthy vested interests who can afford to outspend their opponents and that the campaigns frequently distort the facts and arguments on the issue.

Table 5.1 'Access points' in the American political system

	Legislature	Executive	Judicial	Other agencies
Federal	House of Representatives, Senate, committee members and chairmen	President, Cabinet Secretaries, civil servants	Supreme Court, other federal courts	Independent regulatory commissions
State	State legislature (two houses),* committee members and chairmen	Governor, department heads, state officials	State supreme court, Courts of Appeals	State commissions and agencies
Local	Councils, school boards, other local boards	Mayors, other elected officials, local government officials	Other state courts	Local commissions

* Except Nebraska.

Different types of pressure group

The literature on pressure groups, particularly in America, has often been somewhat confused by the lack of an agreed terminology among the political scientists who have studied this form of political activity. However, we shall find it useful to apply the term 'pressure group' to all those organisations concerned with political objectives, while attempting to subdivide these groups into two major categories. Those pressure groups who are primarily self-interested, and whose goals are to protect, defend and promote the interests of their own members are known as 'interest groups'. Frequently such groups have important economic power and generally they comprise the most influential pressure groups in the United States. They tend to have a clearly defined clientele which is often restricted to those with specific occupations, financial interests or qualifications. Examples of 'peak' business interest groups which seek to represent a wide range of commercial organisations include the National Association of Manufacturers and the US Chamber of Commerce which speaks for some 180,000 businesses, many belonging to local, state and regional chambers. They have been joined by the Business Round Table, representing the largest corporations, and the National Federation of Independent Business which puts forward the interests of over 600,000 small businesses. The NFIB has a strongly conservative ideology and usually opposes government regulation and subsidies. It has developed close ties with conservative Republicans and in recent years has been seen as one of the most influential pressure groups in the country. There are also numerous trade associations such as the American Petroleum Institute which speaks for the major oil companies, and the National Association of Realtors, the estate agents' group, as well as individual corporations that lobby on their own behalf.

The AFL-CIO (American Federation of Labor-Congress of Industrial Organizations) is an alliance of trade unions established in 1955 from the craft-based AFL and the industrially based CIO. As a peak organisation it represents the interests of organised labour, with over 13 million members. However, the influence of the AFL-CIO declined over the last two decades so that by the mid-1990s only 15 per cent of the workforce belonged to trade unions, less than half the proportion of the 1950s. Unions failed to win support in the Southern and Sunbelt states and there are concentrations of membership in the traditional heavy industries of the North-East. However, while unions in the private sector have been in decline, public employee unions, such as the American Federation of Teachers and the American Federation of State, County and Municipal Employees, have grown rapidly in the last two decades. The AFL-CIO saw some revival in its influence in the late 1990s under its new president, John Sweeney, who was committed to modernising the trade union movement. Its strengths continue to be the size of its overall membership, the large number of paid organisers and its huge financial resources.

Professional bodies are prominent among the ranks of interest groups; the American Medical Association is the main organisation representing doctors and has had a long history of lobbying on health issues, while we have already seen in Chapter 4 the importance of the American Bar Association, the lawyers' professional body, and how it has had influence within government, particularly over the appointment of judges.

America's farmers traditionally had considerable political influence in states where agriculture was a major part of the economy but this has reduced as the numbers working on farms have declined. The American Farm Bureau Federation is the largest of the general membership or peak groups but its influence and that of the National Farmers' Union has declined as the number of specialist commodity associations has increased. Examples include the Associated Milk Producers, the National Wool Growers' Association and the American Cattlemen's Association.

The largest pressure group in America is the American Association of Retired Persons. Founded in 1958, its membership increased from one million in 1968 to 34.8 millions by 2001, that is more than half of all Americans over 50 years of age. The 'grey lobby' has not only formidable voting power but the ability to organise immediate and effective grassroots campaigns whenever it sees a threat to, for example, social security or Medicare services. It has a large and effective lobbying operation run by its Federal Affairs Department in Washington.

The second category of pressure groups includes those who are attempting to secure political objectives which are in the interests of people other than themselves, or are concerned with promoting a cause which in their view will help society as a whole. These associations are often called 'promotional groups' based around an idea and at times a single issue with no occupational basis of membership. About a third of these groups have been formed since 1975 and have contributed to a huge expansion of pressure group activity. This growth has also included 'citizens' groups', such as neighbourhood associations and senior citizens groups, which often act as advocates on behalf of the public and as watchdogs over government agencies, and 'public interest groups' which seek to further the collective or public good without selectively benefiting their own members. Burdett A. Loomis and Allan J. Cigler claim that a 'participation revolution' has occurred as large numbers of citizens have become active in an increasingly diverse range of protest groups, citizens' organisations and specialist associations.[3] In addition to those who wish to play an active role in such bodies, increased affluence has created a large potential for 'cheque book' or 'credit card' membership, where people can make an expressive statement of support for a group at the cost of a relatively small subscription without incurring other time-consuming obligations. Loomis and Cigler note that it has been mainly white, educated, middle-class voters who contribute to citizens' groups.[4]

Common Cause, 'a national citizens' lobby' has advocated liberal reforms in the governmental and electoral systems, having been a particularly strong proponent of changes in the seniority system for congressional chairmanships and for statutory limits on campaign expenditure and public funding in elections. Common Cause was one of the most prominent public interest groups that were particularly active in the 1970s and 1980s in trying to influence policy in areas such as consumer protection, the environment, health and minority rights, often opposing the views of business corporations and government agencies. Ralph Nader, the best-known public interest lobbyist, is head of an umbrella organisation called Public Citizen which has contacts with more than a dozen organisations such as Congress Watch, the Health Research Group and the Center for Auto Safety. The League of Women Voters has also been interested in government, but on a less partisan basis; its main concerns have been to promote civic responsibility and participation in politics. The American Civil Liberties Union has taken up the cause of accused persons and has advocated reforms in the administration of justice and strongly opposed the use of capital punishment. The Sierra Club and the Friends of the Earth have been organised across the country to campaign for conservation of the environment while the National Organization for Women has been very vocal in advocating the passage of the 'Equal Rights Amendment' to the Constitution, the greater representation of women in government, and equal treatment in employment, housing and other areas. The National Association for the Advancement of Colored People and the National Urban League have been active in civil rights and racial desegregation campaigns while the 'religious right', through groups such as Christian Coalition, has emphasised 'family issues' with its strong opposition to abortion, to bans on prayers being said in state schools and to what it regards as pornographic literature and television programmes.

In recent decades there has also been the growth of 'think tanks' and policy institutes such as the Heritage Foundation, the American Enterprise Institute and the Progressive Policy Institute which have submitted arguments on a range of issues. Whereas some of the most well-established think tanks, such as the Hoover Institute and the Brookings Institution, had discernible political leanings their research has been essentially scholarly and serious. Many of the more recent think tanks have become more overtly partisan and ideological and give priority to issue advocacy.[5] There are also a variety of other ideological groups ranging from the left-wing Americans for Democratic Action to many of the 'new right' groups such as the Free Congress Foundation.

There has been a very significant increase in the number of 'single issue' groups active in American politics in recent years. They are intensively organised for or against particular policies such as abortion or gun control and have caused concern by their campaigns to unseat politicians who disagree with them on one emotional issue. They have been able to use appeals for money carefully directed at those who have been identified as sympathisers and to raise substantial funds for their cause.

Many organisations are principally interest groups but have a promotional aspect which helps them justify their objectives to the public at large. In this way they can claim that they are not merely self-interested but are concerned with the welfare of the community. Other groups are 'hybrids' in the sense that some members join to defend an economic interest while others advocate the same cause but on ideological grounds. For example, the National Rifle Association numbers among its membership those who have a direct commercial interest in selling guns and who therefore object to attempts by government to regulate the trade. However, it also has considerable support from gun owners and political conservatives who argue that the Second Amendment to the Constitution guarantees the right of citizens 'to bear arms'. These people argue that such a right is fundamental to the maintenance of a free society, that any monopoly of arms by the government could lead to a tyranny, and that regulation would take away the right of citizens to defend themselves against criminal attacks. In the mid-1990s attacks on the extremist positions taken by the NRA led to the resignation of former President George Bush and thousands of other members. With the threat of more regulation of guns in the late 1990s and the actor Charlton Heston taking over as president of the group, membership of the NRA soared to over 3.6 million in 2000. By 2001 the NRA was seen by many political observers as the most powerful pressure group in Washington, with considerable influence both within Congress and the new Bush administration (see Box 5.1).

Box 5.1 The most powerful pressure groups in Washington

Since 1997 the business magazine *Fortune* has carried out surveys to discover which pressure groups are widely regarded by those involved in Washington politics as the most influential. In 2001, for example, every member of Congress, Capitol Hill staff, senior White House aides, professional lobbyists and senior officers of lobbying firms were sent a questionnaire and asked to assess on a scale of 0–100 the political strength of 87 trade associations, trade unions and other organisations. From the responses the top pressure groups were identified. The surveys have shown remarkable consistency over the years, with only six groups having been in the top five over the period. These organisations took the top six places in the 2001 survey shown below. The AARP was first until 2001 when it was overtaken by the NRA.

Ranking 2001		Ranking 1999
1	National Rifle Association of America	2
2	American Association of Retired Persons	1
3	National Federation of Independent Business	3
4	American Israel Public Affairs Committee	4
5	American Association of Trial Lawyers	6
6	AFL-CIO	5
7	Chamber of Commerce of the United States of America	7
8	National Beer Wholesalers' Association	19
9	National Association of Realtors	15
10	National Association of Manufacturers	14

Source: *Fortune* magazine, 28 May 2001.

Methods of pressure group influence

The American political system provides numerous opportunities for pressure groups to influence the official decision-makers, but the methods used by a particular group will depend upon the objectives it is seeking to achieve and its position with regard to size, finance and the strategies of its leaders.

Electioneering

Clearly any group has an advantage if decision makers in the relevant areas are sympathetic to the organisation's interests, and many pressure groups attempt to influence the outcome of elections by advancing the campaigns of friendly politicians or trying to bring about the defeat of hostile opponents.

Fighting elections can be very expensive and many pressure groups, particularly wealthy interest groups, provide campaign contributions. The election finance reforms of the 1970s put limits on the amounts any one contributor could give but provided a vehicle – the political action committee – to circumvent the new spending restrictions. Federal law limits direct PAC contributions to $5,000 to each candidate for each election, primary or general, but there is no limit on the number of PACs that can be formed or their own independent expenditures on campaigns. Independent expenditures are those made without the knowledge of or consultation with the candidate or his managers. The great bulk of money from political action committees goes to congressional candidates who, unlike presidential candidates, are not eligible for public campaign financing (see Chapter 7).

Congressional candidates are not limited in the overall amount of money they can accept from PACs. While many pressure groups are eager to support their friends at election time they are also finding that they themselves are subject to a form of reverse lobbying in which legislators do the wining, dining and cajoling for campaign contributions. The outcome of these factors is that in 1999–2000 PACs dispensed $247.9 million to candidates in Senate and House races.[6] In total candidates for Congress spent $1,005.6 million, with the rest of the money coming from individual voters, the political parties and the candidates themselves. In Senate races 61 per cent of PAC contributions went to Republicans and 39 per cent to Democrats; in House elections the Republicans, who controlled both houses, were favoured by 51 to 49 per cent.

There was a tremendous growth in the number of PACs after the campaign finance reform of 1974 which followed the Watergate scandal. In that year 608 PACs were registered with the new Federal Election Commission. Most of the growth was in the 1970s and the peak year was 1988 when 4,268 PACs were registered. In the 1990s the number stabilised at just under 4,000. On 1 January 2003 4,027 PACs were registered with the FEC.[7] Business corporations' PACs soared from 89 to 1,528 in 2003. Their largesse is shared by both parties' candidates but with some bias to the Republicans. The 320 trade union PACs are far more partisan with almost all their contributions going to Democratic candidates.

The percentage of PAC contributions going to incumbents seeking re-election rose from 57 per cent in 1978 to 79 per cent in 1989–90, fell to 67 per cent in 1995–6 but rose again to 75 per cent in 1999–2000. This variation is explained principally by the number of open races, where no sitting member is on the ballot, in particular years. PACs contributed 14 per cent of their donations to candidates in open elections in 1999–2000, but gifts to those challenging incumbents fell to 11 per cent of the total. PACs are therefore tending to try and keep in office the members they know and with whom they feel comfortable. However, the actual percentage of PAC contributions to campaign funds varies widely. In the 1999–2000 election cycle PACs gave $193.4 million to House candidates which constituted 32 per cent of overall income, whereas they donated $51.9 million to Senate races which accounted for only 12 per cent of the total receipts. Senate candidates have larger constituencies and a more diverse range of wealthy contributors and PACs have traditionally played a more limited role than in House elections.

There was growing criticism of the amounts of special interest money involved in American election campaigns and bills were presented to Congress limiting spending by both candidates and PACs at elections. Some proposals even sought to ban PAC contributions altogether. In the 1990s this concern was exacerbated by the large amounts of 'soft money' given by pressure groups to political parties, which had no limits placed on it and was not regulated by law.[8] In Chapter 7 we shall examine the attempts to reform America's campaign finance laws.

There have been sharp differences of view concerning PACs, their role and impact on American politics. Opponents have argued that their gifts come with strings attached and that the legislative process is tainted by the buying of Congressmen's votes. PACs are also criticised for being internally undemocratic and unaccountable for their actions, for undermining the role of political parties and for the growth of divisive and negative single-issue politics. Supporters of PACs, on the other hand, argue that they are merely the modern method of channelling money to pay for expensive election campaigns, that limits and public disclosure of contributions prevent corruption and that the banning of PAC funding would simply lead to rich individuals having more influence, with more undisclosed gifts. They claim that the range of PACs reflects the diversity of American society and competition between them prevents the dominance of any particular groups. It is also argued that PACs have increased political awareness and participation among the electorate. PACs claim that their contributions at most help them to gain access to legislators and an opportunity to make their case on issues of concern to them.[9] Given the range of factors that influence congressional voting decisions (see Chapter 2), political scientists have found it very difficult to identify causation, as opposed to correlation, between PAC donations and the votes of legislators on bills.

Groups who contribute to campaign funds hope that in return they will receive a sympathetic hearing after the election but it should be noted that big money does not necessarily guarantee success at the polls for the candidate. Pressure groups can also provide something else at elections which is occasionally even more important than money – voluntary manpower. As we have seen, organisations with large memberships, such as trade unions, can provide an invaluable source of campaign workers, people who will actually mobilise the voters by knocking on doors, delivering publicity or providing transport to the polls. Christian Coalition regularly distribute millions of voter guides to churchgoers, informing them of candidates' positions on issues important to the organisation. It is also worth remembering that large numbers of individuals who identify with, or belong to, particular groups, such as Hispanics, gays or the elderly, may comprise a substantial proportion of the electorate in particular districts or states. Candidates will have to take account of the views of pressure groups that claim to speak on their behalf. The endorsement of a candidate by a group leader may also be helpful if the group has a large following, but such support from extremist or minority groups can be an embarrassment and more of a hindrance than a help to the candidate.

Lobbying

Most large pressure groups either employ full-time lobbyists in Washington or hire lobby-ists on a part-time basis to represent their interests. In 1998 $1.42 billion was spent on lobbying activities, an increase of 13 per cent on the previous year. Lobbying is the institutionalised form of the traditional right of petitioning government, and the 'professional persuaders' work permanently in Washington and the 50 state capitals, as well as communicating with local government when necessary. To be effective, a lobbyist must know the workings of the political system very well and have personal contacts with decision-makers in the relevant policy areas. It is not surprising that many lobbyists are former government officials, congressional aides who have the expertise and have built up these relationships over a number of years, or are members of prestigious Washington law firms. In 2001, 158 former members of Congress were registered as lobbyists, a 22 per cent increase on the number so employed just two years earlier.[10] They are in high demand by lobbying firms because they retain access to the Capitol's inner sanctums, such as the members' only dining room and gymnasium and even the floor of the chamber, after they have left office. The former legislators also have an intimate knowledge of congressional procedures and personalities.

The number of lobbyists has increased substantially in recent years and concern has also grown about their influence. The annual publication *Washington Representatives* listed more than 5,000 people in 1979 and by 1991 this had increased to 13,500. By 2002 an estimated 14,000 lobbyists were working in Washington. In November 1989 Congress passed a new restriction on Cabinet members, White House staff and Congressmen from lobbying former colleagues until one year after leaving office. This followed the much publicised case of Michael Deaver, the former Reagan aide, who was accused of exploit-ing his contacts with the White House on behalf of clients immediately after leaving the administration. In 1995 Congress passed new regulations tightening the rules on lobbying and banning members or their staffs from accepting gifts from pressure groups (see 'The Checks on Pressure Group Influence' below, on page 180).

It has not been only domestic pressure groups that have employed lobbyists in Washington. Foreign governments have increasingly sought to influence American foreign policy in this way to supplement their official embassy representation.The White House and federal government departments also employ a number of full-time officials whose job is to persuade Congressmen to support particular programmes. Many state and city governments maintain permanent representatives in Washington to look after their interests. Therefore, although it would be misleading to describe such formal governmental institutions as pressure groups, they do lobby on behalf of their policies.

It should be emphasised that, for private pressure groups, lobbying does not merely mean trying to persuade legislators; often it is even more important to contact and per-suade civil servants, administrators of state governments, or officials of regulatory agencies who formulate and execute policy.

Lobbyists are communication links between pressure groups and politicians and officials. They let government know the views of the group they represent, hoping to persuade decision-makers to promote these policies. They also inform the group's head-quarters of any moves or developments in government circles which may affect the organisation's position, so that leaders have an 'early warning system' and do not suddenly find themselves facing the prospect of hostile policies which have already been formulated and are too far advanced to change. Lobbyists can provide legislators with information and drafts of legislation, and their hope is that by being helpful and constructive they will be able to build a relationship of trust and mutual convenience which will pay dividends in the long term. Lester Milbrath, in his book *The Washington Lobbyists*, showed that, in the 1960s, most Congressmen felt that they obtained useful information from pressure groups on both legislation and administration, and that few felt that lobbyists tried to exert an unreasonable pressure on them.[11] Robert H. Salisbury argues that by the 1990s the increasing number of pressure groups and today's complex world of interdependent interests and policies means that it may often be unclear what the 'true interests' of a group actually are. Lobbyists have been forced to shift much of their energy and activity from advocating policies and influencing government officials to information gathering and analysis. He concludes that organisations in Washington:

> are engaged in a never-ending process of learning, assessment and calculation; and timely information, much of it available only from government, is the sine qua non of this process.[12]

Salisbury suggests that we should not ignore the extent to which pressure groups have come to Washington out of need and dependence rather than because they have influence.

Use of court litigation

The American judiciary has an important role in interpreting the Constitution and the law, and pressure groups occasionally attempt to use the courts as a method of influencing policy. An organisation can seek a court injunction as a tactical manoeuvre, for example, to delay a decision until further pressure can be exerted on the legislative and executive branches, and can also help finance and provide legal counsel for a defendant or plaintiff in a court case. The tradition of *amici curiae* (friends of the court) allows a pressure group's spokesman to give evidence to the court, thus publicising the objectives of the group. In *Brown* v. *Board of Education*, the National Association for the Advancement of Colored People saw the case as a test of the constitutionality of segregation laws in general. The American Civil Liberties Union also backed the attempt to challenge the 1974 federal election funding laws by obtaining a Supreme Court ruling that the regulations were 'unconstitutional'. In an era of divided party control of the elected branches of government, intense partisanship and narrow majorities, the courts have been seen by many pressure groups as an alternative way of promoting their causes and bypassing the slow congressional legislative process.

Business organisations have often retained prestigious law firms to represent them in the courts whenever it is necessary. Business groups tend to be frequent users of the courts because the vast amount of regulatory legislation, such as tax and anti-trust law, can often be challenged on technical or narrow legal grounds. Public interest groups have also been active in pursuing class actions and other lawsuits through the courts. We have seen in Chapter 4 the way that pressure groups increasingly use the judicial system as part of their overall political strategy and a number have sought to influence the appointment of the federal judiciary, including justices of the US Supreme Court.

Grass-roots pressure by members

Although many of the tactics used by a pressure group require initiative and action by the elite of the organisation, the leaders are aware that it can often help their cause if the feelings of the ordinary members in support of the group's policies can be demonstrated.

They can then avoid the charge that they are not representative of the mass membership, and elected politicians are impressed by the size or strength of popular support or opposition to particular policies. Pressure groups frequently urge their members to write to their Congressmen, although legislators can easily distinguish between the spontaneous messages from individual citizens and a large mailbag of similar letters which are part of a carefully orchestrated pressure group campaign. The technology of direct mailing has had a considerable impact on pressure group politics and there are companies which specialise in orchestrating telephone and mail blitzes to drum up constituent support for an issue in key congressional districts.[13] Groups have also encouraged the use of modern technology, with e-mail and fax messages to legislators complementing and to a large extent replacing traditional means of communication. The number of e-mail messages sent to members of Congress rose dramatically from 20 million in 1998 to 48 million in 2000, often overwhelming congressional offices attempting to deal with the huge influx of communications.[14]

Occasionally associations will organise demonstrations and marches in Washington or in state capitals to show the strength of feeling among their members. A large turnout will draw attention to the group's aims and television coverage will provide publicity to the wider electorate as well as obtaining the notice of the policy-makers. Following a number of shootings on school campuses the 'Million Mom' march in May 2000 was a large-scale demonstration of concern, particularly among women, about the gun culture prevalent in the United States and a call for more restrictive laws on the sale of weapons. The marches and peaceful protests of the civil rights movement in the Southern United States attracted considerable publicity and contributed to the atmosphere of reform which eventually led to the passage of the Civil Rights Act in 1964. However, demonstrations that are poorly organised or attended, or which spill over into violent confrontation can do the group's objectives far more harm than good.

Promotional groups, which may have less funds but more active members, find it more difficult to use other more direct methods and tend to use the tactic of grass-roots pressure more frequently than do interest groups who see it as a supplementary device to their more important lobbying activities, or as a last resort when they have failed to convince the decision-makers by use of other channels. Indeed single-issue groups such as the National Right to Life Committee rely upon the zealotry and commitment to the cause of their members to pursue the whole range of grass-roots methods available to influence decision makers.

Publicity and advertising

Pressure groups use public relations campaigns in order to inform the nation of their objectives and to create a favourable, or at least neutral, climate of opinion so that it will be more difficult for government adversely to regulate their activities. Although the public does not decide directly what legislation or policies are adopted at the national level, no pressure group can afford to face generally hostile public opinion for any length of time as this will eventually be reflected in the decisions of government. However, as we have seen, in states that allow referendums and initiatives on important issues direct appeals to the public have even greater significance.

The extent and actual methods of publicity will inevitably depend upon the financial position of the group. Publicity in newspapers and journals is common but television commercials are very expensive and only wealthy pressure groups are able to afford this kind of publicity. Radio provides a cheaper and in some cases more effective alternative.

While TV advertising may be used to promote a positive message about the group and its goals, in recent years there has been a huge growth in 'issue advertising', much of which has been negative in tone. The Health Insurance of America's television campaign helped to kill President Clinton's health care proposals by stirring up opposition to the plan and portraying it as an expensive, bureaucratic nightmare that would restrict patients' choice of doctors. The commercials became known as the 'Harry and Louise' ads after the fictional couple shown reading the Clinton plan and realising their health care would supposedly worsen as a result. In 1994 Americans for Limited Terms were credited with helping to defeat the then Speaker, Tom Foley, in his Washington district, by attacking his strong opposition to legislative term limits. Some groups have targeted their radio and television advertising in the districts or states of key legislators they are seeking to influence. Specialist companies also identify opinion leaders in members' home districts and recruit them to star in the commercials in the hope that their stature and influence locally will help sway legislators.[15]

Pressure groups have made extensive use of advertising during election campaigns attacking a lawmaker's record in office or his stand on particular issues while not specifically calling for the election or defeat of a candidate. The Supreme Court has determined that, unless the adverts do so, they are not covered by campaign finance laws and expenditure on them is not regulated. For example, in 1996 the AFL-CIO was estimated to have spent $20 million on commercials targeting particular Republican legislators and attacking their stands on issues such as Medicaid and the minimum wage.[16] Legislation passed in 2002 placed restrictions on the use of issue ads which mentioned candidates by name in the run-up to an election, a move that was condemned as an unconstitutional infringement on free speech by many politicians and pressure groups and which was inevitably challenged in the courts (see Chapter 7 for details).

Relations with political parties

Most pressure groups try to avoid too close an identification with a particular political party so that they may more easily work with whichever government is in power and with Congress, whatever its political composition. However, many promotional groups in particular have been increasingly involved in seeking to influence the platforms of one or both of the major political parties which are drawn up at the national conventions every four years. Groups for and against abortion, feminists for ERA, the gay rights lobby and those supporting the disabled are just some of those in evidence at party gatherings. They realise that their presence at these events will provide them with a great deal of media publicity and that if a plank advocating their cause is included in the party programme this may well strengthen their position. However, party platforms in America are not firm policy commitments in the way that British parties often treat their election manifestos and therefore inclusion does not by any means guarantee eventual legislative success.

Although Democratic candidates rely a great deal on trade union contributions for their campaign funds there have not been the close historical and institutional links that one sees in Britain between the Labour Party and the trade union movement. Organised labour (or individual unions) do on occasion support Republican candidates.

During the 1990s the Christian Right, and the Christian Coalition in particular, became an influential force within the Republican Party, having supporters in leading positions in many state parties and an estimated 25 per cent of the delegates at the 1996 national convention in San Diego as members. It spent $1 million on phone banks, advertising and direct mail to drum up support for the House Republicans' 'Contract with America' and was particularly influential in pressing legislators to enact a proposal in the document to cut tax for families with children. The Coalition was also active in ensuring that the party platform's commitment to a pro-life position on abortion was not diluted in 1996.

Violence and disorder

All the tactics we have examined so far are accepted as the normal ways in which pressure groups can influence policy so long as they stay within the law and avoid, for example, bribery or illegal industrial action. However, there are occasionally incidents when groups with extreme political opinions, or those who have been frustrated by their lack of progress through the normal channels, resort to promoting a violent demonstration or disorder so that their views may be brought to the attention of politicians and the public in a dramatic way. In a society where the mass media immediately reflect any violent confrontation or crisis, it is a certain way of obtaining publicity, if not the successful implementation of the group's goals. Militant Indians in the American Indian Movement, for example, took over and occupied the Bureau of Indian Affairs in November 1972, and a few months later seized the village of Wounded Knee in South Dakota, in protest against poverty, the federal government's policy towards the Indians, and the fact that the Bureau was run almost exclusively by white officials. In the last occupation a battle ensued between Indians and federal marshals during which two people were killed, before the Indians surrendered in May 1973.

Since the 1980s there have been a number of incidents where extreme opponents of abortion used physical intimidation and violence against clients and staff of abortion clinics. In some cases the clinics themselves have been destroyed and hospital staff murdered. The bombing of the federal office block in Oklahoma City in 1995 highlighted the clandestine activities of extremist militia groups that have been formed in certain parts of the country. Their conspiracy theories and hostility to the federal government in all its forms raised concern about the dangers of domestic terrorism being used as a political weapon. The anti-capitalist demonstration against the World Trade Organisation in Seattle in November 1999, which spilled over into violent confrontation with the police, is an example of how new technology can be used to mobilise support for events which are coordinated by a disparate array of groups. These protesters see themselves as part of a broad social movement rather than as traditional organised pressure groups.

The role of pressure groups in the American system

Pressure groups are accepted by most political scientists and politicians as being an inevitable and necessary part of the democratic process, but it is also true that they generally have a bad image with the general public who often feel that pressure groups can be harmful to representative government. What are the reasons for this apparent contradiction?

Political scientists feel that, although there are certainly defects in the way the pressure group system operates, on balance these organisations fulfil important functions for the working of American government which cannot be satisfactorily performed by other formal or informal institutions. Pressure groups carry out the function of 'interest articulation', which means that they express the views and represent the interests of specialised sections of society. Political parties inevitably have to appeal very broadly to a large number of groups and a cross-section of society in order to win elections, and consequently their programmes have often tended to be a series of rather vague compromises. Pressure groups, it is argued, are not seeking power for themselves, and they can afford to give voice to special interests without having to worry about offending voters or other groups, even though they may take these factors into account when formulating their own policies. Pressure groups not only complement the activities of parties in representing more exclusive interests, but also supplement the official geographical system of representation by an expression of functional or ideological interests and ideas. Congressmen are elected from compact geographical territories within one state and have to attempt to articulate the views of a heterogeneous population within their constituencies. It can be argued that often a section of the population who wish to give vent to their feelings or protect their common interests do not live neatly within one constituency or state. Pressure groups therefore speak on behalf of these people and provide an additional, if subordinate, tier of representation that intersects with and overlaps the official system. Trade unions, professional bodies, business associations, farmers, ethnic minorities and environmental protection groups have members all over the country and they seek to speak on behalf of interests that cut across geographical boundaries.

Pressure groups also provide, as we have seen, a great deal of information and specialised knowledge which is put at the disposal of the formal institutions. Pressure groups make a positive contribution to policy-making and administration by meeting legislators and officials on a regular basis, by submitting proposals for examination and by appearing before congressional hearings to provide evidence on specialised areas. They also act as intermediaries between government and the public, and relate the reactions of various sections of the community to official policies and current issues. Pressure groups are channels of communication by which government is kept permanently responsive to public opinion between election campaigns, as they ensure that all the 'access points' of the formal structure are fully informed on the state of the body politic.

If these positive benefits result from pressure group activity, what explains the continuing suspicion among the public? Even the name, 'pressure' group, implies to some people the use of undue or illegitimate influence, and others feel that these organisations are invariably selfish and must be advocating policies which conflict with the general or public interest, however that is construed. The media often use the term 'special interests' to suggest that certain groups have been given a special and advantaged position in the policy-making process. Perhaps the most trenchant criticism of pressure group politics is the fact that, unlike the formal system of democracy, in which there are equal voting rights, there is often grossly inequitable representation. A major problem of the pluralist system is that those groups with large memberships or financial resources tend to have a much more powerful voice and more open access to the decision-makers. Large interest groups, such as business organisations and trade unions, have, it is often argued, a disproportionate amount of influence, while others, such as the disabled, the ethnic minorities, the unemployed and low-income groups, are difficult to organise into effective pressure groups, have insufficient financial support, or are inarticulate and unable to promote and defend their interests as well. One consequence of this has been, of course, the establishment of many promotional groups so that these less powerful elements of society do not go totally unrepresented.

A second major criticism of the working of pressure group politics in America is that the diffuseness of the formal structure of government and the checks and balances in the system provide major built-in advantages to those groups who wish to preserve the *status quo* and prevent change. The possibilities of delay and obstruction in the legislative, administrative and judicial processes provide opportunities for pressure groups intent on blocking social reforms desired by the majority of the nation.

Some groups are thought by the public to be too powerful, and often criticism is levelled at the leaders of such groups not only for threatening to control an area of policy-making but also for being unaccountable to society for the way in which they exercise their authority. Elected representatives have to stand for renomination and re-election, and they can be defeated if they have used their official positions unwisely or irresponsibly. But many citizens feel that pressure group leaders are elected or appointed by a small minority of the organisation's membership and that they frequently become self-perpetuating oligarchies with little accountability to their own members, let alone the general public.

Some critics argue that America's economic performance has suffered from the increasing burden of government regulations and mounting public expenditure commitments which Congress and the executive branch have implemented as a result of pressure group influence. What is more, attempts to balance the budget have been hampered by special interests anxious to protect their particular programmes and privileges, no matter the cost to the overall public interest.

Finally, it can be said that there is fairly widespread feeling among the American public that the methods used by pressure groups to influence government are often immoral, if not actually illegal. There is much disquiet about pressure groups' large electoral contributions to candidates; even though there may be no bribery intended, the relationship between donor and recipient is liable to be the object of suspicion. The secrecy involved in pressure group lobbying activities, where negotiations take place behind closed doors in a legislator's office or a government department, also arouses fears. The public is understandably concerned about behind-the-scenes deals from which everybody apart from the decision-makers and special interests is excluded.

Although only a small minority of pressure groups ever resort to the use of violence, direct action or law-breaking to promote their goals, the great publicity which accompanies these tactics also helps to create a bad impression in the minds of the public. A riot or demonstration that leads to violence tends to linger in the memory, whereas daily consultations between government and pressure groups either are not reported by television which seeks news with a visual impact, or are easily forgotten.

The checks on pressure group influence

Although there may be some substance to public anxiety in America about the influence and methods of major interest groups, it should not be assumed that these organisations are free from political constraints and enjoy an unlimited and uncontrolled power. The system of checks and balances works not only to dilute the power of formal institutions but also to restrict the influence of pressure groups.

First, there is a decentralisation within the formal decision-making bodies created by the separation of powers system and the federal structure. Although these factors provide numerous access points and opportunities to influence government, they also act as checks on pressure groups achieving their goals. Groups find that, even if they have mobilised support in the Senate by lobbying, they may well fail to marshal sufficient votes in the House or one of its committees; if they do obtain congressional approval, a presidential veto or a government department's administering the statute in a particular way may thwart the group's objectives.

There are also a number of legal restrictions on pressure groups. The Federal Regulation of Lobbying Act (1946) required registration of lobbyists and a record of who employs them, although many groups bypassed this control by claiming that lobbying was not their 'principal purpose'. Some state governments have enacted stricter regulation laws, and there are also penalties for bribery, exerting unlawful influence on politicians and breaking election contribution laws. The general unwillingness of politicians to enact even more stringent regulation of pressure groups has stemmed from the fact that they feel that most of these organisations are generally helpful to the efficient government of the country, the difficulty of imposing meaningful restrictions without infringing on the constitutional rights of free speech, press, assembly and petition and the highly effective opposition of lobbies. Some members may also wish to keep open for themselves the possibility of a future lobbying career. However, public pressure and concern about the role of special interests spurred Congress to pass tougher lobbying registration and disclosure legislation in 1995. Under the new statute those who spend at least a fifth of their time meeting with top executive branch officials, members of Congress or their staff have to disclose the names of their clients, the issues on which they are lobbying and the amounts they are spending. The legislation exempts all grass-roots lobbying and that of tax-exempt religious organisations from the disclosure requirements in order to meet the objections that helped kill a similar bill in the 103rd Congress. Congress also adopted a $50 value limit on gifts – including meals and entertainment – that members or staff could accept from individuals or organisations and a total of $100 from any one source in a year. The previous limit had been $250 but had not included meals. However, private organisations may still pay the travel expenses and costs of trips for legislators and their aides to attend meetings, conferences and other fact-finding visits related to their duties. This is seen as an ethics loophole by many and a survey conducted by *Congressional Quarterly* found that private interests had spent nearly three million dollars on 2,042 trips for members and their staffs over a 17-month period in 1998–9.[17]

It should also be remembered that most pressure groups do not have an unrivalled influence with government. There is often the countervailing pressure of other groups with conflicting objectives: women's movements such as the National Organization for Women, who wish to see the passage of the 'Equal Rights Amendment', are opposed by those women who see it as a threat to their existing position in society; those wishing to ban nuclear energy plants are resisted by the energy and power companies. This does not mean that in all political issues the pressure groups on each side or the resources they control are equally matched. Where a threat to a section of the population exists, either from another group or from government, there is likely to be the mobilisation of that interest into a new pressure group.

Opposition from other organisations is an obvious check on pressure group influence; less obvious, perhaps, are the constraints operating within the group itself. Not all pressure groups are united and cohesive forces working in an efficient manner and taking every opportunity to advance their causes. Many organisations suffer from divisions within their membership, possibly on functional, ideological or tactical lines, which weaken the effectiveness of the groups. Internal conflicts can be enhanced by rival leaders struggling to control the group's policy or by a large and disparate membership that causes difficulties in coordination. Pressure group members may also have overlapping membership with other groups and this tends to dissipate their loyalty and dedication. Lack of money, experienced leadership or efficient administration will also be major constraints on the activities and effectiveness of a pressure group.

The mass media, of course, also provide an invaluable check on the power of pressure groups. Journalists and investigators are vigilant for any scandals, evidence of corruption or the use of intimidation by pressure groups in pursuing their goals. A pressure group uses the media to advance its cause, but all its efforts and expenditure can be wasted if there is a revelation which tarnishes the group's image in the eyes of the politicians or the public.

Public opinion can act as a constraint on the power of even the most deeply entrenched and influential pressure groups. Public suspicion means that groups' claims are often regarded with scepticism and their motives and policies are constantly being examined and questioned. Pressure groups may be able to delay action for a while, but if there is widespread public support for a particular policy, as evidenced by opinion polls and legislators' constituency soundings, it may prove impossible to prevent legislation or the execution of a policy indefinitely. For example, the American Medical Association spent millions of dollars in their campaign against federal 'socialized medicine' but the strength of public support ensured the eventual passage of Medicare legislation in 1965.

Chapter summary

- The American political system is particularly open to the influence of pressure groups. The diversity of American society, the size of the country and the complexity of its economy have all helped to create a vast array of different groups seeking to influence public policy. The political culture, the decentralised nature of the political system which allows many access points where groups can lobby and persuade, and the relative weakness of political parties have all enabled pressure groups to play an important role in the policy-making process. In states that allow referendums and initiatives as forms of direct democracy pressure groups can influence the voters who can make decisions on policy matters themselves.

- Pressure groups fall into two main categories: interest groups whose goals are to protect, defend and promote the interests of their own members and promotional groups which are trying to secure political objectives which are in the interests of people other than themselves or to promote a cause which they believe is in the interests of society as a whole. Some organisations are also variously described as 'citizens' groups', 'public-interest groups' and 'single-issue groups'.

- There are a number of methods which pressure groups legitimately use to influence government and public policy. These are electioneering and contributing financially to candidates' campaigns, lobbying, court litigation, grass-roots pressure by their members including participation in marches and demonstrations, publicity and advertising through the media and seeking to influence the policies of the political parties. A small minority of groups is willing to break the law and resort to violence and the promotion of civic disorder in order to achieve their goals.

- There has been considerable debate as to whether pressure groups play a positive role in democratic politics or not. Political scientists have generally argued that they perform important and necessary functions for the political system such as representing interests within society, encouraging participation in the political process and keeping the government in touch with public opinion in the country. Critics of pressure groups counter that they are often selfishly promoting their own interests at the expense of society as a whole, that the methods they use encourage public cynicism about how policy is made and that the inequality of resources available to different groups leads to those rich and powerful ones exercising disproportionate influence.

- The checks and balances within the American governmental system work to restrict the influence of any particular group. These constraints are supplemented by factors such as regulatory controls, scrutiny by the media, internal divisions within organisations and campaigns run by opposition groups to counter those of their rivals.

Think Points

* Overall do you think pressure groups are a help or hindrance to American democracy?
* Why is the American political system often seen as being particularly susceptible to the influence of pressure groups?
* Is the United States a pluralist political system?

Some further reading

Jeffrey M. Berry, *The Interest Group Society* (Longman 1997).

Allan J. Cigler and Burdett A. Loomis (eds), *Interest Group Politics* (Congressional Quarterly Press 1998)

Kenneth Goldstein, *Interest Groups, Lobbying and Participation in America* (Cambridge University Press 1999)

Alan Grant, 'Political Action Committees in American Politics', in *Contemporary American Politics*, Alan Grant (ed.) (Dartmouth 1995)

Ronald J. Hrebener, *Interest Group Politics in America* (Sharpe 1997)

Lester Milbrath, *The Washington Lobbyists* (Rand McNally 1963)

Anthony J. Nownes, *Organized Interests in American Politics* (Houghton Mifflin 2001)

Mark Petracca (ed.), *The Politics of Interests* (Westview 1992)

Jonathan Rauch, *Demisclerosis* (Time Books 1995)

Larry Sabato, *PAC Power: Inside the World of Political Action Committees* (Norton 1984)

B. Wolpe and B.J. Levine, *Lobbying Congress* (Congressional Quarterly Press 1996)

Weblinks

Policy News and Information Service: www.policy.com

American Association of Retired Persons: www.aarp.org

National Rifle Association: www.nra.org

Center to Prevent Handgun Violence: www.handguncontrol.org

National Federation of Independent Business: www.nfib.com

ALF-CIO: www.afl-cio.org/home.htm

American Israel Public Affairs Committee: www.aipac.org

National Right to Life Committee: www.nrlc.org

National Abortion and Reproductive Rights Action League: www.naral.org

The Sierra Club: www.sierraclub.org

National Organization for Women: www.now.org

6   Party politics

Political scientists have frequently emphasised that democratic government in a modern industrial society would not be possible without political parties. Parties are not simply appendages of representative government; they are central to its effectiveness and play a positive role in it. They are organised attempts to select candidates for official positions, promote certain goals and objectives, and gain government power. The Constitution of the United States does not mention these informal institutions and George Washington warned against the 'baneful effects of the spirit of party'. Since that time an American political culture has developed which has traditionally been suspicious of strong parties and concentrations of authority, but political parties have been an integral and essential part of the American political system since its early days. In examining the workings of the three branches of the federal government, we have already seen the importance of party for an understanding of American politics. American political parties have to operate within a very diverse society and a federal system of government; they have therefore tended to be broadly based coalitions of interests organised in a decentralised way rather than tightly disciplined hierarchical structures. American parties have traditionally been rather weak organisations compared to their counterparts in European democracies. American political scientists have often been concerned that this weakness has adversely affected the ability of parties to perform some of the key functions that they normally fulfil and, what is more, they have been organisations in decline, making them even less relevant to the American political system in recent decades. In this chapter we shall examine some of the characteristics of American parties and the party system, and investigate how far these concerns are justified.

The structure of American parties

A number of diffuse elements make up what is usually known as the American party 'organisation'. Discussion of political parties can be complicated by the fact that they generally do not have fee-paying or card-carrying members. We therefore have to distinguish between the vast array of people with different sorts of connection and relationship to the Democratic or Republican parties. Parties comprise the following groups:

1 *The party's voting support.*   Every election there are millions of Americans who vote regularly or sporadically for one of the parties' candidates. These people, therefore, include both hard-core supporters and 'independents' who have decided to vote for the party in that specific year.

2 *Registered party supporters.* In identifying on a regular basis with one of the major parties, millions of voters are prepared to register themselves on the electoral list as

'Democrats' or 'Republicans' where state laws allow them to do so. Although they pay no subscription to the party, these registered supporters are the closest to being party 'members'. In return for this public expression of support, they usually receive the right to participate in the selection of party candidates in primary elections.

3 Party activists. A much smaller number of Americans regularly play an active role in party politics. These people provide the voluntary labour at elections to mobilise voters, contribute money to campaigns, and may hold local committee positions. Party activists may also attend party conventions as delegates.

4 Party leaders outside government. In both parties there are leadership positions at local and state level as well as within the national organisation which are sought by the most dedicated activists. These leaders are often referred to as the party 'professionals' and they often exert considerable influence over the party's administration and finance.

5 Party leaders holding government positions. For many Americans political parties are, in practice, the government office-holders who carry the party label at elections. The President is, of course, the national leader of one of the parties and the parties have their own leaders in each congressional chamber but there are also many important Governors and Congressmen who are seen as the party leaders within their own states and who can exercise control over the running of state and local parties. What is more, the voters' image of the parties is, to a large extent, shaped by the personalities of its best-known political and governmental leaders.

Political parties are often subject to very detailed regulation of their affairs by state laws, mostly originating from the Progressive era at the beginning of the twentieth century when there was considerable concern about political corruption. Many local elections, as well as those for Nebraska's unicameral legislature, are required by law to be non-partisan.

As a result of the federal system and the plethora of elections that are fought on a state and local basis, American party organisations have traditionally been very decentralised and have lacked a strong central authority. Power over nominations for office, finance and policy-making has been the prerogative of state and local party organisations, and any attempts by the national party headquarters to interfere in these areas have been greatly resented. This decentralisation, diffuseness of authority and lack of clear hierarchy of command has led to party organisations that have been described in the past as 'confederative' rather than federal, although in recent decades the national party organisations' roles have been strengthened in a number of ways, as we shall see later.

The main functions of political parties, nominating candidates for the thousands of elected offices and mobilising voter support to secure victory and the control of government, dictate the structure of the institutions. In the 1960s V.O. Key Jr described the organisation as a system of layers with each successive layer having an individual concern with elections within its geographical jurisdiction. For each higher level of the party to accomplish its ends there had to be collaboration with the lower layers of the organisation. However, the cooperation came from a common sense of purpose rather than from the execution of commands from national to local units in the structure.[1] American parties therefore have not been disciplined armies but rather loose coalitions of state and local organisations which have their own followings and areas of independent action free from external control.

As parties are primarily electoral structures, it is not surprising that the main organisational units develop within electoral constituencies. There may be a dozen or so top officials who are elected at the statewide level, such as the Governor, Treasurer, Attorney-General, Lieutenant-Governor and the two US Senators, but there are hundreds of politicians who represent districts within the state. These include the US Congressmen, state legislators, county and city council members, mayors and sheriffs.

Formal organisational structures can vary considerably from state to state owing to local traditions and electoral laws. They can also be misleading as guidelines to the actual distribution and control of political power, and official positions may be more or less important depending upon the personalities, energies and leadership qualities of the holders. In some areas party organisation may not exist or be in skeleton form only, with many official positions being left unfilled through lack of volunteers. All state parties have state committees and there are almost always county committees, but these may be elected by primaries among all the registered party voters or selected by conventions of activists.

The most local units of organisation are normally the precincts which are administrative subdivisions of cities and counties. Meetings of all party supporters who care to attend elect *precinct chairmen* (or 'captains') who have the responsibilities of directing local fund-raising and mobilising voters at election time. Ward caucuses meet in many areas to select a *ward committee* to run the party's affairs over a number of precincts; wards are also usually the electoral constituencies for city or county council members.

The *county committee* has an important coordinating role in local party administration and its members select a county chairman who will probably become a major figure in state as well as local politics. In some parts of the country there are separate committees for geographical areas which form, for example, congressional districts or state senate constituencies, and these overlap with the county organisations. At the state level conventions are held which usually last for two or three days and are major political events. Party platforms may be adopted and the *state party committee* may be selected by the delegates representing county and ward areas. A smaller executive committee and the state party chairman will often act in the name of the state committee as this body may be too large and unwieldy to be an effective decision-making institution in practice. In those states which do not have presidential primaries, the state conventions and caucuses also select the delegates to attend the party's national nominating convention. At one time state conventions would also select candidates for statewide offices but today the vast majority of states use primary elections in the nominating process. Primaries may be closed, where participation is limited to those registered as party supporters, or open, where voters can decide on the day of the election in which party's primary they wish to take part. Primaries have led to a weakening of party organisation because the state and local officials have little or no control over who is selected to represent the party in the general election. It is rare for more than a quarter of those eligible to turn out to vote in primaries and those who do vote tend to select candidates who are more ideologically in tune with the more partisan and activist supporters of the party than the general electorate. On the other hand, they do have the advantages of allowing greater involvement by the public and opening up the nomination process to a wider range of issues and candidates. Only a small number of states, such as Connecticut, Delaware and Utah, provide for state conventions to nominate candidates for statewide offices and even in these states conventions are combined with primaries when a substantial minority of delegates supports one of the defeated candidates.

One of the formal roles of the national convention is to select a *national committee* with overall administrative responsibilities. In practice, each state party determines who its representatives will be and these are endorsed by the full convention. National committees are made up of one man and one woman from each state, plus a number of additional members. The Democrats have included representatives of the party's Governors and Congressmen and the Republicans have added state party chairmen. The effect has been historically to make the committees far too large to fulfil any function other than a symbolic unifying one. The national committees are concerned with overseeing the presidential campaign as well as selecting the site and making the arrangements for the next convention. However, the national party chairman and the office staff in Washington carry out most of the functions and are involved in fund-raising, publicity and administration. The national chairman is formally selected by the committee but it ratifies the choice made by the presidential nominee of the party. If the presidential candidate suffers a heavy defeat in the November election, the national committee may decide to replace the chairman with one of its own choosing. However, if the candidate becomes President, despite his lack of a formal role in the national committee, his informal control over its leaders and activities is nearly total and if he wants to change the national chairman the committee will promptly elect his choice, usually without dissent.[2]

Until the 1980s American national parties could be said only to come into practical operation once every four years when there was a presidential election. The rest of the time the state parties had no real reason to cooperate and the national committees' Washington offices were run by small skeleton staffs. The national parties then took steps to develop their organisations and roles so that they could make a difference in national politics. In 1972 the Republican National Committee had only 30 staff; by the time of the 1984 presidential election it employed 600. Even in the non-presidential year of 1990 there were 400 people who worked at the RNC headquarters in Washington. The Democratic National Committee's staff rose in numbers from 30 in 1972 to 130 in 1990. As John H. Aldrich observed of the national party organisations: 'They have become more truly national parties, better financed, more professionalized and more institutionalized, with greater power to shape the actions of their state and local organizations.'[3]

The Republican National Committee, particularly during the chairmanship of William Brock between 1977 and 1981, took the lead and was involved in raising money, recruiting and training candidates against Democrats thought to be vulnerable and conducting centralised polling and advertising campaigns, while the National Republican Congressional and Senatorial Committees have provided funds, advice and support to favoured Republican candidates for marginal and electorally competitive seats in the House and Senate respectively. The RNC has also sought to coordinate business and corporate PAC contributions to Republican candidates. These roles came about as an indirect result of the weak position of the Republican Party in the mid-1970s and the RNC's determination to improve both its financial and technical capacity as well as the fact that the party became more ideologically unified.

Large amounts of money, raised principally by direct mail solicitation of supporters, allowed the Republicans nationally to become involved in party-building activities and in strengthening the organisation in the country. The Democrats began the process later and also concentrated on fund-raising to develop their organisation. The Democratic National Committee as well as the Democratic Congressional Campaign and Senate Committees have all been very active in this area. By the 1990s both parties were raising huge sums of money through their national committees to support their candidates' campaigns as well as generic party advertising and other electoral activities. Much of the money raised nationally is actually spent by state and local party organisations but decisions made at national headquarters determine the allocation of resources between and within states. Parties target funds to those key states whose voters may have a pivotal influence in the presidential race and the fight to control Congress. With the closeness of recent elections, exemplified by both the 2000 and 2002 contests, such strategic use of campaign money is an essential tool for the party leaderships.

National parties have raised money from supporters across the country in two forms: 'hard money' where individual donations have been limited by electoral law to a maximum of $1,000 in each election and 'soft money' where there have been no limits on what individuals, companies or interest groups could give to party coffers. Soft money was originally allowed under a 1979 law in order for political parties to strengthen their grass-roots organisations. It was supposed to be spent on 'party-building' activities such as registration drives and 'get out the vote' mobilisation efforts. However, by the 1990s it was being used to support the campaigns of individual candidates, including the presidential nominees, with the largest amounts being spent on television and radio advertising and direct mail campaigns and less than 10 per cent on traditional voter mobilisation activities. In 1999–2000 the two main parties raised a total of $1.2 billion between them, almost double that in 1997–98 and over a quarter more than in the previous presidential election cycle in 1995–96. Whereas the Republicans have had a distinct advantage in raising hard money, the parties attracted almost equal amounts of soft money in the run-up to the 2000 elections, a total of $487 million, almost double that of four years earlier.[4] Critics of soft money argued that it was corrupting the political system by allowing wealthy individuals and special interests to bypass the hard-money limits and to use parties as intermediaries in order to buy influence with important politicians. However, many political scientists have seen soft money as having the beneficial effect of strengthening political parties and allowing them to play a more significant role in elections. Indeed, some would like candidates to be even more dependent on party funding in the belief that it would make legislators more accountable to their parties and lead to more responsible party government. We shall consider issues of campaign finance and its reform in more detail in Chapter 7.

The Democratic National Committee also gained power over state parties by the establishment of binding party rules on the composition of delegations to the national convention. Starting in 1964, when it resolved a challenge to the seating of an all-white Mississippi delegation in favour of a compromise that bound all future Democratic delegations to a rule of non-discrimination, the party has determined acceptable delegate-selection procedures. The rules have actually been very unstable with frequent changes over the years. The McGovern-Fraser Commission in 1969 emphasised the greater participation of minorities, women and young people and dramatically changed the nature of delegations to the 1972 convention which selected George McGovern. In the 1980s, after the poor results in presidential contests the party moved in the opposite direction by requiring the representation of so-called 'super delegates' comprising elected officials who would bring experience and political realism to the conventions, while still requiring state delegations to reflect the demographic profile of the states.

Whether the party organisation at state, county and ward level works hard to secure the election of the party's presidential candidate depends on how local activists feel about him. With voters being willing to 'split their tickets' when voting for the presidency and other offices, the 'coat-tails effect' has been reduced with the effective uncoupling of presidential from other elections (see Chapter 2). When President Nixon won a landslide victory in 1972 while the Democrats remained firmly in control of both houses of Congress, 30 per cent of voters supported different parties' candidates for the presidency and for the House of Representatives. In more recent elections around a fifth of voters have split their tickets in presidential election years.

Party activists would obviously prefer to have a popular presidential candidate such as Ronald Reagan in 1980 and 1984 or Bill Clinton in 1996 at the head of the party's ticket than one who seems destined to lose such as George McGovern in 1972, Walter Mondale in 1984 and Robert Dole in 1996. Party workers at state and local level will then concentrate on securing the positions of their gubernatorial, congressional and local candidates and distance themselves from a presidential candidate who is unpopular in their state. The Democratic Party has had particular problems in this regard because its national conventions have often selected presidential candidates who are far more liberal than the candidates the state and local parties, particularly in the South, often select themselves.

While examining American party organisations it should also be noted that, despite the increasing importance of national party organisations, in many respects, parties have become less important than they used to be in the actual running of campaigns. Party nomination and the party label will be necessary for election to most offices, but candidates for positions ranging from the presidency to local sheriff have increasingly relied upon personal organisations to run their campaigns. We are now in the age of candidate-centred campaigns; activists often prefer to work on behalf of individual men and women and are concerned solely with their victories rather than with the success of the party ticket as a whole. The main reason for this phenomenon is that increasingly primaries are being used to nominate party candidates; as we have seen, this weakens the influence of the party organisation, the committees, the chairmen and the 'professionals'. It also means that aspirants for office inevitably have to set up their own organisations in order to win the party's nomination. They have their own offices, staff, fund-raising and campaign workers and they are likely to hire independent campaign consultants, pollsters, direct mail specialists and media advisers. The cost of hiring highly paid political consultants has fuelled the mounting expenditure levels in recent campaigns; by the 1990 elections this growing industry earned $188 million from congressional candidates. These consultants are usually responsible for strategy and are heavily influenced by opinion poll findings on what issues to emphasise and what approach to take to the opposition. Candidates are increasingly political entrepreneurs who will keep this campaign structure in operation during the general elections because they feel they can trust it as well as exercise greater control over it. Philip John Davies concludes:

> It is not so much a case of candidates being chosen to represent the party line by party loyalists, as it is of candidate organisations capturing the party nomination, thereby eliminating some competitors, and gaining the use of party assets, on the way to a personal victory.[5]

Therefore one may find a large degree of overlap and duplication of work by personal and party organisations, and occasionally friction and conflict between the two.

The relative decline of American party organisation has been the result of a number of other factors. Earlier in the twentieth century American parties, particularly in the cities, were famous for their tight and well-disciplined organisations. Precinct captains and ward chairmen would be proud of their capacity to know the inhabitants in their areas and to get out the vote on election days. 'Machine politics' became a common phenomenon in many Eastern cities, and organised local politics, often under the influence of a political 'boss', became as much a tradition as the unorganised national party system. Tammany Hall in New York was the best known of these local machines; machine politics itself was really the result of dense urban populations, the fragmentation of city government, and the democratic right to vote of large numbers of people, particularly new immigrants to the United States, who had no tradition of political participation. The machines acted as intermediaries who would help provide informal welfare services, such as jobs and housing, in return for electoral support. The system disintegrated because patronage jobs were no longer so easily available, there was closer vetting of city funds, the introduction of government welfare programmes meant that the poor were no longer dependent on local party politicians and the trading of votes also largely ended with changing political morality. The importance of the mass media as a basis of communication and a method of campaigning reduced the impact of the door-to-door contacts made by the local machine. What is more, increasing mobility and the growth of the sprawling suburbs and the decline of the cities as residential areas also contributed to the breakdown of the city machines. The death in 1976 of Mayor Richard Daley of Chicago, often seen as the last of the old-style city bosses, marked the end of an era in the history of American party organisation.

The American two-party system

The historical development

There are two major parties which operate successfully within the American political system, as indeed there have been for most of the nation's history. This does not mean that there are only two parties or that the same two parties have continued to contest elections with each other since the Union was created. In fact there are, and have been, many minor parties, most of which had a fleeting and transitory existence, and there have been several party systems over the last two centuries of American political life. V.O. Key Jr has observed:

> A salient characteristic of the American party system is its dual form. During most of our history power has alternated between two major parties. While minor parties have arisen from time to time and exerted influence on governmental policy, the two major parties have been the only serious contenders for the Presidency. On occasion a major party has disintegrated but in due course the biparty division has reasserted itself.[6]

The first American two-party system lasted a relatively short time after 1787. Despite Washington's and Adams' dislike of party politics, it was inevitable that in a free society groups would coalesce to try to obtain control of government and, in particular, of the presidency. The Democratic-Republicans led by Thomas Jefferson formed an alliance of agrarian and business supporters and created a party organisation to challenge the Federalists, the supporters of Alexander Hamilton, and the idea of a strong national government. The Federalists sank into oblivion within a couple of decades because of their restricted elitist appeal to the well-to-do in society and their opposition to political democracy. For some time after the demise of the Federalists, the United States experienced the 'Era of Good Feelings' when the Democratic-Republicans were the only viable party; but the strong reaction to the policies and personality of Andrew Jackson led to the eventual formation of an opposition party known as the Whigs. The Whigs lasted from 1832 to 1852 but had no real hope of long-term survival because they were, in Clinton Rossiter's words:

The coalition to end all coalitions, a patchwork party with few premonitions of immortality, a loose alliance of every section and interest that was sure to crack under the first hard blow.[7]

The traumatic question of slavery nearly led to the dissolution of the Union, but it actually did lead to the disintegration of the party system and the destruction of the Whigs. The Democratic Party came under the control of Southern interests dedicated to the preservation and expansion of slavery. The Republican Party emerged from the confusion of the 1850s as a grass-roots democratic movement which managed to bring together an alliance of smaller parties as well as disillusioned Whigs and Democrats. The Republican Party's origins were radical and its opposition to the extension of slavery to the territories destined it to be a sectional Northern party. The antipathy in the South to the Republican Party had its political repercussions for well over a century after these events.

After the Civil War the Democratic Party made a recovery and in the period 1876–96 there was intense competition between it and the Republicans for control of both Congress and the presidency. However, social changes in America inevitably were reflected by modifications of the party system. With rapid industrialisation, the growth of big business and the increasing pressure of large-scale immigration, there was growing agrarian discontent which was articulated by small parties like the Populists. In 1896 the Democrats moved to absorb the Populist movement's ideas while their candidate, William Jennings Bryan, ran on a 'free silver' presidential platform. The Republicans, under William McKinley, emerged victorious from the election and were strengthened as a result of becoming a coalition of businessmen, urban workers and Midwestern farmers. The Republicans became recognised as the more conservative and business-oriented party and managed to dominate American politics until 1932. They controlled both the White House and Congress and the only real Democratic success was achieved when Woodrow Wilson was elected twice to the presidency in 1912 and 1916. Even this was mainly as a result of a split in the 'Grand Old Party' (as Republicans call it) between the conservative supporters of William Howard Taft and the progressive followers of Theodore Roosevelt.

The onset of the Great Depression in the period 1929–31 had as disastrous an effect on the fortunes of the Republicans as the Civil War had had on the Democratic Party. Herbert Hoover suffered a massive defeat in the 1932 presidential election and Franklin D. Roosevelt began the first of three full terms in the White House. Roosevelt died in 1945 after being elected a fourth time to the office, but his establishment of the 'New Deal Coalition' was to have repercussions on American politics long after his death. It seems that only major national crises lead to the widespread reassessments of loyalties and attitudes that result in large numbers of Americans changing their party identification on a long-term basis and creating a realignment of political forces, but the Depression and the New Deal era led to the transformation of the traditional Republican majority in the country into a situation where a Democratic majority was normal.[8] Box 6.1 examines the concept of party realignment.

The Democratic dominance of American politics lasted until the late 1960s but gradually the New Deal coalition began to crack. This first became evident in presidential elections from 1968 onwards. Between 1932 and 2000 the Democrats won ten presidential contests to the Republicans' eight. However, the Republican victories have included six of the last nine since 1968, the exceptions being when the Democrats nominated Southern moderate candidates in 1976 (Carter), 1992 and 1996 (Clinton) and were able to counteract the growing attractiveness of the Republican Party to white voters in the South. Table 6.1 shows the 'most Democratic' and 'most Republican' states in

---

Box 6.1 Party realignment

Political scientists have often viewed American political and electoral history in cyclical terms where one party has dominated the political system, controlling both the presidency and Congress as well as most of the state governments, for a period of approximately 30 years and has then been supplanted by a new party. Realignment takes place when new issue concerns and social change are coupled with political or economic crisis causing groups of voters that have traditionally supported one party to transfer their loyalties to another. A 'critical election' occurs which leads to the dominance of a new party. The creation of a new governing coalition results in major changes in government and in policies and can be seen as a turning point in American politics.

Examples of party realignments took place in 1800, after which the Democratic (or Jeffersonian) Republicans were dominant; in 1828 when the Democrats led by Andrew Jackson took control; in 1896 when William McKinley's election as President began a period of Republican dominance until 1932. In that year the Great Depression created the conditions for Franklin D. Roosevelt's election and a period of Democratic control for most of the period until 1968. Since that time, despite the fact that the electorate has become more conservative in its views and the Republicans have been more successful in presidential elections and in congressional elections since 1994, there has not been a clear realignment of the type seen in earlier periods and no great crisis which would create such a major upheaval in voting behaviour. The Democrats in 1992 and 1996 adapted to the more conservative political environment and won the presidency, while the 2000 elections showed an electorate divided almost equally between the parties. Is one of the two parties likely to dominate the American political system over the next decade or so? Republicans can point to their success in the 2002 midterm elections as demonstrating their ability to control both houses of Congress and the presidency, the more conservative mood among the electorate and the fact that their party has been doing well in areas in the country which have experienced population growth and benefited from the reapportionment of House seats. Democrats on the other hand take some comfort from knowing that demographic changes resulting from immigration and higher birth rates among Hispanic and other minority groups could well work in their favour in the longer term as the white population loses its majority status in the nation as a whole.

---

presidential elections over the period 1968–2000. It is notable that no state has voted for the Democratic candidate in all nine elections, if we exclude the District of Columbia; on the other hand, 11 states have given their Electoral College votes to the Republicans in every election over the period.

In congressional elections the period of Democratic dominance meant that the party controlled both houses of Congress from 1932 to 1980 with the exception of only four years – the 80th (1947–48) and 83rd (1953–54) Congresses. Between 1981 and 1987 the Republicans had a majority in the Senate and there was split control of the two houses of Congress. Divided party control of the presidency and Congress became increasingly common and in the watershed mid-term elections of 1994 the Democrats lost their majority status in both houses. The Republican won control of the House of Representatives for the first time in 40 years and have retained their control of the chamber in four further elections, most recently in 2002, albeit with very small majorities. In the Senate the Republicans have had a majority since 1994, with the exception of the period 2000–2 when, following a 50–50 split in the 2000 elections, the defection of one of their members gave the Democrats a one-seat advantage. The Democrats lost their majority status primarily because of Republican gains in the South where many white voters increasingly have supported conservative GOP candidates. What is more, the Republicans benefited

Table 6.1 Party strengths in the states: the 'most Democratic' and 'most Republican' states in presidential elections 1968–2000

Most Democratic		Most Republican
Minnesota	1	Alaska
Hawaii	2	Idaho
Massachusetts	2	Indiana
Rhode Island	2	Kansas
Maryland	3	Nebraska
New York	3	North Dakota
West Virginia	3	Oklahoma
Pennsylvania	4	South Dakota
Washington	4	Utah
Wisconsin	4	Virginia
		Wyoming

Note: The 'Most Democratic' states are those whose Electoral College votes went least often to the Republican candidates in presidential elections 1968–2000; the figures indicate how many times out of the nine elections the state voted Republican. The 'Most Republican' states are those whose Electoral College votes went to the Republican candidates in all nine elections during the period.

Source: Adapted from Harold W. Stanley and Richard G. Niemi, *Vital Statistics on American Politics 1997–8*, Congressional Quarterly Press, 1998, p. 17.

from the effects of reapportionment in 1990 and the creation of districts where minority group voters were concentrated in particular constituencies in order to make the election of ethnic minority representatives more likely (see Chapters 1 and 4). A consequence of this policy was that other seats contained overwhelmingly white electorates with a propensity to vote Republican. This gradual realignment of Southern white voters has not in itself, however, been sufficient to create a clear Republican majority in the national electorate as a whole.

The American two-party system has therefore experienced periods of one-party dominance. The national party system is normally described as a 'two-party system' because, although in any period one party may control government, the other party continues to draw large support in terms of both popular votes and congressional seats. At presidential elections the two main parties normally share well over 90 per cent of the popular vote, although in 1992 and 1996 between 10 and 20 per cent of the voters opted for alternative candidates. Congressional representation is still shared almost exclusively between the two parties. Despite the decline of voter identification and commitment to the parties and the rise in the number of 'Independents', the parties have demonstrated remarkable durability. However, in the early twenty-first century there is no dominant party: the parties are almost evenly balanced in their electoral support and political representation, a fact most vividly demonstrated by the 2000 presidential and congressional elections.

Patterns of state party competition

In addition to the national party system, the United States has 50 other state party systems in which there is a great variety of partisan competition. In the vast majority of states, the two major parties contest most important political offices and the extent of competition depends upon the particular traditions and social composition of the individual states. In some areas there is a close struggle for power, with Democrats and Republicans both winning at various times the gubernatorial elections and control of the state legislature. In other areas there is uneven competition, where one party usually controls the

Table 6.2 The party composition of Congress 1959–2004

	President		Congress	The House		The Senate	
				Maj. party	Min. party	Maj. party	Min. party
1959–60	Eisenhower	(R)	86th	D 283	R 154	D 66	R 34
1961–62	Kennedy	(D)	87th	D 263	R 174	D 64	R 36
1963–64	Kennedy	(D)	88th	D 258	R 176	D 68	R 32
	Johnson	(D)					
1965–66	Johnson	(D)	89th	D 295	R 140	D 67	R 33
1967–68	Johnson	(D)	90th	D 248	R 187	D 64	R 36
1969–70	Nixon	(R)	91st	D 243	R 192	D 58	R 42
1971–72	Nixon	(R)	92nd	D 256	R 179	D 55	R 45
1973–74	Nixon	(R)	93rd	D 243	R 191	D 57	R 43
1975–76	Ford	(R)	94th	D 291	R 144	D 62	R 38
1977–78	Carter	(D)	95th	D 292	R 143	D 62	R 38
1979–80	Carter	(D)	96th	D 276	R 159	D 59	R 41
1981–82	Reagan	(R)	97th	D 243	R 192	R 53	D 47
1983–84	Reagan	(R)	98th	D 269	R 166	R 54	D 46
1985–86	Reagan	(R)	99th	D 253	R 182	R 53	D 47
1987–88	Reagan	(R)	100th	D 258	R 177	D 54	R 46
1989–90	Bush	(R)	101st	D 260	R 175	D 55	R 45
1991–92	Bush	(R)	102nd	D 267	R 167	D 56	R 44
1993–94	Clinton	(D)	103rd	D 258	R 176	D 57	R 43
1995–96	Clinton	(D)	104th	R 230	D 204	R 53	D 47
1997–98	Clinton	(D)	105th	R 227	D 207	R 55	D 45
1999–2000	Clinton	(D)	106th	R 223	D 211	R 55	D 45
2001–2	Bush	(R)	107th	R 221	D 212	R 50	D 50
2003–4	Bush	(R)	108th	R 228	D 204	R 51	D 48

Note: The 102nd to 108th Congresses included one independent from Vermont in the House of Representatives. Republican strength in the 104th Congress was increased by Democratic defections. Before the 1996 elections the Republican lead was 236–198 in the House. In the Senate, Richard Shelby (Alabama) and Ben Nighthorse Campbell (Colorado) also defected to the Republicans in November 1994 and March 1995 respectively.

In the 107th Congress the Senate was initially controlled by the Republicans with the casting vote of the Vice-President. In May 2001 the defection of James Jeffords from the Republicans to become an Independent gave the Democrats control.

Table 6.3 Party control and the state Governors 1980–2003

	Governors		
	Dem.	*Rep.*	*Ind.*
1980	31	19	–
1985	34	16	–
1987	26	24	–
1990	29	21	–
1993	30	18	2
1995	19	30	1
1997	17	32	1
1999	17	31	2*
2001	19	29	2
2003	24	26	–

*Includes one Reform Party

legislature for long periods but is not permanently in a majority. Elections for Governor are more competitive and are often won by the party in the legislative minority. In other states there is a virtual monopoly, where one party has long-term dominance of the legislature and the minority may, on occasions, win the gubernatorial race. As at national level, divided party control of the legislature and executive has become more common. Whereas in 1960 only 37.5 per cent of states had different parties in control of the two branches, by 1990 this had risen to 61 per cent.[9] In 2001, 22 states had a single party in control and 27 demonstrated divided party control with the Governor facing opposition party majorities in one or both of the legislative chambers (with Nebraska having a non-partisan legislature).

The other main trend in the 1990s has been the growing Republican strength at state level. The party has made considerable gains in both gubernatorial and state legislative elections. With the large swing to the Republicans in 1994, the GOP held the governorships of 30 states, including the largest and most populous states in the Union such as California, New York and Texas, compared with only 16 a decade earlier. In the same period states where the Republicans controlled both houses of the state legislatures increased from 11 to 19. Following the 2000 elections the Republicans held 29 governorships and controlled 17 state legislatures; however, the Democrats made up some ground at state level in 2002 by increasing their number of Governors to 24 to the Republicans' 26.

In those Southern states which until the 1980s could be described as 'one-party systems' and had been solidly Democratic since the Civil War, the Republicans historically put up only token resistance in most state elections or did not compete at all. The reasons for the overwhelming domination of one party were historical and social. In the last two decades there has been a weakening of sectionalism and one-partyism due to the increasing urbanisation and pluralism of social groups and interests even in these areas. As we have seen, this has been demonstrated both by the tendency of the Southern states to support Republican candidates for the presidency in preference to liberal Democrats, and also by the increasing number of Republican Congressmen and Governors elected in Southern states. In 1984 71 per cent of Southern whites voted for Ronald Reagan and 59 per cent for Republican congressional candidates. In 2000 66 per cent of these voters supported George W. Bush. Democratic strength in the South has suffered severe erosion and it appears that more voters have accepted that their conservatism fits more comfortably with the Republicans than a regionally based Democratic ideology. This has led not only to ordinary voters, but politicians themselves, switching party; for example, in the 104th Congress five Southern Democrats in the House and one in the Senate defected to the Republicans.

In 1961 Republicans held only nine (7.5 per cent) of the 120 House seats in the 13 Southern states. By 1993 these states had 137 House members, of whom 52 (38 per cent) were Republicans; by 1997 Republicans had won 82 or 60 per cent of the Southern seats. Similarly in the Senate, the GOP's share of the seats rose from 7.7 per cent in 1961 to 42 per cent in 1993 and 69 per cent (with 18 of the 26 members) in 1997. In 1961 all the Governors in the South were Democrats; by 1993 there were three Republicans, whereas in 1997 nine of the 13 state houses were controlled by the GOP.

Why a two-party system?

When one considers the heterogeneity of the United States and the diversity of social, ethnic and regional interests, it is perhaps surprising that there are only two major parties. Multi-party systems are, in fact, more common in liberal democracies than two-party structures, and one could reasonably expect that America would exhibit the former pattern of competition. The explanation is not to be found in one factor, but rather in the historical, cultural, constitutional and social experience of the country.

V.O. Key Jr has argued that the circumstances that happened to mould the American party system into a dual form at its inception had a long-term effect because there is a tendency in human institutions for a persistence of initial form.[10] There was the great debate about the adoption of the Constitution which was an issue that was bound to divide the country into two blocs. There was the rivalry between agrarian and commercial interests that tended to unite in two broad coalitions, and there was, of course, the slavery issue and the Civil War which reinforced a dual division.

The electoral system used in the United States for congressional and state elections encourages the persistence of a two-party system. With a 'simple plurality' or 'first past the post' system, representatives are elected in single-member constituencies by winning more votes than any opponent. Minor parties may be said to be at a disadvantage in that they may contest a large number of elections but not finish at the top of the poll in any constituency and thus remain unrepresented in the legislature. Under a proportional representation electoral system, used by many European democracies, these parties would obtain a number of seats roughly equivalent to the proportion of the popular vote they acquired overall. Minor parties in the United States have therefore found it virtually impossible to beat both the major established parties and win seats in Congress. The system of electing the President encourages the same tendency to dualism. An absolute majority of Electoral College votes is required to win the presidency outright and therefore a pressure exists on voters to coalesce around two main candidates. When further serious contenders do compete in the presidential election, there is the danger of a deadlock in the Electoral College and of the decision being thrown into the House of Representatives. In addition, the very nature of the single-man executive makes it impossible for coalitions of more than one party to win control of the government, as can happen with a Cabinet system.

Further institutional problems exist for minor parties because there is a great diversity of state laws and regulations concerning elections and the qualifications that have to be met before a candidate's name can go forward for the ballot, such as securing thousands of signatures on a petition. Perhaps even more important than the complexity of election laws is the actual cost of campaigning. In elections where large campaign expenditure is necessary to secure television, radio and press advertising, candidates and parties with few financial backers and meagre resources of their own are obviously at a grave disadvantage in attempting to break into the system.

While not running as a party candidate, Ross Perot was backed by a mass movement of volunteers who successfully worked to place his name on the ballot paper for the 1992 presidential election in every state. Perot used his personal wealth to finance his campaign, but even though he won 19 per cent of the popular vote he did not come close to winning any state's Electoral College votes. In 1996 Perot ran again, but this time as the candidate of the Reform Party, winning only 8.4 per cent of the popular vote (see Box 6.2).

The United States also does not have the class-conscious or ideological style of politics so common in many countries that experience multi-partyism. The nature of American political culture means that there is a large degree of consensus on the fundamentals of the political and economic systems. Despite the social and ethnic diversity there is basic support for the Constitution and the principles of liberal democracy based on a private enterprise or capitalist economic structure. This means that traditionally the two major parties have existed with differences of style and approach but with no deep ideological divisions between them. The Democrats and Republicans have been flexible and prepared to adapt themselves to social change, where necessary by broadening their coalitions to absorb any minor parties that have arisen. The absence of a major socialist party dedicated to the transformation of the social and economic order has also been a factor in the creation and persistence of parties which exhibit 'dualism in a moving consensus'.[11]

The Democratic and Republican Parties

One commonly heard complaint about American parties over the years has been that they fail to offer a real choice to the electorate and that voters are in practice often asked whether they prefer 'Tweedledum' or 'Tweedledee'. The existence of a broad national consensus and the absence of strong class divisions have meant that American parties have reflected those social facts of life by not exhibiting such clear-cut ideological differences as most European party systems. In attempting to win control of government, particularly at national level, political parties are obliged to appeal to broad coalitions of interests and win votes from all sections of society. Both parties have tended to try to move to the 'middle ground' in order to win the support of independent voters who do not identify with either party, and the result has been that both parties have usually offered broad and moderate policy proposals, often with a great deal of similarity.

American experience has indicated that, when parties have chosen candidates, formulated policies or projected images that could be criticised as 'extreme' or 'outside the mainstream', they have suffered heavy defeats at the hands of the voters. Barry Goldwater, a conservative Republican who promised to provide 'a choice not an echo' in his presidential campaign of 1964, and George McGovern, a Democrat on the left wing of his party who was nominated as his party's standard-bearer in 1972, were both tagged as 'extremists'. Both challengers, who were fighting incumbent 'safe' Presidents, were decisively defeated. Jimmy Carter tried unsuccessfully to use this tactic in his 1980 campaign against conservative Republican challenger, Ronald Reagan.

There can be little doubt that in the 1980s the two parties moved further apart politically than for many years and that in Ronald Reagan the Republican Party and the American people had a President who was far more ideologically committed than any of his recent predecessors. The differences in 1984 between the avowedly right-wing platform of the Republican Party and the essentially liberal programmes adopted by the Democratic convention were more clear-cut than they probably had ever been. Many of the activists in both parties and the pressure groups associated with them appeared to be far more strident and in some cases more extreme than has traditionally been the case in American politics. However, opinion polls do not indicate that the nation as a whole is necessarily more ideologically committed and many voters from a wide range of social groups who supported President Reagan were attracted to him on personality grounds rather than because they supported his conservative policies and they continued to vote for Democratic candidates elsewhere on the ticket. American politics in the 1990s continued to be increasingly partisan in nature, as we noted in Chapter 2 when examining the working of Congress. For example, the 1994 House Republican candidates' programme 'The Contract With America' was designed to emphasise the differences between the parties and had a distinctively conservative set of policy priorities. Similarly in the 2000 presidential election the Republican and Democratic party platforms differed markedly on issues ranging from tax cuts, the funding of schools and social security to abortion and gay rights.

American parties have always had their differences and their own distinctive bases of support even though they have had to appeal to the country at large and have generally been moderate and non-ideological. After the Great Depression, the Democratic Party managed to become the majority party by winning the regular support of a disparate and heterogeneous coalition of groups. The very nature of this alliance meant that there were constant threats to its stability, but the enduring nature of voter identification and a mixture of good luck and judgement enabled it to survive. The Democrats gained most support from people in the lower socioeconomic groups; the New Deal programmes enabled the party to project the image of caring for the security and welfare of the poor, the unemployed and the ordinary worker. Roosevelt managed to add the votes of the cities, the recent immigrants, the minority ethnic groups and small farmers to those of the traditional Southern white electorate, the unions and liberal academic establishment in the universities. With upward social mobility, many Americans obtained middle-class status but retained their Democratic Party identification.

Until the 1980s the Republican Party's dilemma was that it had become very much the second party in terms of voter identification. The party was therefore more homogeneous than the Democratic Party in terms of social support. It tended to draw votes from non-manual workers and their families and particularly the upper middle classes, the business community, large farmers and college graduates. Republican support came primarily from WASPs (White Anglo-Saxon Protestants) rather than other ethnic groups. Despite the fact that more Americans were working in non-manual jobs and living in the suburbs, the Republicans did not seem to be benefiting to the extent one would have expected. This was at least partially explained by the image of the two parties that the voters tended to have. The Republican Party was often identified as 'the party of the rich' and this rather exclusive image deterred many middle-class Americans. The Democrats were more often seen as 'the party of the ordinary or working people' and, although Americans are less class-conscious than European voters, most do see themselves as 'working people'.

However, the Reagan years enabled the Republican Party to project an image of being the party of peace and prosperity and to improve its position in terms of voter identification. In 1980 the Democrats outnumbered Republicans by 22 per cent but in a Gallup survey in July 1989 the gap had narrowed to 4 per cent.[12] In the last three presidential elections (1992, 1996 and 2000) the gap between those identifying themselves to exit pollsters as Democrats and Republicans has been remarkably consistent at 3–4 per cent.

For example, 39 per cent of voters in 2000 said they were Democrats and 35 per cent Republicans. Approximately 60 per cent of the electorate say they identify with one of the two main parties. In all three recent elections 26–27 per cent of those voting claimed to be 'independents'. However, in 2000 92 per cent of these people actually voted for Bush or Gore. Even in 1992 when there was a prominent and well-financed Independent candidate only 30 per cent of self-identified 'independent' voters supported Ross Perot, while 38 per cent backed Clinton and 32 per cent Bush Senior.[13] The relatively high percentage of the electorate calling themselves 'independents' is in some respects misleading. Surveys such as those carried out by the University of Michigan's Center for Political Studies show that, apart from 'strong' and 'weak' party identifiers there are also independents who 'lean to' the Democrats or Republicans and will probably vote for the party's candidates. Therefore close to 90 per cent of the electorate identify to some extent with one or other of the two parties.

During the 1980s and 1990s there was also been a marked increase in the number of voters identifying themselves as conservatives when compared with those who say they are liberals. In the 1996 exit poll, 33 per cent were conservatives, 20 per cent liberals, while 47 per cent declared themselves to be moderates; in 2000 the numbers were 29 per cent, 20 per cent and 50 per cent respectively. These figures have been fairly typical since the mid-1980s, but are very different from the post-war period when liberalism was more attractive.

The two main parties have differences of emphasis in their policies and programmes which have been inevitably interrelated with their traditional sources of social support in the country. The Democrats have tended to favour government regulation of the economy, large spending programmes such as Social Security, Medicare, federal aid to education and welfare, as well as legislation supported by the trade unions and ethnic minorities. They have advocated reform and change initiated by a strong federal government, where necessary pushing state and local governments to implement interventionist policies. They have seen an activist President and executive branch as the main mechanism for experimentation and social change. Democrats have seen themselves as 'the party of progress', being prepared to look to the future and attempt bold new methods of achieving welfare, security and national prosperity. The Republican Party, on the other hand, has advocated a far more limited role for the federal government in the economic and social affairs of the country. It has opposed large and inflationary spending programmes, particularly in areas that it regards as being much more suitable for state and local policy-making, while resisting intervention in the economy and regulation of business activity. Republicans have often opposed Democratic legislation since the 1930s and then had to accept the major programmes as they have become part of the *status quo* supported by the American consensus.

One of the prices of unity in obtaining support for presidential candidates is the tolerance of diverse shades of opinion within both parties and this overlapping of political orientations has tended further to blur the differences between them. However, it is fair to say that the 'centres of gravity' within the parties are distinct. The Republican Party today can be fairly described as overwhelmingly a conservative party. The orientation among its presidential candidates, its congressional representation and its active supporters has been to the right of the political spectrum and the influence of Ronald Reagan in consolidating the influence of conservatism within the party in the 1980s has been very significant. It is notable that all six of the potential Republican successors to Reagan in the presidential primaries of 1988 were conservatives of various shades; the last liberal Republican to seek the presidential nomination, John Anderson in 1980, left to run an

Independent campaign after failing in the primaries. It was not always this way: until the 1960s the party's liberal wing with its supporters based in the big cities of the Eastern United States and the 'Eastern liberal establishment' of the GOP succeeded in dominating the party's presidential conventions. The nomination of Arizona Senator Barry Goldwater in 1964, over New York Governor Nelson Rockefeller, was a landmark in the wresting of control of the party by the conservative wing. The death of Rockefeller big-government liberalism was also witnessed in Congress, and gradually the ranks of moderate Republicans have also been depleted. The remaining moderates (the term 'liberal' has become taboo in the Republican Party), around 30 in the House and a handful in the Senate, mostly represent constituencies in the North-East. Their ranks have declined as retirements have led to more conservative replacements, by defeats in primaries and by Democratic successes in the region. Overall, the House and Senate Republican Conferences have become far more conservative, with many more members from the West and South and far fewer from the North-East and Midwest.[14] With the collapse of communism and the Soviet threat which had been a uniting factor for Republicans, factional fights in the 1990s were principally between those social conservatives and supporters of the Christian Right who have wanted to emphasise social and moral issues and traditional family values and see a role for government in regulating personal behaviour, and those free market conservatives who believe the party's main attraction to the electorate is its stands on economic policy, less government and reduced taxes. Although some observers argued that the conflicts between social conservatives and the free market-libertarian wing of the party would lead to damaging disunity and electoral disaster, this does not appear to have been borne out by events, with Republican successes in congressional and state elections in the mid-1990s.[15] George W. Bush has to some extent redefined the conservative agenda with his advocacy in 2000 of 'compassionate conservatism'. 'Comcons' see conservatism as showing concern for the disadvantaged that the free market has failed to help and is more positive about the potential role of government in enabling individuals to improve their lives and those of their families. They want to go beyond cutting government and reducing its powers and display a more caring image than that shown by Newt Gingrich and his hard-nosed conservative 'revolutionaries' who alienated much of the American electorate in the mid-1990s. Bush's policies such as the provision of publicly funded education vouchers to enable parents, particularly in poor areas, to choose private education for their children and the use of faith-based and voluntary associations in partnership with government to deliver social services exemplify the compassionate conservative approach.

The Democratic Party has been more heterogeneous in ideological terms and remains so today. The New Deal coalition put together by Roosevelt consisted of a wide variety of groups with sometimes mutually inconsistent political views. The general orientation of the party among its presidential candidates, congressional representation and party activists outside the Southern states has been liberal and interventionist. The party's conservative wing has been based mainly in the South and it remained within the Democratic Party even though it often opposed to the policies endorsed by the congressional leadership and its presidential candidates. George Wallace became the main spokesman for the distinctive Southern segregationist viewpoint of the 1960s, articulating a 'states' rights' doctrine and opposition to federal government intervention in social matters, particularly those pertaining to civil rights and race relations. In the 1980s Democratic candidates in the South moderated their views on these issues, reflecting both the changing socioeconomic position of the South and the recognition that they needed the votes of the increasingly significant black electorate there. In 1986, for example, the

Democrats won back control of the Senate partly because of the influence of black voters in the South in a number of key elections. The nomination and eventual election in 1976 of Jimmy Carter, the former Governor of Georgia, was the result of a calculated appeal to both liberals and conservatives within and outside the party. He managed to project the image of the 'moderate liberal Southerner' when campaigning in the North, while convincing his fellow Southerners that he was really a 'moderate conservative'! Edward Kennedy's challenge to Carter in the 1980 primaries was based on the claim that the President had failed to continue in office the liberal New Deal traditions of the party. The Democratic Party's candidates in the presidential primaries have tended to cover a wider spectrum of views than the Republicans but the nomination process generally favoured liberals consistent with the philosophy of most Democratic Party activists (although not most voters or even those who identify with the Democratic Party).

Following the defeats of Walter Mondale in 1984 and Michael Dukakis in 1988, the influence of the Democratic Leadership Council, a group within the party comprising moderate and mostly Southern politicians, increased considerably. The DLC argued that the party could only win a presidential election if it moved towards the centre, distanced itself from 'old-fashioned liberalism' and nominated a candidate who could appeal to the growing populations of the Southern and Western states, which had been won by the Republicans in recent campaigns. Two prominent members of the DLC were Governor Bill Clinton of Arkansas and Senator Al Gore of Tennessee. In 1992 Clinton campaigned as a 'new kind of Democrat', drawing a distinction with the 'tax and spend liberals' of the past. He argued for welfare reform to increase individual responsibility, supported a tax cut for the 'forgotten middle class' and favoured capital punishment. 'New Democrats' saw themselves as redefining liberal-left politics; by espousing the 'Third Way' as an alternative to free market conservatism and 'big-government' liberalism they argued that their approach was most appropriate in the information age, an era of globalisation and a predominantly middle-class electorate. As Dean McSweeney points out, for New Democrats the values of opportunity, responsibility and community have supplanted the liberals' attachment to equality, rights and government intervention.[16] By stressing the need for job training and an industrial strategy, Clinton was also able to appeal to the 'neo-liberals' within the party who, during the 1980s, had emphasised the necessity of the American economy adapting to the technological revolution. The neo-liberals, such as Gary Hart who ran in the 1984 primaries, argued for a tough-minded and non-ideological approach to dealing with problems, which recognises the fiscal and other limits on government action, while seeking to promote greater equity and social justice.[17]

In the Democratic primaries in 1992 the candidate most associated with 'New Deal liberalism', Senator Tom Harkin, did very poorly and was forced into an early withdrawal from the race. The radical wing of the Democratic Party had its most effective and charismatic spokesman in Jesse Jackson, who campaigned in the 1984 and 1988 primaries. Jackson argued that a more determined attempt to appeal to the disadvantaged groups in American society and the creation of a 'rainbow coalition', most of whom are currently alienated and do not vote, would pay greater electoral dividends than trying to appeal to white middle-class voters by forsaking traditional Democratic policies. In 1992 Jerry Brown, in the absence of Jackson, represented the most radical faction in the Democratic primaries. Nicol Rae's typology of Democratic Party factionalism identifies the New Left/Minorities (the radicals); the Neo-Liberals; the New Deal Regulars and the Southern Democrats.[18]

President Clinton's record of governing as a New Democrat was distinctly mixed, constrained as he was by regular opposition on the one hand from liberal Democrats in

Congress and on the other by Republican conservatives who became the majority party in the legislature after the 1994 midterm elections. Indeed, Republican successes in those elections was in large part due to the failures of Clinton's first two years in office, highlighted by his ill-fated health care reform proposals which bore all the hallmarks of extensive federal regulation and tax increases which New Democrats were supposed to have jettisoned. When Clinton did come to terms with the new political environment in which he was working after 1995 his 'triangulation' strategy allowed him to reassert his moderate credentials. This approach saw the President taking positions on issues midway between the liberal Democrats who dominated the congressional caucus and the Republican conservative majority. By compromising with the Republicans over welfare reform and measures to balance the federal budget Clinton could claim to have acted as a check on extremism and he appealed to the middle ground in the 1996 election. Clinton's successes in these areas appeared to marginalise his Republican opponent, Robert Dole on the right.

In the 2000 elections Clinton's Vice-President Al Gore, an early supporter of New Democrat policies, faced a challenge for the party nomination from former Senator Bill Bradley. Bradley's appeal in the primaries was to the traditional liberal constituencies within the Democratic Party and, in seeing off the challenge, Gore himself moved to the left. Despite his selection of Senator Joseph Lieberman, the chair of the Democratic Leadership Council, as his running-mate and the party platform praising fiscal responsibility as well as a tax cut for the middle classes, Gore continued to present himself in the general election campaign as an 'us *versus* them' populist, attacking big business and advocating federal programmes to solve social problems. This appeal was at least in part motivated by Gore's concern that he might lose crucial liberal support in key states to the Green candidate, Ralph Nader. However, New Democrats criticised Gore for conducting what they saw as an old-fashioned campaign based on class politics which discouraged many centrist voters from supporting the Democratic candidate.

The Democratic and Republican parties, therefore, do differ in their approaches to the central political question of how much government should do in a modern industrialised society and at what level. There are also internal divisions within each party on doctrinal and geographical lines. It is worth noting that there are greater differences between the leaders and activists of the political parties on policy questions than exist between the ordinary voting supporters of the parties. The leaders and activists, not surprisingly, hold more ideologically consistent views than the general population. Delegates attending the Republican and Democratic conventions also differ markedly in terms of ideology and attitudes on specific issues as well as in their socioeconomic backgrounds and membership of pressure groups.

Party leaders are aware that the general public are not deeply divided on ideological lines and therefore often make efforts to moderate internal doctrinal differences in order not to risk offending large sections of the electorate.

Minor parties and independent campaigns

We have already examined some of the underlying reasons for the dominant dualism of the American party system. Minor parties have had great difficulty achieving success in terms of gaining government office because of the electoral system, the cost of campaigning, the difficulty of securing a place on the ballot, the enduring nature of party identification and, perhaps most of all, the flexibility of the two main parties in being prepared to modify their own policies and programmes. In recent times, despite these problems, more minor party candidates have appeared on the ballot across the country and received a higher share of the votes. In 2000 over 50 minor parties ran candidates in congressional and gubernatorial races and the presidential election. One recent survey reported that 37 per cent of Americans said that they had voted for a minor party or independent candidate at some time. Support for minor parties has at various times demonstrated the lack of appeal and failure to aggregate interests by the two major parties. Republican and Democratic party leaders have tended to react to such movements in a typically pragmatic fashion: they hate to see much-needed electoral support going to minor parties.

> One of the persistent qualities of the American two-party system is the way in which one of the major parties moves almost instinctively to absorb – thus to be somewhat reshaped by – the most challenging third party of the time.[19]

In some states there have been local parties that have enjoyed some measure of success, such as the Progressives in Wisconsin and the New York Liberal and Conservative parties. At the national level, there have been two types of minor party. There are the ideological or doctrinal parties that have a long history of competing in elections, and there are the transient third parties that have a rapid rise and decline.

Doctrinal parties tend to operate on the fringes of the political consensus and advocate consistently ideologies or principles that do not find broad support among the electorate. They are therefore not prepared to compromise their basic policies in order to appeal to the voters; they would rather wait for the voters eventually to see the futility of supporting the two main parties and for them to desert in large numbers to an ideologically pure and consistent alternative. They do not seek or expect to govern immediately but think in the long term. Their candidates, therefore, often obtain a derisory percentage of the vote and have no real hope of winning elections. Examples of these parties would include the Socialists, the Socialist Workers Party and the Prohibition Party. Two of the most prominent ideological parties in recent times have been the Libertarians and the Greens. The Libertarian Party, which was founded in 1972, argues for a massive reduction in the powers of government at all levels. Its candidate, Ed Clark, won almost a million votes in the 1980 presidential election while in 2000 Harry Browne obtained over 384,000 votes. In 1996 the new Green Party, with a campaign based on environmental issues and the dangers of corporate power, had the well-known consumer advocate, Ralph Nader, as its candidate. Nader secured 684,871 votes – 0.7 per cent of the total – despite raising little money, campaigning only intermittently and being on the ballot in only 21 states. More than half his votes came from the three Pacific Coast states of California, Oregon and Washington. In 2000 Nader and the Greens won 2.9 million votes or 3 per cent of the total vote and had a significant impact on the election. Earlier in the campaign Nader appeared to be attracting considerably more support and some state polls showed him in double figures. As we have seen, Al Gore managed to lure some liberal voters back to the Democratic cause but not without alienating some moderate voters and at a cost of diverting campaign resources from key marginal states to shore up his support in what are normally safe Democratic strongholds.

The transient third parties, on the other hand, can be seen as part of the two-party system, as their national prominence is usually as a result of the inadequacies of that system and their speedy decline is due to their reabsorption within one or both of the major parties. They may be parties of economic protest such as the Populists in the 1890s or the Progressives in the 1920s whose rise was a reaction to increasing unemployment.

Table 6.4 Minor party candidates in the 2000 presidential election

Candidate/Party	Popular vote	%
Ralph Nader (Green)	2,882,955	2.74
Pat Buchanan (Reform)	448,895	0.42
Harry Browne (Libertarian)	384,431	0.36
Howard Phillips (Constitution)	98,020	0.09
John Hagelin (Natural Law)	83,714	0.08
James Harris (Socialist Workers)	7,378	0.01
L. Neil Smith (Libertarian)	5,775	0.00
David McReynolds (Socialist)	5,602	0.00
Monica Moorehead (Workers World)	4,795	0.00

Source: Federal Election Commission, www.fec.gov/pubrec/2000presgeresults.htm. Figures are official results, updated December 2001.

They may be secessionist parties who have broken away from one of the two main parties because of dissatisfaction with the majority coalition's policies or candidates. In 1912 the Progressive 'Bull Moose' movement split from the Republicans because former President Theodore Roosevelt mobilised opposition to President Taft's conservative policies. In 1948 some Southern Democrats refused to support Harry Truman's presidential campaign and broke away to launch the 'Dixiecrat' candidacy of South Carolina's Strom Thurmond. Twenty years later an even more serious division within the Democratic coalition led to the formation of George Wallace's American Independent Party. Wallace obtained 45 Electoral College votes in the South in 1968 under the AIP banner. The flexibility of the American party system is demonstrated by the fact that four years later he was back in the Democratic Party, and was shot in an assassination attempt while seeking its nomination in the primaries. The 1968 vote was, in effect, a personal vote for George Wallace and most of these supporters returned to the two-party system, leaving the American Independent Party to continue as a right-wing segregationalist doctrinal party. John Schmitz, the party's candidate for the presidency in 1972, obtained approximately 1 per cent of the popular vote, compared with Wallace's 13.5 per cent in 1968, and former Georgia Governor Lester Maddox fared even more disastrously in 1976, obtaining a mere 170,673 votes across the nation. By 1988 the AIP candidate polled only 27,818 votes.

In addition to minor party campaigns for the presidency there have also been two independent candidates in recent elections who polled substantial numbers of votes. In 1980 John Anderson, a liberal Republican Congressman from Illinois, ran as an Independent, having failed to win his party's nomination. He obtained 5.6 million votes or 7 per cent of the total. As we have seen, 19.7 million Americans, or 19 per cent of the total voting, backed Ross Perot in 1992.

Political parties today

Much of the academic debate about political parties has been over their declining influence within the political system, particularly noticeable in the 1960s and 1970s, and how far there have been signs of revival in the last couple of decades. It has been argued that the political parties have traditionally carried out important functions, and they have been regarded by political scientists as essential tools of democratic government. There has therefore been concern that a decline in political parties would damage their ability

---

Box 6.2   The Reform Party

Following Ross Perot's independent bid for the presidency in 1992 he formed an organisation of activists who had supported him, United We Stand America, with the stated intention of influencing congressional races in 1994 by defining issues and possibly by endorsing candidates. Perot later converted this structure into a new political party, the Reform Party, which called for major changes in the way the federal government is run to make it more accountable to the people. It also supported protectionist policies to defend American jobs and business from foreign competition and called for the repeal of NAFTA (the North American Free Trade Agreement).

Perot, not surprisingly, won the Reform Party nomination in 1996, defeating the former Governor of Colorado, Richard Lamm. However, Perot's vote in the presidential election went down from 19 per cent in 1992 to 8.4 per cent and showed a decline in every state. In 1998 the party had 184 candidates running in elections for the House, Senate and state government. It secured a famous victory when the former wrestler, Jesse 'The Body' Ventura, was elected to become the Governor of Minnesota.

Although Perot's vote in 1996 had been disappointing for party supporters it did exceed the 5 per cent minimum threshold required by law to qualify for federal funding for the party's candidate in 2000. The $13.4 million available to the Reform Party candidate made winning its nomination an attractive proposition for a politician who wanted a national platform from which to publicise his views. Pat Buchanan, who had unsuccessfully sought the Republican nomination in the previous two presidential elections, announced his candidacy for the Reform Party nomination. Buchanan's aggressive brand of social conservatism and nationalism was unacceptable to the more liberal members and Ventura left the party. In the summer of 2000 the party split into two distinct factions which even held separate conventions. Both groups laid claim to the federal funds which the Federal Election Commission eventually agreed should go to Buchanan. A significant number of Reform Party activists left to support John Hegelin, the Natural Law Party's candidate.

In the presidential election itself Buchanan received little media interest and he won less than 1 per cent of the vote, less than a half million nationally. His name was mostly in the news when, with the hotly disputed Florida election determining the national result, some voters who were confused by the design of the ballot paper in their county claimed afterwards that they had mistakenly voted for him when they had intended to vote for Gore.

It seems unlikely that the Reform Party will survive the trauma of the 2000 election. Ironically, whereas lack of financial resources has normally been seen as a major factor explaining the lack of success of alternatives to the two main parties, in the case of the Reform party it was the struggle to control the financial resources which the taxpayer was providing for it which led to its electoral suicide.

---

to perform these roles within the political system. What then are the functions that parties have fulfilled to make representative government viable?

First, the peaceful transfer of power from one administration to another, which is one of the characteristics of a stable democracy, is helped by the existence of parties. One President and his staff leave the White House as a new Chief Executive and his party move in. The transition requires cooperation but the new President can find people to take over the vacant offices by rewarding party notables and supporters. In this sense, the parties are huge personnel agencies to be drawn on for filling government posts, judicial appointments and congressional offices.

Political recruitment of potential government leaders also occurs through the political parties. Candidates for local, state and federal offices normally have been active in party politics and emerge as people with leadership qualities. Although it is possible in American politics to become a government leader, and even President, without close ties and a long history of party connections (as Dwight D. Eisenhower did), the vast majority of the political elite, elected and appointed, have risen through the party system.

Parties, therefore, find potential leaders, nominate them for office and provide choices of candidates for the electorate. They also simplify the choice by providing party labels as a frame of reference and guideline for the voters. Fred Greenstein has pointed out that the majority of American citizens' actual information and knowledge about issues and government policies are very vague and that political party labels allow the voters to respond to complex events by simple criteria. Without such a structuring of the choices, detailed research on the issues and the candidates' backgrounds would be necessary for a meaningful choice.[20] It is also worth remembering that American voters are required to select candidates for dozens of federal, state and local positions on the same ballot and that, without the party guideline to help them sort out the vast array of hopefuls, most electors would be totally lost. The effect would be to reduce voting turnout and increase the importance of less relevant criteria such as the names of the candidates or their positions on the ballot paper. It can be argued, therefore, that parties encourage both electoral participation and accountability of government office-holders to the voters.

The American parties also provide a series of programmes and policies in their platforms and documents. They may not be as specific and clear-cut in terms of sharp differences as some critics would like, and may not be able to be carried out as effectively as party manifestos in a parliamentary democracy where the government can count on the support of a disciplined legislative majority (although the House Republicans' 'Contract with America' came close to it in 1994–95), but the parties do perform the function of interest aggregation by putting forward coherent programmes of broad appeal. By doing so they can help reconcile the interests of conflicting groups in a diverse society. Parties organise voters into coalitions whose interests are loosely but perceptibly linked to policies proposed by groupings of politicians under the same party label. As we pointed out in Chapter 1, parties also may help to bridge the institutional gaps created by the separation of powers and the Constitution.

Evidence of the decline of political parties occurred in a number of different areas.[21] In organisational terms there was a declining number of activists and many official positions in the party structures remained unfilled. The parties to a large extent lost direct control of their nomination processes as more candidates were selected by the primaries. American parties cannot even exclude from their nomination process candidates who are totally outside the mainstream of the party's beliefs or who have run against party nominees in the past. Racist politician David Duke not only campaigned for the Republican nomination for state office but also entered the 1992 presidential primaries, to the embarrassment of party leaders who roundly condemned his extreme views. Duke, who had been the Populist Party's presidential candidate in 1988 when he received almost 47,000 votes, appeared in 16 Republican primaries and won over 10 per cent of the votes in Mississippi, although few elsewhere. As the use of primaries increased so did the number of candidate-centred organisations actually running election campaigns. PACs have taken a bigger role in funding candidates, further reducing the influence of parties. The role of grass-roots activists carrying out traditional electioneering declined, to be replaced by campaigns conducted increasingly through the use of television.

As far as the electorate is concerned, there is considerable evidence pointing to partisan dealignment, that is the weakening of identification with and attachment to a political party. More voters have said they were independent of party although, as we have noted, around 90 per cent of the electorate still have some sort of identification, no matter how weak, with one or other of the two major parties. Of those who do identify with one of the parties there has been an erosion in the commitment of many to their party and split-ticket voting has become common. Split-ticket voting has had a direct effect on the working of government, with more frequent occurrences of divided party control of the legislative and executive branches at state as well as at national level, thus making it more difficult for parties to bridge the gap created by the separation of powers system. In the 1970s parties also declined within Congress, as we saw in Chapter 2, with party cohesion weakened and greater independence among legislators making governing more problematic for both party leaders in Congress and for the President.

Despite these trends there have been signs of party renewal and revival in the 1980s and 1990s. We have seen that the Republican Party led the way in strengthening the capacity of its national organisation. In doing so, it offered services to candidates in competition with political consultants and other providers while, at the same time, it built up grass-roots structures at state and local level. Although they may not act as governing bodies over the rest of the party organisation in the country or exert disciplinary control over candidates, political scientists such as Larry Sabato believe that the national parties are stronger than they have ever been in their history.[22] There is also evidence that party activists have started to rebuild and revitalise local party organisations in some parts of the country. Most voters still do identify with parties and support their candidates for office and, as we saw in Chapter 2, party cohesion in Congress increased markedly in the 1980s and 1990s.

With regard to the selection of candidates the Supreme Court has supported the right of political parties to control their nomination processes and determine who can compete in them. In *California Democratic Party* v. *Jones* (2000) the justices decided that a state law which imposed a blanket primary on the parties was unconstitutional. In a blanket primary candidates from all parties compete in one primary election and the top two qualify to contest the general election even if they happen to be from the same party. The Court ruled that this type of primary infringed the parties' First Amendment right to freedom of association. In 2002 the potential power of the national party leadership over the nomination processes of state parties was demonstrated in an unusual way when President George W. Bush intervened directly to recruit Republican candidates for key Senate races and the White House was seen to be supporting particular candidates for the party's nomination. Bush's interest in securing Republican majorities in both houses of Congress led him to promote attractive moderately conservative candidates over those who were seen as too far to the right to win crucial seats. Bush's vigorous campaigning on behalf of Republican candidates was also unusual for a President in midterm elections when his party normally suffers setbacks. Bush's popularity appears to have had a significant effect in his party achieving control of both houses in 2002 and he demonstrated the President's role as a national party leader who can unite the disparate elements into an effective campaign organisation.

James W. Ceaser sees the parties as being flexible bodies that are able to adapt by using the new technology and campaign methods that have often been said to have been instrumental in their decline. He believes that parties could be strengthened by developments in areas where political leaders can have influence: by changing the prevailing opinion among elites and the public about the proper role for parties, particularly in their relationship with candidates, and by altering party rules and election laws at state and federal level that bear on how the parties function, especially with regard to the financing of campaigns. He concludes:

A consideration of parties today reveals a number of tendencies and counter-tendencies at work at the same time. In different ways, parties are declining, stabilizing, and resurging. The fluidity of this situation is reinforced by forces driving party development, which leave a great deal to human choice. . . . The future of the American political party depends greatly on what people decide its future should be.[23]

As we have seen, the parties have raised large amounts of 'soft money' to spend in support of their presidential campaigns as well as on party-building activities at state level, the use for which it was originally intended. This money has also been used extensively to support congressional campaigns as well, although legislation passed by Congress in 2002 bans soft money contributions to parties after the 2002 elections (see Chapter 7). A Supreme Court decision in 1996, *Colorado Republican Federal Campaign Committee* v. *FEC*, allowed parties to raise and spend unlimited amounts to support their congressional candidates so long as these expenditures were not coordinated with their campaigns. However, in a 2001 case the Court upheld strict spending limits on how much hard money parties could spend in conjunction with their candidates; this was carried by a 5–4 vote and disappointed those advocates of stronger political parties playing a more prominent role in election campaigns.

Chapter summary

- American political parties have to operate within a diverse society and a federal system of government. They have tended to be broadly based coalitions of interests organised in a decentralised manner. US parties have traditionally been rather weak organisations compared with those in European democracies.
- As political parties are bodies which are set up to fight and win elections their main organisational units are based within electoral constituencies at state and local levels. Until recent decades the national party organisations really only came into play in presidential election years. However, both main parties have strengthened their national committees' staffing and resources since the 1980s and expect them to play a more active role on a permanent basis.
- Political party organisations have been weakened by the use of primary elections to select candidates for office. This not only takes away the control of nominations from the party leadership but also requires candidates to set up their own electoral organisations to win the primary which are then kept in operation for the general election campaign.
- The United States has had a two-party system during most of its history, although there have been periods when one party has been dominant. Since the 1970s the Democrats have gradually lost the dominance they enjoyed in the period after the Great Depression in the 1930s. In the early twenty-first century it appears that the two main parties are almost evenly balanced in terms of popular support and political representation, although the Republicans had control of the presidency and Congress by narrow majorities in 2003.
- Although American parties have traditionally been less ideological in nature than their European counterparts and have accommodated people with a diverse range of views, today the Republican Party is principally and overwhelmingly a conservative party and the Democratic Party, while still more heterogeneous than their rivals, has a clear majority of those who see themselves as liberals.

- Minor parties have had difficulty in making an impact on American politics because of the first-past-the-post electoral system, the cost of campaigning, the problems of securing a place on the ballot paper and the willingness of the two main parties to adopt policies espoused by smaller parties if they prove to be popular with the electorate.
- Despite their relative weakness American political parties fulfil to some extent important functions for the political system. They allow for a peaceful transfer of power from one administration to another, they recruit candidates for elective offices and for appointed positions in government, they structure electoral choice for the voters and they develop policies and programmes.
- Evidence of the decline of political parties in the 1970s, such as the rising number of independent voters and the incidence of split-ticket voting, has been counterbalanced in more recent times by signs of party revival and renewal. These include the rebuilding of local party organisations, the strengthening of the national party committees and their roles and the ability of parties to raise large amounts of campaign money.

Think points

- People often used to say that the Democratic and Republican parties did not offer the voters a real choice. How far is that true today?
- Political scientists have often bemoaned what they have seen as the decline of political parties. Is this concern still justified and, if so, why?

Some further reading

John H. Aldrich, *Why Parties? The Origin and Transformation of Party Politics in America* (University of Chicago Press 1995)

John J. Coleman, *Party Decline in America: Policy, Politics, and the Fiscal State* (Princeton University Press 1996)

John C. Green and Daniel M. Shea, *The State of the Parties: The Changing Role of Contemporary American Parties* (Rowman and Littlefield 1999)

William J. Keefe, *Parties, Politics and Public Policy in America* (Congressional Quarterly Press 1998)

Dean McSweeney and John Zvesper, *American Political Parties* (Routledge 1991)

L. Sandy Maisel, *The Parties Respond: Changes in American Parties and Campaigns* (Westview 1998)

Nelson Polsby, *Consequences of Party Reform* (Oxford University Press 1994).

Larry Sabato, *The Party's Just Begun* (Scott, Foresman 1988)

Frank J. Sorauf and Paul Allen Beck, *Party Politics in America* (Scott, Foresman 1988)

Martin P. Wattenberg, *American Parties in Decline* (Harvard University Press 1990)

Weblinks

Democratic National Committee: www.democrats.org
Democratic Congressional Campaign Committee: www.dccc.org
Democratic National Senate Committee: www.dnsc.org
Republican National Committee: www.rnc.org
National Republican Congressional Committee: www.nrcc.org
National Republican Senatorial Committee: www.nrsc.org

Green Parties: www.greenparty.org and www.greenparties.org
Libertarian Party: www.lp.org
Reform Party: www.reformparty.org

7 Elections and voting

No nation in the world has as many elections as the United States. In a presidential election year, American voters across the country select a total of over half a million officials in addition to the President, the members of the House of Representatives and a third of the Senate. Altogether there are over a million elected positions, the vast majority of which are at the local level for school boards, county boards of supervisors, sheriffs, and so on. As well as electing politicians to national, state and local offices Americans in many states are asked to vote on a wide range of issues in state and local referenda when propositions are submitted to the electorate for approval in accord with state constitutions. Before these general elections there are also primary elections which in most states determine who will represent the parties in the November contests.

Elections are not only a method of deciding who shall govern and hold office but are also important in the process of political communication. Candidates and parties have to attempt to identify the interests of the people in their campaigns; not only do they speak about what they intend to do if elected, they are also obliged to listen to the views of the voters. Politicians who seek election or re-election need to be responsive to public opinion and American legislators are well aware of the 'folks back home'. Elections allow ordinary citizens to participate in politics in a number of ways besides voting. If they are sufficiently interested they can work on behalf of a candidate or contribute money to his campaign funds, and the right to take part in these ways reinforces the feelings of Americans that they live in a liberal democracy.

Who runs for the presidency?

The President's roles and limitations have already been examined in Chapter 3, and it is clear that not only Americans but people throughout the world have an interest in how he is selected and what kind of individual is given legitimacy by the electoral process to control the powers of the presidency. For the parties the presidency is the big prize; it is the only nationally elected office (along with the vice-presidency), and each party hopes not only that one of its members will lead the nation in order to determine domestic and international policy priorities, but also that the future will in addition bring the fruits of office in the shape of appointments and favours to state and local organisations.

James Bryce said in 1910 that American parties were more concerned that their nominee for the White House should be a good candidate than that he should turn out to be a good President. What sort of person makes a 'good candidate' and who actually runs for the presidency of the United States? The formal qualifications are clearly stated in the Constitution: the President must be 35 years of age or over, must have been a resident of the country for 14 years, and must be a natural-born American citizen. This last condition excludes millions of Americans who are immigrants and naturalised citizens as well as the many aliens who live and work in the country. Henry Kissinger and Madeleine Albright, both naturalised citizens born in Germany and the Czech Republic respectively who served as Secretary of State, have been excluded from the presidency on this basis although not, of course, from having considerable influence within the White House. However, there are many more millions of Americans who technically are qualified to become President, but who in practice are ineligible because they lack the 'political' qualifications.

First, presidential candidates are almost always male and white; certainly all the 43 Presidents have had these characteristics. In 1984 and 1988 the Rev. Jesse Jackson made a major impact in the Democratic Party's nomination process. After winning two primaries and 18 per cent of the votes cast in 1984 primaries, Jackson extended his support in 1988 beyond black voters in the cities and came top in seven primaries and won a total of 29.1 per cent of the votes cast, second only to the eventual nominee, Michael Dukakis. The high regard with which Margaret Thatcher is held in America has almost certainly helped to prepare the electorate for the possibility of a woman in the White House and in 1984 Geraldine Ferraro was the first woman vice-presidential candidate. Elizabeth Dole, a Cabinet Secretary in the Reagan administration and wife of the 1996 Republican presidential candidate, ran a brief campaign in 2000 for the party nomination before withdrawing through lack of money.

Presidential candidates are normally middle-aged. Americans are thought to want a mature and responsible individual as President, and therefore the candidate will preferably be in his middle to late forties or fifties. He cannot be too young or he will be accused of being inexperienced, and if he is over 65 there will be doubts as to whether he is too advanced in years to stand the strains of the office. Ronald Reagan, who was 69 years old in 1980, defused the 'age issue' by vigorous campaigning throughout the Republican primaries. Four years later the issue surfaced briefly after a stumbling performance by the President in the first television debate against challenger Walter Mondale, but Reagan was enjoying a huge lead in the opinion polls at the time and a better showing in the second debate limited the damage. Subsequently he won an easy re-election victory to become America's oldest ever President. In 1996 Robert Dole was 73 years old and, if elected, would have become America's oldest ever first-term President; although fit and appearing younger than his years, the generational gap between him and the 50 year-old President Clinton became an issue during the campaign. No matter what his age, the candidate should be in good health mentally and physically – his fitness for the office may otherwise become a campaign issue later. A wife and family are also generally prerequisites for the aspiring candidate; not only do they provide him with a settled family image but they can also become useful campaigners in their own right. Governor Jerry Brown of California who campaigned in 1976, 1980 and 1992 was unusual in being both relatively young (at 39 in 1976) and a bachelor.

The scrutiny by the media of the suitability of candidates for the presidency, including their past personal lives, reached a new level in 1988 when Gary Hart, who had been the frontrunner for the Democratic nomination, was forced to withdraw from the race after allegations about extra-marital affairs. Although he tried to make a comeback his chances were ruined by the issue. Bill Clinton managed to survive similar allegations in the early stages of the 1992 campaign. He and his wife Hillary were forced to go on television to discuss their marriage and assure voters that any problems they might have had in the past were behind them. Stories about Clinton's personal life continued to circulate during his first term, and a sexual harassment suit brought against the President by Paula Jones, a former Arkansas state employee, caused embarrassment in the run-up to the

1996 campaign. Despite a number of personal, financial and political scandals leading to Clinton's character and integrity being questioned, voters in 1996 largely appeared to ignore such issues and the President enjoyed high public approval ratings for his overall performance in office.

Inevitably presidential candidates tend to be politicians with considerable practical governmental experience. There can be no completely adequate preparation for the presidency as there is no other office quite like it, but perhaps the nearest approximation to the role of the American Chief Executive is that of the state Governors, although their concerns in the state capitals are purely domestic and they have no responsibility for the vital area of foreign affairs. Four of the last five Presidents have served as Governors before entering the White House. Leading Senators may also aspire to the presidency even though the legislative responsibilities of a Senator are quite different from those of the head of the executive branch. The Vice-President may also hope to have the opportunity of heading his party's ticket, and members of the House of Representatives and Cabinet Secretaries also occasionally run. To be serious contenders they will all have to convince the party activists that they can extend their electoral base from the local and state to the national level.

There have been candidates whose main claim to leadership potential was not in the political but the military field. Dwight D. Eisenhower in the 1950s was the most recent example to make it to the White House, but in the nineteenth century several Presidents established their names initially as military heroes. In 1996 the popular former Chairman of the Joint Chiefs of Staff, Colin Powell, was under pressure to declare as a candidate for the Republican nomination but he eventually ruled himself out of the race. Candidates are likely to be drawn from business and professional backgrounds; even though they may have been brought up in modest family circumstances they are likely to have become fairly wealthy in their own right. In 1996 billionaire businessman Steve Forbes sought the Republican nomination in a self-financed campaign that was based principally on promoting the merits of a flat-rate income tax system. Presidential candidates, like Congressmen, have often been lawyers, although Jimmy Carter had been a Georgian peanut farmer and businessman, and Ronald Reagan was a Hollywood actor before becoming Governor of California. In 1988 two church leaders were prominent candidates although neither Jesse Jackson nor Pat Robertson, the right-wing evangelist, had any experience of public office.

It seems that the religious background of a candidate is much less important today than it has been in the past. It was often said that a presidential candidate had, in practice, to be a Protestant to be successful; John Kennedy became the first Catholic President in 1960 and disposed of that argument. Jimmy Carter's Baptist religion was discussed in the 1976 election and may have had a marginal effect on voting behaviour, but it was not a major problem for his campaign. In 2000 Al Gore selected Senator Joseph Lieberman as his running mate and he became the first Jewish candidate on a presidential ticket. Lieberman had been chosen with his strong moral views in mind but after a flurry of public comment about his religion when he was first nominated thereafter it did not appear to be a significant factor in the campaign.

Serious candidates for the presidency normally strive to win the nomination of one of the two main parties; minor party candidates may exert an influence on the eventual outcome of the election, although this is rare, but they have little real chance of winning themselves. Ross Perot's candidacy in 1992 was the most successful independent or third party campaign since 1912; he obtained 19 per cent of the popular vote nationally, although he failed to gain any Electoral College votes.

Any presidential aspirant has to win two main contests to take occupancy of the White House: first, the nomination of his own party in competition with other potential candidates, and then the presidential 'general' election against the other party's nominee. Together these contests make for a long and arduous struggle, a battle that will tax the energies and finances of even the most dedicated and ambitious politician. They will test his stamina, his nerve and the loyalty of his family as he criss-crosses the nation in order to build the foundations of a party and electoral coalition. In recent years many well-qualified potential candidates have decided not to seek the presidency because of their reluctance to submit themselves and their families to the intrusive scrutiny of the media which involves making public personal, financial and even medical records. The rigours of a long campaign and an unwillingness or inability to raise the large amounts of money necessary to make a viable run have also been factors. The battle for the party's nomination can almost be seen as a four-year process, because as soon as one election is resolved speculation starts among the politicians and pundits as to who will be the candidates at the next election. Following the midterm congressional elections the guessing game reaches new heights as a field of candidates emerges when declarations are made, disavowals of interest stated and organisations are developed in those states holding early presidential primaries. Some politicians prefer to sound out opinion in the country by personal tours before formally announcing whether they are in the running. In December 2002 the defeated Democratic nominee in 2000, Al Gore, declared that he would not be a candidate again in 2004. After undertaking a national tour, ostensibly to promote books he had written with his wife, and consulting party notables around the country, he concluded that he would not have the crucial support from Democratic opinion leaders and fund-raisers that he would need to make a further run for the presidency. Those who have retired from office the previous year have more time and opportunities to sound out opinion and make earlier campaign sorties than those currently in government. Both Jimmy Carter and Ronald Reagan ceased to be Governors in January 1975 and used the next year marshalling support and travelling in readiness for the 1976 campaigns. Table 7.1 shows the main dates on the timetable leading to the election.

Table 7.1 The presidential election timetable

Before election year: 1–3 years before the election	Candidates sound out opinion, prepare organisations and declare interest
	Campaigning begins in those states with early primaries and caucuses
January to June	State primaries and caucuses select delegates
July–August	National conventions – formally nominate party candidates
September to early November	Election campaign between parties' candidates
First week in November	Presidential election day
December	Formal count of Electoral College Votes
January	Inauguration of new President

The nomination process

The objective for any candidate in the nomination process is to obtain the support of a simple majority of the delegates to the party's national nominating convention that is held in the summer of election year. For example, in 1996 the Republican candidates required 996 votes and at the Democratic convention 2,145 was the magic figure for victory. Each state party has the right to send a number of delegates to represent its views and this will be approximately proportional to the population size of the state. However, some states may be given extra delegates as a reward for supporting the party's candidate for Governor or presidency at the last election. The delegates at national conventions tended to be overwhelmingly white, middle-aged and male until the 1960s and pressures grew from minority groups for fairer representation. Challenges against some Southern Democratic states' delegations on the basis of racial bias led to protest walk-outs. In 1972 the Democratic Party adopted a 'quota system' and demanded that each state delegation reflect the proportions of women, young people, blacks and other minorities in the population at large. After the disastrous 1972 McGovern defeat the system was dropped and a compromise formula established which lays down only that state parties must seek to achieve a fair cross-section of social groups within their delegations.

The Democratic Party's emphasis on the representation of grass-roots activists at the national convention and the increasing use of primaries for delegate selection in 1972 and 1976 resulted in the exclusion from the convention of many leading party figures in Congress and state politics as well as the charge being made that delegates were out of touch with the views of ordinary Democratic voters. In 1982 the National Committee accepted the recommendations of a party commission chaired by North Carolina Governor, James Hunt, that about 14 per cent of the delegate votes in the 1984 Convention (566 out of a total of 3,933) would be elected office-holders uncommitted to any candidate and this would renew the national party's ties with its estranged congressional wing.[1]

In subsequent elections the Democratic Party increased the number of so-called 'super-delegates' to around 750 to include members of Congress, state Governors, the Democratic National Committee and elder statesmen, such as former presidential candidates. In 1992 almost one in five of the delegates to the New York convention were super-delegates. When this change was first made there was speculation that these delegates might hold the balance of power at the convention in a race where no candidate secured a clear lead in the primary elections, but this has not proved to be the case so far.

There are two main methods for electing delegates to the national conventions:

State caucuses and conventions

Until the 1970s the caucus-convention method of selecting delegates was the dominant form. Caucuses are mass meetings of active party supporters who gather on a precinct basis in schools, village halls and private homes to express their preferences for the presidential nomination. The caucus-convention method provided for the election of delegates by rank and file party activists from one level of the party to the next – from precinct caucuses to county conventions to the state convention and from there to the national convention. During the 1970s the number of states using this process declined so that by 1980 only one-quarter of the delegates to the national convention coming from 17 or 18 states were selected in this way. In 1988 675 out of 4,160 Democratic delegates were selected by the caucus method while 471 Republican delegates out of 2,277 were chosen this way. In 1992 Democrats in 17 states and Republicans in 14 used caucuses. By 2000 caucuses and conventions were held in only 13 states by the Democrats and in six states by the Republicans, including in one state by each party where caucuses were used in conjunction with primaries.

State caucuses tend to reflect the more clearly defined doctrinal views of interested grass-roots supporters and local politicians. They also favour candidates who have a long record of working for the party in the country and whose efforts have been appreciated by party workers.

State caucuses do not obtain as much media attention as presidential primaries but since 1976, when Jimmy Carter first came to public notice in the Iowa caucuses, held even before the first primary in New Hampshire, more interest has been focused upon them. The Iowa caucuses have now become the first major battleground of the nominations process, with some candidates spending months of their time and considerable resources in personally wooing the relatively small number of activists who attend the party meetings. In 2000 Al Gore won 63 per cent of the 1,969 votes cast in the Iowa Democratic caucuses. Candidates invest so much time and money in Iowa in the hope that a good performance in the state will give them an early breakthrough and the momentum to succeed in the New Hampshire primary. In 1992 the estimated attendance at Democratic meetings varied from around 1,100 in Alaska to 60,000 in Minnesota and Washington. Candidates try to ensure that there is a maximum turnout of their own supporters at these caucuses and the effectiveness of the candidates' organisations in the state is often the key factor in determining success.

The presidential primaries

In 1968 presidential primaries were used by Republicans in 16 states and Democrats in 17; by 1980 this had grown to 32 and 33 respectively with three-quarters of national convention delegates selected in this way. A small number of states combined the use of primaries and caucuses. In 1996 the Republicans held 42 primaries in which 13.8 million people participated, while 8.6 million took part in the Democratic contests even though President Clinton was unopposed.

The rules for primaries vary considerably, are complicated and forever changing, particularly in the Democratic Party. Voters elect delegates by casting ballots directly for them or by expressing a preference for a particular candidate. In some states delegates' names appear on the ballot and are elected directly; any preference vote for a candidate is non-binding on the delegates. In closed primaries registered party voters only may participate in their party's election. In open primaries party registration is not a factor and electors can vote in either party's event. In other states registered party voters may only take part in their own party's primary and independent voters can participate in either.

As far as the allocation of delegates is concerned, the Democratic Party now insists upon proportional representation, with all candidates who reach a threshold of 15 per cent in a state obtaining a share of the delegates. The Republicans allow a greater variety of approaches. States may use a 'winner-takes-all' system, with the leading candidate state-wide acquiring all the at-large delegates and other delegates going to the top candidate in each congressional district.

The increasing number of primaries has led to several significant developments. Candidates are obliged to develop personal organisations in a large number of states, making them more independent of the formal party hierarchy. Primaries, therefore, tend to weaken the influence of the state party elders and 'bosses' and there is little or no scope for the 'smoke-filled room' decision-making at the party convention, as in the past. The tactic that has been used in the past, of avoiding the primaries and hoping that a dead-locked convention will allow one's emergence as the compromise candidate, is also very unlikely to be successful. Candidates who are serious presidential contenders now have to enter the primaries at the beginning to pick up delegate support because generally one candidate builds so great a lead that he or she is impossible to stop.

Primary campaigns traditionally began in the cold North-Eastern state of New Hampshire in late February and went on to the climax in sunny California, the largest state with the most delegates, in June. The increasing number of primaries has stretched candidates' resources, particularly as they will be fighting in a number of different states on the same day. In 1988 an important development took place in that 16 states, mostly in the South, agreed to hold their primaries on 8 March and this became known as 'Super Tuesday'. The move had been initiated by Southern Democrats who had hoped that by establishing a regional contest on the same day the candidates would be obliged to take more notice of their interests and that their influence would be strengthened in relation to the Northern liberal states. If it was intended to prevent the eventual nomination of a liberal Democrat it was a failure because Michael Dukakis won in Texas and Florida and thus established himself as a broad-based candidate, while Jesse Jackson won five Southern states. Senator Albert Gore of Tennessee also won in five Southern Border states after a concentrated campaign in the area but failed to do well elsewhere in the country. George Bush swept the Super Tuesday primaries to virtually assure himself of the Republican nomination while his rival Robert Dole failed to win a single primary on 8 March.

In 1992 a number of states, particularly in the West, moved their caucuses and primaries to the week before Super Tuesday in an attempt to increase their own influence on the nomination. In practice, the results of 'Junior Tuesday', as it became known, proved to be indecisive on the Democratic side and it was not until Super Tuesday on 10 March that Bill Clinton, by winning throughout the Southern states, emerged as the clear frontrunner. Therefore, although Super Tuesday in 1992 was reduced to eight primaries and four caucus states, its influence was considerable. In 1996 each Tuesday throughout the month of March saw a number of primaries clustered in a particular region: on 5 March New England; 12 March the South; 19 March the Midwest; and, finally, 26 March the Western states.

In recent elections there has been an increasing tendency to 'frontloading' in the delegate-selection process. In 1980 only nine states held their primaries before April. Approximately a third of all Democratic delegates in 1992 were chosen in the eight-day period of 3–10 March and half of the total were selected by the end of March (compared with 38 per cent in 1984). This trend was developed further in 1996 when two-thirds of the Republican delegates were selected by the end of March. In 2000 Republicans in 27 states held their nominating events before the end of March, with 11 taking place before the end of February and a further 13 on Super Tuesday, 7 March. By the end of March approximately 70 per cent of the delegates to both party conventions had been selected.[2] The effect of this development is that, once a frontrunner does emerge from the pack, he or she appears to be unstoppable. Frontloading has also led to politicians announcing their candidacies for the presidency far earlier than used to be the case. By early January 2003, almost two years before the election, Howard Dean, the former Governor of Vermont, Senator John Kerry of Massachusetts, Rep. Richard Gephardt of Missouri, Senator John Edwards of North Carolina, Senator and former vice-presidential candidate Joseph Lieberman and radical black preacher Rev. Al Sharpton had all declared their intentions to seek the Democratic nomination for 2004. This is partially the result of candidates having to build a very substantial war-chest of campaign funds well before the primary season starts. There is now little chance of building on the momentum from early successes and raising money later in the process because the vital contests are concentrated into such a short period.

Voters in states which hold their primaries at the end of the season have often understandably complained that they are virtually disenfranchised in the process because most of the candidates have withdrawn by then and they are left only to endorse the presumed nominee or to cast what is effectively a protest vote. Disagreements on alternative dates, requirements of state laws and the need to hold primaries for state and local offices have prevented these potentially powerful states from having more influence, although California did move its primary in 1996 from June to the end of March and in 2000 to 7 March.

The trend of holding larger numbers of primaries earlier in the year also means that, after months of personal campaigning in the small states of Iowa and New Hampshire where there is both massive media coverage and also the opportunity to meet voters and address meetings to gain momentum from early victories, the frenetic pace of the campaign thereafter inevitably leads to most of the states being fought principally through the use of television and advertising.

Presidential primaries serve a major purpose apart from the selection of delegates; they demonstrate something which the parties are clearly concerned to discover before entrusting the nomination to a candidate: who can and who cannot win votes. Victory in a primary can remove fears about a candidate among the party 'professionals' and activists. John Kennedy's win in the mainly Protestant state of West Virginia in 1960 showed that his Catholic religion was not as much a handicap as his opponents had forecast. Jimmy Carter's victory in Pennsylvania, a Northern industrial state, allayed suspicions that he was merely a Southern regional candidate, while Clinton's victories outside his own region, in Illinois and Michigan, a week after Super Tuesday consolidated his position as the Democratic frontrunner in 1992.

The early primaries play an important role in weeding out those contenders who have little real public support within their own parties. Candidates tend to enter the primaries in which they feel they can do quite well, and victory or a second place showing in a large field can be a major boost to an individual's chances and enhance the morale of his supporters. Perhaps most importantly, it will impress party leaders and voters in other states. On the other hand, a poor showing in one of the early primaries may lead to a candidate dropping out of the race altogether as his organisation crumbles and his financial resources dry up.

The media here is important, not only in reporting campaign news and events, but also in their interpretation of what is happening. Journalists tend to focus on the 'horse race' aspects of the nomination process: who is in the lead, who is behind and so on, but they do so through the lens of expectations.

> Expectations of candidate performance are crucial to interpreting the evolution of the race. Primary and caucus results are reported not just in terms of raw data but in terms of how the candidates performed against what was expected of them.[3]

It is a remarkable aspect of American presidential politics that someone who is virtually unknown nationally at the beginning of election year, such as Jimmy Carter in 1976 and Bill Clinton in 1992, can have an unassailable lead and become his party's nominee within a few months. In 1992 Governor Douglas Wilder of Virginia withdrew from the Democratic race even before the primary season had begun, while Senator Bob Kerrey of Nebraska and Senator Tom Harkin of Iowa dropped out after disappointing early results. Former Senator Paul Tsongas of Massachusetts, who had been the first Democrat to declare his candidacy in 1991 at the height of George Bush's popularity, bowed out after the Super Tuesday contests, having run out of money and energy. Only former California Governor Jerry Brown who, in the absence of Jesse Jackson, sought to appeal to the party's radical wing and those disillusioned with orthodox party politics, continued his lonely campaign against Clinton to the convention in July. Although the party establishment may have less control of the nominations process as a result of popular involvement through the primary system, it may still influence events. In 1996 the Republicans had an original field of nine candidates, although only five (Dole, Buchanan, Forbes, Senator Phil Gramm of Texas and former Tennessee Governor Lamar Alexander) could be said to be serious contenders. Dole suffered some early setbacks with defeats in New Hampshire (to Buchanan) and in Delaware and Arizona (to Forbes) but, with the party hierarchy rallying to his cause and opposing what they saw as the dangers of the extremist Buchanan gaining further success, he won the vital South Carolina primary on 2 March and throughout that month went on to sweep the remaining primaries to secure the nomination. Overall, Dole won 59 per cent of the total votes cast in the primaries and 1,477 convention delegates. Pat Buchanan continued to campaign after all the other candidates had dropped out, amassed 21 per cent of the popular vote and received 141 delegates.

In 2000 Clinton's Vice-President, Al Gore, was always seen as the favourite to win the Democratic Party's nomination. He was, however, challenged by former Senator Bill Bradley who came close to upsetting the Vice-President when he won 48 per cent of the vote in the New Hampshire primary. After it was revealed that Bradley was suffering from a heart problem his campaign faltered and Gore went on to win all of the party's primaries and caucuses. On the Republican side, the Governor of Texas and son of the former President, George W. Bush, became the clear favourite to win the Republican nomination, having the considerable benefits of name recognition and huge fund-raising ability. Observers have commented in recent elections that the 'invisible primary' plays an increasingly important role in the nomination process. By this they mean that, before any formal votes are cast, one candidate has secured sufficient money, endorsements from party leaders and media coverage to hold a lead in opinion polls and in straw polls of party activists to emerge as the likely winner. The Republican nomination process in 2000 was a good example of this. A number of potential or declared candidates, such as Elizabeth Dole and Dan Quayle, dropped out when they realised that they could not mount an effective challenge to Bush. Steve Forbes was again prepared to spend vast amounts of his own money but, as in 1996, he made little impact. Senator John McCain, who had established a reputation as a reformer but who was regarded by many Republicans as a maverick, obtained very positive media coverage because of his accessibility and willingness to speak candidly on controversial issues. McCain won the New Hampshire primary and six others, doing well in those states which allowed Democrats and independent voters to participate in the Republican contests. However, he withdrew from the race after Super Tuesday when Bush won all the big states and he only did well in a few New England states.

The party that already controls the White House usually has fewer problems in finding a candidate if the President is eligible and wishes to run again. No incumbent President who actively sought it has been denied his party's nomination since 1884. Therefore in some cases the primary elections and state caucuses are merely formalities with either no opposition or purely token resistance from a minor faction within the party; Johnson in 1964, Nixon in 1972, Reagan in 1984 and Clinton in 1996 were all renominated in conventions that were uncontested. However, the strength of the opposition to an incumbent President in an early primary may lead him to decide not to fight again. President Truman in 1952 and Johnson in 1968 both determined to retire from politics rather than face a struggle for their own party's nomination. The opposition to the Vietnam War policies and the support for Eugene McCarthy in the first primaries in 1968 were undoubtedly major factors in Johnson's decision. A consequence of the increasing importance of primaries in the nomination process is the greater political vulnerability of presidential incumbents seeking a second term in office. In 1976 the incumbent but non-elected President Gerald Ford suffered a number of humiliating defeats at the hands of his rival, Ronald Reagan, and neither emerged as the clear victor from the primaries; it was only at the Kansas City convention itself that Ford's slender majority of delegates was confirmed. In 1980 the challenge by Senator Edward Kennedy to President Carter's renomination was carried to the convention itself. Carter won 24 primaries to Kennedy's ten, giving him an eventual majority of 2,123 to 1,150 in the roll call of delegates. In 1992 President George Bush was challenged for the Republican nomination by right-winger Patrick Buchanan. The fact that Buchanan won 37 per cent of the vote in the New Hampshire primary and between one-fifth and one-third of the vote in 17 other states demonstrated Bush's potential vulnerability. Although he only won 18 delegates in the convention his attacks on the President, particularly over taxation and the economy, damaged Bush's standing and developed themes the Democrats were able to capitalise on later in the campaign.[4] In 1996 Bill Clinton was unchallenged for his party's nomination despite the fact that he had been very unpopular during much of his first term, and was widely blamed for contributing to the Democrats' disastrous performance in the 1994 midterm elections. He achieved this by first building up a huge campaign fund that deterred internal challengers and, second, moving to the centre politically and confronting the Republican-controlled Congress over budget cuts, thereby securing rising approval ratings in the opinion polls. The record of twentieth-century presidential elections shows that a smooth path to renomination is essential for incumbents seeking re-election. Those Presidents who were unopposed or faced relatively weak opposition within their own party have all won another term, but those that faced significant opposition for renomination all ended up losing in the general election, as Table 7.2 demonstrates.

The national conventions

The climax of the nominations process is the national party convention which takes place in July or August and formally selects the party's candidate for the presidency. Both parties have succeeded in nominating a candidate on the first ballot in every convention since 1956; the last occasion when more than one ballot was needed was in 1952 when the Democrats required three votes before finally choosing Adlai Stevenson. Although there have been hotly contested conventions, for example, the Republican one in 1976 referred to above – in recent times the nominations process has led to one candidate emerging with a substantial majority of the delegates, and the conventions have merely endorsed the verdict of the primaries and caucuses.

The conventions are important political events insofar as they demonstrate that parties do exist on a national basis and they provide rare opportunities for party activists to meet fellow supporters from other parts of the country. Delegates spend much of the four days in social as well as political gatherings with meetings of state, ethnic and other caucuses. Pressure groups will use the opportunity to lobby on issues of importance to them as many delegates hold influential positions in their own states. A site committee selects a

Table 7.2 Presidential incumbents and re-election contests

Nomination contest		Incumbent's primary vote	Percentage of convention delegates	General election result
Minor or no opposition				
William McKinley	(1900)*	–	100	Won
Theodore Roosevelt	(1904)	–	100	Won
Woodrow Wilson	(1916)*	99%	99	Won
Calvin Coolidge	(1924)	68	96	Won
Franklin D. Roosevelt	(1936)*	93	100	Won
Franklin D. Roosevelt	(1940)	72	86	Won
Franklin D. Roosevelt	(1944)	71	92	Won
Harry S. Truman	(1948)	64	75	Won
Dwight D. Eisenhower	(1956)*	86	100	Won
Lyndon B. Johnson	(1964)	88	100	Won
Richard M. Nixon	(1972)*	87	99	Won
Ronald Reagan	(1984)*	96	100	Won
Bill Clinton	(1996)*	87.3	100	Won
Major or significant opposition				
William H. Taft	(1912)*	34%	52	Lost
Herbert Hoover	(1932)*	33	98	Lost
Gerald R. Ford	(1976)	53	53	Lost
Jimmy Carter	(1980)*	51	64	Lost
George Bush	(1992)*	73	98	Lost

Source: Modified from: *Congressional Quarterly Weekly Report*, 4 February 1984, p. 224.

* Presidents completing first full four-year term when seeking re-election.

city to host the convention which can accommodate not only the delegates and other guests but also the media commentators, journalists and television crews from all over the world. In 2000 the Democrats met in Los Angeles, while the Republicans convened in Philadelphia. For the 2004 conventions the Democrats announced that they would go to Boston and the Republicans that they had selected New York.

A platform committee draws up a set of policy statements which the convention can endorse. The party platform is made up of various 'planks' on different issue areas; sometimes these have been vague and non-specific, but on other occasions they have been more ideologically defined, indicating the strength of the faction that has control of the convention. Austin Ranney has pointed out that most delegates and party leaders, including Presidents running for office, take the platform seriously because it serves two important functions. One is the external role of appealing to as many voters and offending as few as possible and the other, more important function in recent years is the internal one of helping to unite the party's various factions behind the ticket so that they will support it enthusiastically.[5]

Party conventions offer great opportunities for national exposure of the party's candidate and policies to the electorate with free publicity in the national media in a system that requires other political messages to be paid for. In many cases the proceedings have appeared as well-choreographed events played out for the benefit of the television cameras rather than as conferences where real debates take place and important decisions are made. Delegates become spectators and cheer-leaders while the coronation of the candidate takes place. Slick video presentations celebrating the life and achievements of the candidate, short speeches by the party's leading politicians and celebrities, an emphasis on entertainment and the avoidance of controversy have become the order of the day, with the 1996 and 2000 conventions of both parties particularly exemplifying this trend. As a result, the national television networks have reduced their coverage, the number of viewers has declined and it has been suggested that the conventions should be reduced to two or three days in future.

Party managers have increasingly wished to prevent conflict and the appearance of disunity because they recognise that the image of a divided party will stay in the voters' minds and will diminish the chances of success in November. In 1968 the violence outside the Democrat convention centre in Chicago as anti-war protestors clashed with police was mirrored by ugly scenes of rancour and hostility between delegates inside the convention itself. Hubert Humphrey's campaign was severely damaged in the general election as a result. In 1992 the divisive issue of abortion and the emphasis on 'family values' promoted by the Christian Right dominated much of the media coverage of the Republican convention, giving the impression of a narrow and exclusive party that was not reaching out to the wider electorate. Pat Buchanan, who had made a controversial and extreme speech in 1992, was refused an opportunity to address the convention in 1996 by Republican leaders, intent on avoiding a repeat of the public relations disaster of four years before.

The selection of the vice-presidential candidate is eagerly awaited, even though the convention merely endorses the choice of the presidential nominee. Since 1992 presidential candidates have named their running-mates before the convention has commenced to maximise media coverage. The announcement had in the past usually been made during the convention, partly to increase interest in its proceedings (see Box 7.1). In 1980 there was considerable speculation at the Republican convention in Detroit that Ronald Reagan would invite former President Gerald Ford to become his vice-presidential nominee. In the event negotiations broke down as Ford appeared to be demanding too powerful a role in a future Reagan White House and the candidate turned instead to George Bush, who had been his main rival for the presidential nomination.

Box 7.1 Selecting the vice-presidential candidate

In the past when a presidential candidate finalised his choice of vice-presidential running-mate during the party's national convention this was occasionally done with inadequate scrutiny, miring the campaign in controversy and embarrassment, diverting media attention from the candidate while raising questions about his judgement. In Chapter 3 we noted the examples of Thomas Eagleton in 1972 and Dan Quayle in 1988. In 1984 Walter Mondale decided to take the bold step of selecting a woman as vice-presidential candidate in an attempt to revive his lacklustre campaign. Although the selection of Rep. Geraldine Ferraro of New York initially heightened interest and support for the Democratic ticket, subsequent press stories about her financial affairs and her husband's business connections created further problems for the Mondale campaign and considerably reduced the impact of her presence on the ticket.

Learning from these mistakes, presidential candidates now try to ensure that any potential running-mates do not have 'skeletons in their cupboards' and more time and effort is spent checking their backgrounds and records before an announcement is made. Presidential candidates have usually sought to 'balance the ticket' so that the vice-presidential candidate has attractive and vote-winning qualities, which they themselves may lack, in areas of the country from which they come or among particular groups of electors.

Vice-presidential candidates 1988-2000

Democrats

1988 Lloyd Bentsen

Bentsen was a very experienced member of Congress, having served in both houses over the period from 1948. He became Chairman of the Senate Finance Committee in 1987 and later went on to be Treasury Secretary in Clinton's first administration. As a fiscal conservative and a Southerner from Texas, Bentsen was seen as complementing the liberal Governor of Massachusetts, Michael Dukakis. Bentsen is best remembered for his devastating put-down to Dan Quayle in the televised debate between the vice-presidential contenders. When the relatively youthful Quayle tried to compare himself in terms of political experience with the late President Kennedy, Bentsen retorted: 'Senator, I knew Jack Kennedy. Jack Kennedy was friend of mine. Senator, you're no Jack Kennedy.'

1992 and 1996 Al Gore

The son of a US Senator who had been raised to become a politician, Al Gore was a Senator for Tennessee and had run for the presidency himself in 1988. Gore in many respects mirrored rather then complemented Clinton: both were in their mid-forties, both were from the South and were centrists within the party and founders of the Democratic Leadership Council, as well as sharing the same religious and ethnic background (WASP). However, Gore did offer experience that Clinton did not have: he was a Vietnam veteran, had worked in the federal government in Washington and was an acknowledged specialist on environmental and defence policy. Gore was able to reinforce the image of generational change from the Bush era and his nomination was well received by both the party and the media.

2000 Joseph Lieberman

Joseph Lieberman, a Senator from the North-Eastern state of Connecticut since 1988, was selected by Al Gore as a well-respected centrist and the first of the few Democrats who openly criticised Bill Clinton for his behaviour in the Lewinsky affair. The choice was seen as an attempt by Gore to distance himself as far as possible from the scandals of the Clinton White House. Lieberman was also known for his strong views more generally on moral issues and had criticised the Hollywood movie industry for what he saw as excessive sex and violence. As an Orthodox Jew, Lieberman's religion inevitably aroused considerable interest and comment when the announcement was made as he became the first Jewish person on a presidential ticket.

Republicans

1988 and 1992 Dan Quayle

George Bush selected Dan Quayle, a conservative Senator from the Midwestern state of Indiana, in the belief that he would appeal to the right of the party with whom Bush himself had never been very popular, and that he would add a youthful image to the ticket. However, Quayle appeared ill-prepared for the public spotlight and media scrutiny which inevitably followed. A row over allegations that he had evaded military service in Vietnam and a general perception that he lacked the maturity to become Vice-President embarrassed the Bush campaign but ultimately did not prevent the incumbent Vice-President from succeeding Ronald Reagan. Despite speculation to the contrary, Bush remained loyal to Quayle and kept him on the ticket in 1992.

1996 Jack Kemp
Robert Dole chose Jack Kemp, a former American football star, Congressman from New York and Secretary of Housing and Urban Development under Bush, in an attempt to appeal to both conservatives within the Republican Party, with whom Kemp had been very popular since the late 1970s, and to women and minority voters. Kemp, who had been close to and influential with President Reagan, was a supply-side advocate of tax cuts and had in the past come into conflict with Dole who had emphasised the need for balanced budgets and deficit reduction. Dole put aside these personal differences in his belief that Kemp would energise the party activists and also broaden the appeal of the ticket. Kemp's liberal views on immigration and affirmative action and his record as a Congressman for an urban area were thought to be attractive to minority voters. In the campaign, however, Kemp made disappointingly little impact and the Dole-Kemp ticket went down to a heavy defeat.

2000 Dick Cheney
George W. Bush selected Dick Cheney, a former Congressman from Wyoming and Defense Secretary in his father's administration, principally to provide the insider experience of Washington and gravitas that the presidential candidate himself was accused of lacking. Cheney also added important expertise in the foreign and defence policy areas. He was chosen despite a history of heart problems which probably would have kept a less valued adviser from being on the presidential ticket. Cheney in fact played a key role in scrutinising the short-list of potential candidates for the job he eventually was awarded himself.

All that remains for the convention to do is to hear the acceptance speeches of the candidates which are important in setting the tone and the agenda of the general election campaign and to give rapturous applause to the party standard-bearers and their families on the platform. This emotional moment is the reward for the presidential candidate and his supporters after the long months of work and planning. Hopefully the party is not too divided at the end of the convention and the losers accept their defeat gracefully. This factor may well decide the ultimate success or failure of the party at the next stage of the process – the presidential election campaign itself. In both 1976 and 1980 incumbent Presidents' hotly disputed victories led to their parties being divided and weakened during the election campaigns. On the other hand, as challengers, Jimmy Carter in 1976 and Ronald Reagan in 1980 led remarkably united parties to victory in the November elections. In 1992 the Democratic delegates left their convention in New York in high spirits with their candidate enjoying a substantial lead in the polls. They had put on a display of public unity and projected a positive image to the public of the Clinton-Gore ticket. The Republicans, in contrast, left their convention in Houston a month later knowing that the convention had damaged the party in the eyes of uncommitted voters and with Bush still trailing in post-convention polls. Normally a candidate receives a 'bounce' in the polls following the near-monopoly of media coverage he has received during convention week. In 1996 Robert Dole, who had lagged well behind Clinton since the beginning of the year, reduced the lead to around 7 per cent after the San Diego convention and a well-received acceptance speech but, following the meeting of the Democrats in Chicago in late August, the margin again widened to double that figure. In 2000 polls showed Bush's lead over Gore increasing by around 5 per cent to 11–16 per cent after the Republican convention. Gore's 'bounce' following the Democratic convention converted this to a 1–3 per cent lead for Gore. Although there were fluctuations thereafter, the race remained finely balanced until election day.

Traditionally the two parties' nominees took a short vacation following the conventions and began their general election campaigns in earnest after the Labor Day holiday in early September. However, in recent elections campaigning is almost continuous and voters are not treated to even a short break in hostilities. The Democrats learned the lesson from the Dukakis campaign in 1988 when the candidate frittered away a large post-convention lead and disappeared from public view for several weeks, while the Republicans were able to monopolise the media. In 1992 Clinton and Gore, determined to capitalise on their successful convention, set out immediately on one of a number of 'meet the people' tours by coach, thus ensuring that they remained in the public eye throughout the summer and consolidating their poll lead by the time the Republicans met in Houston.

The presidential election campaign

Strategies and organisation

American presidential campaigns therefore last for several months, and with hundreds of meetings, speaking engagements and television appearances it may seem an unnecessarily long time. However, the sheer size of the country, the need for the candidates (particularly a challenger) to become known nationally and the problem of defining more specifically the issues and the candidates' policies within the broad party platforms are determining factors. There is also a need for the cracks in party unity which may have been opened during the nomination process to be papered over, as well as for the coordination of the party and candidate organisations, and all these things can take considerable time.

A presidential candidate has to recognise that the winning of the party's nomination, often achieved by factional support within the party, and achieving success in the actual election, when all the nation's voters are entitled to participate, are two different propositions. He will therefore often try to modify his positions on the issues or change his image so that he can broaden his appeal to the mass electorate. A candidate who fails to move to the centre and win the support of the 'middle ground' risks being labelled an 'extremist' or 'radical'. At the same time a candidate must avoid the other pitfall: if he moves too clearly away from the positions he supported in the primaries he may alienate and disillusion his original supporters whose backing helped him win the nomination. The activists, who have clearer ideological preferences than the majority of the electorate, dislike any watering down of commitments or fuzziness on the issues but those candidates who maintain only this factional party support are doomed to defeat in November. In 1988 Michael Dukakis was attacked by George Bush for his 'liberal' positions which Republicans calculated were unpopular with the majority of voters. It was only in the last stages of the campaign, by which time Dukakis had lost his early lead in the polls, that the Massachusetts Governor tried to turn this charge to his advantage by admitting that he was in the 'New Deal' tradition of the Democratic Party. He thus enthused and motivated Democratic activists in a way that he had noticeably failed to do until that point.

The objective of the presidential campaign is to win an absolute majority of the nation's Electoral College votes. Each state is allocated a number of votes equivalent to its number of Congressmen (that is House members plus two Senators) and the candidate who wins the majority of the popular vote in each state takes all the Electoral College votes of that state. There are, in practice, 50 separate presidential elections (51 if we include the District of Columbia which has three votes) and the Electoral College is a device to record the preferences of each state electorate. There are 538 Electoral College votes and the candidate has to obtain 270 to win. With this system it is inevitable that the largest states with the biggest number of College votes (California 54, New York 33, Texas 32, Florida 25, Pennsylvania 23, Illinois 22 and Ohio 21) are the most valuable prizes as even a narrow victory in the popular vote in these states will give the winning candidate a size-able bloc of votes. It is also important to note the impact reapportionment for the House of Representatives each decade has on the Electoral College votes of the states (see Chapter 1). Therefore the number of votes each state has will help determine where the candidates and their organisations concentrate their efforts; the presidential aspirants, the running-mates and the candidates' families will spend a great deal of their time in the larger states, and particularly in the big cities, with the objective of winning these 'swing-states'. Bill Clinton, for example, made numerous visits to California, not only during the 1996 campaign but during his first term in the White House, in order to consolidate his support in this key state which he had won by a large majority in 1992. Under the 'winner-takes-all' Electoral College system, there is little point in campaigning extensively in areas that are either safe or hopeless for a particular candidate or party; it is in the marginal states that the election will be won or lost. The weakness of George Bush's campaign in 1992 was demonstrated by the fact that he had given up California and its 54 votes as hopeless early in the summer, despite the state's record of having supported Republican candidates in every presidential election since 1968. On the other hand, candidates do not want to appear complacent, and to show that they are not neglecting any one section they will probably make at least fleeting visits to all areas of the nation. Harry Truman's famous 1948 'whistle-stop tour' – a nationwide campaign by train stop-ping at small towns and villages to visit the voters in the country as well as the big cities – added the personal touch to the normal canvassing for support, but in modern elections candidates usually fly by jet plane from one major city to another to give speeches to party rallies where they are assured of a good reception.

In terms of campaign planning, the candidate's personal organisation set up during the primary contests will have to work alongside the official party organisation which is headed by the party chairman at the national level. It is important for the smooth running of the campaign that these two structures – one with loyalty solely to the presidential candidate and the other with interests in elections at all levels – should be able to integrate their efforts into a coordinated and harmonious relationship. The candidate's personal office will probably organise press and television coverage, brief him on the most important issues in particular areas of the country, draft speeches and research areas for new policy statements. It will also be responsible for ensuring that his meetings are well publicised in advance and attended by large enthusiastic audiences. The leading members of the successful candidate's campaign staff will often be given important positions in the new administration.

An incumbent President who is running for a second term in the White House clearly has some major advantages over his rival. He can claim to be experienced in the job, is a recognisable national figure at the beginning of the campaign and can appeal to the voters' respect for and trust in the presidential office. He can make strategic policy moves, such as President Nixon's visit to China, or his peace initiative in the Vietnam War in 1972, which can influence the campaign issues and to which the challenger can only respond without shaping events. He usually has to campaign less and can argue that he is getting on with the job of being President while staying in the Oval Office. The media will report whatever he does anyway, because the President's actions are always news. On the other hand, if the nation's economic position is not healthy the President may take the brunt of public dissatisfaction, as George Bush clearly did in 1992. The 'hostage crisis' in Iran was a continuing problem for President Carter during 1980 and a constant reminder to the voters of foreign policy failures. The challenger to an incumbent will probably have to make the running in his strategy and attack the presidential performance, at the same time convincing electors that he has the ability and experience to do better. In some cases Presidents have succeeded in turning the tables on the challenger and making *him* the major issue. Barry Goldwater and George McGovern both found their own suitability for the presidency seriously questioned, and Bill Clinton's character and experience were also themes in the 1992 election.

Perhaps the worst position a presidential candidate can be in is when he is attempting to follow a President of his own party, if the administration has seriously declined in popularity. Hubert Humphrey, the Democratic nominee in 1968, had been Johnson's Vice-President and thus was connected with the government's unpopular Vietnam policy. He was therefore in a position of either having to defend policies for which he was not personally responsible, or seeming to be disloyal to the President if he criticised them. What is more he could not claim the experience of an incumbent President. Vice-President George Bush's problem in 1988 was rather that of establishing his own identity after serving eight years in the shadow of a popular President. Although opponents tried unsuccessfully to connect him with the Iran-Contra scandal in the minds of the public, Bush had to establish a new image as his own man with his own ideas and policies. On the other hand, being Ronald Reagan's heir-apparent undoubtedly helped him both in securing the Republican nomination and in the election campaign itself. In 2000 Al Gore tried both to bask in the reflected glory of a successful economy and the general public approval of the President he had served for eight years, while at the same time establishing himself as his own man and distancing himself from the scandals that had afflicted the Clinton White House. Gore, who mentioned Clinton only once in his acceptance speech at the convention, was later criticised by many Democrats for not utilising Clinton's charismatic campaign skills more in the final weeks before the election. Clinton was generally restricted to mobilising core Democratic voters such as African-Americans among whom the President was particularly popular. Gore had decided that too prominent a role for Clinton risked overshadowing his own campaign events and alienating swing voters who disapproved of the President's personal behaviour, particularly in the Lewinsky affair.

The media and the election

Perhaps the most significant development in the method and style of campaigning, however, is the use made of television by all candidates in modern presidential elections. A personal appearance is often made to appeal not simply to the voters who are present in the stadium or hall where the meeting is held, but principally to the millions who will see extracts of it that evening on the television news. In 1988 George Bush proved to be far more effective in obtaining this sort of coverage than his opponent, Michael Dukakis; the 'sound-bites' of a few seconds taken from his comments often summed up in a sentence a theme or issue he wanted to develop that day in the news programmes. In 1988 the average direct quote from a presidential candidate on news programmes was a mere 8.9 seconds, compared with 43.1 seconds in 1968.

Television today is the main method by which Americans find out about politics, and therefore the candidates not only try to obtain as much news coverage as possible, but also spend a very large proportion of their total budgets on television advertising. The organisations buy commercials of a few seconds' to several minutes' duration at very expensive rates in order to reach the peak viewing time audiences. As the campaign goes on the number of commercials increases steadily, with saturation coverage in the pivotal states immediately prior to election day itself. Inevitably in the short slots that are mostly used there is very little that can be said about policies, and the campaign public relations advisers try to project an image of the candidate to which the electorate will respond favourably. They emphasise the man's honesty, integrity, strength of character, concern for the needy and other perceived virtues. The candidate is filmed while campaigning, talking to voters, working in his office or relaxing at home with his family. Occasionally the intention of the commercial will be to communicate a short sharp message on an issue (for example, a brief clip of film or some statistics on criminal offences with the accompanying indication that the candidate favours a strong 'law and order' policy) or to launch an attack on the other candidate's policies. The most famous (and criticised) pro-Bush commercial in 1988 featured the case of a black murderer, Willie Horton, who had been released on a prison furlough programme in Massachusetts and had committed further crimes. The commercial implied that Governor Dukakis was 'soft on crime' and it appeared to be effective with the voters. In 1992 Bill Clinton's team were prepared for similar campaigning and were determined not to repeat the mistake the Dukakis campaign made in allowing such attacks to go unanswered, which enabled the Republicans to paint a very negative image of the Democratic candidate. A number of officials were commissioned to issue immediate rebuttals of any charges they felt distorted Clinton's record or position on the issues so that the news media would feel obliged to present their side of the story, if indeed the story was used at all. Frequently campaign managers like to encapsulate the main theme of their candidate's appeal to the voters by the use of an easily identifiable slogan. Gerald Ford, for example, claimed that among his achievements in office he had rescued America from the nightmare of Watergate and restored decency to and trust in the presidency. His television commercials and campaign literature repeated the slogan 'He's making us proud again'.

The 1992 election saw several developments in the way the media covered the campaign and in how they were used by the candidates; these characteristics have been evident in the 1996 and 2000 campaigns. Candidates sought new and alternative ways of getting their message across. They appeared for longer interviews on morning and late evening news programmes, as well as on talk shows with more relaxed formats than the traditional political interview programmes and which often included audience participation. By the end of the campaign the three major candidates had made more than a dozen appearances on 'Larry King Live', a CNN talk show. Bill Clinton often led the way, for example, by appearing on MTV, the cable music channel, to appeal to younger voters, and even playing his saxophone and wearing dark glasses as a guest on the Arsenio Hall late night show. He answered voters' questions directly at dozens of 'town hall meetings' across the country which were each carried live by local television stations, while his staff distributed hundreds of thousands of videocassettes about the candidate and his policies. Ross Perot spent over $60 million of his own money to pay for his campaign which included half-hour 'infomercials', in which he lectured millions of television viewers about the federal budget deficit and poured scorn on his opponents. The diversity of the new or 'alternative' media, including cable and satellite channels, enabled the candidates to some extent to bypass the major television networks which had dominated election coverage in the past. This diversification of the news media and in particular the increasing importance of cable news channels was vividly demonstrated in the 2000 election; a plurality, 35 per cent of Americans now obtain the majority of their political information from cable channels such as CNN, Fox News and MSNBC, with only 28 per cent relying principally on the networks and 22 per cent on newspapers.[6]

News coverage of presidential elections overwhelmingly focuses on the 'horse race' aspect of the campaigns: who is ahead, who is behind and by how far, and the strategies of the candidates. This was particularly true in 2000 because of the closeness of the race, with 71 per cent of news stories about the election taking this approach according to research conducted by the Center for Media and Public Affairs on behalf of the Brookings Institution. Generally television coverage provides relatively little in the way of serious discussion and in-depth analysis of the issues and policy positions of the candidates.

By the 2000 elections the use of the Internet by presidential candidates, as well as by political parties, pressure groups and candidates for other offices, had become a familiar part of the campaign season. Candidates use their websites to provide information on issues and policies, news about their campaign events, photographs and details about themselves and to raise money for their campaigns. John McCain was particularly successful in fund-raising via his website in 2000. Approximately 40 per cent of American households had access to the Internet in 2001 and it is estimated that around a third of adults either browse for or inadvertently discover political news on the web. The number of people claiming that they have been influenced by such information is increasing, although Tim Hames points out that the consensus among party professionals is that very few undecided voters can be located or converted by use of the Internet.[7] Despite this pessimism there is every indication that such new campaign tools will play a growing role in future presidential elections.

It has been said many times that in recent decades America has experienced the era of 'market politics', and critics have drawn attention to the dangers of selecting a man for the most powerful national office on the basis of 'images' created by Madison Avenue public relations and advertising people who package and sell candidates as if they were dealing with a new soap powder or soft drink.[8] However, it would surely be unrealistic to expect presidential candidates not to make maximum use of the modern media which can so easily take them into millions of American homes.

The televised presidential debates

Television can be used by voters in a mature, responsible way to help them decide on the respective merits of the contenders for the presidency. In 1960, there was a series of television confrontations between Republican candidate Vice-President Richard Nixon and Democratic Senator John Kennedy, and these programmes dealt with policy issues in a number of important areas. Kennedy was able to use these occasions to convince the voters that he was not as inexperienced as his opponent had suggested, and Nixon not only did not 'win' the debates as he had confidently expected but also projected a rather shifty appearance that did not help his image. In every election since 1976 televised debates between the main contenders have become part of the ritual of presidential elections. In 1992, with greater public interest in the election, it is estimated that 92 million Americans tuned in to the final televised debate, compared with 71 million in 1988. However, the size of the audience for the debates has shrunk dramatically in the last two elections. In 2000 it was estimated that 46 million Americans watched the first debate and that this dropped to 38 million for the third.

In 1992 the debates were seen as the most important opportunity for President Bush to make a breakthrough in the campaign. However, his team managed to give the impression that they were afraid of letting their man in the ring with Clinton (the 'Oxford debater' as Bush called him) by refusing for weeks to agree the number of debates, rules and procedure. Eventually, three 90-minute programmes featuring the presidential candidates were arranged, with one featuring the vice-presidential contenders, all to take place over a ten-day period in mid-October.

In the past, over-rehearsed candidates, constrained by a format of questions and answers from hand-picked journalists within rigid time limits, have restricted the opportunity for real debate. The contrived drama, the prepared one-liners and effective sound-bites tend to stay in the memory. In 1992 the first debate was based on the traditional pattern. The main winner was Ross Perot. Appearing on the same platform with the two main party candidates raised his stature, and his good-humoured folksy wisdom played well with the viewers. In addition, it was noticeable that in all three debates Bush and Clinton concentrated their fire on each other and at times seemed to defer to the independent candidate in the hope of not alienating Perot supporters and with an eye to eventually winning them over to their own cause. A *Newsweek* poll after the first meeting reported that 43 per cent felt Perot had won, 31 per cent Clinton and only 19 per cent backed Bush. Perot's support in the opinion polls jumped from 7 per cent to 14 per cent almost overnight.

The second debate provided a welcome variation in format with a talk-show setting and the candidates being questioned by an audience of uncommitted voters. Candidates could move around the platform while answering questions in a more informal style, an approach that had been suggested by Clinton and suited him well as he set out specific proposals to deal with the wide range of issues raised by the voters. Bush, who was chastened by a voter chiding him for negative attacks on his opponent, appeared ill at ease and on several occasions was caught by the camera glancing at his watch. Viewers began to tire of Perot's hectoring style and lack of specific answers, and a CBS poll showed that 53 per cent judged Clinton to be the winner, 25 per cent Bush and 21 per cent Perot. It was only in the third debate that Bush gave a combative and forceful performance with a focus on the main themes of his campaign; even then, polls indicated Clinton was judged to have performed better. The vice-presidential debate was notable for the fact that Dan Quayle surprised many observers by being a match for Al Gore and for what ranks as easily the most embarrassingly inept performance ever in such confrontations, by Perot's running-mate, retired Admiral James Stockdale.

In 1996 the bipartisan Commission on Presidential Debates agreed with an advisory panel chaired by political scientist, Professor Richard Neustadt, that Perot should be excluded from participation on the basis that his poll ratings indicated that he did not have a realistic chance of winning the election, in contrast to 1992 when, at one point, he was neck and neck with the two major party candidates. The Dole campaign also wished to deny Perot exposure, believing that any improvement in his fortunes would be likely to be at the expense of the Republican candidate. As predicted, the 1996 televised debates allowed Clinton to exploit his superior communication skills and Dole's last real opportunity to make a breakthrough was lost.

In 2000 the three televised debates were held in the period from 3–17 October. It was widely predicted that Al Gore, as an articulate and experienced Vice-President with a sound grasp of policy questions, would shine in these confrontations with George W. Bush. The low expectations of the Texas Governor worked in his favour. Although opinion polls held immediately after each debate indicated that the viewers felt Gore had 'won' two of the debates, Bush did sufficiently well, particularly in the foreign affairs debate, to overcome many citizens' concerns about his lack of knowledge and experience. While Gore clearly knew more about the details of policy, Bush repeatedly set out his core beliefs in simple terms to appeal to the public, much as Ronald Reagan had done in the past. Bush also appeared more genial and good-humoured while Gore was criticised after the first debate for being overbearing and after the second debate for being too passive and withdrawn. Overall, the debates appear to have had a significant effect on public opinion by making Bush a more credible presidential candidate. Gallup showed a 49–41 per cent lead for Gore before the first debate; this was transformed into a 50–40 per cent lead for Bush immediately after the final debate.[9]

Opinion polls

Another feature of recent presidential campaigns is the growth in the number of opinion polls which are carried out and published. Whereas there were 16 national polls in the peak campaign months in 1960, there were more than 70 in the comparable months of 1988, all gaining wide news coverage and helping to shape the campaign itself. In 1992 Bill Clinton's 15 per cent lead in the opinion polls following the Democratic convention was reduced by a few points after the Republican meeting in Houston, but Bush did not achieve the 'bounce' of the 1988 campaign when he overtook Dukakis after his party's convention and remained in the lead until polling day. Clinton's advantage in the polls remained remarkably consistent from early September until the last week of the campaign, when it appeared to narrow dramatically. It seemed as if Bush's attacks on Clinton's character and the issue of 'trust' were at last paying off, but in the last few days the momentum was lost as the personal abuse became more shrill and unpresidential. Final polls indicated Clinton's lead had widened again to 5–8 per cent; on election day his winning margin in the popular vote was 5 per cent. All but one of the polls under-estimated Perot's final tally by 2–5 per cent.

During 1996 every opinion poll published during the year showed Clinton enjoying a substantial lead over Dole and helped to create a feeling of inevitability that the President would secure a second term. However, as in 1992, Clinton's lead shrunk in the final days of the campaign; of those making up their minds in the last week, Dole won 47 per cent to Clinton's 35 per cent. It appears that revelations of campaign finance abuses may have damaged Clinton, while Dole made a final 96-hour campaign swing that seemed to mobilise many Republican supporters and helped prevent a Clinton landslide, as well as secure vital votes that enabled the party to retain its control of Congress. Almost all the final polls failed to identify this late trend sufficiently well and gave Clinton a much larger lead than the 8 per cent he actually secured in the election.

In 2000, as we have seen, the polls showed a Bush lead up to the Democratic convention and a Gore lead following that meeting. Gore's advantage was reversed by early October and the televised debates contributed to Bush enjoying a lead throughout most of the month. However, many polls also suggested that the outcome of the election would be very close and within the normal margin of error (plus or minus 3 per cent). As the race became even more competitive in many states the national polls became an even less reliable indicator of what might happen in the Electoral College which actually deter-mines the election. There have been concerns expressed about the reliability of polls in a more general sense; not only do organisations now use telephone polls extensively rather than the more expensive face-to-face methods of interviewing, but there has been increased resistance by voters to responding to such polls, giving rise to questions about how representative they are. Overall, however, despite these reservations, the verdict of most of the polls on election day that the race was 'too close to call' was, of course, an accurate assessment of the national mood.

Voting in presidential elections

Any campaign manager planning the strategy for achieving a majority of the Electoral College votes will bear in mind the factors that influence the American electorate in deciding how to vote in presidential elections. The three main criteria are issues, the candidates and party identification.

For an issue to be significant in electoral choice it requires knowledge and feeling on the part of the voter: he has to know about the issue, care strongly about it and know the positions of the candidates on it. Relatively few voters are likely to decide how to vote on the basis of one single issue but a general disenchantment or contentment with the policies of the existing government may have its effect, although in the American system, where the President and Congress are separate and often divided in party control, determining who is to blame or whom to credit with achievements is more difficult for voters. In 1992, however, the state of the economy was clearly the key factor; 43 per cent of electors said that jobs and the economy were the major influences on their vote, and the budget deficit was named by a further 21 per cent. President Bush, successively battered by Buchanan, Clinton and Perot, took the lion's share of the blame from the electorate with fewer than one in three approving of his handling of the issue. In 1996, with rising prosperity, low inflation, falling unemployment and a reduced federal deficit, Bill Clinton undoubtedly benefited from the return of the 'feel good factor' among a substantial proportion of the electorate.

It is quite natural that voters should consider the personalities and characters of the individuals who aspire to become President of the United States. Given the importance of the office to the nation – and the world's security – voters are particularly interested in the candidate's experience, competence and emotional stability. They are also concerned with the honesty and integrity of the candidates, particularly in the post-Watergate era, although it appears that many voters in 1996 were prepared to ignore questions about Clinton's character. Relatively few candidates have had the vote-winning qualities that Roosevelt and Reagan demonstrated in being able to draw support from almost all sections of society, even when in some cases voters did not agree with the candidate's stand on particular issues. Sometimes a candidate wins support because of a negative reaction by voters to the personality of the other candidate. With voters being increasingly willing to split their tickets at presidential elections and the candidates running their own campaigns separately from party organisations, the importance of the individual contenders for the presidency has grown.

Party identification is, however, still a significant factor in presidential elections. As we saw in Chapter 6, around three-quarters of those voting do think of themselves as Republicans and Democrats. Partisan commitment has also weakened and split-ticket voting is common. However, most electors who identify with a particular party support its presidential candidate even in a year when the party does badly. In 1996 80 per cent of Republican identifiers supported the party's candidate, Robert Dole, despite the fact that his defeat seemed inevitable. In 2000 86 per cent of Democrats voted for Gore and 91 per cent of Republicans supported Bush.

The Democratic Party used to enjoy a substantial lead over the Republicans in voter identification and therefore its candidates had to concentrate principally on obtaining a full turnout of the party's supporters, while the Republicans, with a narrower base, had to appeal to independents and disillusioned Democrats in order to win the presidency. Democrats faced the challenge of mobilising voters from social groups who have traditionally had low turnout rates, while the Republican white middle-class voters were

---

Box 7.2 Significant issues in the 2000 presidential election

A number of surveys were carried out during the 2000 campaign for the presidency as well as on election day itself as voters were leaving the polling stations to find out what issues were of most concern to them. While no issue or policy area dominated the campaign and the minds of the electorate there were a number of issues that were significant, although it is difficult, indeed impossible, to say how far they influenced individuals' voting behaviour. The main areas mentioned when voters were asked which issue mattered most were health, Medicare and the cost of prescription drugs, education, the future of social security, jobs and the economy, taxes, moral values, world affairs and crime.

These issues tend to draw voters to one or other of the candidates. For example, 80 per cent of those who thought taxes were the most important voted for Bush, encouraged by the prospect of a large tax cut which he had promised during the campaign. Those seeing world affairs as the most significant issue supported Bush by 54-40 per cent. On the other hand, Gore did well among those most concerned about health care issues (64-33 per cent), the economy and jobs (59-37 per cent) and social security (58-39 per cent). Bush had emphasised the importance of education in his campaign and 44 per cent of those mentioning this issue as their top priority voted for the Texas Governor, while 52 per cent supported Gore. Therefore there was a fairly even split on an issue that has mostly favoured the Democrats in the past.

Which issue mattered most?	All	Gore	Bush	Nader
Economy/jobs	18	59	37	2
Education	15	52	44	3
Social security	14	58	39	1
Taxes	14	17	80	2
World affairs	12	40	54	4
Health care	8	64	33	3
Medicare/ prescriptions drugs	7	60	38	1

Source: www.cnn.com/ELECTION/2000/epolls/US/P000.html

---

more likely to go to the polls. During the 1980s the gap in partisan support narrowed substantially: among white voters it was non-existent in 1984 and just three points in 1986. Only the solid support of the black electorate kept the Democrats from slipping to an even position with their opponents nationwide. According to Martin P. Wattenberg, the Republican strategy for presidential elections has therefore changed dramatically from needing to win Democrat and independent votes to simply maintaining their own base.[10] In 1996 Dole actually enjoyed a 3 per cent lead over Clinton among white voters but, in many states huge leads among blacks and Hispanics provided the President with the popular majorities sufficient to secure their Electoral College votes.

The factor of party identification probably explains why a very large group of voters – 42 per cent in 1980, for example – reported that they decided how to vote before the party conventions officially decided who the candidates would be. However, a further 40 per cent said they made up their minds during the campaign itself and clearly undecided voters hold the key to victory in close elections.[11]

We have already seen in Chapter 6 that certain social groups in the nation tend to support one or the other of the major parties. A candidate for the presidency knows the traditional supporters of his party very well and has to attempt to preserve this base and

Box 7.3 The candidates, personalities and the 2000 presidential election

Voters are obviously interested in the personal qualities and characteristics of the candidates for the presidency. They form a judgment based on a variety of sources: media pundits, what they have seen and read themselves about the candidates' backgrounds, the views of their families, friends and work colleagues to name but a few. The candidates' own advertising and the televised debates also play a significant role in determining whether individuals feel that they 'connect with' the candidate and have a favourable or unfavourable view overall. Voters expect candidates for the presidency to have a range of virtuous qualities and are deterred by less desirable characteristics. In 1996 most voters put aside their misgivings about Bill Clinton the man and voted for Bill Clinton the President who was generally seen as an effective leader. Following the later exposure of his affair with Monica Lewinsky after he had long denied such a liaison many voters may have regretted this earlier indulgence of the President's personal weaknesses.

In exit polling in 2000 voters were asked which personal quality mattered most to them and how they had cast their vote. It is clear that honesty and trustworthiness were seen as easily the most important qualities and Bush had a huge lead among those voters who ranked these highest. He also scored well among voters who were looking for a strong leader and someone who is likeable. Not surprisingly, as the incumbent Vice-President, Gore had strong leads among those who emphasised the need for experience and an understanding of the issues. Gore also did well among those who gave top priority to a candidate who 'cares about people'. Voters who believed that having good judgement was most important split evenly between the two contenders.

Which quality mattered most?	*All*	*Gore*	*Bush*	*Nader*
Honest/trustworthy	24	15	80	3
Has experience	15	82	17	1
Strong leader	14	34	64	1
Good judgement	13	48	49	1
Understands issues	13	75	19	4
Cares about people	12	63	31	5
Likeable	2	38	60	2

Source: www.cnn.com/ELECTION/2000/epolls/US/P000.html

preferably also attract 'independents' and those who are undecided at the beginning of the campaign. Between 1968 and 1988 the Republicans won five of the six presidential elections. Their successes came about as the traditional New Deal coalition cracked and Nixon, Reagan and Bush made inroads into areas of the country and among social groups which had historically supported the Democratic Party. In 1992 and 1996 Bill Clinton succeeded in winning back many of these voters and, in so doing, became the first Democratic President to win re-election since Franklin Roosevelt. If we analyse the vote in presidential elections we can see that the following factors are significant:

Region. Republican victories in the 1980s were built on an electorally solid base of Western and Southern states, many of which were growing economically and expanding in population, thereby increasing their Electoral College votes. Reagan and Bush swept these regions, although in 1988 Michael Dukakis did win Oregon and Washington in the Pacific West. However, in the 1990s Bill Clinton won a number of important Western and Southern states, breaking GOP dominance in these areas. In both 1992 and 1996 he won California with large pluralities of the popular vote. In 2000 Gore also won California as well as Oregon and Washington. The South was the only region in the country in which Dole obtained a majority of the Electoral College votes (104–59) but the Democratic ticket headed by the two Southerners did win in Louisiana, Florida and Kentucky, as well as in their home states of Arkansas and Tennessee. In 2000, on the other hand, Bush swept the South, albeit with the razor-thin plurality of votes in Florida, and Gore failed to win even in Tennessee.

Democratic strength in the North-East was consolidated during the 1990s, and in 1996 Clinton swept every state in the region, winning all 127 Electoral College votes. All these states, with the exception of Pennsylvania, gave Clinton at least a ten-point margin of victory over Dole. In 2000 Gore won all of the North-East with the sole exception of New Hampshire. Dole's only successes in the Midwest were in sparsely populated areas such as his own home state of Kansas and in Indiana which has remained loyal to the Republicans in the 1990s. In 2000 the Midwest and Western states were almost evenly split between Bush and Gore.

Observers have noted that the Democrats have been most successful in those states on America's Atlantic and Pacific coasts, particularly where there are metropolitan regions surrounding large cities such as New York and Los Angeles which have attracted a large number of immigrants and are multi-ethnic in character. In the hinterland of the country where the population is overwhelmingly white, or in the case of the South-East, biracial, voters are generally more conservative and are more likely to support the Republican candidate for the presidency.

Occupation and income. Republican successes were based on the party's traditional support among white collar professional and managerial voters, complemented by winning over large numbers of blue-collar manual workers in the 1980s. In 1984 Reagan had a 9 per cent lead among this group while in 1980 and 1988 the parties attracted this key part of the old Democratic coalition in equal numbers. The votes of blue-collar 'Reagan Democrats', particularly those of skilled workers, were crucial to the Republicans' victory in a number of large industrial states in the North-East and Midwest, but in 1992 this group went back to the Democrats by a margin of two to one. Suburban and middle-income voters also moved decisively to Clinton, while low-income groups remained solidly Democratic. In 1996 only the highest-income groups gave Dole a majority of their votes. The 2000 election demonstrated a strong correlation between income levels and voting. Among those whose family income was less than $15,000 a year Gore enjoyed a 20 per cent lead, whereas Bush had strong leads of 9–10 per cent among the highest-income groups and middle income voters split almost evenly between the two candidates.

Ethnic and religious minorities. The Democratic Party's traditional coalition included many ethnic and religious minorities, but the Republicans made inroads among a number of these groups in the 1980s. For example, Catholic voters, including Italian, Irish and Polish Americans, supported Reagan by 9 per cent in 1984 and Bush by 5 per cent in 1988. However, many returned to the Democrats in the 1990s: in 1992 Clinton enjoyed an 8 per cent lead among Catholics and increased this to 16 per cent in 1996. In contrast, Jewish voters have been loyal to the Democrats throughout, even giving Mondale two-thirds of their votes in the Reagan landslide year of 1984. In 1996 Clinton led by a massive 62 per cent among Jews and in the much closer election of 2000 Gore still had a 60 per cent lead, helped no doubt by the presence of Joseph Lieberman on the ticket. Hispanic and black voters have also provided solid and consistent support for Democratic candidates in every presidential election. For example, in 2000 Hispanics gave Gore 62 per cent of their votes, despite Bush's Texas background and his considerable efforts to attract their support. In the same year nine out of ten African-Americans backed Al Gore.

Age.   One of the most remarkable aspects of Reagan's 1984 victory was that the nation's oldest-ever President enjoyed a huge 19 per cent lead among younger voters between 18 and 29 years in age. This Republican lead was reduced to 5 per cent in 1988, and Clinton secured large majorities among younger voters in the 1990s. Older voters over 60 supported Reagan overwhelmingly in 1984, split their votes almost evenly in 1988 and in the 1990s backed Clinton, although in 1996 his lead over Dole was only 4 per cent compared with a 12 per cent margin four years earlier. In 2000 voters of all age groups were split almost evenly; those over 60 gave Gore a four-point lead, encouraged by the emphasis in the Democratic campaign on Medicare and the cost of prescription drugs, issues of great importance to the elderly.

Gender.   Political scientists have been particularly interested in the phenomenon known as the gender gap that opened up in the 1980s and has become a significant feature of voting behaviour. Women are a larger proportion of the electorate and have a longer life expectancy than men. Female voters are much more willing to support Democratic candidates: Reagan's lead over Mondale in 1984 was 25 per cent among men, but only 12 per cent among women; in 1988 Bush gained 16 per cent more of the male votes than Dukakis but only 1 per cent more of the female vote. In 1992 Clinton had a 3 per cent lead among men but a 9 per cent margin among women, while in 1996 1 per cent more

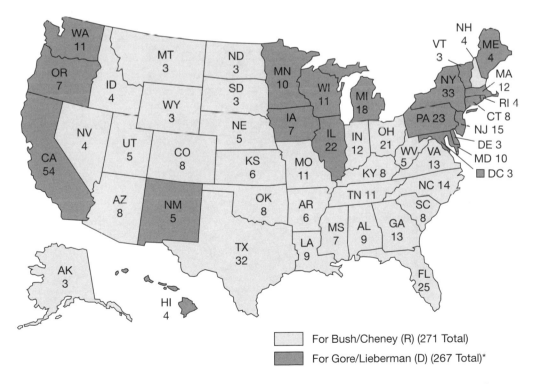

For Bush/Cheney (R) (271 Total)
For Gore/Lieberman (D) (267 Total)*

*In the official total of Electoral College votes, Gore/Lieberman received 266 as a result of the abstention of one District of Columbia Elector.

Figure 7.1 The Electoral College votes in the 2000 presidential election

Table 7.3 Portrait of the electorate 1992, 1996 and 2000

% of 2000 total		Vote in 1992			Vote in 1996			Vote in 2000	
		Clinton	Bush	Perot	Clinton	Dole	Perot	Gore	Bush
	TOTAL	43%	38%	19%	49%	41%	8%	48%	48%
48	Men	41	38	21	43	44	10	42	53
52	Women	46	37	17	54	38	7	54	43
82	Whites	39	41	20	43	46	9	42	54
10	Blacks	82	11	7	84	12	4	90	8
4	Hispanics	62	25	14	72	21	6	67	31
65	Married	40	40	20	44	46	9	44	53
35	Not married	49	33	18	57	31	9	57	38
17	Aged 18–29	44	34	22	53	34	10	48	46
33	30–44	42	38	20	48	41	9	48	49
28	45–59	41	40	19	48	41	9	48	49
22	60 and older	50	38	12	48	44	7	51	47
5	Not a high school graduate	55	28	17	59	28	11	59	39
21	High school graduate	43	36	20	51	35	13	48	49
42	College graduate or more	44	39	18	47	44	7	48	48
47	White Protestant	33	46	21	36	53	10	34	63
26	Catholic	44	36	20	53	37	9	49	47

Jewish	4	78	12	10	78	16	3	79	19
Trade union household	26	65	24	21	59	30	9	59	37
Family income under $15,000	7	59	23	18	59	28	11	57	37
$15,000–$29,999	16	45	35	20	53	36	9	54	41
$30,000–$49,999	24	41	38	21	48	40	10	49	48
over $50,000*	53	40	42	18	44	48	7	45	52
over $100,000*	15	36	48	16	38	54	6	43	54
From the East	23	47	35	18	55	34	9	56	39
From the Midwest	26	42	37	21	48	41	10	48	49
From the South	31	42	43	16	46	46	7	43	55
From the West	21	44	34	22	48	40	8	48	46
Republicans	35	10	73	17	13	80	6	8	91
Democrats	39	77	10	13	84	10	5	86	11
Independents	27	38	32	22	43	35	17	45	47
Liberals	20	68	14	18	78	11	7	80	13
Moderates	50	48	31	21	57	33	9	52	44
Conservatives	29	18	65	17	20	71	8	17	81
First-time voters	9	48	30	22	54	34	11	52	43

Sources: Exit polls 1996 and 2000 from Voter News Services, 1992 from Voter Research and Surveys.

* The 1988 and 1992 figures are based on the income ranges $50,000–$74,999 and over $75,000 respectively.

men voted for Dole than Clinton, while the President had an overwhelming 16 per cent lead among women. This dominance was particularly notable among unmarried women (62–28 per cent) and younger women (58–31 per cent). In 2000 the gender gap was particularly large, with Bush enjoying an 11 per cent lead among men and Gore having the same lead among women. Among white men Bush's advantage was a huge 24 points (60–36 per cent), but a mere 1 per cent among white women.

The explanation for these differences seems to lie in the issue areas that have been of most concern to men and women. Male voters have been attracted to Republican candidates since the 1980s because they gave priority to defence, patriotism and law and order; females have placed more emphasis on social issues, such as health care and education, and perceived the Democratic candidates as better equipped to deal with them. In recent times the Republicans have also been seen as hostile to abortion, affirmative action programmes and increases in the minimum wage, while being in favour of cuts in welfare programmes, all of which are viewed as threatening by many women. More women than men are in low paid or part-time employment, and this economic factor helps explain women's greater tendency to support the Democratic Party in elections. Some observers have argued that too much attention has been paid to women's voting behaviour and insufficient to that of males during the period since the 1980s. They contend that many men, particularly white males, have deserted the Democratic Party in protest at the social changes that have taken place since the 1970s and which in many cases they have seen as disadvantaging them.

The Electoral College

The Founding Fathers established an Electoral College made up of representatives of the states to elect the President of the United States. They did so in order to ensure that the states played an institutionalised role in the election of the nation's Chief Executive and that, as an indirectly elected body in a pre-democratic era, it could, if necessary, ignore the 'popular passions' of the ordinary voters and select the person who, in the view of the Electors, was most appropriate and qualified candidate. In practice the Electoral College has played a formal rather than an active role in the selection of the President, registering the popular preferences of the voters in the 50 states and the District of Columbia.

When voters mark their ballot paper for presidential and vice-presidential candidates, they are really endorsing a list of electors picked by the candidate's party in that state. These party dignatories are authorised to cast all their state's Electoral College votes for their candidate if he wins the majority of the popular vote in the state. In most states the names of the candidates only and not the list of electors appear on the ballot paper. Electors meet in each of the state capitals in December and register their votes which are transmitted to Congress where an official count takes place on the first day of the new session in January, but the nation's Electoral College never meets as a body.

Although academics and politicians have argued about the advantages and disadvantages of maintaining this constitutional procedure established at the end of the eighteenth century in a democratic age, in practical terms the Electoral College has not been a subject of major political controversy in recent times until the 2000 presidential election. In most elections a clear winner has emerged on election night and the television networks have announced which candidate has taken the Electoral College votes of individual states by projecting from the returns of a number of representative precincts and from exit polls, even though the formal casting of votes by the Electoral College members does not take place until several weeks later. In 2000 the closeness of the popular vote in a number of individual states created an unprecedented degree of uncertainty about the outcome nationally. In the final analysis, the miniscule and disputed plurality of votes for Bush in Florida gave the Texas Governor the state's 25 Electoral College votes and one more than the 270 needed to win overall. What is more, serious errors were made on election night both in the collation and interpretation of voting returns and exit polling data. The television networks first declared Gore the winner in Florida and then retracted, only to 'call' the state for Bush before having to renounce that as well when it became clear that the state's popular vote was so evenly divided that no firm conclusion could be reached without a recount (see Box 7.4).

Box 7.4 Television and election night coverage

In recent presidential elections whichever television station viewers tuned into to watch the latest news and results and whichever presenters and pundits they listened to, they would be essentially obtaining their information from the same source. In order to save the costs of each company running their own operations, in 1993 six major news organisations created a consortium, Voter News Service, by merging separate companies that counted votes and conducted exit polls on election day. The three main television networks, ABC, CBS and NBC, combined forces with cable network news channels, CNN and Fox News, and the Associated Press news agency.

Although they worked together in this way the television companies are, of course, still in competition with each other for viewers. There is an inevitable tension, especially in a close election, between those whose job it is to analyse the data in a cautious way to make the correct prediction of electoral outcomes and the television executives who want to get the news out as quickly as possible and do not wish to be beaten to announcing the winner by their rivals. In 2000 both the television networks and Voter News Service were implicated in errors at various stages in the process which led to two incorrect declarations on election night.

After the 2000 election fiasco Voter News Service contracted with an Ohio-based research company to rebuild its system but this was not ready for the 2002 midterm elections. VNS was not able to provide its members and other clients with results from exit poll surveys which are used to supplement the vote count in order to make projections of winners in various races. Exit polls are also essential for political scientists and journalists analysing which voters voted for whom and what factors influenced the way they voted. Therefore although the impact on election night coverage was not particularly apparent to viewers, apart from delaying some of the declarations in close run races, it did mean that no reliable national data on voting behaviour exists for the 2002 elections.

In January 2003 the six news organisations announced that they were disbanding VNS and considering alternative options for their coverage of the 2004 elections. One possibility was to entrust the election night count to the Associated Press which had for many years conducted its own count separate from VNS and was the only consortium member not to have declared Bush the winner in Florida early in the morning after the election. Members were also reported to be thinking about alternative ways of establishing a new exit poll organisation, but time was short with the presidential primaries only a year away.

Source: www.cnn.com, 'News groups disband Voter News Service', 13 January 2003.

In 48 states a candidate can win all of the state's Electoral College votes by securing a plurality of the votes cast, that is, more votes than any other candidate even if this is less than an overall majority. The 'winner takes all' system usually means that there is a tendency for the Electoral College result, which really counts, to exaggerate the margin of victory as compared with the popular vote. For example, in 1984 Ronald Reagan won 59 per cent of the popular vote in his landslide victory over Walter Mondale; because he won 49 states (all except Mondale's own state of Minnesota, plus the District of Columbia) Reagan took 98 per cent of the Electoral College votes. In 1996 Bill Clinton won 70 per cent of the College based on 49 per cent of the popular vote. Two states use a proportional system that awards two votes to the statewide winner and allocates the remaining votes by congressional districts. Maine has used this system since 1969 and Nebraska since 1992. In theory therefore their Electoral College votes could be split between the candidates, although this has not happened in practice. Because states can adopt their own election rules such a change in the ways votes are allocated does not require a constitutional amendment at national level. There are four main criticisms that are made about the Electoral College:

1   There is the possibility that the candidate who wins most votes in the country will actually lose the election because his rival has accumulated his support in such a way that he wins more Electoral College votes. This has happened four times – John Quincey Adams (1824), Rutherford B. Hayes (1876), Benjamin Harrison (1888) and George W. Bush (2000). In 23 of the nation's presidential elections the winner has had an uncomfortably close victory and even Jimmy Carter, who had a 1.7 million vote plurality, would have lost in the Electoral College if a mere 9,245 votes in Ohio and Hawaii had gone to Ford.[12] In 2000 Bush's eventual victory came despite the fact that Al Gore won more than 540,000 more votes nationwide.

2   It is necessary for a candidate to win an overall majority of Electoral College votes to become President. If no such clear majority is obtained because of the intervention of a strong minor party candidate, then the House of Representatives has the constitutional right to decide, voting in state blocs with one vote each. Many critics see such an eventuality as a threat to the democratic wishes of the people. The House had to resolve the issue in 1800 and 1824, and there were fears that George Wallace's 1968 campaign might also produce a deadlocked situation. However, Wallace did not obtain sufficient Electoral College votes to deny Nixon victory (see Table 7.4).

3   The system deters voters from supporting minor party or independent candidates. Even when they attract considerable public support, as Ross Perot did in 1992, this is not reflected in the Electoral College unless they have concentrated their votes in particular states.

4   Although the party officials who become state electors are supposed to vote for their own party's candidate sometimes an individual will go against the popular wishes of the state's electorate and vote for a different candidate. For example, in 1972 a Virginian Republican voted for the Libertarian party's John Hospers rather than for Richard Nixon and in 1976 one Republican elector supported Ronald Reagan rather than Gerald Ford. In 2000 one of the Washington, DC Electors abstained in protest against the lack of congressional representation for the District. In 24 states plus the District of Columbia Electors are required to cast their votes according to the popular will either by state law or by pledges made to political parties. However, nobody has ever been prosecuted for failing to honour this commitment.

There have been hundreds of proposals for constitutional amendments that would either modify the rules of the Electoral College or abolish it altogether. In 1969 the House of Representatives, encouraged by President Nixon, voted by 338–70 to abolish the Electoral College and replace it with a direct election but the proposal died after a filibuster in the Senate by Republicans and Southern Democrats. Early in his presidency,

Table 7.4 Electoral College and popular votes

		Electoral College votes	Popular vote	
1968				
	Nixon (R)	302	37,770,237	(43.4%)
	Humphrey (D)	191	37,270,533	(42.7%)
	Wallace (AIP)	45	9,906,141	(13.6%)
1976				
	Carter (D)	297	40,827,394	(50.0%)
	Ford (R)	240	39,145,977	(47.9%)
	McCarthy (Ind.)	—	745,042	(0.9%)
	Others	1	965,505	(1.2%)
1984				
	Reagan (R)	525	54,455,093	(59.0%)
	Mondale (D)	13	37,567,331	(41.0%)
1988				
	Bush (R)	426	48,881,278	(53.4%)
	Dukakis (D)	112	41,805,374	(45.7%)
1992				
	Clinton (D)	370	44,908,233	(43.2%)
	Bush (R)	168	39,102,282	(37.7%)
	Perot (Ind.)	0	19,741,048	(19.0%)
1996				
	Clinton (D)	379	47,401,054	(49.2%)
	Dole (R)	159	39,197,350	(40.7%)
	Perot (Reform)	0	8,085,285	(8.4%)
2000				
	Bush (R)	271	50,456,062	(47.9%)
	Gore (D)	266	50,996,582	(48.4%)

Jimmy Carter threw his weight behind the reform movement by stating that he would like to see the archaic system replaced by direct popular election. The best-supported proposal in recent times has been put forward by Senator Birch Bayh of Indiana, who suggested direct elections of the President with a run-off election between the two top contenders if no one secured more than 40 per cent of the popular vote in the first poll. In July 1979 the Senate passed a proposal for a constitutional amendment on these lines by 51–48 votes but this was well short of the two-thirds majority necessary. There have been less radical suggestions to modify the 'winner-takes-all' nature of the Electoral College. There could be a system of dividing the Electoral College votes of a state in proportion to the popular vote attained by each individual, although this would make it more difficult for one candidate to secure an absolute majority, or partially by congressional districts in the way Maine and Nebraska do.

Why has the present system survived so long? This is most easily explained by the lack of consensus behind any particular method of reform. Direct popular election across the nation would undermine federalism, taking away from the states their role in presidential elections; the US Constitution was designed to safeguard their interests and reform would also remove the influence of small states and less populated areas.[13] Some opponents have argued that African-Americans and other minority groups could see their influence diluted if a popular vote system were adopted because under the current system such voters have a crucial role in determining the direction of many states' Electoral College votes and candidates have to pay attention to their interests. Some people also fear that popular election would further weaken the two-party system and encourage minor party candidates. For all these reasons reform of the electoral system is assured of strong opposition in Congress and the state legislatures, which have to approve any constitutional changes. In the immediate aftermath of the 2000 presidential election there was, not surprisingly, a heated debate about the future of the Electoral College. However, Republicans were reluctant to support any proposal to abolish the institution in case it appeared that they were casting doubt on the legitimacy of George W. Bush's presidency. It is not possible to pass a constitutional amendment without overwhelming and bipartisan support and interest in the issue faded.

Participation in elections

At the national level the voting turnout in presidential elections has not been impressive when contrasted with many European democracies. A survey on electoral turnouts showed the United States with the second lowest of 24 democratic states with only Switzerland having lower levels of participation in elections.[14] The 1960 figure of 62.8 per cent in the Kennedy-Nixon election was very good by American standards. In the 1992 presidential election 55.2 per cent of Americans of voting age turned out – the highest since 1968 with a record increase in new voters (nearly 13 million) and the largest ever total (over 104 million). However, in 1996 only 49 per cent went to the polls, the lowest turnout since 1924 when women first had the right to vote. This national figure obscures the fact that turnout varied from a high of 71.9 per cent in Maine to 38.3 in Nevada. In 2000, despite the closeness of the race, just over half, 51.2 per cent, of those of voting age actually went to the polls. In the midterm congressional elections, when there is no presidential election to stimulate voter interest, under 40 per cent of eligible voters usually take part (see Figures 7.2 and 7.3).

Evidence suggests that groups given the right to vote do not immediately exercise that right. After the passage of the Nineteenth Amendment in 1920 many women were slow to use their new right and, since the early 1970s, turnout rates have been affected by the low participation rate of young voters, always well below 50 per cent, following the ratification of the Twenty-Sixth Amendment in 1971. Turnout rates are not as low as they may first appear. In the US they are calculated as a percentage of the total number of eligible adults in the country. However, the census figures used do not distinguish between those of voting age who are citizens and therefore qualified to vote and those who are resident non-citizens who are not. Given the large number of immigrants in the country, the system inevitably underestimates turnout. In addition, many states have residence requirements which people have to meet before they are allowed to vote

The most important factor in America is the effect of registration laws. The United States is the only democracy in the world where voter registration is initiated by the individual; in other countries the Government (in whole or part) draws up the list and usually makes efforts to obtain as complete a register as possible. In most states each individual has the responsibility of registering himself as a qualified voter well before election day. Those who fail to do so by a specific date are ineligible to vote on election day even if they are technically qualified to vote in other ways. Six states allow same-day registration and they tend to have higher turnouts than the others. The turnout rate for those who are actually registered was approximately 66 per cent in 1996 compared with 49 per cent of adults of voting age.

Table 7.5 Number of Electoral College votes and percentage of popular votes for Gore and Bush in 2000

	Popular vote %		EC vote	
	Gore	Bush	Gore	Bush
Alabama	41.6	56.5		9
Alaska	27.8	58.8		3
Arizona	44.7	51.0		8
Arkansas	45.9	51.3		6
California	53.5	41.7	54	
Colorado	42.4	50.8		8
Connecticut	55.9	38.4	8	
Delaware	55.0	41.9	3	
District of Columbia	85.2	9.0	2	
Florida	48.8	48.9		25
Georgia	43.2	55.0		13
Hawaii	55.8	37.5	4	
Idaho	27.6	67.2		4
Illinois	54.6	42.6	22	
Indiana	41.0	56.7		12
Iowa	48.6	48.3	7	
Kansas	37.2	58.0		6
Kentucky	41.3	56.4		8
Louisiana	44.8	52.6		9
Maine	49.1	43.8	4	
Maryland	56.6	40.2	10	
Massachusetts	59.9	32.6	12	
Michigan	51.3	46.1	18	
Minnesota	47.9	45.5	10	
Mississippi	40.7	57.6		7
Missouri	47.1	50.4		11
Montana	33.4	58.4		3
Nebraska	33.3	62.2		5
Nevada	46.2	49.8		4
New Hampshire	46.9	48.2		4
New Jersey	56.1	40.3	15	
New Mexico	47.9	47.9	5	
New York	60.2	35.2	33	
North Carolina	43.2	56.0		14
North Dakota	33.1	60.1		3
Ohio	46.4	50.0		21
Oklahoma	38.4	60.3		8
Oregon	47.1	46.7	7	
Pennsylvania	50.6	46.4	23	
Rhode Island	61.0	31.9	4	
South Carolina	40.9	56.9		8
South Dakota	37.6	60.3		3
Tennessee	47.3	51.2		11
Texas	38.0	59.3		32
Utah	26.5	67.2		5
Vermont	50.7	40.8	3	
Virginia	44.5	52.5		13
Washington	50.2	44.6	11	
West Virginia	45.6	51.9		5
Wisconsin	47.8	47.6	11	
Wyoming	28.3	69.2		3

Note: Table based on official election returns. Figures rounded to nearest decimal point.

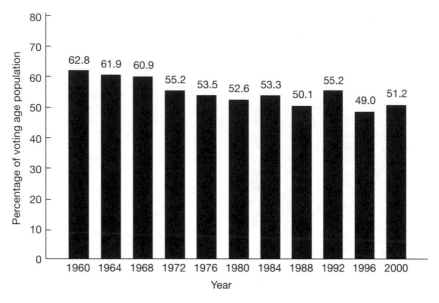

Figure 7.2 Voting turnout in presidential elections 1960–2000

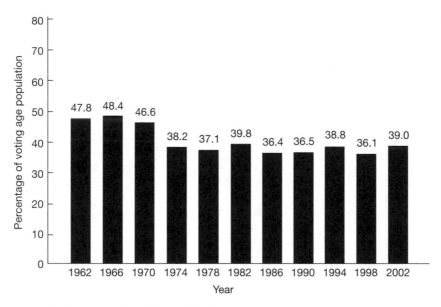

Figure 7.3 Voting turnout in midterm elections

In 1993 Congress passed and President Clinton signed into law a measure, the National Voter Registration Act, that became known as the 'motor voter' bill because its main provision requires states to allow people to register to vote when applying for a driving licence. The law, which came into effect in 1995, also requires states to provide registration through the mail and at state offices that assist the disabled and distribute welfare payments. Despite easier procedures resulting in an additional five million people being registered, the 1996 election saw almost ten million fewer citizens exercising their right to vote than in 1992. Although voter turnout in general was down, the number of blacks voting was greater and they comprised 10 per cent of the voting electorate compared with 8 per cent four years earlier.

In 1998 Oregon voters passed an initiative requiring the state to conduct its elections by postal ballots and these have now replaced voting at traditional polling stations. Although advocates of the reform argued that, by making voting more convenient, participation would increase, there have been concerns that such a change affects the privacy and secrecy of the ballot and could lead to greater voter fraud. Postal votes also take longer to count and can get lost in the mail. Oregon was one of the last states to certify its results in the 2000. Apart from Oregon, about half the states allow early ballots to be cast before election day and 21 states permit 'no excuse' absentee ballots where voters can request a postal ballot for convenience's sake rather than because they will be away on election day. These developments are having a significant impact on the conduct of American elections even if they do help to increase the number of people voting.

In the 1984 election 92.6 million people did vote and a further 84 million Americans of voting age did not. After the election the Gallup poll issued a breakdown of non-voters and the reasons they gave for not voting, with the percentages from sample projected into numbers of people. This is shown in Table 7.6.

Some of the reasons given for non-voting would undoubtedly be similar to those in other countries, although the mobility of American society with up to 20 per cent of the population moving home each year is likely to exacerbate the trends. Institutions that have traditionally mobilised voters such as political party organisations and trade unions have been in decline, and campaigns that were once principally conducted at grass-roots level by party activists are now waged through the more impersonal medium of television. A number of variables may apply to a particular election: in 1972, 1984 and 1996 the result was in many people's minds a foregone conclusion and it may not have seemed worth voting. In 1988 and 1996 there was a lack of feeling that the election was a really important choice between two clear and divergent philosophies; in 1996 Clinton ran on what, in many respects, was a conservative programme that made the differences with Dole seem minimal. The campaigns stimulated little voter interest, and the negative tone of much of the advertising may well have acted as a deterrent. At the same time the lack of major issues worrying the electorate also seems likely to have depressed turnout levels.

Table 7.6 Reasons for non-voting

---

54 million were not registered.
17.4 million did not like the candidates.
14 million were not interested in politics.
14 million had no particular reason.
12 million were ill or disabled.
12 million said they could not leave their jobs.
12 million said it was inconvenient.
10.4 million were not American citizens.
10.4 million were not residents in their community and had not met residence requirements.
8.7 million were travelling and away from home.
5 million had no way to get to the polls.
1.7 million had not obtained an absentee ballot.
1.7 million mentioned a variety of other reasons.

Source: Figures are those for the 1984 election as set out in a Gallup Poll press release, 9 December 1984. As some people gave more than one reason, the number of responses is greater than 84 million not voting.

A former US Census Bureau Director said:

> Peace and prosperity can generally operate to keep the vote down as well as to help the incumbent. In a sense low turnout is consent. A pool of discontent may be valuable for a democracy.[15]

In 1992 the increased turnout resulted from a number of factors. Polls indicated that 79 per cent of respondents said they were interested in the presidential race compared with 64 per cent in 1988. The efforts made by candidates to use new and alternative methods of communication with the electorate, the recession and the intervention of Ross Perot all helped stimulate interest. A number of states had also eased their registration rules since 1988, while many states had controversial issues on their ballots as referendums which also encouraged a higher turnout.

Education seems to be the most significant factor in determining voter turnout. Not surprisingly, better educated citizens are more likely to be interested in elections and to vote in them. The greater people's sense of political effectiveness, in that they feel they can understand and influence politics, the more likely they are to vote. Nationally surveys have shown a loss of political efficacy among many voters. For example, in the mid-1990s over half of those asked agreed with the statement that people do not have a say in what government does, compared with just over a quarter in 1960.[16] The non-voting citizen is more likely to be very young or very old, have only elementary education, live in a rural area, be a Southerner, have a manual occupation, be black and have little interest in politics.

Two concerns about the incidence of non-voting should be noted. First, if those who do vote come disproportionately from the middle classes and those who are financially better off and the non-voters are predominantly from the poor and disadvantaged sections of society, how far does this affect the political agenda and the issues with which politicians are concerned? What is more, some critics have claimed that incumbent legislators are unlikely to push for measures which will encourage even higher levels of turnout when those sections of the electorate who already vote put them in office. Second, and of more general and long-term significance to the constitutional order and health of the nation, is how far high levels of non-voting affect the legitimacy of the political system and the feeling among Americans that they live in a democracy?

Congressional elections

Although there is a tendency in the media, particularly outside the United States, to focus almost exclusively on the presidential election, it is important to remember that the political landscape in Washington DC depends as much on the results of the congressional elections and which party secures a majority of seats in the House of Representatives and the Senate as who occupies the White House.

We have seen in Chapter 2 the importance of incumbency in legislative elections and noted the trend in recent elections for competitive elections to result principally from the creation of open seats when existing members decide to retire. In 2002 all but a few dozen of the 435 seats in the House were regarded as 'safe' for one party, with reapportionment after the 2000 census reducing electoral competition even further. Despite this, as all House seats and one-third of the Senate are elected every two years members are constantly keeping a wary eye on the next election.

A legislator will try to establish a solid record of achievements and a reputation as an effective constituency representative so that voters will be inclined to return him or her regularly to Washington. Many members play down their party attachment in their campaigns in order to appeal to as wide a cross-section of voters as possible. Name recognition and seniority in Congress are important and many congressional elections have been fought on what are essentially local issues and have focused on local personalities. Opinion polls that ask a generic question about which party voters will support in congressional elections have been notoriously unreliable indicators of actual results because they do not take account of these local factors.

The 1994 midterm elections were therefore unusual insofar as the Republican House candidates, led by Newt Gingrich, ran a more coordinated national campaign based on the 'Contract with America' which most of them signed. The document became a manifesto of commitments and was designed to draw out differences between the parties. The Republicans' campaign attacked the record of the Democrats who had been in control of Congress and exploited the current unpopularity of Bill Clinton. Gingrich believed that the traditional locally based campaigns enabled Democratic members to exploit their incumbency advantages while avoiding accountability for their actions as the majority party. The sweeping Republican victories, with 52 net gains in the House and an additional eight seats in the Senate, gave them control of Congress for the first time in 40 years. No Republican incumbent lost his seat while Democratic leaders such as Speaker Tom Foley (Washington), Dan Rostenkowski (Illinois), Jack Brooks (Texas) and Senator Jim Sasser (Tennessee), who had hoped to become the new Senate Majority Leader, were swept from office.

In 1996 the Democrats attempted to turn the tables on their rivals by running a nationally oriented campaign exploiting the unpopularity of Speaker Gingrich and voters' concerns about Republican plans for cuts in social programmes. Vulnerable Republicans, especially those freshmen who had won their seats in 1994 by small majorities, were targeted and their association with, and support for, Gingrich highlighted. Although neither party produced a campaign document similar to the Contract, the Democrats' 'anti-Newt' message was projected nationwide. Republican candidates generally emphasised their records in serving their constituents and distanced themselves from the Speaker, who concentrated on fighting his Georgia district and was almost invisible as a national campaigner, in stark contrast to two years earlier.

With Dole's defeat appearing inevitable and concerns that he might drag down many Republican congressional candidates with him, the national party decided to take a gamble late in the campaign and run commercials that emphasised the need to re-elect a Republican Congress to act as a check on Clinton during a second term. In the event, the late swing to the Republicans meant that, of the party's 73 House freshmen, only 14 were defeated and the GOP retained control of Congress, albeit with a reduced majority in the House. The GOP share of the national vote in House elections was down 3.5 per cent compared with 1994 and at 48.9 per cent was the lowest for a party winning a majority of seats since 1938; their lead over the Democrats in the popular vote was only 0.33 per cent. Despite the closeness of the elections, the Republicans actually improved their position by two seats in the Senate where the party won 2.3 per cent more of the votes than their rivals.

American midterm elections have usually seen the President's party suffering losses in congressional seats. For example, from the end of the Second World War to 1998 the party controlling the White House lost an average of 27 house seats. However, in 1998 the Democrats confounded the pundits with a surprisingly strong showing and became the first presidential party to increase their number of House seats in midterm for more than six decades.[17] The campaign had been overshadowed by the confession by President

Clinton that he had concealed his affair with former White House intern, Monica Lewinsky, and the subsequent calls for his impeachment and removal from office. Democratic candidates had been worried that, with the President himself not on the ballot paper in 1998, many voters would vent their anger on those Democrats who were running for office and that many of the party's traditional supporters would stay home in disgust. Republicans, on the other hand, were hopeful of adding at least 10–20 seats to their House majority and improving on their 55–45 majority in the Senate. In the event, although the Republicans kept control of the House for a third consecutive term for the first time in 70 years, it was with a reduced majority, whereas in the Senate the existing balance was maintained. The strong economy and the public's general contentment with the status quo proved to be much more significant factors in determining voting behaviour than the Lewinsky affair. It was ironic that the elections actually strengthened Clinton's position and made his removal from office less likely, while the Speaker Newt Gingrich was obliged to resign as Republican members blamed the party leadership for the disappointing performance.

As we have seen, the 2000 congressional elections reflected the dead heat presidential race and the Senate was evenly balanced with each party having 50 members. In 2002 the Republicans bucked the trend, as the Democrats had in 1998, by making gains in the midterm elections. Helped by the energetic campaigning and personal popularity of George W. Bush, the Republicans moved to a 51–49 majority in the Senate and increased their slim majority in the House to 229–205 with one independent. The elections were seen as a personal triumph for Bush who spent far more time and effort than most presidential incumbents in campaigning and fund-raising for his party's candidates. They resulted in the Republican Party having outright control of the presidency and majorities in both houses of Congress for the first time in 50 years. What is more, Bush became the first President in his second year in office to recapture control of a chamber of Congress, and only the second since the Civil War to see his party make midterm gains in both houses, Franklin D. Roosevelt being the other in 1934.

Therefore, although national issues, such as the impeachment crisis in 1998 and the war on terror and possible US intervention in Iraq in 2002, are important in understanding the results of midterm elections and Presidents can play a major role even when they are not on the ballot paper directly, many of the individual races are most affected by and can only be explained by the peculiar circumstances of those constituencies and the personalities of the individual candidates. For example, in 2002 in Minnesota the Republicans were victorious in the Senate race after the incumbent Paul Wellstone was killed in an air crash a few weeks before the election and his Democratic replacement, former presidential candidate Walter Mondale, could not hold on to the seat. In New Jersey, however, the former Democratic Senator Frank Lautenberg returned to the upper house and beat his Republican opponent after taking over the party's candidacy from incumbent Senator Richard Torricelli who was forced to resign after accepting expensive gifts from a businessman.

The administration of elections

The disputed 2000 election result in Florida highlighted two important aspects of the administration of elections in the United States. First, as we have seen, states in the federal system are given the power to make their own laws on electoral practices and procedures, as long as they do not conflict with the requirements of the US Constitution. This has meant that states have adopted very different rules on everything from registration procedures to the actual mechanics of voting.[18] Although some states still make limited use of ballots completed by hand, as in Britain, most use other approaches. Some states use electronic means by which the voter touches a screen, while others have optical scanners that read ballots filled in by the voter's pencil mark. The traditional methods used involve the use of lever-and-curtain machines or those with punch cards; however, these are using increasingly obsolete and unreliable technology. In Florida in 2000 many voters using the punch card system failed to push the stylus completely through the card, leaving the problem of 'pregnant' and 'hanging' chads,[19] terms which have become part of the folklore of the election, and the officials with the difficult task of ascertaining whether the votes should be counted as valid ballots.

As Florida also demonstrated, making policy over election procedures has been de-centralised even further with individual counties within the state making their own decisions, for example, on the design of the ballot paper. The use of 'butterfly ballots' in one county whereby the names of candidates were printed on both sides of the ballot paper confused a number of mostly elderly citizens. As a result they voted accidentally for Pat Buchanan rather than Al Gore or disqualified their vote by double punching the card. The different practices adopted by the various county boards in the manual recounts of votes led to the issue of unequal treatment of voters coming before the Supreme Court in *Bush* v. *Gore*.

The second feature of the Florida election was the prominent role played by elected partisan officials in the administration and oversight of the electoral process. In Britain a senior and non-political local government officer is appointed as returning officer for elections and ensures that they are conducted legally and fairly. In 22 states there are provisions for officials or boards who are appointed by the Governor, the legislature or a combination of both to supervise elections and they are expected to be non-partisan in carrying out their duties. However, in the other 28, including Florida, elected officials, usually the Secretary of State, is responsible. Kathleen Harris, the Florida Secretary of State is a prominent Republican and was co-chair of Bush's campaign in the state. She had the duty of certifying the official vote in Florida. The county electoral boards, which were overseeing the conduct of the election and administering the recounts, were also led by elected politicians. It is not surprising that in such a hotly contested election many voters were sceptical about whether party politicians could be trusted to administer the process fairly.

In 2002 Congress passed the Federal Voting Standards and Procedures Act in order to try to deal with some of the criticisms of practices that came to light in the 2000 elections. The new law, which was heralded by its proponents as the 'first civil rights act of the twenty-first century', sets broad standards for the conduct of federal elections and is the first time that Congress has legislated in detail in an area traditionally left to the states and local governments.[20] The statute authorised $3.9 billion in federal aid to help states meet the new standards. In order to qualify for the grants states will have to develop plans for modernising their machinery by replacing the old punch card and lever voting systems and have specific procedures, such as centralised and computerised voter registration databases in place. They will also have to commit themselves to extensive new training programmes for election officials and voter education projects. Under the new law a voter whose eligibility is questioned must be allowed to cast a provisional ballot which would be counted later if election officials determined that the individual was qualified to vote. This provision was included to satisfy Democrats who claimed that many Americans, particularly from minority groups, had been denied a vote in 2000. Republicans, on the other hand, insisted that there should be new protections against voter fraud, and election officials must be able to verify the identities of voters when they register, using a wide variety of methods of identification. The Act also created a new Election Assistance Commission to distribute the grants and offer advice and information to the states. Its four members would be nominated by the President and confirmed by the Senate although Republicans insisted it was not intended to be a regulatory agency. Despite the widespread support for the legislation there was concern that Congress might not appropriate sufficient funding over the next three years for its effective implementation if the federal budget deficit grew as predicted. Whether these concerns are justified remains to be seen.

Financing elections

Traditionally, American elections have been financed by private donations, both large and small, to a candidate's campaign or by a combination of such gifts with the candidate's own money. In 1974, after the Watergate scandal and revelations that illegal and undisclosed contributions had been made to the Nixon campaign, Congress passed amendments to the Federal Election Campaign Act of 1971 and, in so doing, introduced the most sweeping reforms of campaign finance in American history. The major components of the bill included limits on campaign contributions and spending by candidates, a system of public funding for presidential elections and the establishment of a new regulatory agency, the Federal Election Commission, to enforce the law. A challenge to the constitutionality of the Act led to the Supreme Court upholding some parts of the law but overturning others in the case of *Buckley* v. *Valeo* in 1976.[21]

The Supreme Court argued that, while there had to be safeguards against corruption of the electoral system with the improper use of money, this had to be done without infringing the constitutional freedoms of both candidates and citizens. In modern elections candidates need money to pay the costs of communicating with the voters through the media. It therefore ruled that it was unconstitutional to impose mandatory expenditure limits on campaigns, to restrict the amounts candidates could spend of their own money or prevent independent campaigns for or against particular candidates. However, the justices did accept that voluntary spending limits could be established as a condition for receiving public funding, that public financing of elections by taxpayer contributions was legal and that it was permissible to place limits on the amounts which individuals and groups could donate. The law restricted individual citizens to a maximum of $1,000 to any campaign with an overall annual limit of $25,000; political action committees (PACs) could give up to $5,000 to a particular candidate but no aggregate limit was imposed. These figures were not raised to take account of inflation over the period since 1974 and their real value therefore by 2000 had depreciated by two-thirds.

In presidential elections until 2000 the scope of public financing available led to candidates, with the exception of the very wealthy Ross Perot in 1992 and Steve Forbes in 1996 who funded their own campaigns, accepting money from the taxpayer check-off fund set up by the 1974 legislation, and, in so doing, they were technically obliged to comply with the 'voluntary' spending limits laid down. These have been index-linked to reflect the effects of inflation. Candidates in the nomination process raise money from private contributors and, once they demonstrate they can do so on a broad basis, they become eligible for matching public funds. This condition was included so that only serious contenders on a national basis could receive taxpayers' money. Public funding was made available to the parties to pay for their national conventions and to the candidates to provide the bulk of their spending in the general election campaigns. In

1996 Clinton and Dole each received $62 million and their parties were restricted to spending $12 million on their presidential campaigns.

However, in recent presidential elections both major parties have routinely circumvented these limits with the use of so-called 'soft money' to supplement the public funding. In 1979 Congress passed legislation designed to help political parties revive their grass-roots activities, such as registration drives and 'get-out-the-vote' efforts, by allowing them to raise and spend money for general campaigning outside the limits on federal contributions. Individual, corporate and trade union donors could give large sums to party committees and bypass the limits on contributions to campaigns. Critics claim that this allowed the return of 'fat cat' influence in the electoral process that the post-Watergate reforms were supposed to have prevented. Since 1980 party committees have used this soft money to support their presidential candidates. In the 1990s the extent of this spending increased so dramatically that the official limits were effectively ignored altogether, giving rise to new demands for reform of the legislation applying to election funding. In 1996 party committees raised $264 million in soft money – three times more than in 1992 and more than 13 times what they raised in 1980. The Democratic Party raised $102 million in soft money in 1996, 232 per cent more than in the previous presidential election. Revelations that President Clinton had encouraged his fund-raisers with promises to meet wealthy donors personally, even allowing some of them to stay overnight at the White House as a reward for their generosity to the Democratic cause, coupled with allegations that illegal contributions had been received from foreign businessmen who may have sought to influence American trade or foreign policy, highlighted the way this type of election funding had been abused.

Some commentators have argued that soft money became important in presidential elections because the official limits for spending were set unrealistically low. In 1996 Robert Dole spent practically all his permitted funds in the early months of the nomination process fighting off the challenge of Steve Forbes who was not restricted in the amounts he spent as he was not in receipt of federal funds. Subsequently Dole was left without official funding for many months until the start of the general election campaign, at a time when Clinton was spending freely, particularly on television advertising. Dole was therefore forced to rely on spending by Republican committees to keep his name before the public in the period up to the convention. In learning from this lesson, George W. Bush in 2000 refused public funding in the nomination process so that he would not be restricted by spending limits. With the advantages of his name and his father's contacts Bush raised record amounts of hard money in contributions from individuals of $1,000 or less. Altogether his war-chest of over $100 million deterred other a number of candidates from entering the race and easily saw off the challenges from Forbes and Senator John McCain whom he left trailing in his financial wake.

In congressional elections there are no overall statutory limits on the amounts candidates may spend on their campaigns and, as there is no public funding available, there are no 'voluntary' limits either. Candidates are able to raise and spend as much as they feel they require to run a winning campaign or as much as they can persuade contributors to give them. Wealthy candidates can spend their own resources without constraint, although Michael Huffington's 1994 Senate campaign in California demonstrates that this does not necessarily guarantee success. Having used over $26 million to pay for his campaign, the Republican candidate still lost the race to incumbent Democratic Senator, Dianne Feinstein.

Congressional candidates draw money from individual supporters, from party committees and from PACs. There has been concern over the increasing costs of running for Congress and the growing gap in the funding available to incumbents and challengers. This has been a major factor in explaining the high success rate of incumbent members and the decline in competitive elections. In 1974 the average House incumbent spent $56,000 and the average challenger $40,000, a gap of only $16,000. By 1992 the figures were $580,000 and $180,000 respectively, a margin of $400,000. After remaining fairly static during the 1980s, overall campaign expenditure in congressional elections rose sharply in 1992 to $678 million and in 2000 totalled just over a billion dollars.

In 1996 political parties extended the use of soft money to support congressional campaigns as well as their presidential candidates. A Supreme Court ruling in June 1996 also paved the way for additional party funding of legislative races; the justices decided that parties could spend as much as they wished in congressional campaigns, so long as they acted independently of the candidates. One consequence of this ruling was that parties were given the green light to spend large amounts on negative advertising. This is because such commercials are generally felt by the parties to be safer than spending money on positive messages on behalf of their own candidates which may be claimed to have been coordinated with their campaigns and thus count as illegal expenditure.

Campaign finance reform proposals in the decade up to 1997 tended to focus on introducing limits on spending with some form of public finance or subsidy as the inducement to candidates to comply, as well as restrictions on the contributions from PACs. All efforts to pass such legislation failed as a result of deep divisions both between and within the political parties in Congress as well as differing priorities between House and Senate members. In September 1997 Senators John McCain (R. Arizona) and Russell Feingold (D. Wisconsin), the main sponsors of reform legislation in the Senate, drastically scaled back the scope of their bill in the hope of overcoming opposition. They stripped the proposal of most of the provisions that had formed the basis of comprehensive reform bills in the past to concentrate on what they saw as the key problems. The new McCain-Feingold bill focused on a ban on soft money donations to political parties and the introduction of new regulations affecting issue advocacy commercials mentioning a candidate by name in the run-up to an election.

As we saw in Chapter 5, many pressure groups have used issue advertising during election campaigns to support or more usually to criticise a candidate's stand on particular issues of interest to them, while not specifically calling for the election or defeat of the candidate on election day. Unless they 'expressly advocate' such a course of action the Supreme Court has held that these commercials could not be regulated by election law. Therefore there were no limits on how much groups could spend on issue ads and corporations and trade unions which are banned from contributing directly to campaigns (as opposed to through political action committees) could spend as much as they liked in support of or in opposition to a candidate, a situation that reformers saw as a major loophole through which vast *de facto* campaign contributions could pass unregulated. Therefore the new bill included a ban on corporations and unions from buying issue advertising on television or radio which mentions a candidate by name within 30 days of a primary or 60 days of a general election. Other groups buying such commercials would be required to disclose who had funded them.

Over the next four years campaign finance reform bills were effectively blocked by Republicans in the Senate who used the filibuster weapon to prevent a vote on McCain-Feingold's proposals. Although a small majority of members, 52–54 of the 100 Senators including 7–8 Republicans, regularly supported the reforms they were well short of the 60 votes needed to pass a cloture motion. However, in March 2001 the Senate voted 59–41 in favour of the legislation and opponents reluctantly accepted defeat in the chamber. The Senate was evenly split following the 2000 elections and the additional Democratic votes proved vital to the passage of the bill. Important amendments were agreed during the legislative process. These included an extension of the ban on issue ads before elections to include all pressure groups which was passed despite the opposition of McCain and Feingold, and the raising of the limits on hard money donations by individuals from $1,000 to $2,000.

The House of Representatives had passed reform bills in previous years but these had not progressed because of opposition in the Senate. In February 2002 the chamber supported a similar bill to that passed in the Senate by 240–189, overcoming the resistance of the Republican leadership. The Enron scandal, with the exposure of accounting malpractices by a giant corporation which had regularly given soft money gifts to both parties, provided a major impetus for congressional passage of the legislation. The final bill was signed into law later in 2002 by President Bush who, while unenthusiastic about the proposals, did not want to be seen to be opposing 'reform' and was anxious to avoid a confrontation with Senator McCain, his rival for the Republican nomination in 2000 and a possible challenger in the future.

Opponents of the new law immediately launched a challenge to its constitutionality, claiming that it violated First Amendment rights, and the Supreme Court was expected to hear the case in the Spring of 2003. The law came into effect after the 2002 elections and political parties were coming to terms with the need to raise more hard money donations to replace the soft money that was now banned. Many observers expected them also to try and find ways of circumventing the new rules, for example by establishing new committees that could accept larger contributions.

Chapter summary

- Most presidential candidates are white, male, middle-aged and have considerable experience in politics. Most recent Presidents have formerly been Governors of states.
- The battle for the presidential nominations of the two parties commences about two years before the election itself. Politicians sound out opinion, declare their candidacies, make media appearances and seek endorsements and money.
- Successful nomination requires a candidate to secure a simple majority of votes from the delegates who attend the national party convention in the summer of election year. State parties use either caucuses or primaries to select their delegates.
- Primaries are now used by the vast majority of state parties. Primaries in those states which hold their primaries early in election year act to narrow the field of candidates because those with little support drop out of the race.
- 'Frontloading' of the primaries has led to more states bringing their contests forward to earlier in the calendar so that a substantial majority of the delegates are now chosen before the end of March. Candidates have thus been forced to organise and raise funds well before election year starts.
- National party conventions offer the opportunity for the country to see the candidate and hear about the party's programme. They are now carefully synchronised events to maximise media exposure and provide a favourable impression of the party and its candidate who normally receives a 'bounce' in the opinion polls following the convention.
- In the general election campaign both parties' candidates are striving to win a majority of the votes in the Electoral College (270 out of 538). In all but two states the winner of a simple plurality of the popular vote statewide wins all of the Electoral

College votes of that state. The strategy for winning a majority in the Electoral College usually involves concentrating resources in the largest states and those that are likely to be very close in the popular vote count.

- Television plays a key role in presidential campaigns but here has been a diversification of the news media in recent times which affects how candidates try to reach the voters.
- The televised debates can have a significant impact on the voters' perceptions of the candidates and therefore the way people vote.
- The three main factors affecting voter choice are party identification, issues and the personalities and qualifications of the candidates. Most voters support the candidate of the party they generally identify with, even if that candidate is unlikely to be successful.
- Analysis of voting behaviour over a number of presidential elections demonstrates that the Republicans and Democrats draw their strongest support from different areas and social groups within the United States. Region, occupation and income, ethnic and racial background, age and gender all play a part in explaining the parties' and their candidates' electoral performances.
- The 2000 election highlighted the role of the Electoral College in determining who becomes President and revived the debate as to whether it should be replaced by a direct popular election.
- Voting turnouts in the US have been relatively low; a key factor in explaining this phenomenon is the impact of voter registration laws.
- Congressional elections are dominated by incumbents seeking re-election. Seats which change hands between the parties are usually those where there is an open race. Turnout is lower in midterm elections than in presidential election years. Although national events can affect congressional elections and the President's popularity or lack of it can influence the political climate, many individual races are determined by local issues and the personalities involved in those elections.
- After the 2000 elections Congress passed legislation in 2002 to help the states modernise their electoral procedures and practices.
- After many years of debate in 2002 Congress passed a major reform of the campaign finance system, introducing a ban on the soft money donations to political parties which had grown dramatically since the early 1990s.

Think points

- What does a politician need to have if he or she is to become a serious presidential candidate?
- Should the Electoral College be replaced by a direct popular election for the presidency?
- Why do only a half of the voting age public in the United States turn out to elect the most important government office in the world?

Some further reading

M. Margaret Conway, *Political Participation in the US* (Congressional Quarterly Press 1991)
Philip John Davies, *US Elections Today* (Manchester University Press 1999)
Philip John Davies, 'Elections, Voting and Campaigning at the Start of the Twenty-first Century', in *American Politics: 2000 and Beyond*, Alan Grant (ed.) (Ashgate 2000)

E.J. Dionne, Gerald M. Pomper and William G. Mayer, *The Election of 2000: Reports and Interpretations* (Chatham House 2001)

J.C. Doppelt and E. Shearer, *Non-Voters: America's No-shows* (Sage 1999)

William H. Flanigan and Nancy H. Kingale, *Political Behavior of the American Electorate* (Congressional Quarterly Press 1998)

Alan Grant, 'The Reform of Election Campaign Finance', in *American Politics: 2000 and Beyond*, Alan Grant (ed.) (Ashgate 2000)

Paul Herrnson, *Congressional Elections: Campaigns at Home and in Washington* (Congressional Quarterly Press 1998)

Gary Jacobson, *The Politics of Congressional Elections* (Harper Collins 1992)

R.G. Niemi and H. Weisberg, *Controversies in Voting Behaviour* (Congressional Quarterly Press 1993)

Nelson Polsby and Aaron Wildavsky, *Presidential Elections* (Scribner's 1991)

Gerald M. Pomper (ed.), *The Election of 1992* (Chatham House 1993)

Gerald M. Pomper (ed.), *The Election of 1996* (Chatham House 1997)

Jack N. Rakove, Alex Kaysaar and Henry Brady, *The Unfinished Election of 2000* (Basic Books 2001)

Byron Shafer (ed.), *The End of Realignment? Interpreting American Election Eras* (University of Wisconsin Press 1991)

Frank J. Sorauf, *Inside Campaign Finance: Myths and Realities* (Yale University Press 1992)

Weblinks

National Election Studies (University of Michigan): www.umich.edu/~nes/
Federal Election Commission: www.fec.gov
Center for Responsive Politics: www.opensecrets.org
Gallup Organization: www.gallup.com
Project Vote Smart: www.vote-smart.org/index.phtml

8 Federalism, the states and local government

The federal principle

The Founding Fathers established a system of government at the Philadelphia Convention in 1787 which was the result of the compromises necessary to reconcile the conflicting political and economic interests present. Federalism was in fact a 'half-way house' between the concept of a centralised unitary state that was unacceptable to the 13 states jealous of their own independence and that of a confederation which was a weak association of autonomous states of the kind that had proved unsatisfactory between 1781 and 1787. Federalism arose out of a desire to bolster national unity while at the same time accommodating regional diversity. The Constitution itself does not mention anywhere the terms 'federalism' and 'federation' but the United States has been recognised ever since as the major example of this compromise form of unity. Many other nations later attempted to adopt the federal principle which K.C. Wheare describes as: 'The method of dividing powers so that the general and regional governments are each, within a sphere, co-ordinate and independent.'[1]

Wheare says that the fundamental characteristic of the United States as an association of states is that the Constitution establishes an arrangement whereby powers are divided between a general (that is national or federal) government, which in certain matters is independent of the governments of the associated states, and state governments, which in certain matters are independent of the general government. Both national and state governments operate directly upon the people and each US citizen is subject to two governments.

The American federal system should not be seen therefore as a pyramid structure with the federal government at the apex, the states below it and the local governments as the base, because in constitutional terms at least the federal and state governments are of equal status with their own distinctive areas of authority. What is true, however, is that local government units are subordinate bodies and creatures of the states; their boundaries and powers can be altered as the state determines, because the 50 states are unitary systems in their own right.

There are certain institutions and practices which are essential for a federal system to exist and operate as an effective policy-making and administrative structure. First, a written constitution has to be accepted as supreme so that the terms of the division of power are binding upon all governments. The 'supremacy clause' (Article VI) makes it clear that the American Constitution and the laws of the United States shall be the supreme law of the land. Therefore, particularly in areas where concurrent legislative powers exist, the Constitution provides that federal statutes shall prevail in the event of a conflict with state laws.

It is also important that a single body be recognised as being able to settle disputes which arise about the division of powers. The US Supreme Court has developed this function of constitutional adjudication and, after some early opposition, its judgments have been accepted as binding upon both federal and state governments.

If federalism is to work satisfactorily, the power of amending the Constitution cannot be left exclusively to either tier of government; to do so would, of course, lead eventually to the subordination of one to the other. In the United States, both Congress and the state legislatures (or conventions) are involved in the amendment process. The federal relationship also entails the acknowledgement that states may not secede unilaterally from the Union, and that a state cannot be expelled from the association against its will. In most federations, the interests of the smaller states are protected either by equal representation or by additional members to those warranted by the size of their population in the upper house of the legislature. The US Senate was a very important part of the federal compromise at Philadelphia and was established to secure the support of the less populated states.[2]

As the Founding Fathers assumed that the states would continue to perform the major domestic roles of government, such as the maintenance of law and order, the Constitution does not deal in any detail with the functions of the states. The document is more specific on what the states could not do – the limitations on their freedom of action which was the price of greater national unity – and what the newly created federal government could and could not do. The powers of government can therefore be described in the following ways:

(a) *The 'enumerated' powers of the federal government.* Congress was given the right to legislate in certain specific areas in Article 1 Section 8, such as defence, currency, the Post Office and naturalisation of citizens;

(b) *The 'inherent' powers of the federal government.* The federal government has the right to do certain things because these are 'inherent' in its role as a national government; most important are the rights to conduct foreign relations and wage war;

(c) *The 'implied' powers of the federal government.* Having listed specific areas where Congress may legislate, Article 1 Section 8 of the Constitution says that it has the right to make all laws that are 'necessary and proper' for carrying into execution the enumerated powers;

(d) *The 'concurrent' powers of federal and state governments.* In some fields, such as taxation, both federal and state governments can legislate simultaneously;

(e) *The powers specifically denied to the federal government.* There are constitutional prohibitions on the Congress, for example, taxing exports, creating titles of nobility or favouring the ports of one state over another (Article 1 Section 9);

(f) *The powers denied to the states.* Article 1 Section 10 restricts the activities of state governments in certain fields; they cannot, for example, enter into treaties with foreign powers, or impose import or export duties;

(g) *The 'reserved' or 'residual' powers of the states.* The Tenth Amendment was included as part of the Bill of Rights as the price for the ratification of the Constitution. It provides that anything not delegated to the federal government or denied to the states be left to the authority of the states or to the people.

It has not always been easy to say which matters in practice are within the spheres of the federal or state governments because, as new issues have arisen, there have been disputes over the meaning of words in the constitutional document. The Supreme Court has had to interpret the Constitution and settle disputes in individual cases, but, as Wheare has noted, once it is granted that a government is acting within its allotted sphere, that government is not subordinate to any other in the United States.[3]

The development of modern federalism

In the early days of the Republic, there was a major political controversy concerning the nature of the federalism which had been created at the Philadelphia Convention. The Jeffersonian Democratic-Republicans wanted to see a restricted national authority and were concerned to protect the rights of the states against encroachment and centralising tendencies. The Hamiltonian Federalists were equally convinced of the need to strengthen the powers and status of the national government if America was to avoid the dangers of disintegration.

Although most Americans would have accepted the view that the Constitution established a relationship between independent and coordinate federal and state authorities, an important body of opinion argued that the federal government was not an equal partner, but was rather the creation of the states and thus subordinate to them. In the Southern states particularly, it was frequently asserted that the state legislatures had the right to nullify any Act of Congress with which they disagreed, and that if this was done the statute would have no force of law within their boundaries. Only after the Civil War was this view discredited. With the defeat of the South, Chief Justice Samuel Chase stressed the permanence of the Union: 'The Constitution, in all its provisions looks to an indestructible Union, comprised of indestructible States.'[4]

In the period since the Civil War, government regulatory activity has expanded at all levels, but the most striking development has been the increasingly important role of the federal government in its relationship with the states. A number of underlying social and economic factors have influenced the growth of responsibilities in Washington and contributed to the shift in the balance of power in the federal system. First, there has been the development of a strong national identity, which has helped provide the cultural background making the national government's expanded role acceptable. There are also much better communications and a greater degree of geographical mobility than ever before, so that, despite the size of the country, Americans are far more aware of social conditions in other parts of the nation. One of the effects of the modern mass media has been to provide further pressures towards uniformity of standards and provision of services.

The federal government's influence has also been considerably strengthened by the United States' twentieth-century role as a world super-power. This had led to vast increases in its budget and an expansion of its personnel in both civilian and military capacities and, because it is a major contractor and provider of jobs in private defence-related industries, the government's decisions vitally affect the economic well-being of the states and their people. The Great Depression of the 1930s also increased the expectation that the federal government would intervene to deal with the major social and economic ills of the country. Washington's attempts to ameliorate the problems by direct works programmes and unemployment insurance schemes filled a vacuum left by many state governments, which either were unable to act themselves as a result of the pressures on their own finances or seemed unwilling to do so. Some of the unreformed and rurally dominated state legislatures tended to neglect urgent problems afflicting the nation's urban areas. It is not surprising that city administration which found the state authorities unprepared to help looked instead to the federal government. The lack of a positive approach by some state governments to the crisis of the cities was an exacerbating factor encouraging centralisation. Indeed, the very nature of the problems in a highly complex industrialised society provides a challenge to the federal system. The federal government has often stepped in to coordinate governmental programmes when the problems cut across state and local boundaries.

These social and economic factors have led to pressures over the last two centuries for changes in the constitutional and political relationships within the federal system. A number of different methods have been adopted by reformers to bring about this transformation.

Constitutional amendments

The most obvious way of changing the constitutional relationship is by altering the written document, and four of the amendments passed since 1787 have significantly affected the federal system. After the Civil War, the Fourteenth Amendment gave the federal government the power to ensure that the states provided 'due process of law' and 'equal protection' of the laws to all their citizens. The Bill of Rights, initially a restriction on the federal government, was from that time on to apply to the states as well, and the federal government had the duty to enforce these provisions, a responsibility which would allow direct intervention in the affairs of the states.[5] The Fifteenth Amendment (1870) preventing citizens from being denied the right to vote on the basis of race or colour has allowed federal supervision of states' electoral practices under the Voting Rights Act of 1965 where there was evidence of past discrimination.

The Sixteenth Amendment, passed in 1913, was possibly the most important constitutional change in shaping the modern federal system. The federal government was given the right to raise a graduated tax on individual incomes, and this transformed its financial position. Without this lucrative source of revenue, the federal government would have found it increasingly difficult to raise sufficient money to pay for its defence and foreign policies and would have been unable to take action in the social and economic spheres. It might have had to approach the states for grants or subsidies to cover its expenditure. In practice, the federal government tended to squeeze the states out of the income tax field as its own demands on the taxpayers grew, and eventually state legislatures were obliged to accept grants from the federal government.

The Seventeenth Amendment, also passed in 1913, introduced the direct election of Senators by the people and broke the link between the Senate and state legislatures which had until that time elected members of the upper house.

Judicial interpretations of the Constitution

The decisions of the Supreme Court also have led to important changes in the federal relationship. In the period until the 1930s the Court restricted the powers of the federal government by stressing the provisions in the Tenth Amendment; however, in modern times it has allowed a considerable expansion of national intervention by its emphasis on the broad permissive clauses of the Constitution. The three most relevant sections have been:

(a) the 'necessary and proper' clause;
(b) the Congressional power to 'tax for the common defence and general welfare' of the United States;
(c) the 'inter-state commerce' clause.[6]

From the New Deal to the 1990s the Court did little to protect the states' constitutional position. In the 1941 case of *US* v. *Darby* the Court expressed the view that the Tenth Amendment was 'a mere truism', while in *Garcia* v. *San Antonio Metropolitan Transit Authority* (1985) the majority in a 5–4 ruling decided that Congress could constitutionally tell the states and local governments how much they should pay their own employees. The justices even argued that the states could not expect the courts to protect their powers from encroachment by the federal government through invoking the Tenth Amendment; they should instead lobby Congress to safeguard their interests in the same way as any other pressure group. By its decision in *Garcia* the Court was in effect abdicating its historic role in upholding the constitutional balance of power in the federal system.

The financial relationship

As the Sixteenth Amendment allowed the federal government to raise income taxes there was a considerable improvement in its tax base after 1913 and this led to a great expansion in the size of its budget and the scope of its activities. In 1913 federal government spending had been just over a third of the total outlay of state and local governments. In 1929 public spending in the United States totalled $10.2 billion,[7] of which the federal government spent $2.6 billion and state and local governments $7.6 billion. Fifty years later, in 1979, total public expenditure amounted to $764.5 billion; the federal government spent $507 billion while state and local governments paid out $257.5 billion from their own funds.[8] By that time federal spending made up about two-thirds of all public spending and the American people paid 60 per cent of their total taxes to Washington, 21 per cent to the states and 19 per cent to local governments.

As demands for more health and welfare services, education, police protection and environmental services fell heavily on the states and local authorities, the federal government increased the amounts of financial aid from its treasury to make up the cost of performing these functions. Over the two decades to 1978 federal grants had been increasing rapidly and at a faster rate than the state and local governments' own sources of revenue. In 1964 federal aid comprised 15.4 per cent of state and local governments' outlays; by 1978 this had grown to 26.5 per cent. The last years of the Carter administration saw the beginnings of a reversal of this trend and Ronald Reagan's period in office continued that process. Federal aid as a percentage of total state and local expenditure dropped from 25 per cent in 1981 to approximately 18 per cent in 1990.[9] Under Bush and Clinton there was further growth in such aid so that by the mid-1990s it accounted for approximately 22 per cent. The dependence of the states on federal financial resources to support their services inevitably coloured the relationship.

The main form of federal finance since the Great Depression has been the 'grants-in-aid' system. Although six such programmes were established before 1900, it was after the 1930s that the major development took place. The balance of aid has shifted in more recent times from supporting programmes for places, such as urban renewal or highways, to assistance directly to individuals in the form of programmes such as Medicaid and food stamps. By 1995 almost two-thirds of the $225 billion in federal aid was dedicated to programmes to persons, compared with approximately a third in the 1970s. The system has led to federal government supervision in areas which would otherwise not be within its powers, because these categorical grants, the most common form of aid, have strings attached to them. The states and local governments may only spend the money on the conditions laid down and must make matching funds available themselves in order to receive the federal finances. The actual proportion or percentage which Washington pays will depend upon the programme, but the system is designed so that state and local governments have to commit their own money to the schemes. The federal government also has the right to approve the plans, lay down minimum standards and inspect the results of any programme to which it has contributed. The grants-in-aid system has led to more government activity at all levels because, although they are not compelled to take part, a refusal by the states to do so would mean that they were, in effect, cutting themselves off from the tax money raised from their own citizens. As John Lees wrote:

> The key to the acquisition of funds is . . . intensive state activity. The more a state is prepared to develop programmes, the more it is likely to receive national funds or contracts.[10]

Despite its longevity and established status as part of the modern federal relationship, cogent political criticisms are made of the grants-in-aid system. Conservatives have not liked these programmes for a number of reasons. It is argued that they stimulate a considerable amount of unnecessary government regulatory activity and encourage the states to initiate schemes that they do not really need simply to obtain federal funds that are on offer. What is more, conservatives feel that the system has led to widespread federal government intervention in the affairs of state and local authorities and has resulted in the decline of the states as coordinate and independent units of government. Grants-in-aid therefore encourage centralisation and the abridgement of states' rights under the Tenth Amendment. Critics also point to the high costs of administering the system and argue that grants-in-aid have led to wasteful and inefficient bureaucratisation. They feel that revenues could be better raised and spent at the state and local level rather than have the federal government collecting and redistributing the funds, with the attendant problems and delays. Finally, it is argued that the system developed as a response to the crisis of the Depression and that there is no real justification for Washington's retaining and expanding these powers in the more prosperous times since the Second World War.

However, supporters of the grants-in-aid system have been convinced that, far from destroying the federal relationship and eroding the responsibilities of the states, it rescued federalism from the verge of collapse and placed it on a sounder basis. They feel that the alternative would have been the direct control by the federal government of services and functions, whereas under the grants-in-aid system the states are heavily involved in planning and administering the programmes and a great deal is left to local initiative. Liberals who have promoted the grants-in-aid system also argue that it encouraged the reactionary or backward states to meet their responsibilities in providing services for all their people as well as ensuring basic minimum standards throughout the country. They believe that without some safeguards the resulting inequalities would have threatened the stability and unity of the American nation. The system, therefore, has particularly helped the poorer areas of the country whose state governments would otherwise have been unable to pay for satisfactory public services. It has also allowed the federal government to promote social objectives such as the elimination of discrimination in public services and to meet problems without apparently increasing the size of the federal bureaucracy.

Dual federalism and cooperative federalism

The arguments between conservatives and liberals about the value of grants-in-aid can be broadened to demonstrate two different approaches to the workings of modern federalism. The popular view of the federal system before the New Deal, and still supported by many conservative Americans, is that of 'dual federalism'; this is a belief that the Constitution created two separate tiers of government which should be independent, with their own clearly defined areas of responsibility. In such a system there would inevitably be a certain amount of tension and competition, and the Supreme Court would have the role of arbiter in cases of conflict and would protect the constitutional division of powers. It is argued that the Supreme Court abandoned this responsibility and has since allowed considerable encroachment by the federal government into the areas reserved for the states. Grants-in-aid have been mechanisms for extending this intervention, a process which conservatives would like to see reversed. They feel that, for the constitutional division of powers to become a reality once again, the federal government must give up many of its present responsibilities and return the powers of effective decision-making and revenue-raising to the states.

Since the New Deal an alternative approach has been articulated by supporters of the expanded federal government role. 'Cooperative federalism' emphasises the partnership between the different levels of government providing effective public services for the nation.

> The various levels of government are seen as related parts of a single government system, characterized more by co-operation and shared functions than by conflict and competition.[11]

Some writers have argued that dual federalism not only does not exist today, but in fact never did exist in a pure form, because even in the early nineteenth century the federal government provided some grants to the states for internal improvements such as new roads. Morton Grodzins said that the national, state and local governments have always shared activities, powers and responsibilities. He did not see American government as symbolised by a neat 'layer cake' of three distinct and separate planes but rather as a 'marble cake', an inseparable mixture of differently coloured ingredients.[12] Daniel Elazar, Grodzins' associate, argued that, given the existence of a national economy in which people and goods flow freely across boundaries, state governments are simply unable to cope with certain problems without federal assistance. Major highways construction, water pollution control and unemployment insurance, for example, could not be undertaken alone, even by those states that can afford to support them. He summed up this theory by saying:

> In the years since the establishment of the Republic, inter-governmental co-operation has been progressively expanded to include virtually every function. From public welfare to public recreation, from national defense to local police protection, the system of sharing has become so pervasive that it is often difficult for the uninitiated by-stander to tell just who is doing what under which hat. The highly institutionalized system of federal-state co-operation that has developed has become part of the nation's constitutional tradition. Under this co-operative system, the federal government, the states and the localities share the burden for the great domestic programs by making the larger governments primarily responsible for raising revenues and setting standards and the smaller ones primarily responsible for administering the programs.[13]

The proponents of cooperative federalism argued that in the nature of the relationship the role of the federal government is to supplement, stimulate and assist the states, not to pre-empt their functions and act as a superior partner. Therefore the states have had considerable discretion as to how they administer programmes such as welfare schemes that have been financed by both federal and state authorities. Apart from federal-state cooperation, grants-in-aid programmes which involve Washington directly with the local governments also developed, as well as those which are jointly administered by federal, state and local agencies. The officials of all three tiers of government had frequent communications with one another, and it is worth remembering that almost 90 per cent of federal civil servants work outside the capital and administer policy in regional offices. There is also a great deal of informal cooperation between different governments, and formal contracts also exist for cooperative action by different governments.

During the 1960s, particularly as a result of President Johnson's 'Great Society' legislation, there was an official recognition of the existence of cooperative federalism and a marked expansion of the role of the federal government in not only initiating programmes but also using various forms of pressure to ensure state and local government compliance with its wishes. Johnson described this relationship as 'creative federalism', but in fact the vast proliferation of various forms of grant programmes resulted in large-scale confusion and over-bureaucratisation. States and local governments found it difficult to decide which programmes would be valuable to them and many opened offices in Washington to represent their interests before federal government departments. This presence was particularly valuable in securing project grants, a special form of categorical grant, designed to handle specific problems and made selectively to those states and cities which submitted proposals for developments within federal guidelines and then successfully lobbied for their approval by the department concerned. There were also complaints that some federal agencies tried to reduce the areas of state discretion and increase the degree of national uniformity in administering policies. There were long and frustrating delays before states obtained decisions from federal offices, and also direct contacts between Washington and local governments which bypassed the states tended to create tension and worsen relations between the states and the cities. Therefore those who saw co-operation and partnership as being the key to the federal relationship recognised that all was not harmony and that 'squeak-points', as Grodzins called them, existed. One student of the federal system, Michael D. Reagan, went further than the proponents of 'cooperative federalism' by saying that the growth of federal aid to the states had created a 'nationally dominated system of shared power and shared functions'.[14] With his colleague, John G. Sanzone, he argued that a new label should be given to the system as it operated in the 1980s – 'permissive federalism'.

> That phrase conveys the notion that there is a sharing of power and authority between the national and state governments, but that the states' share rests upon the permission and permissiveness of the national government . . . The national government unquestionably possesses the legal authority to impose whatever degree of restrictiveness it wishes. It should be clear at once that this is not federalism at all in its classic conception. Federalism in that sense is dead.[15]

New federalism, revenue-sharing and block grants

In the late 1960s there was a reaction against the continuing expansion of the federal government's activity and expenditure. Despite the vast amounts of money spent by Washington it appeared that the problems of the cities in particular were actually getting worse. President Nixon, in his first year of office, declared that there was a need for a 'new federalism' so that the proper balance of power between the state capitals and Washington could be restored. He looked forward to a decade of decentralisation when power would be shifted away from the centre and handed back to the state and local governments. He argued on nationwide television:

> For a third of a century, power and responsibility have flowed towards Washington, and Washington has taken for its own the best sources of revenue.
>
> We intend to reverse this tide and to turn back to the states a greater measure of responsibility – not as a way of avoiding problems but as a better way of solving problems.[16]

Nixon was a managerial conservative who was not against increasing federal government authority in principle but believed that improving the efficient implementation of programmes was the most important priority. Nixon's principal legacy in the development of federalism was the introduction of revenue-sharing as a way of distributing aid to other levels of government and which was a major initiative designed to begin the process of decentralisation. The plan was that Congress should assign a set proportion of revenues from its taxes to be passed back to the states with scarcely any restrictions on how the money should be used, and a certain percentage of these funds should be channelled directly to the local governments. The philosophy of this approach was that state and local authorities knew how to deal with their own problems better than the more remote federal bureaucracy, and that these funds should not have the strings attached to them that traditionally accompanied grants-in-aid. Nixon found that his original proposals ran into opposition in Congress. Liberals were opposed to giving unconditional grants to the traditionally conservative state legislatures, while committee chairmen, such as Wilbur Mills (Ways and Means), were reluctant to give up their own discretionary powers on how federal taxes should be spent.

However, in 1972 Congress did eventually pass a Revenue Sharing Act which provided for $6 billion a year of federal revenues to be distributed to state and local governments. By 1975 revenue-sharing accounted for 14.3% of total federal aid and a number of extensions of the legislation were passed until the late 1980s when the Reagan administration, having reduced the funds over the years, cut out the programmes as part of its reductions in federal government expenditure. Treasury Secretary James Baker, referring to the federal deficit, said that there was 'no revenue to share'. The programme, which was never very popular on Capitol Hill, was easy prey when the search for spending cuts became an urgent priority.

Another development in the financing of the federal relationship which allows the states more discretion was the introduction of block grants as a form of grant-in-aid programme. In 1966, categorical grants with their many conditions made up 98 per cent of all federal aid, but by 1975 this had declined to just under three-quarters of the total amount. There were about 600 categorical grant programmes in operation that year costing approximately $40 billion. Block grants, on the other hand, are sums of money with few strings attached but which must be spent by the states in one of five broad subject areas (community development, manpower services, law enforcement, social services or health). The block grant system was first tried in 1966 but was expanded greatly in the period 1972–75, so that by 1975 over $5 billion (approximately 10 per cent of total federal assistance to state and local governments) was transferred in this form. Block grants have developed either as new programmes with broad functional aims or through the merging of separate categorical grants. By 1985 'flexible funding' through revenue-sharing and block grants accounted for about one-fifth of total federal aid. The continuing preference of Congress for categorical grants over which it exerts more control is demonstrated by the fact that, a decade later, in 1995 they numbered 618 and accounted for 85 per cent of federal aid, while only 15 block grants existed at that time.

Box 8.1 Associations representing state and local government

States and local governments have found it necessary to lobby like pressure groups to ensure their collective views and interests are heard in Washington, DC when national government policies are being formulated which affect them. The most influential organisation in recent times has been the National Governors' Association which has had a Republican majority among its members since the party gained control of most of the state houses in the mid-1990s. It has been consulted by Republican legislators in Congress, and George W. Bush, as the Governor of Texas, was a leading member before he entered the White House.

The main associations are:

Council of State Governments. The Council was established in 1933 to provide a forum by which states share resources and ideas. State leaders of both legislative and executive branches cooperate through this body.

National Association of Counties. Founded in 1935 it speaks on behalf of the county level of local government with a membership of almost 2000 authorities representing three-quarters of the nation's population. Its headquarters are in Washington and it provides legislative, research and technical advice to its members.

National Conference of State Legislatures. The Conference was established in 1975 as a bipartisan organisation committed to helping state legislators and the staffs of the fifty state legislatures. It carries out research, publishes papers and conducts seminars and conferences.

National Governors' Association. The NGA is a bipartisan national organisation set up in 1908 to represent the views of the state governors. Since 1967 it has had an Office of State-Federal Relations in Washington.

National League of Cities. The NCL was created in 1924 and represents more than 18,000 municipal governments, including large and small cities, towns and villages. It encourages membership and participation from councillors as well as mayors.

United States Conference of Mayors. This body is a non-partisan association of cities with populations of over 30,000 of which there are approximately 1,100 today in the US. It was founded in 1933. Each city is represented in the conference by its mayor.

All of these organisations have their own websites which provide information about their activities. See website references at the end of the chapter.

President Reagan and new federalism

Ronald Reagan, unlike Nixon, was an ideological conservative, and opposition to government intervention at all levels, but particularly by the federal government, was the cornerstone of his political philosophy. His eight years of experience as the Governor of California had reinforced his belief that Washington's interference in state and local affairs was not only undesirable and led to inefficiency but was also in many cases unconstitutional. For him, government was more often the cause of a problem rather than its solution. Taking up the theme of the need to re-establish a form of dual federalism, President Reagan vowed in his inaugural address to 'demand recognition of the distinction between the powers granted to the federal government and those reserved for the states or to the people'. In April 1981 he established an advisory committee chaired by Senator Paul Laxalt of Nevada to draft legislation to 'restore a proper constitutional relationship' between the three levels of federal, state and local government. Demands for a realignment of powers had been developing for several years; the Advisory Commission on Intergovernmental Relations and the National Governors' Association were among the bodies urging a review of the federal system which most agreed had shifted too much power and decision-making to Washington. They argued that state and local governments could manage programmes more effectively and efficiently than the federal administration. In his first year in office Reagan announced that the federal departments of Energy and Education would be dismantled (although this did not happen in practice because of opposition within Congress) and that there would be major reductions in the number of federal regulations. He established the Office of Information and Regulatory Affairs within the Office of Management and Budget (OMB) to evaluate proposed federal regulations, and departments and agencies were required to justify any new orders as well as an assessment of costs of implementation. The administration also restricted the power of federal civil servants in reviewing the activities of state and local governments, insisting that they defer to states' own policies on standards wherever possible, rather than imposing uniform national standards of provision.

The President's budget cuts led to a decline in federal aid to state and local governments from $95.9 billion in 1981 to $86.8 billion in 1982, the first reduction in federal grants since 1946. In the decade up to 1988 the money transferred in grants-in-aid fell by a quarter and, as a proportion of state and local revenues, by more than a fifth. The number of government employees at federal, state and local level also fell in 1981 for the first time since the First World War. Congress voted to establish nine block grants to replace 57 individual grants-in-aid in the areas of education, social services and health care, thus devolving more discretionary powers to the states.

In his state-of-the-union address in January 1982, President Reagan called for the creation of a 'New Federalism' which would lead to a major upheaval in the administration of many government programmes. The major proposals were:

(a) From October 1983 the federal government would take over completely Medicaid, the health cost programme for the poor, currently shared with the states. At the same time the states would assume full responsibility for the costs of the major welfare programmes, Aid to Families with Dependent Children and food stamps.

(b) Federal excise taxes and part of the tax on oil profits would be put into a trust fund. Approximately $28 billion a year from the fund would go to state and local governments to finance 43 additional programmes currently funded by the federal government. These programmes included vocational education, local transport and water and sewage services.

(c) The trust would be phased out by 1991 and states and localities would have to increase their own taxes or discontinue the services.

It was immediately evident that the President would encounter many obstacles in obtaining the coalition of support necessary to ensure passage of these radical proposals in their original form. Many politicians at all levels sympathised with the general philosophy of shifting power and responsibility to the states and localities but there was concern about the detailed implementation of the policy.

The National Governors' Association was particularly opposed to taking over the very costly welfare programmes and was also worried about having the responsibility for other social services without sufficient revenue to pay for them. Many Democrats argued that the New Federalism proposal was bound to be given a cautious reception as it was part of the Reagan administration's overall retrenchment in social policy. There was also the familiar concern among liberal politicians that many state legislatures would be insensitive to the needs of the urban areas, ethnic minorities and the poor, and would not support the continuation of services currently financed by the federal government. Some Republicans were worried about the complexity of services such as the food stamp programme being administered by 50 separate authorities and also that large variations in state welfare benefits might prompt mass migration of recipients seeking more generous provision. Many observers also questioned whether Congress would be prepared to give up the power implicit in the Reagan plan, particularly as it would reduce the scope for legislators to claim that they had brought federal funds and favours to their constituencies.

The administration's $21 billion legislative package consolidating 34 programmes into four 'mega-blocks' was never reported out of committee on Capitol Hill and a consensus on the major swap of health care and welfare responsibilities did not materialise. In practice the problem of the federal budget deficit in the 1980s meant not only a reduction in federal aid to state and local governments but a reluctance at the national level to initiate programmes that would lead to greater federal expenditure on activities that could be considered to be basically state or local matters. In this respect there was a movement towards a *de facto* sorting out of responsibilities. As John Shannon, the former executive director of the US Advisory Commission on Inter-governmental Relations, has said:

> The creation of a fiscal environment that forces state and local officials to become more self reliant stands out as the primary impact the Reagan administration has had on our federal system . . . Federal policymakers are being forced by fiscal and political realities to allocate an increasing share of their resources for strictly national government programs: defense, social security, medicare and interest on the $2.4 trillion debt . . .[17]

Shannon describes this as a return to the competitive 'fend-for-yourself' federalism of the pre-'Great Society' kind.

The 1980s were therefore a decade during which there was considerable discussion about the future of American federalism. The Reagan administration frequently stated that it wished to recast the roles and responsibilities of the federal government and, in May 1986, the President signed a statement of federalism principles developed by his Domestic Policy Council. However, because this policy occasionally came into conflict with Reagan's overall commitment to the deregulation of business, pressure groups representing business interests managed to persuade the administration that it would be preferable to have one national regulatory standard with which they had to comply rather than a patchwork quilt of 50 different sets of rules. Timothy Conlan has pointed out that when the goal of rebalancing federalism came into conflict with other competing priorities, such as reducing the federal deficit, deregulating the private sector or advancing the conservatives' social agenda, policies supportive of devolving power to the states invariably lost out.[18]

The Reagan administration used the pre-emption powers given to the federal government under the supremacy clause of the Constitution (Article VI) to set national policies in such areas and to short-circuit more demanding state laws passed by liberal Democrats. The regulation of truck weights and sizes, the enforcement of the national 55 mph speed limit and the withdrawal of highway funds from those states failing to adopt a minimum drinking age of 21 years were all examples of the Reagan administration ignoring its own federalist objections to regulation by Washington.

Reagan left his mark on American federalism but did not succeed in securing the fundamental shift he was seeking, principally because of political opposition in Congress, among state officials nervous of the consequences and because public opinion was not yet prepared for such radical reformation of the post-New Deal governmental system.

Reagan's New Federalism did have the overall effect of reversing the trend towards the nationalisation of the federal system by restraining, to some extent, the intervention of government in Washington and stimulating the revitalisation of the states. State governments, which had reformed and professionalised their activities in recent decades, were usually willing and able to play a more activist role. Conservatives, who wished to see less government at all levels, were often disappointed with the effects of their federal budgets cuts as the results were invariably more state spending and tax increases to replace much of the federal funding and many of the programmes. Richard Nathan has argued that the period of conservative retrenchment in Washington led to a 'ratcheting up' effect with more liberal activist government promoted by Democratic administrations at state level.[19] By 1990 the states and local governments were raising $1 trillion in taxes, on a par with the federal government, according to Census Bureau figures.[20]

While this increase in state activity was possible during the growth years of the 1980s, the effects of recession, the rising costs of programmes and voter resistance to further tax increases forced many states to make spending cuts of their own in the early 1990s in order to balance their budgets, as required in state constitutions.[21] The phasing out of direct federal aid to local governments during the Reagan years made the local authorities more dependent on support from the states which were responsible for the distribution of federal block grants.

Federalism in the 1990s

In the continuing debate about the nature of federalism, John Kincaid, the Executive Director of the US Advisory Commission on Intergovernmental Relations at the time, wrote in 1994 that it was marked by a seeming paradox: federal dominance coexisted with the resurgence of the states.[22] He argues that, in the early 1990s, the federal government was exercising more power over more aspects of domestic policy than ever and, although the states occupied the leading position in fiscal and administrative areas, they did so within a significant regulatory framework established at national level. Increased federal intervention had been accompanied by increased activity at state and local levels as all governments have broadened their involvement with society and, as we have seen, many federal programmes have been in practice implemented by other tiers of administration in a complex system of intergovernmentalism.

Kincaid states that the system has become less cooperative and more coercive since the 1960s because Washington has sought to harness state and local capacities to its own policy ends. He argues that 'coercive federalism' has a number of key characteristics. Among these are the reduction in total federal aid and the change in the balance of aid from programmes based on location to those supporting persons, to which reference was made earlier in this chapter. He points out that, despite the encouragement of block grants with more discretion for the states during the Reagan years, Congress still prefers to attach conditions to federal money. The federal government has also imposed numerous mandates so that state and local officials must perform functions laid down in statutes or face criminal or civil actions. However, in an era of federal budget deficits these regulations were usually unfunded, and no federal money is provided to enforce compliance with the mandates. The growth of 'unfunded mandates' became a source of considerable tension between the federal and sub-national governments. State and local authorities had to levy taxes to pay for policies over which they had no control. What is more, many of these new obligations, in areas such as environmental protection and the provision of facilities for disabled people, were extremely expensive to implement.

Furthermore, Congress has passed many laws which pre-empt state authority; over half of all the explicit pre-emption laws enacted by Congress from 1789 to 1991 were passed after 1969. Federal laws overrode state legislation in areas such as commerce, health and safety, banking and finance, civil rights, natural resources and taxation. Statutes may direct the states to initiate specific actions, pass laws or meet minimum standards in a particular area of regulatory policy. Joseph Zimmerman has argued that congressional pre-emption has become the principal method by which power has become more centralised in Washington, although the revolution in intergovernmental relations it has produced has not been as widely recognised as the impact of financial measures.[23]

Other features of coercive federalism have included the intrusion of the federal government in the traditional tax bases of state and local governments, the decline of genuinely cooperative programmes, the role of the federal courts in requiring state or local action or institutional changes and the federalisation of criminal law – traditionally a state preserve – with over 3,000 federal crimes being established. 'Cross-over sanctions' have also been used to persuade states to adopt uniform laws by threatening them with loss of a grant-in-aid authorised by an earlier law if they fail to comply. For example, the Reagan administration eventually gave in to public and congressional pressure and supported the loss of highways grants to states that failed to enforce a common standard age of 21 for the purchase of alcohol as a way of countering the dangers of drunk driving among young people. The Supreme Court backed the use of such sanctions in *South Dakota* v. *Dole* (1987), arguing that participation in grants-in-aid programmes was voluntary and if states did not like the conditions they could choose not to take part.

It was against this background that the Republicans won control of both houses of Congress in the 1994 midterm elections with the commitment to reshape the federal relationship and devolve power back to the states.[24] The elections were widely interpreted as a rejection by the public of 'big government'; public opinion had swung in recent years against federal institutions, and confidence in the federal government had declined. President Clinton's ambitious health care initiative in 1994 failed to progress largely because of fears that Washington would not be able to run an efficient health care system. Clinton himself had recognised the need to streamline federal bureaucracy and create a more responsive and efficient national government and had placed Vice-President Gore in charge of the 'Reinventing Government' initiative (see Chapter 3). In 1996 the President declared in his State of the Union address that 'the era of big government is over', even though the message was unwelcome to the more liberal members of his own party. In practice the Clinton administration's approach to federalism issues was to give sub-national governments more flexibility in the running of federal programmes rather than a genuine devolution of power to the states.

The Republican-controlled 104th Congress developed proposals for a radical re-structuring of federalism, balancing the federal budget over a seven-year period with huge cuts in expenditure at the national level in many areas and the scrapping or reduction of many programmes and agencies. The plans had to be scaled back because of the threat of Clinton's veto. Although the conservatives within the party did not achieve all they wanted, particularly in terms of the dismantling of government departments, they were able to go a great deal further than Reagan had managed. This was a result not only of the Republicans' legislative majority, the determined leadership of Speaker Newt Gingrich and the transformation of public opinion in the intervening period but also because Republican Governors now controlled the majority of the state houses around the country, including the largest states. Republican politicians at state level were enthusiastic in their support for devolution, were regularly consulted by congressional leaders and involved in developing legislative proposals.

One of the first acts of the new Congress was to pass legislation restricting the federal government from imposing new 'unfunded mandates'. A consensus had developed during the previous session that this practice had to be checked and President Clinton, a former Governor himself and aware of the resentment they caused at state and local levels, signed the bill into law in March 1995. The statute requires the Congressional Budget Office to signal when any bill creates mandates involving more than minimal expenditure by states, localities or the private sector and forces Congress to debate the merits of such requirements. While providing exemptions in the areas of conduct relating to civil rights, disability and discrimination and not banning unfunded mandates altogether, the new law was intended to curb the tendency of Congress to impose expensive new regulations and pass the costs on to others. One early study showed that the primary impact of the legislation was not the blocking of new laws but rather its effect as a deterrent to expensive mandates being introduced during the drafting of bills. Taking account of the CBO estimates, sponsors were likely to make significant amendments to bring the costs below the $50 million threshold.[25]

Congress also repealed all national speed limits, leaving it to the states to decide the most appropriate rules for their own areas and, in overhauling the Safe Drinking Water Act, it gave states and local governments more flexibility in implementing the policy and ended the requirement that the federal government create new regulations every three years.

The most important legislation devolving power was the welfare reform bill, reluctantly signed by President Clinton in August 1996, which ended the federal government's 61 year-old guarantee to provide welfare cheques to all low income mothers and children and instead gave the states considerable discretion over eligibility and benefits. It was the first time that a major individual entitlement programme had been transformed into a block grant to the states although Congress retained the right to regulate state plans and laid down limits on the time people could receive welfare payments. It also required states to make progress in moving welfare recipients into jobs. The Republicans argued that capping the federal government's commitment on welfare expenditure was essential if their objective of a balanced budget was to be achieved; the new law was expected to save $54.1 billion in the period up to the year 2002, mostly by cutting the food stamps programme and denying a variety of benefits to legal immigrants. However, the Republican proposal to turn Medicaid, the federal-state health insurance system for the poor, into a similar block grant programme and to end the guarantee of coverage for all those who qualify, failed to pass into law, despite the eagerness of Republican Governors to exercise more control of the policy which is more costly to the states than welfare. Clinton and the Democrats were more resistant to ending individual entitlement to Medicaid coverage, which enjoyed wider public support, than in ending entitlement to welfare payments.

However, in other areas the Republican majority, as in the Reagan era, confounded expectations and consolidated authority in Washington when it appeared to be the best way to implement their political agenda. Legislation passed in the 104th Congress established national criteria for state-issued drivers' licences, ended state registration of mutual funds, created national food safety standards, nullified state laws that had restricted telecommunications competition and extended federal criminal penalties to cover certain violent crimes.[26]

Political pressure from voters encouraged conservative legislators to take at least symbolic action in areas such as crime and education, even though they generally argue that these are issues which rightly come under state and local jurisdiction. At the same time as they were giving states more authority in social and environmental policy, Republicans also found that their efforts to reduce government interference in the marketplace and protect business from a variety of state regulations more stringent than the federal one resulted in them designating the federal government as the sole regulator in a number of areas.

President George W. Bush and federalism

As the Governor of Texas, George W. Bush had been encouraged to run for the presidency in 2000 by Republican colleagues in the National Governors' Association who were confident that he shared their convictions and would support pro-devolution policies if he were to enter the White House. Following his election Bush appointed a number of Governors, Mayors and those with experience at local government level to his Cabinet (see Chapter 3). After the 11 September attacks he chose former Governor of Pennsylvania, Tom Ridge, to become the new Director for Homeland Security. He also created an inter-agency working group to find ways of promoting federalism and to draft a new executive order on relations between the federal and state governments.

Although it would be difficult to question Bush's credentials in terms of his general support for a continuation of the rebalancing of the federal relationship begun in the 1980s and 1990s, it is also true that the new President faces similar conflicting priorities to Ronald Reagan and Republican congressional leaders. Business groups continue to press for federal pre-emption of state laws when it suits their interests to comply with one set of regulations rather than 50 separate ones. Social conservatives continue to argue that the federal government should intervene to block what they see as undesirable and ultra-liberal state laws such as the one in Oregon which permits physician-assisted suicides. Bush himself has placed improving school standards at the top of his political agenda. Unlike Reagan who tried unsuccessfully to abolish the national Education Department, Bush wants to use the power and influence of the federal government to increase accountability and raise levels of attainment among pupils. In doing so the potential inevitably exists for increasing tensions between Washington and the traditional providers of education services at state and local levels.

The economic slowdown in the period since 2000 also led to many states experiencing a serious decline in their tax revenues, limiting their scope for new initiatives and making it difficult to meet the costs of existing commitments. The *Fiscal Survey of the States* published by the National Governors' Association in 2002 showed that states' financial reserves had fallen from $48.8 billion in 2000 to a projected $14.5 billion in 2003. All but a handful of states were reported to be in financial difficulties or even crisis. California, for example, was facing a $21 billion budget shortfall in 2003 and the prospect of major cuts in services, following the stock market slump and a recession in the computer industry.

Finally, the War against Terrorism that Bush declared following 11 September has strengthened the hand of the federal government and led to demands for greater national coordination of security policies (see Box 3.3).

Despite these counter-pressures President Bush's chances of making his own personal mark on American federalism and advancing the pro-devolution agenda were substantially improved by the successes of his Republican Party in the 2002 midterm congressional elections. Control by conservatives of both houses of Congress as well as the White House provide opportunities not seen since the New Deal era, despite the loss of some gubernatorial elections to the Democrats with the resulting weakening of Republican control at state level. What is more, conservative dominance of the elected branches of the federal government is matched by a sympathetic majority of justices on the Supreme Court, to which we now turn.

The Rehnquist Supreme Court and contemporary federalism

Writing in 1990, Richard Nathan described the Supreme Court under Chief Justices Warren and Burger as 'an aggressive nationalizing force' in the federal relationship.[27] As we saw in Chapter 4, the conservative majority on the Rehnquist Court began to take a different approach and since 1991 has provided increased judicial protection for the states. It has also questioned the constitutional basis for congressional legislation; for example, between 1995 and 2000 provisions in 24 separate federal laws were struck down by the Court.

In 1992 in *New York* v. *United States* the Supreme Court declared unconstitutional part of a law which compelled states to enact legislation providing for the disposal of radioactive wastes or assume liability for the damages generated. Justice O'Connor, for the majority, argued that the broad authority which Congress possessed under its commerce and spending powers did not extend to 'commandeering' the states' legislative processes.

In 1995 the Court decided that a federal law violated the commerce clause for the first time since the New Deal era. The justices had previously allowed federal regulation of any internal state economic activity that might have a substantial impact on inter-state commerce. In *United States* v. *Lopez* the Court declared that the 1990 Gun Free School Zones Act, which regulated the possession of guns near a school, represented an unacceptable extension of federal authority into the area of law and order which was traditionally a state and local preserve. It rejected claims that possession of guns in or near schools had an impact on inter-state commerce, stating that the law had nothing to do with economic activity but was clearly designed to fight crime. In 1997 the Court declared unconstitutional a provision in another high-profile law and order statute, the Brady Handgun Violence Prevention Act, which directed state and local law enforcement officers to conduct background checks on those seeking to buy handguns. In *Printz* v. *United States* the justices ruled that the federal government could not mandate state and local government officials to implement its administrative orders. In the case of *United States* v. *Morrison* (2000), the Supreme Court found that Congress had exceeded its authority when it passed the 1994 Violence Against Women Act by allowing women who were victims of violence to sue their attackers in the federal courts.

The Rehnquist Court has not only invoked the Tenth Amendment and reinterpreted the commerce clause but has also used the Eleventh Amendment, which provides states with immunity from suits by individuals in federal courts, in a number of cases in recent years. In 1996, for example, in *Seminole Tribe* v. *Florida* it ruled that a federal law that allowed Indian tribes to sue states in the federal courts in order to force negotiations over gambling on Indian reservations was unconstitutional, while in *Alden* v. *Maine* (1999) the Court found that a federal law could not be used by a private citizen to sue a state in a state court. In *University of Alabama Board of Trustees* v. *Garrett* (2001), the majority held that Congress had exceeded its authority when it included in the American With Disabilities Act a provision allowing state employees to sue in the federal courts; the justices held that state employees could only sue in the state courts.

The majority's construction of a doctrine of states' 'sovereign immunity' from lawsuits was heavily criticised by the minority and many commentators. The effect of these rulings is to severely restrict citizens who wish to use a federal law to seek damages against a state in any court, state or federal. They limit the ability of citizens to seek redress for the failure of a state to enforce federal legislation across a number of areas such as age discrimination and labour and disability rights.

The Supreme Court has also made it clear that it will not allow states to encroach on the powers of the federal government. In *US Term Limits* v. *Thornton* (1995), a 5–4 majority decided that states' attempts to limit the number of terms their congressional representatives could serve was unconstitutional because they were seeking to add to the qualifications for federal legislators set out in the Constitution. In *Crosby* v. *National Trade Council* (2000) the justices unanimously agreed that Massachusetts could not pursue its own trade sanctions against the government of Myanmar (formerly Burma)

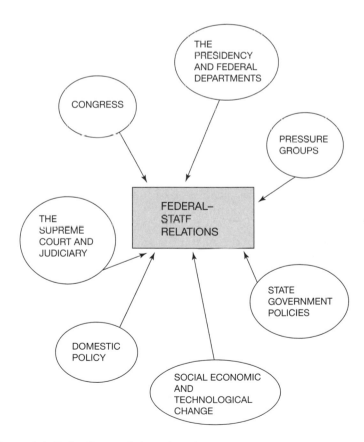

Figure 8.1 Federalism and the political environment

because foreign policy is the exclusive preserve of the federal government. We have seen in Chapter 4 that in *Bush* v. *Gore* (2000) the Court's willingness to intervene to overturn the judgment of the Florida supreme court was contrary to its normal practice of deferring to state decisions on electoral matters.

Overall, however, there is little doubt that the Supreme Court under Rehnquist is determined to show that there are constitutional limits on the powers of the federal government and Congress has been served notice that the majority is prepared to invoke them in a way not seen since the 1930s. In this sense the Court has been willing to resume its role as arbiter of the Constitution on federalism issues from which it appeared to have withdrawn in the *Garcia* case in 1985.

The organisation of state and local governments

The states in the American federal system have therefore been widely perceived as resurgent in the last decade. Far from being the poor relations, with low public visibility and having a reputation for being backward and less concerned for the well-being of the people than either the federal or local governments, as they were in the past, John Kincaid claims that they are now largely seen as 'competent, innovative and fiscally responsible'.[28] The states have acted as laboratories of experimentation, finding new ways of dealing with problems, and the new generation of Governors have earned a reputation as path-finders for the federal government. For example, Tommy Thompson, the Republican Governor of Wisconsin, earned a national reputation as an innovative reformer of the welfare system in his state and in 2001 was rewarded by being appointed as Secretary for Health and Human Services in the federal government by President George W. Bush. It is important to note that in 2000 the federal government employed only 2.8 million civilian workers out of a total of 20.2 million working in the public sector, mostly for state and local governments. This comprises 10.4 per cent of the total public employees, compared with 19 per cent in 1980 and 17 per cent in 1990.[29]

The states

All the states have 'republican' forms of government with the separation of powers principle written into their constitutions. All but Nebraska have bicameral legislatures (usually called the Assembly and the Senate) and all have state Governors in charge of the administration and separate judicial systems. The 50 states have written constitutions which are on average three times the length of the federal Constitution, and many are very detailed and restrictive of government initiative and spending powers. Frequently power is divided not only between the three branches of government but also between numerous agencies and commissions, which exacerbates tendencies to fragmentation of authority.

Despite these similarities of structure, there has been a considerable diversity in the actual workings of state politics. The position and powers of the Governor vary considerably from state to state. 'Weak' Governors typically have had short terms, cannot succeed themselves in office and share executive power with a number of other elected officials such as the Lieutenant-Governor, Treasurer and Attorney-General. They also have had little power in formulating the state budget and very restricted appointment powers. In other states the Governor is in a much better position to influence policy if he has a four-year term, is able to seek unlimited re-election to the office, has strong appointment and budgetary powers and shares executive authority with few other elected officials. The Governor in all states except North Carolina and North Dakota have a veto power over legislation and in 43 states have the right to an 'item veto' over single parts of appropriations bills; in three states the item veto extends to other bills as well. During the twentieth century the trend was for more states to provide four-year terms for their chief executives; today only two states (New Hampshire and Vermont) retain a two-year term. Governors in 39 states have a limitation on the number of terms they can serve, most of them restricted to two four-year periods in office as the President of the United States is.

Since the 1960s there has been a trend for the modernisation of state governments to take place so that they may more adequately deal with the responsibilities they have acquired. Constitutions have been reformed to allow state legislatures to have longer and more frequent sessions to study legislation. The legislatures themselves have streamlined their committee structures, have become more professional, taken on more support staff and have reapportioned their constituency boundaries. The tight control of state legislatures by rural elites has been broken and city dwellers and minorities are better represented. This has led to what David B. Walker calls 'the remarkable and largely unheralded renaissance of the states'.[30] However, there is still great diversity across the country in the way that state legislatures work. At one end of the spectrum stands California with its relatively small number of legislators for its 34 million people (40 in the Senate and 80 in the Assembly), large salaries ($75,000 per annum in 1997) and fully professionalised operation with substantial legislative branch staffing in Sacramento. At the other extreme, New Hampshire has 400 members in its lower house and 24 in its Senate serving a population of only 1.2 million. Its representatives are part-time, are paid only $200 a year and have minimal staff support.[31]

The moves towards the professionalisation of government and the growth of career politicians led to a backlash in the 1990s, with many states adopting term limits for legislators as well as for executive officials where they did not already exist. In contrast to the federal level where the Supreme Court ruled that such restrictions on service were unconstitutional, state constitutions have been amended or interpreted to allow term limits. Supporters hope this will lead to the return of 'citizen legislators' who will serve in public office and then go back to their former careers and become ordinary members of the public again. However, many 'termed out' legislators do remain in politics and seek other elective or appointive offices. The full impact of such developments on the working of state government will only become fully apparent over the next decade.[32]

Local governments

Local governments have those powers which the states delegate to them and they carry the responsibility for much of the day-to-day administration of major services. Although they are elected in their own right, they are subordinate governments and are essentially the administrative agents of the states. Each state is free to organise its local governments as it wishes and there are differing patterns throughout the nation. The main units are:

(a) The municipalities. These include cities, villages, boroughs and some towns. Most cities elect a council which makes policy and a mayor who is responsible for carrying out the administration of the area, or elect a council that employs a professional 'city manager' to run the city.

(b) The counties. Outside the city areas, the county is the basic unit of organisation within the states. The number, size and powers of the counties vary from one state to another, but in the majority of counties there are elected 'Boards of Supervisors' which

make policy, and also elected executive officials such as the Sheriff, Treasurer and Coroner. The council-administrator system, in which an elected commission passes laws and appoints an administrator to carry out policy, is used in some areas and the remaining counties have an elected administrator who acts as chief executive and a council that determines legislative policy.

(c) *Special districts.* These districts have been established to deal with one particular service which, it is argued, may be more efficiently administered through separate functional areas. Therefore elected 'Boards of Trustees' run, for example, special park, harbour, school and college districts. They are the fastest-growing form of local government. Excluding the 13,726 school districts the number of units has risen from 8,299 in 1942 to 34,683 in 1997 (see Figure 8.2), and critics have argued that the fragmentation of local government in this way hinders effective coordination and administration of services.

The roles of state and local governments

In 1998 state and local governments in America spent a total of $1,529 billion in providing public services. Education was by far the most expensive function with $450.3 billion allocated for its administration. The states normally are responsible directly for running the universities and higher education institutions, while local governments administer the schools and other colleges. Public welfare, which includes payments to the elderly, the poor and the handicapped, as well as unemployment insurance and the maintenance of institutions, accounted for $204.6 billion, while highways cost $87.2 billion and hospitals and health $114 billion. The other major areas of state and local government spending are police and fire protection, sewerage, prisons and the administration of justice, parks and recreation, housing and urban renewal.[33]

To finance these services there are a number of different sources of revenue. Federal aid to state and local governments is still a significant factor although in the last two decades it has declined as a proportion of their overall revenues. In 1980 18 per cent of state and local governments' income came from Washington; by 1990 this had been reduced to 13

	Units
Federal	1
States	50
Total local governments	87,453
Counties	3,043
Municipalities	19,372
Townships	16,629
School districts	13,726
Special districts	34,683
Total	87,453

Figure 8.2 Government units in the United States 1997

Source: *Statistical Abstract of the United States* 2001, p. 258.

per cent and in 1998 stood at 14.8 per cent. The most lucrative independent forms of income raised within the states are property taxes and sales taxes. Property taxes are levied normally by local governments to pay for their services but revenues have not always kept pace with inflation and the pressures of increasing demand, while many states have given way to public pressure for property tax relief to home owners. In 1998 state and local governments levied $773.9 billion in taxes of which the states raised $473 billion. Of these state revenues over half came from sales taxes, either in the form of a general levy on all goods and services, sold within the state (68 per cent of the total) or specific taxes on items such as gasoline, alcohol and tobacco. Given their reliance on sales taxes, it is not surprising that the states have been very concerned about the development of e-commerce and the increasing number of purchases of goods and services via the Internet. It has been difficult for state governments to keep track of online sales and obtain taxes payable by customers for purchases from companies with a physical presence, such as an office or factory, in their states. What is more, pro-business groups and many Republican legislators in Congress support proposals for federal laws which would ban taxes on online sales as well as pre-empting state laws on consumer protection. State income taxes accounted for 18.6 per cent of total revenues from their own sources and corporation taxes a further 3.6 per cent, although these are at lower rates than the equivalent federal taxes. Additional income in some states come from running public utilities, lotteries and liquor stores.[34]

The problems of modern federalism

The United States has changed beyond all recognition in the two centuries since the original 13 states formed the federal union in 1787. Many of the developments that have taken place since that time, such as the expansion of the federal government's domestic functions, the increased activity of state and local governments, and the development of grants-in-aid and 'cooperative federalism', have been responses to the industrialisation and urbanisation of the nation. More than three-quarters of the population now live in cities, towns or the suburbs and urbanised living has brought new problems with which governments have to deal.

Today the United States really has too many governments for effective policy-making. In addition to the federal government and the 50 states, there are over 80,000 local government units (see Figure 8.2), each with its own territorial area and jealous of its own jurisdiction. This hotch-potch of cities, townships, counties and special districts with overlapping boundaries and responsibilities complicates considerably the coordination of policies designed to deal with these twenty-first-century problems. The separate jurisdictions of police forces in an area can hinder effective crime fighting, while individual local and even state governments often have inadequate resources or are insufficiently broad in area to deal with the issues of pollution control or transportation policy.

However, even with more active and well-financed state governments, sources of tension between state legislatures and city administrations often still exist, and these can lead not only to difficulties in executing policy efficiently but also to the cities looking to Washington for more sympathy and assistance. Not least of these conflict areas is the question of how the cities should be financed. Many American cities, particularly the larger and older ones in the North-East and Midwest, found themselves in an increasingly precarious financial situation. Their populations steadily became socially unbalanced so that racial ghettos developed. Demands on the city services, particularly welfare provision, housing and police protection, grew dramatically at a time when their tax bases

Table 8.1 State and local government finances 1998

	State	Local
Revenue	1,103,239	909,661
Intergovernmental revenue	240,789	306,270
Total revenue from own sources	862,450	603,391
Total taxes	473,051	300,912
Property taxes	10,659	219,492
Individual income	160,115	15,515
Corporation income	31,089	3,323
Sales and gross receipts	226,643	48,240
General	155,272	33,481
Selective[1]	71,371	14,759
Motor vehicle and operator licences	14,919	1,223
Death and gift	6,939	32
Charges and miscellaneous[2]	149,682	187,068
Interest earnings	32,715	32,702
Utility and liquor store revenue	7,687	73,439
Insurance trust revenue	232,029	41,972
Expenditure		
Direct expenditure	651,098	874,664
Education	118,563	331,802
Elementary and secondary	2,886	315,179
Higher education	96,251	16,623
Public welfare	172,119	32,521
Hospitals	28,486	41,148
Health	23,130	21,261
Highways	51,971	35,243
Police protection	7,165	43,310
Fire protection	0	20,269
Corrections	28,679	13,800
Natural resources	12,883	4,609
Sewerage	1,132	24,515
Solid waste management	1,988	14,130
Housing and community development	2,414	22,284
Governmental administration	29,692	41,035
Parks and recreation	3,893	18,472
Interest on debt	26,776	37,778
Utility	8,365	91,154
Insurance trust expenditure	91,113	17,287
Expenditure by character		
Current expenditure	446,440	682,817
Capital expenditure	64,441	117,430
Salaries and wages	139,970	355,170

Source: Adapted from the *Statistical Abstract of the United States 2001*, p. 268.
Figures are in millions of dollars.

Notes
1 Selective includes motor fuel, alcohol, tobacco and public utility taxes.
2 Charges and miscellaneous includes charges for the whole range of services set out below including school
   lunches, higher education and hospital fees, highway tolls etc.

were declining. Property taxes provided insufficient revenue and, with the middle-class flight to the suburbs, the deterioration of the city centres led to cities having even fewer resources. In some cases the cities have found themselves almost bankrupt although, as in the most famous case of New York City, this may be partially the result of profligate and extravagant spending programmes.

In the mid-1990s the city of Miami in Florida ran into severe financial difficulties, while Washington's long history of mismanagement by city administrations led to a serious crisis affecting basic public services. There were calls for the federal government to take over the running of the police force as crime figures escalated and to provide billions of dollars of additional support for the nation's capital. The cities have traditionally looked to the states to provide more funds, but the legislatures controlled by politicians representing suburban and rural areas have often been reluctant to vote any more aid for the city services. The resistance to providing revenues for the cities occasionally overlooks the fact that many of the suburban voters actually commute to and work in the cities during the day and therefore derive benefit from better facilities in the downtown areas. However, it would be wrong, as Gillian Peele points out, to generalise too much about the plight of the cities. There was much talk of an 'urban renaissance' in the 1990s and cities differ greatly in size and economic position. Many, particularly in the West and South of the country, have grown rapidly and are prosperous centres of the new technology-driven economy.[35]

Another alternative which is often vigorously opposed by county residents is that the city's boundaries be extended to incorporate within its area the surrounding suburbs. In this way the city would have a broader and more lucrative tax base, but suburban residents have generally fought against 'incorporation' on the grounds that it would not only force them to pay higher taxes but would also integrate their school systems with those of the city centres. Many of the white suburbanites feel that the standards of education for their children would be irreparably damaged by such a move. Consolidations between cities and counties are rarely carried out because they usually require the approval of the voters. It is somewhat ironic that, whereas minority ethnic groups have obtained political control of some of the major cities through the demographic changes of the last decade, incorporation of suburban areas into the cities would almost certainly weaken and dilute this influence. Incorporation is in many parts of the United States not merely a question of reforming and making more efficient the organisation of local government, it is also an issue that arouses intense feelings on all sides because it affects political control and the distribution of resources.

Chapter summary

- Federalism was adopted by the Founding Fathers as a compromise between a weak association of states and a centralised unitary system. The federal government was thereafter to have certain 'enumerated' powers, 'inherent' powers and some 'implied' powers. The states have 'reserved' powers under the Tenth Amendment.
- As the United States developed as a nation the federal government strengthened its position in relation to the states. This came about as a result of the passage of constitutional amendments, the interpretation of the Constitution by the Supreme Court and through changes in the financial relationship whereby the states became partially dependent on the federal government for revenues to pay for their services. The Sixteenth Amendment and the subsequent development in federal grants-in-aid, particularly after the Great Depression, were significant here.

- The traditional model of 'dual federalism', whereby there was a clear delineation of the roles of the states and the national government and the two levels were coordinate and independent in their spheres of authority, gave way to a system of 'cooperative federalism', a model that was characterised by shared functions and intergovernmental collaboration.
- Conservative Presidents Nixon and Reagan attempted to reverse this trend of increasing federal intervention in state affairs through the development of new methods of funding which gave the states and localities more discretion over how they spent the money raised by the national exchequer. Reagan also reduced the amount of federal regulation and tried, unsuccessfully, to define more clearly which social programmes were the responsibility of the national and state levels of government.
- 'Coercive federalism' developed from the 1970s onwards. The federal government sought to utilise the state and local governments resources to achieve its own policy goals but there was less involvement by those authorities in the design and implementation of new programmes and little or no funding in the way of grants to pay for them. There was much greater use of the federal pre-emption power to override state laws under the 'supremacy clause' of Article VI of the Constitution. Congress also passed many 'unfunded mandates' which required sub-national governments to act in a specific way but did compensate them financially for the costs incurred in complying with national policy.
- The Republican takeover of Congress in 1995 led to several moves to devolve power back to the states. These included making the passage of new unfunded mandates more difficult and welfare reform legislation which transformed the programme by providing block grants to the states and allowing them more discretion over its administration. However, Republicans were still prepared to pass new laws on education and crime, areas traditionally under state jurisdiction, and to protect business from state regulation of their affairs.
- Since the early 1990s the conservative majority on the Supreme Court has made decisions in a number of cases which show its determination to limit the federal government's powers in relation to the states. In particular they have interpreted the commerce clause more narrowly to restrict federal laws on crime and have frequently cited the Eleventh Amendment.
- The states and local governments are responsible for many important public services and employ the vast majority of those people working in the public sector. In recent times the states have modernised themselves and are widely seen to be playing a more significant role in the federal system.

Think points

- Why is an understanding of state and local government essential for a proper appreciation of the complexities of American politics?
- How far can 'coercive federalism' be seen as being consistent with a 'renaissance of the states'?
- To what extent has the United States experienced a 'devolution revolution' in the last decade or so?

Some further reading

Timothy Conlan, *New Federalism* (Brookings Institution 1988)

Thomas R. Dye, *American Federalism* (Lexington Books 1990)

Daniel J. Elazar, *American Federalism: A View from the States* (Harper and Row 1985)

John A. Ferejohn and Barry Weingast (eds), *The New Federalism: Can the States Be Trusted?* (Hoover Institution 1997)

Alan Grant, 'Devolution and the Reshaping of American Federalism', in *American Politics: 2000 and Beyond*, Alan Grant (ed.) (Ashgate 2000)

Richard P. Nathan, *Reagan and the States* (Princeton University Press 1987)

Lawrence J. O'Toole Jr, *American Intergovernmental Relations* (Congressional Quarterly Press 1993)

Paul E. Petersen, *The Price of Federalism* (Brookings Institution 1995)

Alice Rivlin, *Reviving the American Dream* (Brookings Institution 1992)

Carl E. Van Horn, *The State of the States* (Congressional Quarterly Press 1992)

David Walker, *The Rebirth of Federalism* (Chatham House 2000)

Joseph F. Zimmerman, *Contemporary American Federalism* (Leicester University Press 1992)

Weblinks:

Council of State Governments: www.csg.org

National Association of Counties: www.naco.org

National Conference of State Legislatures: www.ncsl.org

National Governors' Association: www.nga.org

National League of Cities: www.nlc.org

National Conference of Mayors: www.usmayors.org/uscm/

Governing (a periodical concerned with state and local government): www.governing.com and www.governing.com/govlinks.htm

Notes

1 The framework of American politics

1 David Easton, *The Political System. An Enquiry into the State of Political Science* (Knopf 1953).
2 Bronwen Maddox, 'Land of opportunity keeps on beckoning', *The Times*, 6 June 2002.
3 US Census Bureau News Release, 4 June 2002.
4 R.J. Alsop (ed.) *The Wall Street Journal Almanac 1999* (Ballantine Books 1998), pp. 113–15.
5 For a thorough examination of the arguments on the issue see Andrew Wroe, 'Immigration: a Nation State or A State of Nations?', in *Controversies in American Politics and Society*, David McKay, David Houghton and Andrew Wroe (Blackwells 2002).
6 Edward Ashbee, 'America Divided: the Politics of Balkanization', in *American Politics: 2000 and Beyond*, Alan Grant (ed.) (Ashgate 2000).
7 US Census Bureau News Release, 13 August 2001. It should be noted that the 36.4 million black Americans (12.9 per cent of total population) comprises 34.7 million (12.3 per cent) who were reported in the census as being black alone and 1.8 million (0.6 per cent) who described themselves as black with one or more other races.
8 *Statistical Abstract of the United States 1996*, p. 284.
9 Ibid., p. 279.
10 *Congressional Quarterly Weekly*, 29 June 2002, 'Pursuing the Prize of America's Hispanic Vote', p. 1710.
11 *Congressional Quarterly Weekly*, 17 November 2001, 'Immigration Liberalization: Delayed but Not Abandoned', p. 2715.
12 Andrew Wroe, 'Affirmative Action: the Continuing Dilemma', in *Controversies in American Politics and Society*, David McKay, David Houghton and Andrew Wroe (Blackwells 2002).
13 *Statistical Abstract of the United States 1996*, p. 32.
14 'Population Change and Distribution 1990 to 2000', *Census 2000 Brief*, US Census Bureau, April 2001.
15 Ibid.
16 Ibid.
17 Anatole Kaletsky, 'Clinton, Jobs and Keynes', *The Times*, 9 July 1996; Irwin Stelzer, 'Myth of America's Crushed Workers', *Sunday Times*, 12 January 1997.
18 Tim Hames, 'The Budget Process and Deficit Politics', in *Contemporary American Politics*, Alan Grant (ed.) (Dartmouth 1995).
19 For a detailed examination and explanation of the different Articles and Amendments to the US Constitution see Alan Grant and Edward Ashbee, *The 'Politics Today' Companion to American Government* (Manchester University Press 2002), Chapter 2.
20 The District of Columbia, along with Guam, the Virgin Islands and American Samoa, have delegates to Congress; Puerto Rico's Resident Commissioner has similar status. The delegates may vote in committees but not in the full House.
21 *Congressional Quarterly Weekly Report*, 9 May 1992, p. 1230, '1789 Pay Raise Amendment Returns to Haunt Congress' and 16 May 1992, p. 1323, 'James Madison Gets His Way As Congress Ducks Issue'.
22 Alan Grant, 'Legislative Careerism and the Term Limitation Movement', in *Contemporary American Politics*, Alan Grant (ed.) (Dartmouth 1995); Alan Grant, 'The Term Limitation Movement in the United States', *Parliamentary Affairs*, July 1995, pp. 515–29.

23 The use of 'he' and 'his' throughout the book to refer generically to legislators, judges, Presidents, etc. is not intended to imply in any way that a woman may not hold these positions.
24 *New York Times Company v. United States* (1971).
25 'Americans lose faith in federal politics', *The Times*, 30 August 1997.

2 Making the laws: the American Congress

1 Nelson Polsby, 'Legislatures', in *Handbook of Political Science*, Vol. 5, Fred Greenstein and Nelson Polsby (eds) (Addison-Wesley 1975).
2 *Congressional Quarterly Weekly*, 16 February 2002, p. 504, '107th Congress, 1st Session By the Numbers'.
3 Allen Schick, 'Politics Through Law: Congressional Limitations on Executive Discretion', in *Both Ends of the Avenue*, Anthony King (ed.) (American Enterprise Institute 1983), pp. 180–81.
4 Roger Davidson (ed.), *The Postreform Congress* (St Martin's Press 1992), pp. 18–19.
5 Christopher J. Bailey, 'Ethics as politics; Congress in the 1990s', in *Political Issues in America: the 1990s*, Philip John Davies and Fredric A. Waldstein (eds) (Manchester University Press 1991), p. 146.
6 Roger Davidson and Walter Oleszek, *Congress and Its Members* (CQ Press 2000), pp. 407–20.
7 *Congressional Quarterly, Weekly*, 25 January 2003, '108th Congress Becomes First With a Baby Boomer Majority, pp. 190–93.
8 William M. Lunch, *The Nationalization of American Politics* (University of California Press 1987), pp. 14, 102 and 114.
9 *Congressional Quarterly Weekly*, 18 May 2002, 'Safe House: Members Face Worry-Free Election', pp. 1274–86.
10 Ibid.
11 See Chapter 4, p. 146 for discussion on *Baker* v. *Carr*.
12 *Congressional Quarterly Weekly*, 18 May 2002, op. cit.
13 Ross K. Baker, *House and Senate* (Norton 1989).
14 Nelson Polsby, *Congress and the Presidency* (Prentice-Hall 1964), p. 36.
15 Donald R. Matthews, *US Senators and their World* (Vintage 1973).
16 The term 'filibuster' comes from the Spanish *filibustero*, meaning 'pirate'.
17 Three-fifths of the entire Senate (60 if no vacancies) have to vote for a cloture motion for it to be successful. Until 1975 the rule was two-thirds present and voting; from 1917 to 1975 only 24 out of 104 attempts to obtain a cloture were successful.
18 Nicol C. Rae and Colton C. Campbell, 'Party Politics in the Contemporary Senate', in *The Contentious Senate*, Colton C. Campbell and Nicol C. Rae (eds) (Rowman and Littlefield 2001), p. 18.
19 *Congressional Quarterly Weekly Report*, 1 September 1995, p. 913, 'Senate Altering Its Course In Favour of Contract'.
20 Norman Ornstein, 'The Open Congress Meets the President', in A. King (ed.) op. cit., p. 196.
21 William M. Lunch, op. cit., p. 124.
22 Steven C. Smith, 'The Senate in the Post-reform Era', in Roger Davidson (ed.), op. cit., p. 187.
23 Barbara Sinclair, 'House Majority Party Leadership in an Era Of Legislative Constraint', in Roger Davidson (ed.), op. cit., p. 93. See also Daniel J. Palazzolo, 'From Decentralization to Centralization: Members' Changing Expectations for House Leaders', in the same volume, pp. 112–26.
24 However, challenges occasionally happen. In 1970, a move by liberal Democrats to defeat Speaker John McCormack's renomination was defeated, although he subsequently decided to retire. In 1997 there was some internal opposition among Republican members to the renomination of Newt Gingrich because of charges of ethical violations. As we have seen, in the House vote, strong leadership pressure restricted the number of eventual dissidents to four.
25 Barbara Sinclair, 'The Struggle over Representation and Lawmaking in Congress', in *Remaking Congress: Change and Stability in the 1990s*, James Thurber and Roger Davidson (eds), (CQ Press, 1995), pp. 105–7.
26 Barbara Sinclair, 'The Senate Leadership Dilemma: Passing Bills and Pursuing Partisan Advantage in a Nonmajoritarian Chamber', in Colton C. Campbell and Nicol C. Rae (eds) op. cit., p. 72.

27 William Connelly and John Pitney Jr., *Congress' Permanent Minority? Republicans in the US House* (Littlefield Adams 1994).
28 Alan Grant, 'The New Republican Congress', *Talking Politics*, Vol. 7, No. 3, Spring 1995.
29 *Congressional Quarterly Weekly Report*, 4 February 1995, p. 331, 'Speaker Wants His Platform To Rival the Presidency'.
30 *Congressional Quarterly Weekly Report*, 23 November 1996, pp. 3299–302, 'Revolutionary Rhetoric Fades As GOP Softens its Edges'.
31 John E. Owens, 'Congress after the "Revolution": The Continuing Problems of Governance in a Partisan Era', in *American Politics: 2000 and Beyond*, Alan Grant (ed.) (Ashgate 2000).
32 Eric Schickler, 'Congress', in *Developments in American Politics 4*, Gillian Peele *et al.* (eds) (Palgrave 2002); Alan Grant, 'The 1998 US Midterm Elections', *Talking Politics*, Vol. 11, No. 2, Winter 1999.
33 *Congressional Quarterly Weekly*, 30 September 2000, 'Hastert and the Limits Of Persuasion', pp. 2252–54.
34 Eric Schickler, op. cit., p. 102.
35 *Congressional Quarterly Weekly*, 29 June 2002, 'Senate GOP Agrees to "Middle Ground" On Committee Term Limits', p. 1732.
36 Morris Fiorina, *Congress: Keystone of the Washington Establishment* (Yale 1977).
37 Roger Davidson, *The Role of the Congressman* (Pegasus 1969), p. 119.
38 Nelson Polsby, 'Some Landmarks in Modern Presidential-Congressional Relations', in Anthony King (ed.) op. cit., p. 18.
39 Eric L. Davis, 'Congressional Liaison: The People and the Institutions', in Anthony King (ed.), op. cit., pp. 59–95. Also see Joseph D. Hogan, 'Legislative Liaison in the Reagan Administration', in *Reagan's First Four Years*, John Lees and Michael Turner (eds) (University of Manchester 1988), pp. 68–94.
40 Norman Ornstein, Thomas Mann and Michael Malbin, *Vital Statistics on Congress 1999–2000*, (The AEI Press 2000), pp. 129–31.
41 Anthony King, 'A Mile and a Half is a Long Way', in Anthony King (ed.) op. cit., pp. 256–62.
42 *Congressional Quarterly Weekly*, 20 July 2002, 'Daschle's Soft Touch Lost In Tough Senate Arena', pp. 1920–22.
43 Walter J. Oleszek, 'House–Senate Relations: A Perspective on Bicameralism', in Roger Davidson (ed.), op. cit., p. 205.
44 *Congressional Quarterly Weekly*, 20 January 2001, 'Versatility With the Veto', pp. 175–77.
45 Byron York, *National Review*, 17 June 2002, 'The Man Who Won't Veto', pp. 18–19.
46 For a fuller discussion see Tim Hames, 'The Budget Process and Deficit Politics', in *Contemporary American Politics*, Alan Grant (ed.) (Dartmouth 1995).
47 David Mervin, 'George Bush and the 1990 Budget Crisis', *Talking Politics* (Summer 1991), pp. 121–25.
48 James P. Pfiffner, 'The President and the Postreform Congress', in Roger Davidson (ed.), op. cit., pp. 218–21.
49 *Congressional Quarterly Weekly*, 20 May 2000, 'Budget Overhaul's Defeat Leaves Hill Bound by Deficit-Era Rules', pp. 1177–78.

3 Law execution: the President and administration

1 Philip John Davies, 'The Resurgent Presidency', in *Political Issues in America Today* (Manchester University Press 1987), pp. 18–19.
2 David Broder, 'A Tough Act to Swallow', *Washington Post National Weekly Edition* 30 June 1986, quoted in Davies, ibid., p. 18.
3 Austin Ranney, 'The President and His Party' and Anthony King, 'A Mile and a Half is a Long Way', in *Both Ends of the Avenue*, Anthony King (ed.) (American Enterprise Institute 1983).
4 Clinton Rossiter, *The American Presidency* (Harvest 1960), Chapter 1.
5 Clinton Rossiter, op. cit., p. 26.
6 David Mervin, *The President of the United States* (Harvester-Wheatsheaf 1993), p. 130.
7 Aaron Wildavsky, 'The Two Presidencies', in Aaron Wildavsky (ed.) *Perspectives on the Presidency* (Little, Brown 1977).
8 James D. Barber, *The Presidential Character; Predicting Performance in the White House* (Prentice Hall 1985).

9 Colin Campbell, 'Clinton's Encounter with the Separation of Powers: "United" and "Divided" Gridlock', *Government and Opposition*, Vol. 36, No. 2, Spring 2001, p. 164.
10 Richard Nixon, 'The Nature of the Presidency' (radio broadcast, 19 October 1968).
11 Paul Weaver, 'Liberals and the Presidency', *Readings in American Government 1976–77* (Dushkin 1976).
12 James P. Pfiffner, 'The President and the Postreform Congress', in *The Postreform Congress*, Roger Davidson (ed.) (St Martin's Press 1992), p. 231.
13 David Mervin, op. cit., pp. 88–89.
14 'After Two Years – A Conversation with the President' (television and radio interview with John F. Kennedy, 17 December 1962).
15 *Immigration and Naturalization Service* v. *Chadha*.
16 James P. Pfiffner, op. cit., pp. 223–25; *Congressional Quarterly Weekly Report*, 12 January 1991, p. 65, 'Bush Is Given Authorization To Use Force Against Iraq'.
17 *Time*, 5 April 1993, p. 43.
18 *Congressional Quarterly Weekly Report*, 7 January 1989, p. 12, 'Reagan Added Luster but Little Clout to Office'.
19 Michael Foley, 'Congress and Policy-making: Can it Cope with Foreign Affairs?', in *Explaining American Politics*, Robert Williams (ed.) (Routledge 1990), p. 91.
20 John Dumbrell, 'Foreign Policy and Foreign Policy Making' in *American Politics: 2000 and Beyond*, Alan Grant (ed.) (Ashgate 2000), p. 97.
21 For other examples of judicial checks, see Chapter 1, the section on 'Checks and Balances', 'Judicial Checks on the President', on page 22.
22 Carl Bernstein and Robert Woodward, *All the President's Men* (Simon & Schuster 1974).
23 Richard Neustadt,' The Weakening White House', *British Journal of Political Science*, Volume 31, 2001, pp. 1–11; Jonathan Herbert, 'The Presidency', in *Developments in American Politics 4*, Gillian Peele, Christopher Bailey, Bruce Cain and B. Guy Peters (eds) (Palgrave 2002), pp. 75–76.
24 Arthur Schlesinger Jr, *The Imperial Presidency* (Houghton Mifflin 1973).
25 James MacGregor Burns, J.W. Peltason and Thomas E. Cronin, *Government by the People* (Prentice Hall 1987), p. 359.
26 Jonathan Herbert, op. cit., p. 81.
27 David Broder, 'Bush's Desire to Unite Will be Tested', *Washington Post*, 14 December 2000.
28 Charles O. Jones, *The Presidency in a Separated System* (Brookings Institution 1994), pp. 48–51.
29 David Mervin, 'Statecraft in the White House: The Reagan and Bush Presidencies', in *Contemporary American Politics*, Alan Grant (ed.) (Dartmouth 1995), p. 1.
30 Charles O. Jones, op. cit., p. 6.
31 Morris P. Fiorina, 'An Era of Divided Government', in *Developments in American Politics*, Gillian Peele, Christopher Bailey and Bruce Cain (eds) (Macmillan 1992).
32 James L. Sundquist, 'Needed: A Political Theory for the New Era of Coalition Government in the United States', *Political Science Quarterly*, Vol. 103, Winter 1988–89, pp. 613–35.
33 David R. Mayhew, *Divided We Govern* (Yale University Press 1991).
34 Richard Neustadt, *Presidential Power* (Wiley & Sons 1976), p. 102.
35 Ibid., pp. 77–78.
36 Tim Hames, 'Presidential Power and the Clinton Presidency', in *American Politics: 2000 and Beyond*, Alan Grant (ed.), p. 68.
37 Charles O. Jones, op. cit., p. 2.
38 Charles O. Jones, *Separate But Equal Branches: Congress and the Presidency* (Chatham House 1995), p. 101.
39 Jonathan Herbert, op. cit., p. 95.
40 Clinton Rossiter, op. cit., p. 134.
41 James Pfiffner, 'Can the President Manage the Government?', in *Understanding the Presidency*, James Pfiffner and Roger H. Davidson (eds) (Longman 2000), p. 226.
42 James Pfiffner, ibid., p. 232–33.
43 *U.S. News and World Report*, 4 January 1982, p. 26 and 29 March 1982, p. 28.
44 Hugh Heclo, 'One Executive Branch or Many', in Anthony King (ed.) op. cit., p. 26.
45 Quoted in Hugh Heclo, ibid., p. 47.
46 Jonathan Herbert, op. cit., p. 88.
47 Richard Fenno, *The President's Cabinet* (Harvard University Press 1959), p. 248.

48 See Chapter 1, 'Amendments to Alter Government', for full details of the Twenty-Fifth Amendment.

49 B. Guy Peters, 'Public Bureaucracy in the American Political System', in Gillian Peele, Christopher Bailey and Bruce Cain (eds), p. 171.

50 *Congressional Quarterly Weekly*, 8 June 2002, 'Bush's Swift, Sweeping Plan Is Work Order for Congress', pp. 1498–504; 22 June 2002, 'Homeland Security Debate: Balancing Swift and Sure', pp. 1642–47.

51 B. Guy Peters, 'Federal Bureaucracy and Public Management', in Gillian Peele, Christopher Bailey, Bruce Cain and B. Guy Peters (eds), p. 138.

52 Michael Turner, 'The Reagan White House, Cabinet and Bureaucracy', in *Reagan's First Four Years: A New Beginning*, John Lees and Michael Turner (eds) (Manchester University Press 1988), p. 60.

53 Robert Williams, 'Policy, process and power: understanding American bureaucracy', in Robert Williams (ed.), pp. 109–10.

54 David Osborne and Ted Gaebler, *Reinventing Government* (Addison-Wesley Press 1992).

55 B. Guy Peters, 'Federal Bureaucracy and Public Management', op. cit., p. 141.

56 *Washington Post*, 1 June 1993, 'Tracking Staff Trends at the Top'.

57 Michael Turner, op. cit., p. 57.

58 Michael Turner, op. cit., p. 54.

59 *Congressional Quarterly Weekly Report*, 1 May 1993, p. 1059, 'As Administration Fills Its Slots, Congress Plays Waiting Game'.

60 B. Guy Peters, 'Federal Bureaucracy and Public Management' op. cit., p. 144.

61 *Washington Post*, op. cit.

62 Hugh Heclo, *A Government of Strangers: Executive Politics in Washington* (Brookings Institution 1977).

63 William Lunch, *The Nationalization of American Politics* (University of California 1987), p. 184.

4 Law adjudication: the Supreme Court and the judiciary

1 Presidential press statement, 25 July 1974.

2 *United States* v. *Richard M. Nixon* (24 July 1974).

3 There are, in addition, special federal courts for such matters as military cases, taxation, custom and patents.

4 Sheldon Goldman in *Congressional Quarterly Almanac, 2000*, section 15–42.

5 See above, page 130, discussion on *Marbury* v. *Madison*.

6 Robert McKeever, 'In Search of a Role: The Supreme Court in a Post-Civil Rights Era', in *American Politics: 2000 and Beyond*, Alan Grant (ed.) (Ashgate 2000), p. 131.

7 *Congressional Quarterly Weekly Report*, 24 June 1989, p. 1549, 'Flag-Burning, Dial-a-Porn Acts Struck Down by Justices'.

8 Quoted in the *Los Angeles Times*, 23 April 1975, p. 7.

9 *Congressional Quarterly Weekly Report*, 26 November 1988, p. 3392, 'Reagan's Legacy Is Not Only on the Bench'.

10 Ibid., p. 3393.

11 *Congressional Quarterly Weekly*, 28 April 2001, pp. 898–902, 'For Bush's Judicial Nominees, A Tough Tribunal Awaits'.

12 *Congressional Quarterly Weekly*, 9 May 1998, p. 1217 'Agreement on Judgeships No Guarantee Of Quick Confirmations' and 10 April 1999, pp. 845–47, 'Clinton's Deals With GOP on Judgeships Stir Discontent Among Democrats'.

13 *Congressional Quarterly Weekly*, 28 April 2001, op.cit., p. 902.

14 *Congressional Quarterly Weekly*, 19 October 2002, p. 2725, 'Parties Use Judicial Standoff To Play to Core Constituents'.

15 *Congressional Quarterly Weekly Report*, 22 April 1987, p. 897, 'For Robert Bork the Real Test Begins Now'.

16 Richard Hodder-Williams, 'The Supreme Court Nominations of Reagan and Bush', in *Contemporary American Politics*, Alan Grant (ed.) (Dartmouth 1995).

17 *Time*, 21 October 1991; see also *Congressional Quarterly Weekly Report*, 31 August 1991, p. 2360, 'Search for the Definitive Thomas Turns to the Hearings'; 12 October 1991, p. 2948, 'Thomas Drama Engulfs Nation: Anguished Senate Faces Vote'; and 19 October 1991, p. 3026, 'Thomas' Victory Puts Icing on Reagan-Bush Court'.

18 *National Journal*, 4 July 1992, p. 1589, 'Memories of Thomas Fight Haunt Senate'.
19 'The Warren Era: A Conversation with former Chief Justice Earl Warren' (McClatchy Broadcasting, Sacramento, California). Reprinted in Charles Sheldon, *The Supreme Court: Politicians in Robes* (Glencoe Press 1970), pp. xiv–xxii.
20 Archibald Cox, *The Warren Court: Constitutional Decision as an Instrument of Reform*, quoted in Sheldon, ibid., p. ix.
21 Martin Shapiro, 'The Supreme Court from Early Burger to Early Rehnquist', in *The New American Political System*, Second Version, Anthony King (ed.) (AEI Press 1990), p. 58.
22 Earl Warren, in Sheldon, op. cit., p. xviii.
23 Martin Shapiro, op. cit., p. 59.
24 *Congressional Quarterly Weekly Report*, 6 July 1991, pp. 1829–31, '1990–1 Term Marked by Surge in Conservative Activism'.
25 *The Washington Post National Weekly Edition*, 10–16 July 1995, 'The Supreme Court Ronald Reagan Wanted Has Arrived'.
26 Robert McKeever, in *American Politics: 2000 and Beyond*, op. cit., p. 145, footnote 2.
27 Robert McKeever, ibid. pp. 133–135.
28 *Congressional Quarterly Weekly*, 11 August 2001, pp. 1970–71, 'Despite Series of Court Rulings States Officials Are Left Guessing'.
29 *Church of the Lukumi Babalu Aye v. Hialeah*.
30 See Robert McKeever, *Raw Judicial Power? The Supreme Court and American Society* (Manchester University Press 1995), Chapter 4, and Andrew Wroe, 'Abortion: the Right to Life Debate', in *Controversies in American Politics and Society*, David McKay, David Houghton and Andrew Wroe (Blackwell 2002) for detailed discussion of the abortion issue.
31 Robert McCloskey, *The American Supreme Court* (University of Chicago Press 1960), p. 20.
32 *Congressional Quarterly Weekly Report*, 19 September 1992, pp. 2813–16.
33 Archibald Cox, *The Role of the Supreme Court in American Government* (Clarendon Press 1976), pp. 117–18.
34 Richard Hodder-Williams, 'Constitutional Legitimacy and the Supreme Court', in *Developments in American Politics*, Gillian Peele, Christopher J. Bailey and Bruce Cain (eds) (Macmillan 1992), p. 139.
35 Quoted in *Congressional Quarterly Weekly*, 16 December 2000, p. 2854, 'Facing the Judgment of History'.

5 Pressure group politics

1 See Chapter 1, p. 1.
2 Alexis De Tocqueville, *Democracy in America*, Vol. 1 (Fontana 1968), p. 232.
3 Allan J. Cigler and Burdett A. Loomis, 'The Changing Nature of Interest Group Politics', in *Interest Group Politics*, Loomis and Cigler (eds) (Congressional Quarterly Books 1991), p. 10.
4 Allan J. Cigler and Burdett A. Loomis, ibid., p. 22.
5 Steve Reilly, 'Interest Groups in National Politics', in *Developments in American Politics 3*, Gillian Peele *et al.* (eds) (Macmillan 1998), pp. 173–75.
6 Federal Election Commission, *PAC Activity Increases in 2000 Election Cycle*, 31 May 2001.
7 Federal Election Commission, *FEC Issues Semi-annual Federal PAC Count*, 14 January 2003.
8 See Alan Grant, 'The Politics of American Campaign Finance', *Parliamentary Affairs*, Vol. 51, No. 2, 1998, 223–40; Alan Grant, 'Campaign Finance' in *Developments in American Politics 4*, Gillian Peele *et al.* (eds) (Palgrave 2002).
9 Alan Grant, 'Political Action Committees in American Politics', in *Contemporary American Politics*, Alan Grant (ed.) (Dartmouth 1995).
10 *Congressional Quarterly Weekly*, 16 February 2002, p. 458, 'Top Tier Lobbyists: Ex-Members' Special Access Becomes an Issue'; also see *Congressional Quarterly Weekly*, 11 March 2000, pp. 1594–602, 'Grass Greener After Congress'.
11 Lester Milbrath, *The Washington Lobbyists* (Rand McNally 1963).
12 Robert H. Salisbury, 'The Paradox of Interest Groups in Washington – More Groups, Less Clout', in *The New American Political System*, Second Version, Anthony King (ed.) (AEI Press 1990), pp. 225–29.
13 *National Journal*, 27 March 1993, ' Green, Green Grass', pp. 754–57.
14 *Congressional Quarterly Weekly*, 24 March 2001, p. 641, 'Overwhelmed by E-Mail'.

15 *Congressional Quarterly Weekly*, 2 October 1999, 'Hitting Them Where They Live', pp. 2283–84.
16 *National Journal*, 15 June 1996, 'Air Strikes', pp. 1313–15.
17 *Congressional Quarterly Weekly*, 3 July 1999, 'Hill's Privately Funded Trips: Well-Traveled Ethics Loophole', pp. 1594–602.

6 Party politics

1 V.O. Key Jr, *Politics, Parties and Pressure Groups* (Crowell 1964), p. 316.
2 Austin Ranney, 'The President and His Party', in *Both Ends of the Avenue*, Anthony King (ed.) (American Enterprise Institute 1983), p. 133.
3 John H. Aldrich, *Why Parties? The Origins and Transformation of Parties in America* (University of Chicago Press 1995), p. 260.
4 Alan Grant, 'Campaign Finance', in *Developments in American Politics 4*, Gillian Peele, Christopher J. Bailey, Bruce Cain and B. Guy Peters (eds) (Palgrave 2002), pp. 292–94.
5 Philip John Davies, 'Shifting Sands: Developments in Party Politics', in '*Political Issues in America Today*', Philip John Davies and Frederic A. Waldstein (eds) (Manchester University Press 1987), p. 79.
6 V.O. Key Jr, op. cit., p. 205.
7 Clinton Rossiter, *Parties and Politics in America* (Cornell 1960), p. 78.
8 For an interesting analysis of the emergence of the New Deal Coalition and its effects, see Samuel Lubell's *The Future of American Politics* (Harper & Row 1965).
9 Dean McSweeney and John Zvesper, *American Political Parties* (Routledge 1991), pp. 80–82.
10 V.O. Key Jr, op. cit., pp. 207–8.
11 V.O. Key Jr, op. cit., p. 222.
12 *Congressional Quarterly Weekly Report*, 11 November 1989, p. 3098, 'Approval of Bush Is High, But Ratings Are Slippery'.
13 Exit poll data from Voter Research and Surveys; see Table 7.3.
14 See Nicol Rae, *The Decline and Fall of the Liberal Republicans* (Oxford University Press 1989).
15 For an analysis of factions within the Republican Party see Nigel Ashford, 'The Right After Reagan: Crack-Up or Comeback?', in *Contemporary American Politics*, Alan Grant (ed.) (Dartmouth 1995).
16 Dean McSweeney, 'Political Parties' in *Developments in American Politics 4*, Gillian Peele, Christopher J. Bailey, Bruce Cain and B. Guy Peters (eds) (Palgrave 2002), p. 42.
17 Kenneth M. Dolbeare and Linda J. Medcalf, 'The Rising Stars? Neoliberalism and Neoconservatism', in *Political Issues in America Today*, Philip John Davies and Frederic A. Waldstein (eds) (University of Manchester Press 1989), p. 93.
18 Nicol Rae, 'Clinton and the Democratic Party: the 1992 Election and Beyond', in *Contemporary American Politics*, Alan Grant (ed.) (Dartmouth 1995).
19 Clinton Rossiter, op. cit., p. 5.
20 Fred Greenstein, *The American Party System and the American People* (Prentice Hall 1970), p. 39.
21 For a detailed discussion of these trends, see Dean McSweeney, 'Is the party over? Decline and revival in the American party system', in *Explaining American Politics*, Robert Williams (ed.) (Routledge 1990).
22 Larry Sabato, *The Party's Just Begun* (Scott, Foresman 1988), p. 90.
23 James W. Ceaser, 'Political Parties – Declining, Stabilizing or Resurging', in *The New American Political System*, Anthony King (ed.) (AEI Press 1990), p. 137.

7 Elections and voting

1 For an analysis of changes in the nomination process, see Dean McSweeney, 'Parties and Presidential Nominations', in *Contemporary American Politics*, Alan Grant (ed.) (Dartmouth 1995).
2 *Congressional Quarterly Weekly*, 29 July 2000, pp. 69–71, 'Rethinking the Primaries'.
3 Ryan J. Barilleaux and Randall E. Adkins, 'The Nominations: Process and Patterns', in *The Elections of 1992*, Michael Nelson (ed.) (Congressional Quarterly Press 1993), p. 29.
4 Alan Grant, 'The US Presidential Election of 1992', *Parliamentary Affairs*, Vol. 46, No. 2, April

1993, pp. 238–54 and 'The 1992 Presidential Election' in *Contemporary American Politics*, Alan Grant (ed.) (Dartmouth 1995).

5 Austin Ranney, 'The President and His Party', in *Both Ends of the Avenue*, Anthony King (ed.) (American Enterprise Institute 1983), p. 136.

6 Tim Hames, 'The Media', in *Developments in American Politics 4*, Gillian Peele *et al.* (eds.) (Palgrave 2002), pp. 279–82.

7 Tim Hames, op. cit., pp. 284–86.

8 See e.g. Joe McGinniss, *The Selling of the President 1968* (Trident Press 1969), a critical study of Richard Nixon's campaign.

9 Gallup Organization press release, 'Bush gains from debates as presidential campaign enters its final phase', 23 October 2000.

10 Martin P. Wattenberg, 'From a Partisan to a Candidate-centered Electorate', in *The New American Political System*, Second Version, Anthony King (ed.) (AEI Press 1990), pp. 158–60.

11 William H. Flanigan and Nancy H. Zingale, *Political Behaviour of the American Electorate*, 5th edn (Allyn and Bacon 1983), p. 159.

12 *Time*, 4 April 1977.

13 *National Journal*, 18 November 2000, pp. 3650–57, 'Pondering a Popular Vote', and pp. 3658–61, 'Can It Be Done?'

14 Philip John Davies, 'Motivating the US "motor voter"', *Politics Review*, February 2000, pp. 26–9.

15 *Congressional Quarterly Weekly Report*, 21 January 1989, p. 135, 'Turnout Hits 64-Year Low in Presidential Race'.

16 National Election Studies, *The NES Guide to Public Opinion and Electoral Behavior: People Don't Have a Say In What the Government Does 1952–1998*.

17 Alan Grant, 'The 1998 US Midterm Elections', *Talking Politics*, Vol. 11, No. 2, Winter 1999, pp. 118–22.

18 *National Journal*, 12 February 2001, pp. 3720–30, 'Florida Times 50'.

19 A 'pregnant chad' is where a ballot paper has been only slightly indented by the voting stylus, rather than wholly pushed through. A 'hanging chad' is where the voting stylus has only made a partial hole in the ballot paper.

20 *Congressional Quarterly Weekly*, 12 October 2002, pp. 2652–54, 'Election Upgrades Could Prove Expensive For States Seeking Federal Help'; 2 November 2002, pp. 2810–11, 'Provisions of the Federal Voting Standards and Procedures Law'.

21 Alan Grant, 'The Politics of American Campaign Finance', *Parliamentary Affairs*, Vol. 51, No. 2, April 1998, pp. 223–40; 'The Reform of Election Campaign Finance' in *American Politics: 2000 and Beyond*, Alan Grant (ed.) (Ashgate 2000); 'Campaign Finance' in *Developments in American Politics 4*, Gillian Peele *et al.* (eds) (Palgrave 2002)

8 Federalism, the states and local government

1 K.C. Wheare, *Federal Government* (Oxford University Press 1961), p. 10.

2 See Chapter 1, on page 14 'The Historical Framework: From Independence to Philadelphia'; for a discussion of the nature of federalism, see Wheare, ibid., Chapters 4 and 5.

3 Wheare, op. cit., p. 2.

4 *Texas* v. *White* (1869).

5 See, in Chapter 1, 'Amendments to advance individual rights', on page 17.

6 See, in Chapter 4, 'The Supreme Court and the role of government', page 142 for a detailed examination of this development.

7 The American billion (a thousand millions) is used throughout, as figures are from US sources. (In the UK the billion is a million million.)

8 *Significant Features of Fiscal Federalism* (Advisory Commission on Intergovernmental Relations 1980), p. 7.

9 *Statistical Abstract of the United States* 1992, p. 282.

10 John Lees, *The Political System of the United States* (Faber 1975), p. 57.

11 Milton Cummings and David Wise, *Democracy Under Pressure*, 5th edn (Harcourt Brace Jovanovich 1985), p. 69.

12 Morton Grodzins, *The American System* (Rand McNally 1966), pp. 3–4.

13 David Elazar, *American Federalism* (Cromwell 1972), p. 47.

14 Michael D. Reagan, *The New Federalism* (Oxford University Press 1972), p. 145.

15 Michael D. Reagan and John G. Sanzone, *The New Federalism*, 2nd edn (Oxford University Press 1981), p. 175.

16 President Richard Nixon, television address, 8 August 1969.

17 John Shannon, 'A Return to Fend-For-Yourself Federalism: The Reagan Mark', in *State Government 1988/9 (Congressional Quarterly Guide to Current Issues and Activities)*, Thad T. Beyle (ed.), pp. 216, 218.

18 Timothy J. Conlan, 'Federalism and Competing Values in the Reagan Administration', in *American Intergovernmental Relations*, Lawrence J. O'Toole (ed.) (Congressional Quarterly Press 1993) pp. 359–77.

19 Richard Nathan, 'Federalism – The Great Composition', in *The New American Political System*, Second Version, Anthony King (ed.) (The AEI Press 1990).

20 *National Journal*, 3 October 1992, 'Rethinking Federalism', p. 2256.

21 *National Journal*, 2 January 1992, 'Just Saying No', p. 18.

22 John Kincaid, 'Governing the American States', in *Developments in American Politics 2*, Gillian Peele *et al.* (eds) (Macmillan 1994).

23 Joseph Zimmerman, *Contemporary American Federalism:The Growth of National Power* (University of Leicester Press 1992), pp. 11, 55.

24 In the United States the term 'devolution' has come to mean the restoration or reviving of states' powers or rights and a rebalancing of the federal system. It does not mean, as in Britain, the decentralisation of power from a superior to a subordinate level of government as, within a unitary state, the transfer of limited legislative authority to the Scottish Parliament from Westminster. See Alan Grant, 'Devolution and the Reshaping of American Federalism', in *American Politics: 2000 and Beyond*, Alan Grant (ed.) (Ashgate 2000) for a fuller discussion of the issues raised in this chapter.

25 Paul L. Posner, 'Unfunded Mandates Reform:1996 and Beyond', *Publius: The Journal of Federalism*, Vol. 27, No. 2, Spring 1997, p. 71.

26 *Congressional Quarterly Weekly Report*, 5 October 1996, 'Reshaping the Federal–State Relationship', pp. 2824–25 and 2 November 1996, 'GOP Confounds Expectations, Expands Federal Authority', pp. 3117–22.

27 Richard Nathan, op. cit., p. 248.

28 John Kincaid, op. cit., p. 200.

29 B. Guy Peters, 'Federal Bureaucracy and Public Management', in *Developments in American Politics 4*, Gillian Peele, Christopher J. Bailey, Bruce Cain and B. Guy Peters (eds) (Palgrave 2002) p. 138.

30 David B. Walker, 'American Federalism in the 1990s', in *Political Issues in America: the 1990s*, Philip John Davies and Frederic A. Waldstein (eds) (Manchester University Press 1991), p. 130.

31 See Alan Grant and Edward Ashbee, *The 'Politics Today' Companion to American Government* (Manchester University Press 2002), Chapter 9, 'Federalism and the States' and Appendix, 'State Profiles' for analysis and data about state government and politics.

32 See Alan Grant, 'Legislative Careerism and the Term Limitation Movement', in *Contemporary American Politics*, Alan Grant (ed.) (Dartmouth 1995) and Alan Grant, 'Legislative Term Limits in the United States', *The Journal of Legislative Studies*, Vol. 5, No. 2, Summer 1999, pp. 115–35.

33 Figures for state and local government expenditure taken from *Statistical Abstract of the United States 2001*, p. 268.

34 Figures from the *Statistical Abstract of the United States 2001*, pp.267–68.

35 Gillian Peele, 'Federalism and Intergovernmental Relations', in *Developments in American Politics 4*, Gillian Peele, Christopher J. Bailey, Bruce Cain and B. Guy Peters (eds) (Palgrave 2002), pp. 154–55.

Appendix I

The Constitution of the United States

PREAMBLE

WE THE PEOPLE of the United States, in order to form a more perfect Union, establish justice, insure domestic tranquillity, provide for the common defense, promote the general welfare, and secure the blessings of liberty to ourselves and our posterity, do ordain and establish this Constitution for the United States of America.

ARTICLE I

SECTION 1. All legislative powers herein granted shall be vested in a Congress of the United States, which shall consist of a Senate and House of Representatives.

SECTION 2. The House of Representatives shall be composed of members chosen every second year by the people of the several States, and the electors in each State shall have the qualifications requisite for electors of the most numerous branch of the State Legislature.

No person shall be a representative who shall not have attained to the age of twenty-five years, and been seven years a citizen of the United States, and who shall not, when elected, be an inhabitant of the State in which he shall be chosen.

Representatives and direct taxes shall be apportioned among the several States which may be included within this Union, according to their respective numbers, which shall be determined by adding to the whole number of free persons, including those bound to service for a term of years, and excluding Indians not taxed, three-fifths of all other persons. The actual enumeration shall be made within three years after the first meeting of the Congress of the United States, and within every subsequent term of ten years, in such manner as they shall by law direct. The number of representatives shall not exceed one for every thirty thousand, but each State shall have at least one representative; and until such enumeration shall be made, the State of New Hampshire shall be entitled to choose three, Massachusetts eight, Rhode Island and Providence Plantations one, Connecticut five, New York six, New Jersey four, Pennsylvania eight, Delaware one, Maryland six, Virginia ten, North Carolina five, South Carolina five, and Georgia three.

When vacancies happen in the representation from any State, the executive authority thereof shall issue writs of election to fill such vacancies.

The House of Representatives shall choose their Speaker and other officers; and shall have the sole power of impeachment.

SECTION 3. The Senate of the United States shall be composed of two senators from each State, chosen by the legislature thereof, for six years and each senator shall have one vote.

Immediately after they shall be assembled in consequence of the first election, they shall be divided as equally as may be into three classes. The seats of the senators of the first class shall be vacated at the expiration of the second year, of the second class at the expiration of the fourth year, and of the third class at the expiration of the sixth year, so that one-third may be chosen every second year; and if vacancies happen by resignation, or otherwise, during the recess of the legislature of any State, the executive thereof may make temporary appointments until the next meeting of the legislature, which shall then fill such vacancies.

No person shall be a senator who shall not have attained to the age of thirty years, and been nine years a citizen of the United States, and who shall not, when elected, be an inhabitant of that State for which he shall be chosen.

The Vice-President of the United States shall be President of the Senate, but shall have no vote, unless they be equally divided.

The Senate shall choose their other officers, and also a President pro tempore, in the absence of the Vice-President, or when he shall exercise the office of President of the United States.

The Senate shall have the sole power to try all impeachments. When sitting for that purpose, they shall be on oath or affirmation. When the President of the United States is tried, the Chief Justice shall preside: And no person shall be convicted without the concurrence of two-thirds of the members present.

Judgment in cases of impeachment shall not extend further than to removal from office, and disqualification to hold and enjoy any office of honor, trust or profit under the United States: but the party convicted shall nevertheless be liable and subject to indictment, trial, judgment and punishment, according to law.

SECTION 4. The times, places and manner of holding elections for senators and representatives, shall be prescribed in each State by the legislature thereof; but the Congress may at any time by law make or alter such regulations, except as to the places of choosing senators.

The Congress shall assemble at least once in every year, and such meeting shall be on the first Monday in December, unless they shall by law appoint a different day.

SECTION 5. Each house shall be the judge of the elections, returns and qualifications of its own members, and a majority of each shall constitute a quorum to do business; but a smaller number may adjourn from day to day, and may be authorized to compel the attendance of absent members, in such manner, and under such penalties as each house may provide.

Each house may determine the rules of its proceedings, punish its members for disorderly behaviour, and, with the concurrence of two-thirds, expel a member.

Each house shall keep a journal of its proceedings, and from time to time publish the same, excepting such parts as may in their judgment require secrecy; and the yeas and nays of the members of either house on any question shall, at the desire of one-fifth of those present, be entered on the journal.

Neither house, during the session of Congress, shall, without the consent of the other, adjourn for more than three days, nor to any other place than that in which the two houses shall be sitting.

SECTION 6. The senators and representatives shall receive a compensation for their services, to be ascertained by law, and paid out of the Treasury of the United States. They shall in all cases, except treason, felony and breach of the peace, be privileged from arrest during their attendance at the session of their respective houses, and in going to and returning from the same; and for any speech or debate in either house, they shall not be questioned in any other place.

No senator or representative shall, during the time for which he was elected, be appointed to any civil office under the authority of the United States, which shall have been created, or the emoluments whereof shall have been increased during such time; and no person holding any office under the United States, shall be a member of either house during his continuance in office.

SECTION 7. All bills for raising revenue shall originate in the House of Representatives; but the Senate may propose or concur with amendments as on other bills.

Every bill which shall have passed the House of Representatives and the Senate, shall, before it becomes a law, be presented to the President of the United States; if he approves he shall sign it, but if not he shall return it, with his objections to that house in which it shall have originated, who shall enter the objections at large on their journal, and proceed to reconsider it. If after such reconsideration two-thirds of that House shall agree to pass the bill, it shall be sent, together with the objections to the other House, by which it shall likewise be reconsidered, and if approved by two-thirds of that House, it shall become a law. But in all such cases the votes of both Houses shall be determined by yeas and nays, and the names of the persons voting for and against the bill shall be entered on the journal of each House respectively. If any bill shall not be returned by the President within ten days (Sundays excepted) after it shall have been presented to him, the same shall be a law, in like manner as if he had signed it, unless the Congress by their adjournment prevent its return, in which case it shall not be a law.

Every order, resolution, or vote to which the concurrence of the Senate and House of Representatives may be necessary (except on a question of adjournment) shall be presented to the President of the United States; and before the same shall take effect, shall be approved by him, or being disapproved by him, shall be repassed by two-thirds of the Senate and House of Representatives, according to the rules and limitations prescribed in the case of a bill.

SECTION 8. The Congress shall have the power to lay and collect taxes, duties, imposts and excises, to pay the debts and provide for the common defense and general welfare of the United States; but all duties, imposts and excises shall be uniform throughout the United States;

To borrow money on the credit of the United States;

To regulate commerce with foreign nations, and among the several States, and with the Indian tribes;

To establish an uniform rule of naturalization, and uniform laws on the subject of bankruptcies throughout the United States;

To coin money, regulate the value thereof, and of foreign coin, and fix the standard of weights and measures;

To provide for the punishment of counterfeiting the securities and current coin of the United States;

To establish post offices and post roads;

To promote the progress of science and useful arts; by securing for limited times to authors and inventors the exclusive right to their respective writings and discoveries;

To constitute tribunals inferior to the Supreme Court;

To define and punish piracies and felonies committed on the high seas, and offenses against the law of nations;

To declare war, grant letters of marque and reprisal, and make rules concerning captures on land and water;

To raise and support armies, but no appropriation of money to that use shall be for a longer term than two years;

To provide and maintain a Navy;

To make rules for the government and regulation of the land and naval forces;

To provide for calling forth the militia to execute the laws of the Union, suppress insurrections and repel invasions;

To provide for organizing, arming, and disciplining the militia, and for governing such part of them as may be employed in the service of the United States, reserving to the States respectively the appointment of the officers, and the authority of training the militia according to the discipline prescribed by Congress;

To exercise exclusive legislation in all cases whatsoever, over such district (not exceeding ten miles square) as may, by cession of particular States, and the acceptance of Congress, become the seat of the Government of the United States, and to exercise like authority over all places purchased by the consent of the legislature of the State in which the same shall be, for the erection of forts, magazines, arsenals, dockyards, and other needful buildings; – And

To make all laws which shall be necessary and proper for carrying into execution the foregoing powers, and all other powers vested by the Constitution in the Government of the United States, or in any department or officer thereof.

SECTION 9. The migration or importation of such persons as any of the States now existing shall think proper to admit, shall not be prohibited by the Congress prior to the year one thousand eight hundred and eight, but a tax or duty may be imposed on such importation, not exceeding ten dollars for each person.

The privilege of the writ of habeas corpus shall not be suspended, unless when in cases of rebellion or invasion the public safety may require it.

No bill of attainder or ex post facto law shall be passed.

No capitation, or other direct, tax shall be laid, unless in proportion to the census or enumeration herein before directed to be taken.

No tax or duty shall be laid on articles exported from any State.

No preference shall be given by any regulation of commerce or revenue to the ports of one State over those of another: nor shall vessels bound to, or from, one State, be obliged to enter, clear, or pay duties in another.

No money shall be drawn from the Treasury, but in consequence of appropriations made by law; and a regular statement and account of the receipts and expenditures of all public money shall be published from time to time.

No title of nobility shall be granted by the United States: And no person holding any office or profit or trust under them shall, without the consent of the Congress, accept of any present, emoluments, office, or title, of any kind whatever, from any King, Prince, or foreign State.

SECTION 10. No state shall enter into any treaty, alliance, or confederation; grant letters of marque and reprisal; coin money; emit bills of credit; make any thing but gold and silver coin a tender in payment of debts; pass any bill of attainder, ex post facto law, or law impairing the obligation of contracts, or grant any title of nobility.

No state shall, without the consent of the Congress, lay any imposts or duties on imports or exports, except what may be absolutely necessary for executing its inspection laws: and the net produce of all duties and imposts, laid by any State on imports or exports, shall be for the use of the Treasury of the United States; and all such laws shall be subject to the revision and control of the Congress.

No state shall, without the consent of Congress, lay any duty of tonnage, keep troops, or ships of war in time of peace, enter into any agreement or compact with another State, or with a foreign power, or engage in war, unless actually invaded or in such imminent danger as will not admit of delay.

ARTICLE II

SECTION 1. The executive power shall be vested in a President of the United States of America. He shall hold his office during the term of four years, and, together with the Vice-President, chosen for the same term, be elected, as follows:

Each state shall appoint, in such manner as the legislature thereof may direct, a number of electors, equal to the whole number of senators and representatives to which the State may be entitled in the Congress: but no senator or representative, or person holding an office of trust or profit under the United States, shall be appointed an elector.

The electors shall meet in their respective States, and vote by ballot for two persons, of whom one at least shall not be an inhabitant of the same State with themselves. And they shall make a list of all the persons voted for, and of the number of votes for each; which list they shall sign and certify, and transmit sealed to the seat of the Government of the United States, directed to the President of the Senate. The President of the Senate shall, in the presence of the Senate and House of Representatives, open all the certificates, and the votes shall then be counted. The person having the greatest number of votes shall be the President, if such number be a majority of the whole number of electors appointed; and if there be more than one who have such majority, and have an equal number of votes, then the House of Representatives shall immediately choose by ballot one of them for President; and if no person have a majority, then from the five highest on the list the said House shall in like manner choose the President. But in choosing the President, the votes shall be taken by States, the representation from each State having one vote; a quorum for this purpose shall consist of a member or members from two-thirds of the States, and a majority of all the States shall be necessary to a choice. In every case, after the choice of the President, the person having the greatest number of votes of the electors shall be the Vice-President. But if there should remain two or more who have equal votes, the Senate shall choose from them by ballot the Vice-President.

The Congress may determine the time of choosing the electors, and the day on which they shall give their votes; which day shall be the same throughout the United States.

No person except a natural born citizen, or a citizen of the United States, at the time of the adoption of this Constitution, shall be eligible to the office of President; neither shall any person be eligible to that office who shall not have attained to the age of thirty-five years, and been fourteen years a resident within the United States.

In case of the removal of the President from office, or of his death, resignation, or inability to discharge the powers and duties of the said office, the same shall devolve on the Vice-President, and the Congress may by law provide for the case of removal, death, resignation, or in ability, both of the President and Vice-President, declaring what officer shall then act as President, and such officer shall act accordingly, until the disability be removed, or a President shall be elected.

The President shall, at stated times, receive for his services, a compensation, which shall neither be increased nor diminished during the period for which he shall have been elected, and he shall not receive within that period any other emolument from the United States, or any of them.

Before he enter on the execution of his office, he shall take the following oath of affirmation:– 'I do solemnly swear (or affirm) that I will faithfully execute the office of President of the United States, and will to the best of my ability, preserve, protect and defend the Constitution of the United States.'

SECTION 2. The President shall be Commander in Chief of the Army and Navy of the United States, and of the militia of the several States, when called into the actual service of the United States; he may require the opinion, in writing, of the principal officer in each of the Executive Departments, upon any subject relating to the duties of their respective offices, and he shall have power to grant reprieves and pardons for offenses against the United States, except in cases of impeachment.

He shall have power, by and with the advice and consent of the Senate, to make treaties, provided two-thirds of the senators present concur; and he shall nominate, and by and with the advice and consent of the Senate, shall appoint ambassadors, other public ministers and consuls, judges of the Supreme Court, and all other officers of the United States, whose appointments are not herein otherwise provided for, and which shall be established by law: but the Congress may by law vest the appointment of such inferior officers, as they think proper, in the President alone, in the courts of law, or in the heads of departments.

The President shall have power to fill up all vacancies that may happen during the recess of the Senate, by granting commissions which shall expire at the end of their next session.

SECTION 3. He shall from time to time give to the Congress information of the state of the Union, and recommend to their consideration such measures as he shall judge necessary and expedient; he may, on extraordinary occasions, convene both houses, or either of them, and in case of disagreement between them, with respect to the time of adjournment, he may adjourn them to such time as he shall think proper; he shall receive ambassadors and other public ministers; he shall take care that the laws be faithfully executed, and shall commission all the officers of the United States.

SECTION 4. The President, Vice-President and all civil officers of the United States, shall be removed from office on impeachment for and conviction of, treason, bribery, or other high crimes and misdemeanors.

ARTICLE III

SECTION 1. The judicial power of the United States shall be vested in one Supreme Court, and in such inferior courts as the Congress may from time to time ordain and establish. The judges, both of the supreme and inferior courts, shall hold their offices during good behavior, and shall, at stated times, receive for their services, a compensation, which shall not be diminished during their continuance in office.

SECTION 2. The judicial power shall extend to all cases, in law and equity, arising under this Constitution, the laws of the United States, and treaties made, or which shall be made, under their authority; to all cases affecting ambassadors, other public ministers and consuls; to all cases of admiralty and maritime jurisdiction; to controversies to which the United States shall be a party; to controversies between two or more States; between a State and citizens of another State; between citizens of different States; between citizens of the same State claiming lands under grants of different States, and between a State, or the citizens thereof, and foreign States, citizens, or subjects.

In all cases affecting ambassadors, other public ministers and consuls, and those in which a State shall be party, the Supreme Court shall have original jurisdiction. In all the other cases before mentioned, the Supreme Court shall have appellate jurisdiction, both as to law and to fact, with such exceptions, and under such regulations as the Congress shall make.

The trial of all crimes, except in cases of impeachment, shall be by jury; and such trial shall be held in the State where the said crimes shall have been committed; but when not committed within any State, the trial shall be at such place or places as the Congress may by law have directed.

SECTION 3. Treason against the United States, shall consist only in levying war against them, or in adhering to their enemies, giving them aid and comfort. No person shall be convicted of treason unless on the testimony of two witnesses to the same overt act, or on confession in open court.

The Congress shall have power to declare the punishment of treason, but no attainder of treason shall work corruption of blood, or forfeiture except during the life of the person attainted.

ARTICLE IV

SECTION 1. Full faith and credit shall be given in each State to the public acts, records, and judicial proceedings of every other State. And the Congress may by general laws prescribe the manner in which such acts, records and proceedings shall be proved, and the effect thereof.

SECTION 2. The citizens of each state shall be entitled to all privileges and immunities of citizens in the several States.

A person charged in any State with treason, felony, or other crime, who shall flee from justice, and be found in another State, shall on demand of the executive authority of the State from which he fled, be delivered up, to be removed to the State having jurisdiction of the crime.

No person held to service or labor in one State, under the laws thereof, escaping into another, shall, in consequence of any law or regulation therein, be discharged from such service or labor, but shall be delivered up on claim of the party to whom such service or labor may be due.

SECTION 3. New States may be admitted by the Congress into this Union; but no new State shall be formed or erected within the jurisdiction of any other State; nor any State be formed by the junction of two or more States, or parts of States, without the consent of the legislatures of the States concerned as well as of the Congress.

The Congress shall have the power to dispose of and make all needful rules and regulations respecting the Territory or other property belonging to the United States; and nothing in this Constitution shall be so construed as to prejudice any claims of the United States, or of any particular State.

SECTION 4. The United States shall guarantee to every State in this Union a republican form of Government, and shall protect each of them against invasion; and on application of the legislature, or of the executive (when the legislature cannot be convened) against domestic violence.

ARTICLE V

The Congress, whenever two-thirds of both Houses shall deem it necessary, shall propose amendments to this Constitution, or, on the application of the legislatures of two-thirds of the several States, shall call a convention for proposing amendments, which, in either case, shall be valid to all intents and purposes, as part of this Constitution, when ratified by the legislatures of three-fourths of the several States, or by convention in three-fourths thereof, as the one or the other mode of ratification may be proposed by the Congress; provided that no amendment which may be made prior to the year one thousand eight hundred and eight shall in any manner affect the first and fourth clauses in the Ninth Section of the First Article; and that no State, without its consent, shall be deprived of its equal suffrage in the Senate.

ARTICLE VI

All debts contracted and engagements entered into, before the adoption of this Constitution, shall be as valid against the United States under this Constitution, as under the Confederation.

This Constitution, and the laws of the United States which shall be made in pursuance thereof; and all treaties made, or which shall be made, under the authority of the United States, shall be the supreme law of the land; and the judges in every State shall be bound thereby, anything in the Constitution or laws of any State to the contrary notwithstanding.

The Senators and Representatives before mentioned, and the members of the several State legislatures, and all executive and judicial officers, both of the United States and of the several States, shall be bound by oath or affirmation, to support this Constitution; but no religious test shall ever be required as a qualification to any office or public trust under the United States.

ARTICLE VII

The ratification of the conventions of nine States shall be sufficient for the establishment of this Constitution between the States so ratifying the same.

Done in convention by the unanimous consent of the States present the seventeenth day of September in the year of our Lord one thousand seven hundred and eighty seven and of the Independence of the United States of America the twelfth. In witness whereof we have hereunto subscribed our names.

GEO. WASHINGTON,
Presid't and deputy from Virginia.

Amendments

AMENDMENT I

[Ratification of the first ten amendments was completed 15 December 1791.]

Congress shall make no law respecting an establishment of religion, or prohibiting the free exercise thereof; or abridging the freedom of speech, or of the press; or the right of the people peaceably to assemble and to petition the Government for a redress of grievances.

AMENDMENT II

A well regulated militia, being necessary to the security of a free State, the right of the people to keep and bear arms, shall not be infringed.

AMENDMENT III

No soldier shall, in time of peace be quartered in any house, without the consent of the owner, nor in time of war, but in a manner to be prescribed by law.

AMENDMENT IV

The right of the people to be secure in their persons, houses, papers, and effects, against unreasonable searches and seizures, shall not be violated, and no warrants shall issue, but upon probable cause, supported by oath or affirmation, and particularly describing the place to be searched, and the persons or things to be seized.

AMENDMENT V

No person shall be held to answer for a capital, or other infamous crime, unless on a presentment or indictment of a grand jury, except in cases arising in the land or naval forces, or in the militia, when in actual service in time of war or public danger; nor shall any person be subject for the same offence to be twice put in jeopardy of life or limb; nor shall be compelled in any criminal case to be a witness against himself, nor be deprived of life, liberty, or property, without due process of law; nor shall private property be taken for public use, without just compensation.

AMENDMENT VI

In all criminal prosecutions, the accused shall enjoy the right to a speedy and public trial, by an impartial jury of the State and district wherein the crime shall have been committed, which district shall have been previously ascertained by law, and to be informed of the nature and cause of the accusation; to be confronted with the witnesses against him; to have compulsory process for obtaining witnesses in his favor, and to have the assistance of counsel for his defence.

AMENDMENT VII

In suits at common law, where the value in controversy shall exceed twenty dollars, the right of trial by jury shall be preserved, and no fact tried by a jury, shall be otherwise re-examined in any court of the United States, than according to the rules of the common law.

AMENDMENT VIII

Excessive bail shall not be required, nor excessive fines imposed, nor cruel and unusual punishments inflicted.

AMENDMENT IX

The enumeration in the Constitution, of certain rights, shall not be construed to deny or disparage others retained by the people.

AMENDMENT X

The powers not delegated to the United States by the Constitution, nor prohibited by it to the States, are reserved to the States respectively, or to the people.

AMENDMENT XI   [Ratified 8 January 1798]

The judicial power of the United States shall not be construed to extend to any suit in law or equity, commenced or prosecuted against one of the United States by citizens of another State, or by citizens or subjects of any foreign State.

AMENDMENT XII   [Ratified 25 September 1804]

The electors shall meet in their respective States and vote by ballot for President and Vice-President, one of whom, at least, shall not be an inhabitant of the same State with themselves; they shall name in their ballots the person voted for as President, and in distinct ballots the person voted for as Vice-President, and they shall make distinct lists of all persons voted for as President and of all persons voted for as Vice-President, and of the number of votes for each, which lists they shall sign and certify, and transmit sealed to the seat of the government of the United States, directed to the President of the Senate; – The President of the Senate shall, in the presence of Senate and House of Representatives, open all the certificates and the votes shall then be counted; – The person having the greatest number of votes for President, shall be the President, if such a number be a majority of the whole number of Electors appointed; and if no person have such majority, then from the persons having the highest numbers not exceeding three on the list of those voted for as President, the House of Representatives shall choose imme-diately, by ballot, the President. But in choosing the President, the votes shall be taken by States, the representation from each State having one vote, a quorum for this purpose shall consist of a member or members from two-thirds of the States, and a majority of all the States shall be necessary to a choice. And if the House of Representatives shall not choose a President whenever the right of choice shall devolve upon them, before the fourth day of March next following, then the Vice-President shall act as President, as in the case of the death or other constitutional disability of the President. – The person having the greatest number of votes as Vice-President, shall be the Vice-President, if such number be a majority of the whole number of Electors appointed, and if no person have a majority, then from the two highest numbers on the list, the Senate shall choose the Vice-President; a quorum for the purpose shall consist of two-thirds of the whole number of senators, and a majority of the whole number shall be necessary to a choice. But no person constitutionally ineligible to the office of President shall be eligible to that of Vice-President of the United States.

AMENDMENT XIII   [Ratified 18 December 1865]

SECTION 1. Neither slavery nor involuntary servitude, except as a punishment for crime whereof the party shall have been duly convicted, shall exist within the United States, or any place subject to their jurisdiction.

SECTION 2. Congress shall have power to enforce this article by appropriate legislation.

AMENDMENT XIV   [Ratified 28 July 1868]

SECTION 1. All persons born or naturalized in the United States, and subject to the jurisdiction thereof, are citizens of the United States and of the State wherein they reside. No State shall make or enforce any law which shall abridge the privileges or immunities of citizens of the United States; nor shall any State deprive any person of life, liberty, or property, without due process of law; nor deny to any person within its jurisdiction the equal protection of the laws.

SECTION 2. Representatives shall be apportioned among the several States according to their respective numbers, counting the whole number of persons in each State, excluding Indians not taxed. But when the right to vote at any election for the choice of electors for President and Vice-President of the United States, representatives in Congress, the executive and judicial officers of a State, or the members of the legislature thereof, is denied to any of the male inhabitants of such State, being twenty-one years of age, and citizens of the United States, or in any way abridged, except for participation in rebellion, or other crime, the basis of representation therein shall be reduced in the proportion which the number of such male citizens shall bear to the whole number of male citizens twenty-one years of age in such State.

SECTION 3. No person shall be a senator or representative in Congress, or elector of President and Vice-President, or hold any office, civil or military, under the United States, or under any State, who, having previously taken an oath, as a member of Congress, or as an officer of the United States, or as a member of any State legislature, or as an executive or judicial officer of any State, to support the Constitution of the United States, shall have engaged in insurrection or rebellion against the same, or given aid or comfort to the enemies thereof. But Congress may by a vote of two-thirds of each House, remove such disability.

SECTION 4. The validity of the public debt of the United States, authorized by law, including debts incurred for payment of pensions and bounties for services in suppressing insurrection or rebellion, shall not be questioned. But neither the United States nor any State shall assume or pay any debt or obligation incurred in aid of insurrection or rebellion against the United States, or any claim for the loss or emancipation of any slave; but all such debts, obligations, and claims shall be held illegal and void.

SECTION 5. The Congress shall have power to enforce, by appropriate legislation, the provisions of this article.

AMENDMENT XV   [Ratified 30 March 1870]

SECTION 1. The right of citizens of the United States to vote shall not be denied or abridged by the United States or by any State on account of race, color, or previous condition of servitude.

SECTION 2. The Congress shall have power to enforce this article by appropriate legislation.

AMENDMENT XVI   [Ratified 25 February 1913]

The Congress shall have power to lay and collect taxes on incomes, from whatever source derived, without apportionment among the several States, and without regard to any census or enumeration.

AMENDMENT XVII   [Ratified 31 May 1913]

SECTION 1. The Senate of the United States shall be composed of two senators from each State, elected by the people thereof, for six years; and each senator shall have one vote. The electors in each State shall have the qualifications requisite for electors of the most numerous branch of the State legislature.

SECTION 2. When vacancies happen in the representation of any State in the Senate, the executive authority of such State shall issue writs of election to fill such vacancies: *Provided*, That the legislature of any State may empower the executive thereof to make temporary appointments until the people fill the vacancies by election as the legislature may direct.

SECTION 3. This amendment shall not be so construed as to affect the election or term of any senator chosen before it becomes valid as part of the Constitution.

AMENDMENT XVIII [Ratified 29 January 1919. Repealed by the 21st Amendment]

SECTION 1. After one year from the ratification of this article the manufacture, sale, or transportation of intoxicating liquors within, the importation thereof into, or the exportation thereof from the United States and all territory subject to the jurisdiction thereof for beverage purposes is hereby prohibited.

SECTION 2. The Congress and the several States shall have concurrent power to enforce this article by appropriate legislation.

SECTION 3. This article shall be inoperative unless it shall have been ratified as an amendment of the Constitution by the legislatures of the several States, as provided in the Constitution, within seven years from the date of the submission hereof to the States by the Congress.

AMENDMENT XIX   [Ratified 26 August 1920]

SECTION 1. The right of citizens of the United States to vote shall not be denied or abridged by the United States or by any State on account of sex.

SECTION 2. Congress shall have power to enforce this article by appropriate legislation.

AMENDMENT XX   [Ratified 6 February 1933]

SECTION 1. The terms of the President and Vice-President shall end at noon on the 20th day of January, and the terms of Senators and Representatives at noon on the 3rd day of January, of the years in which such terms would have ended if this article had not been ratified; and the terms of their successors shall then begin.

SECTION 2. The Congress shall assemble at least once in every year, and such meeting shall begin at noon on the 3rd day of January, unless they shall by law appoint a different day.

SECTION 3. If, at the time fixed for the beginning of the term of the President, the President elect shall have died, the Vice-President elect shall become President. If a President shall not have been chosen before the time fixed for the beginning of his term, or if the President elect shall have failed to qualify, then the Vice-President elect shall act as President until a President shall have qualified; and the Congress may by law provide for the case wherein neither a President elect nor a Vice-President elect shall have qualified, declaring who shall then act as President, or the manner in which one who is to act shall be selected and such person shall act accordingly until a President or Vice-President shall have qualified.

SECTION 4. The Congress may by law provide for the case of the death of any of the persons from whom the House of Representatives may choose a President whenever the right of choice shall have devolved upon them, and for the case of the death of any of the persons from whom the Senate may choose a Vice-President whenever the right of choice shall have devolved upon them.

SECTION 5. Sections 1 and 2 shall take effect on the 15th day of October following the ratification of this article.

SECTION 6. This article shall be inoperative unless it shall have been ratified as an amendment to the Constitution by the legislatures of three-fourths of the several States within seven years from the date of its submission.

AMENDMENT XXI   [Ratified 5 December 1933]

SECTION 1. The eighteenth article of amendment to the Constitution of the United States is hereby repealed.

SECTION 2. The transportation or importation into any State, Territory, or possession of the United States for delivery or use therein of intoxicating liquors, in violation of the laws thereof, is hereby prohibited.

SECTION 3. This article shall be inoperative unless it shall have been ratified as an amendment to the Constitution by conventions in the several States, as provided in the Constitution, within seven years from the date of the submission hereof to the States by the Congress.

AMENDMENT XXII   [Ratified 1 March 1951]

SECTION 1. No person shall be elected to the office of the President more than twice, and no person who has held the office of President, or acted as President, for more than two years of a term to which some other person was elected President shall be elected to the office of President more than once. But the Article shall not apply to any person holding the office of President when this Article was proposed by the Congress, and shall not prevent any person who may be holding the office of President, or acting as President, during the term within which this Article becomes operative from holding the office of President or acting as President during the remainder of such term.

SECTION 2. This article shall be inoperative unless it shall have been ratified as an amendment to the Constitution by the legislatures of three-fourths of the several States within seven years from the date of its submission to the States by the Congress.

AMENDMENT XXIII   [Ratified 29 March 1961]

SECTION 1. The District constituting the seat of Government of the United States shall appoint in such manner as the Congress may direct:

A number of electors of President and Vice-President equal to the whole number of Senators and Representatives in Congress to which the District would be entitled if it were a State, but in no event more than the least populous State; they shall be in addition to those appointed by the States, but they shall be considered, for the purpose of the election of President and Vice-President, to be electors appointed by a State; and they shall meet in the District and perform such duties as provided by the twelfth article of amendment.

SECTION 2. The Congress shall have power to enforce this article by appropriate legislation.

AMENDMENT XXIV   [Ratified 23 January 1964]

SECTION 1. The right of citizens of the United States to vote in any primary or other election for President or Vice-President, for electors for President or Vice-President, or for Senator or Representative in Congress, shall not be denied or abridged by the United States or any state by reason of failure to pay any poll tax or other tax.

SECTION 2. The Congress shall have power to enforce this article by appropriate legislation.

AMENDMENT XXV   [Ratified 10 February 1967]

SECTION 1. In case of the removal of the President from office or of his death or resignation, the Vice-President shall become President.

SECTION 2. Whenever there is a vacancy in the office of the Vice-President the President shall nominate a Vice-President who shall take office upon confirmation by a majority vote of both Houses of Congress.

SECTION 3. Whenever the President transmits to the President pro tempore of the Senate and the Speaker of the House of Representatives his written declaration that he is unable to discharge the powers and duties of his office, and until he transmits to them a written declaration to the contrary, such powers and duties shall be discharged by the Vice-President as Acting President.

SECTION 4. Whenever the Vice-President and the majority of either the principal officers of the executive departments or of such other body as Congress may by law provide, transmit to the President pro tempore of the Senate and the Speaker of the House of Representatives their written declaration that the President is unable to discharge the powers and duties of his office, the Vice-President shall immediately assume the powers and duties of the office as Acting President.

Thereafter, when the President transmits to the President pro tempore of the Senate and the Speaker of the House of Representatives his written declaration that no inability exists, he shall resume the powers and duties of his office unless the Vice-President and a majority of either the principal officers of the executive departments or of such other body as Congress may by law provide, transmit within four days to the President pro tempore of the Senate and the Speaker of the House of Representatives their written declaration that the President is unable to discharge the powers and duties of his office. Thereupon Congress shall decide the issue, assembling within forty-eight hours for that purpose if not in session. If the Congress, within twenty-one days after receipt of the latter written declaration, or, if Congress is not in session, within twenty-one days after Congress is required to assemble, determines by two-thirds vote of both Houses that the President is unable to discharge the powers and duties of his office, the Vice-President shall continue to discharge the same as Acting President; otherwise, the President shall resume the powers and duties of his office.

AMENDMENT XXVI   [Ratified 30 June 1971]

The right of citizens of the United States, who are 18 years of age or older, to vote shall not be abridged by the United States or by any State on account of age.

AMENDMENT XXVII   [Ratified 7 May 1992]

No law varying the compensation for the services of the Senators and Representatives shall take effect, until an election of Representatives shall have intervened.

Appendix II
Presidents and Vice-Presidents of the United States

Name	Term of office	Party	State of res.	Vice-President
1 George Washington	1789–97	Fed.	Virginia	John Adams
2 John Adams	1797–1801	Fed.	Mass.	Thomas Jefferson
3 Thomas Jefferson	1801–9	Dem. Rep.	Virginia	Aaron Burr, George Clinton (from 1805)
4 James Madison	1809–17	Dem. Rep.	Virginia	George Clinton, E. Gerry (from 1813)
5 James Monroe	1817–25	Dem. Rep.	Virginia	D.D. Tompkins
6 John Quincey Adams	1825–29	Dem. Rep.	Mass.	John C. Calhoun
7 Andrew Jackson	1829–37	Dem.	Tennessee	John C. Calhoun, Martin Van Buren (from 1833)
8 Martin Van Buren	1837–41	Dem.	New York	R.M. Johnson
9 William Harrison*	1841	Whig	Indiana	John Tyler
10 John Tyler	1841–45	Whig	Virginia	–
11 James Polk	1845–49	Dem.	Tennessee	George M. Dallas
12 Zachary Taylor*	1849–50	Whig	Louisiana	Millard Fillmore
13 Millard Fillmore	1850–53	Whig	New York	
14 Franklin Pierce	1853–57	Dem.	New Hampshire	William R. King
15 James Buchanan	1857–61	Dem.	Pennsylvania	J.C. Breckinridge
16 Abraham Lincoln†	1861–5	Rep.	Illinois	H. Hamlin, Andrew Johnson (from 1865)
17 Andrew Johnson	1865–69	Dem.	Tennessee	–
18 Ulysses S. Grant	1869–77	Rep.	Ohio	S. Colfax, H. Wilson (from 1873)
19 Rutherford B. Hayes	1877–81	Rep.	Ohio	W.A. Wheeler
20 James A. Garfield†	1881	Rep.	Ohio	Chester A. Arthur
21 Chester A. Arthur	1881–85	Rep.	New York	–
22 Grover Cleveland	1885–89	Dem.	New York	A. Hendricks
23 Benjamin Harrison	1889–93	Rep.	Indiana	Levi P. Morton
24 Grover Cleveland	1893–97	Dem.	New York	Adlai E. Stevenson
25 William McKinley†	1897–1901	Rep.	Ohio	G.A. Hobart, Theodore Roosevelt (from 1901)

continued

Name	Term of office	Party	State of res.	Vice-President
26 Theodore Roosevelt	1901–9	Rep.	New York	C.M. Fairbanks (from 1905)
27 William H. Taft	1909–13	Rep.	Ohio	J.S. Sherman
28 Woodrow Wilson	1913–21	Dem.	New Jersey	T.R. Marshall
29 Warren G. Harding*	1921–23	Rep.	Ohio	Calvin Coolidge
30 Calvin Coolidge	1923–29	Rep.	Mass.	Charles Davies (from 1925)
31 Herbert Hoover	1929–33	Rep.	California	Charles Curtis
32 Franklin D. Roosevelt*	1933–45	Dem.	New York	John N. Garner, Henry A. Wallace (from 1941), Harry S. Truman (from 1945)
33 Harry S. Truman	1945–53	Dem.	Missouri	Alben Barkley (from 1949)
34 Dwight D. Eisenhower	1953–61	Rep.	New York	Richard M. Nixon
35 John F. Kennedy†	1961–63	Dem.	Mass.	Lyndon B. Johnson
36 Lyndon B. Johnson	1963–69	Dem.	Texas	Hubert Humphrey (from 1965)
37 Richard M. Nixon	1969–74	Rep.	New York	Spiro Agnew, Gerald R. Ford (from 1973)
38 Gerald R. Ford	1974–77	Rep.	Michigan	Nelson Rockefeller
39 Jimmy Carter	1977–81	Dem.	Georgia	Walter Mondale
40 Ronald Reagan	1981–89	Rep.	California	George Bush
41 George Bush	1989–93	Rep.	Texas	Dan Quayle
42 Bill Clinton	1993–2001	Dem.	Arkansas	Al Gore
43 George W. Bush	2001–	Rep.	Texas	Dick Cheney

*Died in office †Assassinated

Appendix III
Glossary

Advice and consent. The power given to the Senate to advise the President and give consent to proposed treaties and presidential appointments. Originally the Senate comprised distinguished citizens elected by the state legislatures and had only 26 members.

Affirmative action programmes. Policies that are designed to favour minorities (for example, in job recruitment) and remedy past discrimination.

Amicus curiae. A person or organisation that is not a party in a case but has an interest in it and is allowed by the court to file a brief and present arguments as a 'friend of the court'.

Appellate jurisdiction. The powers of a court to re-examine or review a case on appeal from a lower court.

Appropriation. The process by which Congress determines the actual amounts of money each government department and agency can spend.

Attorney-General. The chief law officer of the United States who is the head of the Justice Department and a senior member of the President's Cabinet.

Balanced budget. A budget in which revenues are equal to or exceed expenditures. A constitutional amendment to force an end to deficit spending by the federal government has been proposed which would mandate a balanced budget except in particular circumstances such as wartime.

'Balancing the ticket'. The practice of attempting to make a party's candidates attractive to broad sections of the nation by nominating people from different ethnic, religious or regional backgrounds.

Band-wagon effect. The process by which reports of voters' or delegates' intentions can influence the outcome of an election or nominating convention.

Beltway issue. An issue that is of concern to those involved in Washington politics but not to the people outside the Beltway – the interstate highway that surrounds the capital.

Bicameralism. Having a two-chamber legislative body.

'Big government'. The phenomenon of a large-scale federal government with an increased number of departments, civil servants and responsibilities that has existed since the 1930s.

Bill of Rights. The first ten Amendments to the US Constitution, ratified in 1791, guaranteeing individual and state rights.

Bipartisanship. Cooperation between the two parties and their leaders on a political issue.

Blue ribbon commission. A panel of eminent and distinguished citizens, possibly with particular expertise, formed to investigate a problem and make recommendations for action.

Calendar. A list of pending business awaiting legislative action.

Caucus. A meeting of party members to plan strategy or select candidates.

Certiorari, Writ of. An order from a court to a lower court directing that the record of its proceedings be put forward for review – 'to be made certain'.

Checks and balances. The principle of having government institutions exercising certain checks and constraints over one another's activities.

Cloture (closure). The process of setting a time limit and terminating debate on a bill.

Coat-tails effect. The result of voters casting their votes for one popular candidate and also voting for the rest of the party's candidates for other offices.

Concurrent powers. The authority possessed by both the federal and the state governments simultaneously (e.g. taxation).

Confederation. An alliance or league of sovereign states that delegates limited powers on specific issues to a weak central authority.

Conference committee. A committee made up of members of both houses of Congress whose job is to iron out differences between House and Senate versions of a bill and recommend one version to the two houses for final approval.

Continuing resolution. Legislation that provides funding for executive branch activities to continue at a particular level, when the regular appropriation has not been passed by the start of the fiscal year.

'Dark horse' candidate. A candidate for political office who has little support at a convention but who may be a compromise choice if there is a deadlock between the major contenders.

Dealignment. The process by which loyalties of citizens towards, for example, a political party are progressively eroded.

Direct mail fund-raising. A technique to raise money directly from the public using computerised mailing lists.

Divided government. A government where the legislative and executive branches are controlled by different parties.

Due process of law. The right of citizens against arbitrary action by government, protected by following established judicial procedures.

Executive agreement. An agreement made by the President with a foreign power that has the same force as a treaty but does not require Senate approval.

Executive privilege. The argument that the communications between a President and his advisers are confidential and should not be revealed without the permission of the President.

Exit polls. Election-day polls taken as people leave the polling stations, used by media to predict results and for analysis of the way sections of the electorate voted.

Fat cats. Wealthy contributors to political campaigns.

'Favourite son' candidate. A state politician who is nominated for President at a convention by delegates from his own state but is not usually a serious contender. Often used for bargaining purposes or personal publicity.

Federalism. A system of government under which powers are shared between a national (or federal) government and individual states.

Filibuster. The obstruction of Senate action on a bill by taking advantage of the rule of unlimited debate and 'talking the bill to death'.

Founding Fathers. Those individuals who played a major role in the establishment of the new nation, in winning independence and writing the Constitution.

Freshmen. Congressmen serving their first term in office.

Frontrunner. A candidate whom politicians and the media have identified as the likely winner.

Gender gap. A pattern of clear and consistent difference in the voting behaviour or in the opinions on policy issues between men and women.

Gerrymandering. Dividing voters into electoral districts in such a way as to give one party or faction an unfair advantage.

GOP. Grand Old Party or Republican party, which was formed in 1856.

Grand jury. A jury whose role is to investigate whether there is sufficient evidence to justify holding for trial an individual who has been arrested.

Grants-in-aid. A financial subsidy provided by the federal government to state and local governments (or by states to local government) to be used for specific purposes.

Gridlock. A situation where the different branches of government have conflicting objectives or views on a policy and no action is possible. The separation of powers and particularly divided party control of the presidency and Congress can make this possible. The term derives from the position in a city where traffic is so congested it cannot move in any direction.

Hispanic. A term used to include persons of Mexican-American, Puerto Rican, Cuban, Central or South American, or other Spanish origin.

Home Rule. The practice of states allowing their local governments to draft their own charters and manage their own affairs with less direction from the state than is normal.

Honeymoon period. The period, often relatively short, after a President takes office when he experiences harmonious relations with Congress, the media and the public.

Hundred days. The first hundred days of a new administration when it attempts to pass major legislation while support is still strong following election success, such as Roosevelt's policies to counter the Great Depression in 1933.

Impeachment. The formal accusation of misconduct on the part of an executive or judicial official by the House of Representatives, starting the process by which the individual can be removed from office after a trial by the Senate.

Implied powers. The powers Congress has been given to carry out its specified tasks, implied by the 'necessary and proper' clause of the Constitution.

Impoundment. The refusal by the President to spend funds appropriated by Congress for particular purposes.

Incumbent. The person currently holding a particular office.

Initiative. The process by which state laws or constitutional amendments can be enacted by direct popular vote, having been placed on the ballot paper as a result of a petition signed by a specific number of electors.

Interstate commerce. Business or activity between or among several states and subject to federal government regulation.

Intra-state commerce. Business or activity within the boundaries of one state and subject only to regulation by that state authority.

Item veto. The ability of some state Governors to prevent particular sections of a bill from becoming law while allowing the rest to go on to the statute books.

Jim Crow laws. Laws passed by Southern states requiring segregation and racial discrimination between blacks and whites.

Judicial review. The power of the judiciary to declare the actions of the legislative or executive branches unconstitutional.

Keynote address. The major speech at a party national convention, other than the nominee's acceptance speech, that sets out the party's themes and vision for the forthcoming election.

'Lame duck'.   An office-holder who has lost an election but holds power until the inauguration of a successor.

Legislative veto.   A provision of a law in which Congress asserts the power to nullify the actions of the executive branch.

Lobbyist.   An individual who works on behalf of a pressure group and tries to influence the decisions of the legislature or administration on impending legislation or policy.

Log-rolling.   The practice whereby legislators will trade votes in order to achieve their own individual legislative objectives.

Merit system.   The system used in public employment whereby personnel are recruited and promoted on the basis of qualifications and ability rather than by political patronage.

Metropolitan area.   A large area or conurbation made up of several large cities and the areas between them; also known as a 'megalopolis'.

Negative advertising.   Paid commercials which attack an opponent and his policies in an election campaign.

Open seat.   A constituency in which the incumbent member is not seeking re-election.

PAC.   A political action committee set up by a pressure group to raise and distribute campaign finance to particular candidates in elections.

Patronage.   The appointment of positions by executive officials on the basis of party, usually as a reward to friends or supporters.

Pigeon-hole.   To set aside indefinitely; the practice of Congressional committees in not considering bills sent to them.

Platform.   A statement of party policies, made up of clauses on different subjects.

Pluralism.   A theory of government which emphasises the importance of competing groups in a democratic political system where power is dispersed widely within society.

Plurality.   The largest number of votes cast in an election for one candidate who wins whether or not he has an absolute majority over all the other candidates.

Pocket veto.   Refusal by the President to give assent to legislation after the adjournment of Congress. As there is no opportunity for the legislature to override the veto, the bill dies.

Pocketbook issue.   A political issue which directly affects the disposable income of electors, such as taxation and inflation.

Pork-barrelling.   The appropriation of public money secured by legislators for projects which will favour their local constituencies, and help their re-election.

Precinct.   An electoral subdivision of a city, probably small enough for all the residents to be able to vote at one polling station.

Pre-emption.   Under the 'supremacy clause' of Article VI of the Constitution, laws passed by Congress may pre-empt or override those of the states if they are in conflict in the same policy area.

Primary.   An election held before the general election to nominate a party's candidate for office. If it is 'closed', only registered or declared party supporters may vote; if it is 'open', a voter may vote for the nomination of any of the candidates regardless of his party affiliation.

Ranking member.   The member of a political party on a committee who has the longest continuous service on that committee.

Reapportionment.   The redrawing of electoral districts and redistribution of legislative seats to take into account the changes in population settlement.

Recall.   The procedure by which voters can remove an elected official from office before the end of his term if there is evidence of corruption, negligence or incompetence.

About one-quarter of the states provide such a procedure in their constitutions, although such attempts are rarely successful.

Recess appointments.   Appointments made to positions by the President on a temporary basis while Congress is in recess. The post-holder can serve until the end of the following session of Congress without Senate confirmation.

Referendum.   A popular vote on a new state constitution or amendment, or on a statute already approved by the legislature. A petition signed by a specific number of voters is necessary to refer such legislation to the electorate.

Reserved powers.   The powers possessed by the states under the Tenth Amendment to the Constitution, that is all those not delegated to the federal government or denied to the states. Also known as the 'residual powers'.

Revenue sharing.   The allocation of a portion of tax moneys by the federal government to states and local governments to spend with few or no conditions as to how it should be used.

Rider.   A provision included in legislation that is not related to the main subject of the bill it is riding on.

Senatorial courtesy.   The process by which the President consults with Senators of his own party when he makes an appointment to one of the states, thus helping to secure confirmation of the appointment by the Senate.

Seniority system.   The system by which priority or status is given to an individual on the basis of his length of service in an organisation.

Separation of powers.   The principle that power should be distributed between three independent branches of government—the legislature, executive and judiciary.

Smoke-filled room.   A phrase that grew out of the 1920 Republican Convention, symbolising the secret meeting of political bosses to select a candidate.

Soft money.   Money contributed to a political party ostensibly to support its organisational activities but also used to help the party's candidates financially outside of the scope of federal election regulations.

Soundbite.   The use in news programmes of a brief excerpt of a candidate's or politician's speech.

Special districts.   A local government unit that is created to administer one particular service.

Special election.   A by-election that has been specially arranged to fill a vacancy when a member has resigned or died in office before the expiry of his term.

Splitting tickets.   The process whereby a voter selects candidates of different parties for different offices on the same ballot paper.

State of the Union address.   The President's annual speech to Congress setting out his main legislative priorities and the key issues as he sees it in domestic and foreign policy.

States' rights.   The opposition to increasing federal government power at the expense of the states.

Sunbelt.   The southern states, characterised by mild and warm weather, that experienced considerable population growth in the 1980s.

Term limit.   A legal or constitutional restriction on an office-holder serving more than a defined number of terms in the same position.

Treaty.   A formal agreement between sovereign states establishing certain relationships between them. US treaties must be approved by a two-thirds vote in the Senate.

Turnout.   The percentage of the voting age population who cast a vote in a particular election.

Veto.   The power of the President's to prevent legislation passed by the legislature. The President's veto can be overridden if both houses of Congress support the bill by a two-thirds majority.

Whips.   Legislators who can act as communication links between leaders and ordinary Congressmen and who make sure party members are present for crucial votes.

Write-in candidate.   A candidate whose name does not appear on the printed ballot and whose supporters must therefore write his name themselves.

Index

A library at your fingertips!

eBooks are electronic versions of print books. You can store them onto your PC/laptop or browse them online.

They have advantages for anyone needing rapid access to a wide variety of published, copyright information.

eBooks can help your research by enabling you to bookmark chapters, annotate and use instant searches to find specific words or phrases. Several eBook files would fit on even a small laptop or PDA.

NEW: Save money by eSubscribing: cheap, online acess to any eBook for as long as you need it.

Annual subscription packages

We now offer special low cost bulk subscriptions to packages of eBooks in certain subject areas. These are available to libraries or to individuals.

For more information please contact webmaster.ebooks@tandf.co.uk

We're continually developing the eBook concept, so keep up to date by visiting the website.

www.eBookstore.tandf.co.uk